She Is Weeping

Dannelle Gutarra Cordero's expansive study incorporates writers, cultural figures, and intellectuals from antiquity to the present day to analyze how discourses on emotion serve to create and maintain White supremacy and racism. Throughout history, scientific theories have played a vital role in the accumulation of power over colonized and racialized people. Scientific intellectual discourses on race, gender, and sexuality characterized Blackness as emotionally distinct in both deficiency and excess, a contrast with the emotional benevolence accorded to Whiteness. Ideas on racialized emotions have simultaneously driven the development of devastating body politics by enslaving structures of power. Bold and thought provoking, *She Is Weeping* provides a new understanding of racialized emotions in the Atlantic world, and how these discourses proved instrumental to the rise of slavery and racial capitalism, racialized sexual violence, and the expansion of the carceral state.

DANNELLE GUTARRA CORDERO is Lecturer in African American Studies and Gender and Sexuality Studies and the Director of the Archival Justice for the Enslaved Project at Princeton University.

She Is Weeping

An Intellectual History of Racialized Slavery and Emotions in the Atlantic World

DANNELLE GUTARRA CORDERO
Princeton University

CAMBRIDGE
UNIVERSITY PRESS

University Printing House, Cambridge CB2 8BS, United Kingdom

One Liberty Plaza, 20th Floor, New York, NY 10006, USA

477 Williamstown Road, Port Melbourne, VIC 3207, Australia

314–321, 3rd Floor, Plot 3, Splendor Forum, Jasola District Centre, New Delhi – 110025, India

103 Penang Road, #05-06/07, Visioncrest Commercial, Singapore 238467

Cambridge University Press is part of the University of Cambridge.

It furthers the University's mission by disseminating knowledge in the pursuit of education, learning, and research at the highest international levels of excellence.

www.cambridge.org
Information on this title: www.cambridge.org/9781316512203
DOI: 10.1017/9781009057974

© Dannelle Gutarra Cordero 2022

This publication is in copyright. Subject to statutory exception and to the provisions of relevant collective licensing agreements, no reproduction of any part may take place without the written permission of Cambridge University Press.

First published 2022

Printed in the United Kingdom by TJ Books Limited, Padstow Cornwall

A catalogue record for this publication is available from the British Library.

ISBN 978-1-316-51220-3 Hardback

Cambridge University Press has no responsibility for the persistence or accuracy of URLs for external or third-party internet websites referred to in this publication and does not guarantee that any content on such websites is, or will remain, accurate or appropriate.

Contents

Acknowledgments   *page* vii

1. The Emotional Foundations of Racialized Slavery   1
2. Scientific Racism and Emotional Difference   49
3. Atlantic Slavery and Its Passionate Transgressions   112
4. The "Abolition" of an Economic Apparatus of Feelings   168
5. The Racialization of Emotions in Contemporary Slavery   224

Bibliography   259
Index   277

Acknowledgments

Part of the research for this book was performed during a Visiting Fellowship in the Hutchins Center for African & African American Research at Harvard University. I am profoundly grateful to the Department of African American Studies, the Program of Gender and Sexuality Studies, and my students at Princeton University for supporting my teaching and scholarship while I was writing this manuscript. I would also like to express my gratitude to Cambridge University Press, Senior Editor Cecelia Cancellaro, and the anonymous peer reviewers for their outstanding support in the completion of this book.

I dedicate this and all my writing to my mother and my sister.

I

The Emotional Foundations of Racialized Slavery

A mother and a daughter. Their heartbeat drums in sync. She pushes in. She wants to breathe, she wants to be caressed without fear for once, she wants. The pain is unbearable. But it is less pain as long as you are here with me. There is nothing I want more than to see you, and there is nothing I want less. You are my everything, everything I long, I love, I anticipate. You are Life and fear of death. I cannot have you. She is Weeping.

Slavery has always primarily been an emotional economic system.[1] The racialization of emotions in the Atlantic world is the consequence of the historical transcendence of the ancient discourse of "slavery to passions" and the medieval notion of "slavery to sin." Fueling relativism of slavery, these principles were mostly shaped by ancient and medieval philosophical theories about the recognizable biological difference of the "naturally enslaved." The rise of scientific racism in the eighteenth century accelerated the racialization of "emotional difference," arguing that distinct racialized categories feel differently. The theoretical definition of Blackness in scientific racism, and thus in modern economies of racialized

---

[1] As a trigger warning for enslaved people and descendants of enslaved people, this book tells a painful history that sparks painful memories. Quoted primary sources include hateful language and might be misgendering historical figures. English translations of primary sources in other languages were all done by the author and can be found in the footnotes. This book abstains from showing racial slurs in quoted sources as a way to connote the profound indignation the author feels toward the fetishization of this hateful violence and the minimization of the history of the intersection of racial slurs and racialized violence in academia. Translations point to the racial construct targeted by the racial slur, while still abstaining from writing down the racial slur.

slavery, can be summarized in the following tension: Black bodies were thought to be emotionally impulsive and to simultaneously be deceptive about their feelings. This opportunistic ambivalence sanctions the everlasting emotional policing of Black communities. This emotional policing is inescapable and the essence of Black captivity itself, then and now.

The scholarly conversation about the history of emotions has contextualized epistemological approaches to emotional ideas. This scholarship has argued that language about emotions has been historically "poorly suited to the phenomena the terms are intended to describe"[2] and has theorized how discourses about emotions influence the "self-perception of the feeling subject."[3] Emotional expression has been described as impacted by "cognitive reflection" and in turn influenced by historical and social transformations; "performance of affect" then lies at the intersection of individual subjectivity and societal constructs.[4] It has been claimed that the influence of Galenic medical theory in "Western" knowledge production solidified "the cultural and spiritual origins of the heart as a symbol of affect (and affection)," spreading a "heartfelt" language of emotions.[5] Researchers contend that emotional concepts, such as "nostalgia," spark the "affective power" of "heritage"[6] and that the "cultural politics of emotion" propel a dichotomy between the "fear of passivity" and the "fear of emotionality."[7] These politics are differentiated in distinct "emotional communities," societal structures that dictate the "norms" of which emotions are of "value" and the "modes" of expression.[8]

The scholarly exchange about the history of emotions has highlighted the eighteenth century as a turning point of meaning in the Atlantic

---

[2] Jerome Kagan, *What Is Emotion? History, Measures, and Meanings* (New Haven, CT: Yale University Press, 2007), 9.

[3] Jan Plamper, *The History of Emotions: An Introduction* (Oxford: Oxford University Press, 2012), 32.

[4] David Lemmings & Ann Brooks, "The Emotional Turn in the Humanities and Social Sciences," in *Emotions and Social Change: Historical and Sociological Perspectives*, edited by David Lemmings & Ann Brooks (New York: Routledge, 2014), 3.

[5] Fay Bound Alberti, *Matters of the Heart: History, Medicine, and Emotion* (Oxford: Oxford University Press, 2010), 4.

[6] Alicia Marchant, "Introduction: Historicising Heritage and Emotions," in *Historicising Heritage and Emotions: The Affective Histories of Blood Stone and Land*, edited by Alicia Marchant (New York: Routledge, 2019).

[7] Sara Ahmed, *The Cultural Politics of Emotion* (New York: Routledge, 2004), 2.

[8] Barbara H. Rosenwein, *Generations of Feeling: A History of Emotions, 600–1700* (New York: Cambridge University Press, 2016), 2–3.

world.[9] According to this scholarship, during this "Age of Sentimentality," literature on "elocution" engendered definitions of a "well-bred" body that could balance politeness and emotional expressiveness,[10] while "sentimentalist fiction" intensified the commodification of emotions in economic systems, leading to the conceptualization of "goods as objects of emotional attachment."[11] Scholars have affirmed that there is a correlation between the rise of "modernity" as molded by colonialism in the Atlantic world[12] and eighteenth-century thought about the "bodily nature of affect as an aspect of the mind/body/soul relation."[13] Sentimentality represented the "literary mode of empire in the eighteenth century" by disseminating discourses about the "selective recognition of the humanity" of the colonizer versus the colonized.[14] White elites historically elevated their own emotions as "refined feelings" in order to "discredit the emotions of social antagonists."[15] Research on the history of emotions has explored how "Europe's refined bourgeois economy of emotion" mobilized the "export of European standards of emotion to colonial societies."[16] The "emotional narratives" of imperialism validated "legitimate conquest" and racial exclusion, while discourses of "pity," "compassion," and "sympathy" justified "missionary intervention" in indigenous communities as a "form of atonement and redemption."[17] The scholarship has pointed out that it is

---

[9] The notion of the "Atlantic world" has been primarily constructed by historiography, and this historiography has applied different methodologies to analyze imperial history, many through the gaze of the colonizer, and some through the perspective of the colonized. See A. B. Leonard & David Pretel, "Experiments in Modernity: The Making of the Atlantic World Economy," in *The Caribbean and the Atlantic World Economy: Circuits of Trade, Money and Knowledge, 1650–1914*, edited by A. B. Leonard & David Pretel (New York: Palgrave Macmillan, 2016).

[10] Paul Goring, *The Rhetoric of Sensibility in Eighteenth-Century Culture* (New York: Cambridge University Press, 2005), 39–41.

[11] Ute Frevert, *Emotions in History: Lost and Found* (Budapest: Central European University Press, 2010).

[12] Sibylle Fischer, *Modernity Disavowed: Haiti and the Cultures of Slavery in the Age of Revolution* (Durham, NC: Duke University Press, 2004), 24.

[13] Fay Bound Alberti, *Medicine, Emotion and Disease, 1700–1950* (New York: Palgrave Macmillan, 2006), xix.

[14] Lynn Festa, *Sentimental Figures of Empire in Eighteenth-Century Britain and France* (Baltimore, MD: Johns Hopkins University Press, 2006).

[15] Nicole Eustace, *Passion Is the Gale: Emotion, Power, and the Coming of the American Revolution* (Chapel Hill: University of North Carolina Press, 2008), 5.

[16] Ute Frevert, "Defining Emotions: Concepts and Debates over Three Centuries," in *Emotional Lexicons: Continuity and Change in the Vocabulary of Feeling, 1700–2000*, edited by Ute Frevert et al. (Oxford: Oxford University Press, 2014), 7.

[17] Jane Lydon, *Imperial Emotions: The Politics of Empathy across the British Empire* (New York: Cambridge University Press, 2020), 2, 18.

in the nineteenth century when the history of a multiplicity of categories, such as "appetites, passions, affections, and sentiments" culminated in a "single over-arching category of emotions."[18] It is also in the nineteenth century when the categorization of "civility and civilized emotions" structurally determined political participation in imperial jurisdictions.[19]

The historiography of emotions has been mostly focused on the "West."[20] Although a scholarly debate about the intellectual history of racialized slavery as an emotional economy is nonexistent, the scholarship has examined how the intersections of ideas of race, gender, sexuality, class, age, and "disability" have historically impacted which feelings of pain are "othered, sidelined, reduced, justified, condoned, condemned and mythologized."[21] It has been analyzed how, due to the overpowering historical authority of the Aristotelian theorization of the enslaved, an enslaved person is deemed a "vehicle of emotion, but not an origin or end."[22] Scholars have investigated how discourses about emotions cultivated the "sectionalization" of "political allegiances" into "North and South" in the antebellum United States,[23] while also evaluating how, in recent history, public emotional discussion about "criminality," "terrorism," "welfare dependence," and "illegal immigration" has systematically legitimized "military-carceral expansion and the retreat from social welfare goods."[24] Nonetheless, the scholarly production about the history of slavery and of emotions has not yet traced the ascent of racialist thought back to the emotional justifications of slavery in the ancient and medieval worlds, or explored the influence of scientific theories of racialized emotional difference in historical and contemporary racialized criminalization and exploitation.

---

[18] Thomas Dixon, *From Passions to Emotions: The Creation of a Secular Psychological Category* (New York: Cambridge University Press, 2003), 2.

[19] Magrit Pernau & Helge Jordheim, "Introduction," in *Civilizing Emotions: Concepts in Nineteenth Century Asia and Europe*, edited by Ute Frevert & Thomas Dixon (Oxford: Oxford University Press, 2015), 1.

[20] Susan J. Matt & Peter N. Stearns, "Introduction," in *Doing Emotions History*, edited by Susan J. Matt & Peter N. Stearns (Urbana-Champaign: University of Illinois Press, 2014), 5.

[21] Rob Boddice, "Introduction: Hurt Feelings?," in *Pain and Emotion in Modern History*, edited by Rob Boddice (New York: Palgrave Macmillan, 2014), 2.

[22] Daniel M. Gross, *The Secret History of Emotion: From Aristotle's Rhetoric to Modern Brain Science* (Chicago: University of Chicago Press, 2006), 36.

[23] Michael E. Woods, *Emotional and Sectional Conflict in the Antebellum United States* (New York: Cambridge University Press, 2014), 2.

[24] Paula Ioanade, *The Emotional Politics of Racism: How Feelings Trump Facts in an Era of Colorblindness* (Stanford, CA: Stanford University Press, 2015), 1.

The Emotional Foundations of Racialized Slavery

This book argues that the intellectual history of racialized slavery in the Atlantic world has always been and still is defined by the inescapability of emotional policing of racialized bodies. This structural inescapability violently distresses Black lives and propels institutional hatred toward a racialized body that simultaneously feels "too much" and "too little," keeping the Black body at the brink of death. The ancient world relativized slavery with the notion of "slavery to passions," while also propagating ideas about the "biological difference" of an othered "naturally enslaved" person. Ancient intellectual production advocated for the systematization of passions as the fulfillment of political justice through the absolute "emotional subjugation" of the "naturally enslaved." The rise of Christianity led to the extension of the notion of "slavery to passions" toward the discourse of "slavery to sin," which eventually validated religious, colonial, and corporeal conquests. These ancient and medieval emotional justifications of enslavement set the framework for the globalized racialization of the institution of slavery. Eighteenth-century scientific racism built on from this framework and was therefore mainly concerned with "emotional difference," consecrating a racial hierarchy of feelings. Blackness was fatally marked with the synchronicity of emotional impulsivity, emotional resilience, and deceptive emotional performativity. The Black body is judged to be wholly driven by disruptive feelings, and yet deemed more calculated, simulated, imitative. Yet the Black body feels less. Yet the Black body can bear it.

The symbiotic hypersexualization, depersonalization, and suspicion of Black emotionality sustained the imperial emotional economy and systemic sexual violence of Atlantic slavery, sanctioning the institution of racialized slavery as a perpetual stage of paternalistic emotional tutelage and education. This emotional surveillance prescribed the self-containment of emotions within the Black body, which in turn resulted in the legitimization of the continuous escalation of imperial genocidal violence toward the Black "defect" of disorderly emotionality. The "order" of racial inequality guaranteed the protection of "happiness" in colonial societies via this incessant racialized emotional policing, while the resistance of the enslaved was persecuted as transgressions emerging from "passionate" bodies that had to tamed. Even nineteenth-century White abolitionist efforts utilized emotional imagery that othered Black "feelings" and mobilized empathy toward the protection of the "innocence" of White, "loving" familial structures. In contrast, Black antislavery thought and the revolutions of the enslaved vehemently denounced the emotional detachment and morbidity of the imperial slaveholding regimes of the Atlantic world. Throughout the "post-emancipation era," the longings of Black communities for political citizenship and economic mobility were disregarded by structures of power as emotional weakness that went against the value of capitalistic progress and benevolent political agency. The exacerbation of the racialized carceral landscape was grounded on the institutional insistence in the failure of the Black body to diligently serve as a carceral site of suppression of unruly emotions.

During the twentieth century, the emotional policing of the racialized and the colonized fueled the persistence of racially premised enslavement, the expansion of carceral economies, and the propagation of emotional archetypes in politics, economics, health, media, and education. The enlargement of the carceral landscape mirrored the intensification of the institutional antagonism toward "Black rage" and mimicked the imperial reactions to the revolutions of the enslaved. Today, the narrative of the "abolition" of racialized slavery thrives in the preservation of a racially premised, enslaving emotional economy and in the political fascination with "White slavery," framing the recent intellectual history of legal and media emotional responses to "human trafficking." Today, public discourse about racism vividly visualizes the "fear" and "guilt" of White privilege instead of the actually visible structural hate toward Blackness. Today, the racialization of childhood, concretized by scientific racism, still claims "menace" in a murdered Black child and "innocence" in an "emotionally complex" White assassin. The commodification of Blackness is now even more a conduit for White emotional performativity, and the inexorability of racialized emotional criminalization is still intact and drives the capitalistic "order" of White happiness. The institutional dependence on contemporary racialized exploitation and genocidal violence is embodied in the political imagining of an emotional Other that will silently take it and will be better for it.

EMOTIONAL JUSTIFICATIONS OF SLAVERY IN THE ANCIENT AND MEDIEVAL WORLDS

> For a man who is able to belong to another person is by nature a slave (for that is why he belongs to someone else), as is a man who participates in reason only so far to realize that it exists, but not so far as to have it himself – other animals do not recognize reason, but follow their passions.
> —Aristotle, *Politics*

In *Politics*, Aristotle infamously argued for the perceptible existence of the "naturally enslaved" and contended that the condition of slavery can be "advantageous" to the one subordinated to the whim of a master. The philosopher first defines enslaved people as an "animate piece of property,"[25] a "tool" disconnected from a soul, and then proceeds to craft an allegory about the power relations between body and soul: "it is clear that it is natural and advantageous for the body to be ruled by the soul and the emotions by the intellect (which is the part that possesses reason)."[26] Aristotle asserted that these power dynamics "must apply to mankind as a whole,"[27] generating a complex parallelism among the "differences" between man and animal, man and woman, and master and the enslaved. After having affirmed that "men" in their "natural state"[28] are ruled by soul/reason and not body/emotions, the prominent philosopher concludes: "Nature must therefore have intended to make the bodies of free men and of slaves different also."[29] The bodies of "free men" are destined for a public life of citizenship. The bodies of the enslaved are driven by an absence of self-governance, like "animals" that indiscriminately "follow their passions." While *Politics* ambiguously "clarifies" that the enslaved body is not at all times unequivocally identifiable in order to avoid the "illogicality" of the enslavement of "rightful" citizens, Aristotle does proclaim the state of being of a "stronger," generally recognizable, a manifest "naturally enslaved" person.

Both Aristotelian and Platonic thought nurtured a parallelism in the power relationships between reason and passions, soul and body, man and woman, father and child, master and the enslaved, King and the State. It is through these mirrored definitions of political governance that ancient Greek philosophy introduced the concept of "slavery to passions" to both relativize and legitimize the societal practice of slavery. The doctrine of "slavery to passions" normalized the institution of slavery by projecting the link between the body and the soul as a political one that should ultimately aim for the regulation of emotions, regulation that had to mimic the rule of the Father over his Home and the sovereignty of the King over the State. Thus, the principle of "slavery to passions" built an emotional economy grounded on the corporeal control of the "naturally" enslaved for being "emotionally different"

---

[25] Aristotle, "Politics," in *Greek and Roman Slavery*, edited by Thomas Wiedemann (New York: Routledge, 2003), 15.
[26] Aristotle, "Politics," 16.   [27] Aristotle, "Politics," 16.   [28] Aristotle, "Politics," 16.
[29] Aristotle, "Politics," 17.

and "biologically identifiable." Both Plato and Aristotle summoned this reasoning to disseminate ideas about "quality of men" and bodies that are recognizably distinct, setting a racialist precedent for future "biological" hierarchies. Throughout the Middle Ages and the European conquest and colonization of the Atlantic world, this premise of "slavery to passions" extended to the religious concept of "slavery to sin," which in turn progressed into the conceptualization of imperial subjugation as the righteous and predestined consolidation of a global hierarchy of feelings.

SLAVERY TO PASSIONS: EMOTIONAL FOUNDATIONS OF SLAVERY IN THE ANCIENT GRECO-ROMAN WORLD

The connection between exploitative power and the notion of "emotional difference" can be unveiled in the initial artifacts of the history of slavery, unearthing the etymological and mechanical conceptualization of bondage. David Brion Davis contended that the institution of slavery was born in the processes and mechanisms of the domestication of animals, establishing "dehumanization" as a vital component of the enslaved experience.[30] Even in the earliest written sources about slavery, there are references to "emotional difference," from *"dullu,"* the Akkadian word for "corvée" that has been translated to "misery," to texts that disparage enslaved women as having an inclination toward laziness and "constant complaining."[31] The animalization and emotional disavowal of enslaved bodies would later be exemplified in the etymology of multiple ancient terms for enslaved people, such as the Egyptian *hm* "from a word for 'body'"[32] and the Greek *andrapodon,* meaning "man-footed thing,"[33] among the multiplicity of ancient terms[34] that either infantilize the enslaved person or metonymically refer to an unfeeling enslaved body. Homer's *Odyssey* materialized a dominant literary statement on the

---

[30] David Brion Davis, *Inhuman Bondage: The Rise and Fall of Slavery in the New World* (Oxford: Oxford University Press, 2006), 32.
[31] Daniel C. Snell, "Slavery in the Ancient Near East," in *The Cambridge World History of Slavery*, vol. 1, edited by Keith Bradley & Paul Cartledge (New York: Cambridge University Press, 2011), 8–12.
[32] Snell, "Slavery in the Ancient Near East," 16.
[33] T. E. Rihll, "Classical Athens," in *The Cambridge World History of Slavery*, vol. 1, edited by Keith Bradley & Paul Cartledge (New York: Cambridge University Press, 2011), 51.
[34] See Youval Rotman, *Byzantine Slavery and the Mediterranean World* (Cambridge, MA: Harvard University Press, 2009), 82.

condition of slavery: "For half the virtue that the God-head gave, the God resumes when a man becomes a slave."[35] Ancient rationalizations of slavery would indeed cultivate an inexorable tie between the exercise of freedom and the public display of virtuous emotions.

Various ancient Greek didactical texts represented slavery as emerging from the nature of the excluded Other, nature ambivalently marked by a predisposition toward both revenge and complacence. The well-known fables attributed to formerly enslaved Aesop show several slavery tropes and plots of animals becoming enslaved to Men. In "The Horse and the Stag," the Horse "acquires" its servitude by asking for help from Man to exercise revenge on the Stag; instead, Man "mounts" and thus overpowers the Horse, and the Horse becomes "from that time forward the slave of Man."[36] "The House-Dog and the Wolf" creates a dichotomy between the "lean, hungry Wolf" and the "plump, well-fed House-Dog."[37] Similarly, the *Pseudo-Phocyclides* included the aphorism "Provide your servant with the share of food that he is owed. Give a slave his rations so that he may respect you."[38] The discursive distrust toward the "well-fed," and yet potentially vengeful, enslaved person aimed to normalize the notion that the "nature" of slavery arose from the emotional, carnal, self-destructive, and animalized deviance of the enslaved, while simultaneously belittling the lived experience of slavery as a content and "plump" existence.

The ancient Greek literary canon further explored the anxiety between the human and inhuman in the conception of enslaved feelings. In "The Banqueting Sophists," Atheneaus collected diverse slavery tropes already present in the ancient Greek literary tradition, including the imagery of substituting enslaved people with "walking" inanimate objects[39] and the description of enslaved people as "bringers of gifts, trembling before their lords."[40] Multiple ancient Greek plays depicted "comedic" instances of physical punishment toward enslaved people.[41] This spectacle of the

---

[35] Homer, *Odyssey*, vol. 4 (London: Nicol and Murray, 1834), 122.
[36] Aesop, *Aesop's Fables*, edited by W. T. Stead (London: Review of Reviews Office, 1896), 13.
[37] Aesop, *Aesop's Fables*, 22.
[38] "Pseudo-Phocyclides," in *Greek and Roman Slavery*, edited by Thomas Wiedemann (New York: Routledge, 2003), 179.
[39] Atheneaus, "The Banqueting Sophists," in *Greek and Roman Slavery*, edited by Thomas Wiedemann (New York: Routledge, 2003), 82.
[40] Atheneaus, "The Banqueting Sophists," 76.
[41] Peter Hunt, "Slavery in Greek Literary Culture," in *The Cambridge World History of Slavery*, vol. 1, edited by Keith Bradley & Paul Cartledge (New York: Cambridge University Press, 2011), 30.

penalization of the enslaved for the enjoyment of audiences of citizens has been interpreted as a manifestation of the "consciousness of the precarious nature of freedom."[42] The "comedic" portrayal of bodily punishment of the "trembling" enslaved could serve as an emotionally cathartic simulation of the potentiality of falling into slavery and thus dishonor.

The exclusionary politics of honor in ancient Greece were precisely framed with the concept of *atimia*. Within the gradations of disenfranchisement, total *atimia* represented the denial of honor, public life, and political participation.[43] Orlando Patterson notably contextualized the enslaved experience within the concept of "systematic dishonor," reducing the lived enslaved condition to a fixed "social death" and sparking a scholarly debate about the subjectivities of the enslaved.[44] Ancient Greek morality did intertwine the notions of honor and freedom, constructing the condition of slavery as intrinsically dishonorable and granting a high value to the public spectacle of political agency and citizenship as a validation of honor. Within this public spectacle, the hubris code of conduct emphasized civic moderation toward the enslaved, as their public humiliation for the gratification of the master was deemed a moral transgression.[45] Execution of enslaved people by masters was also frowned upon, since it was regarded as a matter of the State.[46] The hubris law encompasses how honor was conceived as the public performance of freedom, morality, and citizenship: the home was a private sphere that theoretically mirrored public life and yet also operated as a space of morbidity. This duality of an emotional economy rooted in paradoxical discourses of honor is central to the connection between the lived experiences of the enslaved subject and the emotional performativity of public and private life. This duality is ever-present and is vital to the examination of the global history of enslaved subjectivities and the suffering they fervently condemned.

---

[42] Rob Tordoff, "Introduction: Slaves and Slavery in Ancient Greek Comedy," in *Slaves and Slavery in Ancient Greek Comic Drama*, edited by Ben Akrigg & Rob Tordoff (New York: Cambridge University Press, 2013), 47.

[43] Deborah Kamen, *Status in Classical Athens* (Princeton, NJ: Princeton University Press, 2013), 74–78.

[44] Orlando Patterson, *Slavery and Social Death: A Comparative Study* (Cambridge, MA: Harvard University Press, 1982), 78.

[45] Demosthenes, "Against Meidias," in *Greek and Roman Slavery*, edited by Thomas Wiedemann (New York: Routledge, 2003), 166.

[46] Antiphon, "Death of Herodes," in *Greek and Roman Slavery*, edited by Thomas Wiedemann (New York: Routledge, 2003), 165.

The Emotional Foundations of Racialized Slavery

In its effort to systematize the power dynamics of the household and society at large, ancient Greek philosophy engendered intricate theoretical frameworks that justified the social practice of slavery. Undeniably, the political understanding of the *oikos*, or household,[47] was driven by the "emotional subjugation" of enslaved people. Xenophon's *Oeconomicus* claimed that heads of households who were not governed by reason lived in a state of unfreedom.

How, said Socrates, can they have no masters, if although they wish to be happy and desire to do what would gain good things for themselves they are hindered from doing so by their rulers? And who are these, said Critobulus, who, although invisible yet rule over them? But, by Zeus, said Socrates, they are not invisible, but very plain to be seen. Even you perceive that they are very wicked, if indeed you consider laziness, weakness of mind, and carelessness to be wickedness: and there are other deceitful mistresses which pretend to be pleasures, and gambling with dice, and profitless conversations, which in process of time clearly show even to their dupes that they are sorrows concealed within an outer crust of pleasure, which gain a mastery over them and keep them from useful works.[48]

Michel Foucault would state that Xenophon's work evinced that "the government of an *oikos* presuppose that one has acquired the ability to govern oneself."[49] Indeed, this passage emphatically represents lack of "control" over one's emotions as a "master" of one's state of being. According to Xenophon, "male" heads of households naturally wish to enjoy happiness, but the inability of emotional self-containment irremediably brings "concealed sorrows." The philosopher personifies pleasure as disguised sadness, propelling an intrinsic anxiety between the body and its passions. While those "enslaved" by their passions do not have the capacity to detect this "wickedness," it is very "plain to see" for the discerned eye of an accomplished head of the household. The "feminine" trope of pleasures as "deceitful mistresses" seems to be premeditated, since Xenophon's construction of marriage within the *oikos* is an allegory for a patriarchal structure of societal power. The motivation behind Xenophon's rhetoric is to explicitly legitimize the power of the

---

[47] See Mark Golden, "Slavery and the Greek Family," in *The Cambridge World History of Slavery*, vol. 1, edited by Keith Bradley & Paul Cartledge (New York: Cambridge University Press, 2011), 135.
[48] Xenophon, *Oeconomicus, or Treatise on Household Management* (Cambridge: J. Hall & Son, 1885), 4.
[49] Michel Foucault, *The History of Sexuality, vol. 2: The Use of Pleasure* (New York: Pantheon Books, 1985), 160.

slaveholder as a source of clemency for the enslaved person inherently "ruled" by emotions.

> We ought, however, Critobulus, to fight against these for our freedom, no less against those who endeavor to enslave us with arms. Nay, ere now, when enemies who are men of honour have taken any men prisoners, they have forced many of them to be better by chastening them, and have made them live more peacefully for the rest of their lives: but such mistresses as these never cease from harassing the bodies, minds, and households of men, as long as they rule over them.[50]

Xenophon's thought minimizes the condition of slavery by claiming the potential for complacency in enslaved people, in turn summoning empathy toward the perpetual struggle for (self-)government that afflicts the head of the household. This rationale conceives questioning slavery as a banal undertaking, since any deviation from an existence ruled by *logos*, or knowledge, represents some degree of enslavement. With the purpose of systematizing slavery, Xenophon's works provide a set of rules for slaveholders to follow in order to promote the "contentment" of enslaved people. An enslaved person with a "will" to be a head of a household had to be submitted to "every kind of punishment" until they could be forced to "serve properly."[51] Enslaved reproduction had to be regulated by separating enslaved people by their prescribed gender in different quarters, as a way to additionally prevent revolutionary resistance.[52] Most importantly, master dominance had to be analogical to the domestication of animals and conceive the unfree as inhuman.

> It is possible to make human beings more ready to obey you simply by explaining to them the advantages of being obedient; but with slaves, the training considered to be appropriate to wild beasts is a particularly useful way of instilling obedience. You will achieve the greatest success with them by allowing them as much food as they want. Those who are ambitious by nature will also be motivated by praise (for there are some people who are as naturally keen for praise as others are for food and drink).[53]

Therefore, Xenophon's work theorizes the discipline and punishment of enslaved people as closer to the one geared to the "obedience" of "wild beasts," which follows his principle of "forcing" the "will" of enslaved

---

[50] Xenophon, *Oeconomicus*, 5.
[51] Xenophon, "Memorabilia," in *Greek and Roman Slavery*, edited by Thomas Wiedemann (New York: Routledge, 2003), 166.
[52] Xenophon, "The Householder," in *Greek and Roman Slavery*, edited by Thomas Wiedemann (New York: Routledge, 2003), 171.
[53] Xenophon, "The Householder," 177.

people into "obedience" through physical violence. According to the philosopher, the enslaved could also be compelled to subservience and complacency through food or the stimulation of "vanity" due to their intrinsic animalized essence. Enslaved people were then doubly dominated by their "carnal desires" without the likelihood of escaping any pleasurable "sorrows." Xenophon's writing hence openly endorsed the political imposition of the "passions," the same "passions" that he alleged naturally lead to the enslaved condition, as a method to systematize slaveholding economies through violence, since discerning the "passions" was solely the domain of the "emotionally superior" slaveholder.

Just as Xenophon's writing stressed the notion of slavery to pleasure (or concealed unhappiness), Plato would also perpetuate the metaphor of "slavery to passions," in this case as the foundation of his envisioned political order. Plato claimed that those enslaved by "desire" and "pleasure" could not control the urge to fulfill sublime gratification. "The man who is under the sway of desire and a slave to pleasure will inevitably try to derive the greatest pleasure possible from the object of his passions."[54] The Platonic definition of the soul conceptualizes its "nature" as the "ruler" of the body, which parallels the order of the Universe, separating the incorporeal from the material. "It is the soul's nature to rule, the body's to serve. In this the soul is more akin to the divine, the body to that which is mortal." Even more, the philosopher uses the trope of slavery to lay a framework for measuring the "quality of men,"[55] since his thought defines enslaved people as having "unhealthy" souls, prone to irrational passions.[56] On the contrary, the soul that mirrors the divine, and can thus rule the State, is one that refrains from undue emotions.

Only the philosopher's soul will join the gods, for only he abstains from lusts for the right purpose – not to avoid property or disgrace or illness, but to avoid the distortion of his sense of values which excessive emotions would create: for intense excitement may lead one to attribute more importance to the material objects that cause it than to that which is divine.[57]

Plato conceives political governance as analogical to self-governance, toward the divine and away from emotional "excess." The Platonic understanding of enslaved people as non-political is best exemplified in

---

[54] Plato, *Phaedrus and Letters VII and VIII* (London: Penguin Books, 1973), 38.
[55] Plato, *Phaedo* (London: Routledge, 1955), 74.
[56] Plato, "Laws," in *Greek and Roman Slavery*, edited by Thomas Wiedemann (New York: Routledge, 2003), 78.
[57] Plato, *Phaedo*, 74.

the use of imagery of slavery in the Allegory of the Cave.[58] Ignorant people who have been deceived by the "shadows" are chained and in a state of continual captivity. Although many scholars contend that Platonic discourse on the "human" potential to utilize reason to achieve immortality made the rise of racial categories "antithetical,"[59] Platonic thought did premeditatedly spread ideas about the "quality of men," as tied to status. "Our best men should make their match with the best women as often as possible; but with men and women of lower status, it's the reverse. We must nurture the offspring of the first group, but not those of the second, if our flock is to be of the highest quality."[60] Hence, the philosopher held that political societies should promote the reproduction of "men of the highest quality," Men who exercise control over their emotions and consequently have intrinsic political leadership. On the contrary, according to the Allegory of the Cave, people of a "lower status" turn the "direction of the soul" away from the divine due to the "weight" of the "passions," arguing that "this part of such a nature had been hammered at in earliest childhood and had been knocked free of attachment to becoming, lead weights, as it were, which, grafted onto it through food and like pleasures and delicacies, turn the soul's sight downward."[61] Plato's Allegory proposes that only self-governance can lead to political order and that only "men of the highest quality" are the ones capable of stepping out of the cave of illusory "pleasures." The chains and the darkness of the cave are the afflictions of the emotional bodies that are not "biologically" capable of "turning their soul."

Aristotelian thought would further solidify and expand the parallelism between emotional self-control and political domination, starting at the level of rhetorical thinking. Aristotle's *Rhetoric* claimed that persuasion could be achieved by understanding the role that emotions play in the shaping of "opinions" and "decisions." "Men's judgments vary with love or hatred, with joy or sorrow; insomuch that writers on rhetoric have hitherto confined the art wholly to address in moving the passions."[62] This text then portrays the "judgments of men" as responsive to "agitations of the mind, and their accompanying pains or pleasures."[63] While rhetorical delivery is constructed as a consciousness of the transcendence

---

[58] Plato, *Republic* (Cambridge, MA: Harvard University Press, 2014), 107.
[59] See Ivan Hannaford, *Race: The History of an Idea in the West* (Baltimore, MD: Johns Hopkins University Press, 1996), 21.
[60] Plato, *Republic*, 487.   [61] Plato, *Republic*, 123.
[62] Aristotle, *Rhetoric* (London: T. Cadell, 1823), 160.   [63] Aristotle, *Rhetoric*, 255.

of emotions over reason, Aristotelian thought establishes categories of emotional difference by status and by age.

Rhetoric asserts that youth is universally a stage of inherent vulnerability to passions, a phase which never culminates within the condition of slavery: "what still remains of the subject, it may be observed that youth is naturally obnoxious to all those passions which originate in the love of pleasure; with these it abounds, hurrying to the gratification of them through every obstacle, and too often indulging in them to the most profligate excess."[64] While children are prone to "excess," "men in the prime of life" and "in power" are capable of controlling their reactions to emotional stimuli. "The same manly temperament will prevail throughout, and regulate all the angry passions, as well as all those originating in the love of pleasure."[65] By conflating age and status, Aristotle demarcates the nature of the enslaved person as innately emotional and infantile. Moreover, the philosopher distinguishes anger as a passion that is universal and particularly fleeting when stimulated by "just punishment" to an act of "misconduct": "thus even slaves may be made to perceive the fitness of their punishment."[66]

Aristotle further explored the universality of anger in *Nicomachean Ethics*, crafting a hierarchy of "incontinence."

And hence anger may, to a certain extent, be said to obey reason, while desire cannot: and hence, to desire is the more disgraceful of the two. He, indeed, who is incontinent of anger is worsted, not by passion alone, but, to a certain extent, by reason also; whereas he who is incontinent of his desires, is worsted by simple lust alone, without any admixture of reason.[67]

The classification of the "incontinence of anger" as less dishonorable than the "incontinence of desires" is vital to comprehend Aristotelian thought on the "irrationality" of the "naturally enslaved." *Nicomachean Ethics* describes enslaved people as inherently "low-minded" and "weak-souled," even depicting flattery as emerging from the "slavish spirit."[68] The thinker consistently establishes connections between the "spirit" of the "naturally enslaved" and the tendency toward "desires," in turn animalizing enslaved people as "brute beasts."

---

[64] Aristotle, *Rhetoric*, 301.   [65] Aristotle, *Rhetoric*, 307–310.
[66] Aristotle, *Rhetoric*, 265.
[67] Aristotle, *Nicomachean Ethics* (London: Longmans, Green, and Co., 1869), 231.
[68] Aristotle, *Nicomachean Ethics*, 120.

But, to return to the point from which we commenced our digression, the many and baser sort give by their lives a fair presumption that their conception of the chief good and of happiness is that it consists in material pleasure: for their only delight is in a life of gross enjoyment. There are, indeed, but three noteworthy modes of life, the one just mentioned, the life of the statesman, and the third, the life of the philosopher. Now the many are clearly in no way better than slaves, in that they deliberately choose the life of brute beasts.[69]

Therefore, Aristotle utilizes the trope of the enslaved person as an archetype for the degrading incontinence of passions for "gross enjoyment." Furthermore, *Nicomachean Ethics* proposes that the relationship between the ruler and the ruled is "that of the craftsman to his tool, or of the soul to the body, or of the owner to the slave; for, in each of these three relations, the owner may be said to confer an absolute benefit upon his property by his use of it."[70] Just as in *Politics*, Aristotle abstracts enslaved people as "tools" for the "absolute benefit" of a master and connotes an allegory about power relations in society and power dynamics between the body and the soul. *Nicomachean Ethics* also distinctively examines the "paradoxical symbiosis" between master and the enslaved, an interpretation that would insistently infiltrate intellectual and popular discourses on slavery to this day.[71]

But justice between master and slave, or between father and son, is not the same as is justice political, but only like unto it. One cannot wrong that which is absolutely one's own. Now one's property, and equally with it one's son (as long as he is of a certain age, and so has not yet separated himself from his parents), is, as it were, an integral portion of one's self. And, since no man can deliberately purpose to do himself an injury, it follows that for a man to commit a wrong against himself is an impossibility.[72]

Aristotle conceives enslaved people and the progeny of free Men not only as property of the Father/Master but also as "surrogate bodies" of the "self" of the Father/Master, theory that would be intensified in the ancient Roman world. Due to their status as "surrogate bodies," the Master cannot hypothetically "injure" these segments of the "self." While Aristotle, who notoriously labeled wives and offspring as "poor men's slaves,"[73] isolates the potential in "male" children to acquire

---

[69] Aristotle, *Nicomachean Ethics*, 7. [70] Aristotle, *Nicomachean Ethics*, 293.
[71] William Fitzgerald, *Roman Literature and Its Contexts: Slavery and the Roman Literary Imagination* (New York: Cambridge University Press, 2000), 6.
[72] Aristotle, *Nicomachean Ethics*, 162. [73] See Rihll, "Classical Athens," 49.

selfhood, the enslaved person is designated as a perennial "portion" of the "self" of the enslaver.

Lastly, by a metaphorical or analogical use of language, we may be allowed to speak of justice as subsisting, not between a man and himself, but between the man as a whole and certain parts of his nature. But yet it will not be every kind of justice that can thus subsist, but only that justice which can subsist between master and slave, or between a father and his family; for a relation of this kind it is that exists between the rational and the irrational parts of the soul.[74]

Aristotelian thought, then, in instances, subdivides the soul into "rational" and "irrational" parts, still echoing the more consistent allusion to the challenging struggle of the soul to conquer bodily desires as "analogous" to governing over an enslaved person, a home, and a State. This plight is represented as an act of political and introspective justice. Thus, "political justice" is premised on the physical identification of a "surrogate body" and the fulfillment of an intrinsically "noninjurious benefit."

Following emotionally charged Greek philosophical precedents, ancient Roman thought stressed the economic productivity and the ethical relativity of slavery through emotional differentiation. In *Agriculture*, Varro argued for the profitability of a self-sufficient household with the "purchase" of specialized enslaved people.[75] Moreover, Varro adapted and perpetuated the Aristotelian conception of the "naturally enslaved" person as a "tool" in his portrait of the instrumentum vocale.[76] The popular sayings of formerly enslaved Publilius Syrus included "Modesty is also a kind of slavery" and "Whoever helps his country is the slave of his people," downplaying the significance of the lived experiences of slavery.[77] Likewise, a recurrent metaphor of slavery in ancient Roman thought referred to "disempowered senators" in light of the ascent of emperors.[78] Cicero's *Republic* preserved the discourse of "slavery to passions" as the failure for self-governance, claiming that the ideal ruler

---

[74] Aristotle, *Nicomachean Ethics*, 180.
[75] Varro, "Agriculture," in *Greek and Roman Slavery*, edited by Thomas Wiedemann (New York: Routledge, 2003), 92.
[76] Sandra Joshel, "Slavery and Roman Literary Culture," in *The Cambridge World History of Slavery*, vol. 1, edited by Keith Bradley & Paul Cartledge (New York: Cambridge University Press, 2011), 215.
[77] "Pubilius Syrus," in *Greek and Roman Slavery*, edited by Thomas Wiedemann (New York: Routledge, 2003), 71.
[78] Sandra Joshel, *Slavery in the Roman World* (New York: Cambridge University Press, 2010), 10.

is the one who can be master of "his" emotions and hence sovereign of all: "What more illustrious than the man, who while he governs others is himself the slave of no bad passions?"[79] According to Cicero, exemplary Men would demonstrate their capacity for (self-)government with "fair" comportment toward enslaved people, "the lowest kinds of people."[80]

Ancient Roman law crafted exclusionary norms that would be inherited by the institutionalization of slavery in the Atlantic world and that were driven by a political agenda against societal "corruption." Slavery fell outside the range of the *ius naturale*, but was legitimized as natural behavior in the *ius gentium*.[81] Yet the acquisition of the condition of slavery could not be specified in positive law, as this would place Men in power at risk of falling prey to slavery. Lex Aelia Sentia fixed limitations to the number of manumissions as a political statement that it was "very important that the people should be kept pure and uncorrupted by any taint of foreign or slave blood."[82] Ancient Roman law also declared that any enslaved person with an assassinated enslaver "deserves to suffer the penalty of death, so that no other slaves may think that they should consider their own interests when their masters are in danger."[83] Furthermore, "corrupting a slave" was regarded as a breach of the code of conduct, whether the citizen was "making a good slave bad, or a bad slave worse."[84] Under Constantine, the boundaries of the penalization of the enslaved would be slightly demystified: while slaveholders possessed the right to punish enslaved people with "sticks, whips, and chains," the use of "stones, lethal weapons, poison, and wild beasts" was purportedly reserved to the sovereignty of the State.[85] These legal norms responded to a general narrative of *"terror servilis,"* encouraging physical violence toward enslaved people and simultaneously targeting "corruption" of

---

[79] Cicero, *Republic* (New York: G. & C. Carvill, 1829), 63.
[80] Cicero, "On Duties," in *Greek and Roman Slavery*, edited by Thomas Wiedemann (New York: Routledge, 2003), 180.
[81] Marcianus, "Institutes," in *Greek and Roman Slavery*, edited by Thomas Wiedemann (New York: Routledge, 2003), 20.
[82] Suetonius, "Augustus," in *Greek and Roman Slavery*, edited by Thomas Wiedemann (New York: Routledge, 2003), 17.
[83] "The Senate Recommendations Proposed by Silanus and Claudius," in *Greek and Roman Slavery*, edited by Thomas Wiedemann (New York: Routledge, 2003), 164.
[84] Ulpian, "On the Edict," in *Greek and Roman Slavery*, edited by Thomas Wiedemann (New York: Routledge, 2003), 30.
[85] "Code of Theodosius," in *Greek and Roman Slavery*, edited by Thomas Wiedemann (New York: Routledge, 2003), 167.

The Emotional Foundations of Racialized Slavery

the enslaved and society as a whole.[86] The notion of "corruption" was rooted in discourses about emotional deviance, foreignness, and bloodlines, setting precedents for Atlantic "terror" mythologies of the "corruptive" nature of the racialized/colonized and in turn the inexorability of emotional policing.

Just as the Greek *oikos*, the Roman *familia*[87] aimed to contain enslaved people, and the enslaved had to be emotionally regulated as if the Home mirrored the State. Now, the institution of the paterfamilias assumed offspring and enslaved people to be under the *patria potestas* of the Father: the paterfamilias had the right of life and death over his children[88] and "paternalistic" dominance over the enslaved.[89] Being accompanied by a large "entourage" of enslaved people was not only a signifier of status, but also the exemplary manifestation of the civic exercise of *potestas*.[90] Following the Aristotelian framework, Roman law constructed enslaved people as "surrogate bodies," decreeing that the injuries of an enslaved person were legally a transgression against the "slaveholder's personal dignity."[91] The patriarchal dominion of the paterfamilias over enslaved and "infantile" bodies augmented their disposability and incited the propensity of exposure of infants, particularly those identified as "female" by the State, which in turn ignited the growth of a pedophilic sex industry.[92] While the enslaved were forced to be subjected to the expectations of sexual gratification of the paterfamilias, sexual relationships between free women and enslaved men were socially regarded as dishonorable.[93]

The ancient Roman code of conduct utilized discourses of emotion to authenticate the nonexistence of enslaved autonomy, setting precedents

---

[86] Keith Bradley, "Slavery in the Roman Republic," in *The Cambridge World History of Slavery*, vol. 1, edited by Keith Bradley & Paul Cartledge (New York: Cambridge University Press, 2011), 261.

[87] See Jonathan Edmondson, "Slavery and the Roman Family," in *The Cambridge World History of Slavery*, vol. 1, edited by Keith Bradley & Paul Cartledge (New York: Cambridge University Press, 2011), 351.

[88] "The Twelve Tables," in *The Civil Law, Including the Twelve Tables: The Institutes of Gaius, the Rules of Ulpian, the Opinions of Paulus, the Enactments of Justinian, and the Constitutions of Leo*, edited by S. P. Scott (Cincinnati: Central Trust Co., 1932), 64.

[89] Edmondson, "Slavery and the Roman Family," 357.

[90] Catherine Hezser, *Jewish Slavery in Antiquity* (Oxford: Oxford University Press, 2005), 125.

[91] Jennifer A. Glancy, *Slavery in Early Christianity* (Oxford: Oxford University Press, 2002), 12.

[92] Davis, *Inhuman Bondage*, 40.

[93] Edmondson, "Slavery and the Roman Family," 352.

for anti-Black enslavement. Enslaved people were essentially attributed a perilous "moral deficiency" that required regulation.[94] While enslaved people were considered the ultimate source of *fastidium* (annoyance), *veracundia* (social worry) was reckoned as out of the range of emotion of enslaved people, and *pudor* (shame) was associated with both slavery and "femininity."[95] However, shame did not translate to the principle of protection of "sexual honor," since the enslaved were forced to grant carnal pleasure to their enslavers.[96] Moreover, Roman slaveholders often denoted enslaved adults as "boys" or "girls" and in turn negated their maturity, while enslaved people could not disobey exhaustive norms of demeanor without being reprimanded, even if their enslavers insulted or taunted them.[97] The perpetual "infancy" of enslaved people was paradoxically grounded on their "brief childhood" or their "early" capacity to "comprehend" their "duties" as enslaved people, since Columella contended that enslaved people should preferably initiate their labor by the age of six.[98] Emancipation did not rid the formerly enslaved of the burden of stigma: the emancipated were subjected to harsher legal punishments, could not vote, and could not serve in the military, among other restrictions.[99] Table X of the Twelve Tables dictated that the "body of no dead slave shall be anointed; nor shall any drinking take place at his funeral, nor a banquet of any kind be instituted in his honor."[100] No emotions could be summoned at the death of an enslaved person: to be enslaved emulated being a *homo sacer*.[101]

Many ancient Roman texts further diffused the conception of the enslaved person as prone to passions and weakness of character.

---

[94] Sandra Joshel & Sheila Murnaghan, *Women and Slaves in Greco-Roman Societies* (New York: Routledge, 1998), 3.
[95] Robert A. Kaster, *Emotion, Restraint, and Community in Ancient Rome* (Oxford: Oxford University Press, 2005), 23, 47, 117.
[96] Matthew J. Perry, *Gender, Manumission, and the Roman Freedwoman* (New York: Cambridge University Press, 2014), 8.
[97] Kyle Harper, *Slavery in the Late Roman World AD 275–425* (New York: Cambridge University Press, 2011), 332.
[98] Hanne Sigismund-Nielsen, "Slave and Lower-Class Children," in *The Oxford Handbook of Childhood and Education in the Classical World*, edited by Judith Evans Grubs, Tim Parkin, & Roslynne Bell (Oxford: Oxford University Press, 2013), 290.
[99] Tristan S. Taylor, "Legally Marginalised Group: The Empire," in *The Oxford Handbook of Roman Law and Society*, edited by Paul J. du Plessis, Clifford Ando, & Kauis Tuori (Oxford: Oxford University Press, 2016), 361.
[100] "The Twelve Tables," 75.
[101] See Giorgio Agamben, *Homo Sacer: Sovereign Power and Bare Life* (Palo Alto, CA: Stanford University Press, 1998), 54.

Horace portrayed the enslaved character as controlled by the "stomach": "Does the man who sells his estates to comply with his stomach's demands have nothing of the slave in him?"[102] Meanwhile, Philo of Alexandria abstracted the enslaved person as an emblem of emotional submissiveness.

> But the slave or the metal lies subdued and unresponsive, ready to suffer all that the one who handles it is minded to do so. This state of being we should never admit into our bodies, much less into our souls, but rather that condition which is characterized by reciprocity, for mortal kind must inevitably suffer. Let us not like effeminate men, invertebrate and unstrung, succumbing before the first shot is fired, our psychic energies drained, sink in utter exhaustion. Invigorated instead by the firm tension of our minds, let us have the strength to lighten and alleviate the onset of the impending terrors.[103]

Philo of Alexandria constructs submissiveness as framed by "terror" and enslaved people as overpowered by suffering. In this passage, enslaved people are analogous to "effeminate men," and the intrinsic "femininity" and "passivity" of the enslaved are regarded as detrimental to body and soul. Meanwhile, dominant "masculinity" is defined as guided by "reciprocity" and a "strong" response to fear. Philo of Alexandria further argues that the institution of slavery is not a natural phenomenon, but that this practice is brought by the irrationality and animalism of the enslaved themselves: "The servants are indeed free by nature, for no man is naturally a slave, but the irrational animals have been made ready for the need and service of men and rank as slaves."[104] Seemingly incongruously, this interpreter of Jewish religious texts later appropriates the trope of slavery to claim that Men must assume their minds and bodies to be "God's possessions": "I am not even master of my senses, but more likely their slave, following wherever they lead, to colors, shapes, sounds, scents, flavors, and the other bodily things."[105] Here, there is a symptom of the later application of the trope of slavery to designate not only the traits that are unwanted in society but also the aptitudes that are desired in religious devotion.

Seneca utilized imagery of the enslaved to articulate the moral expectancy of Stoicism, a philosophical current that would intensify the societal

---

[102] Horace, *Satires and Epistles* (Oxford: Oxford University Press, 2011), 59.
[103] Philo of Alexandria, *The Contemplative Life, The Giants, and Selections* (Mahwah, NJ: Paulist Press, 1981), 189.
[104] Philo of Alexandria, *The Contemplative Life, The Giants, and Selections*, 189.
[105] Philo of Alexandria, *The Contemplative Life, The Giants, and Selections*, 189.

influence of the notion of "slavery to passions." *On Anger* categorized an "outburst of anger from a position of authority" as being "beastly, horrible and bloodthirsty, and unable to be cured except by fear of some greater power."[106] Based on this principle, his denunciation of violence toward enslaved people is fixated with the character of the slaveholding aggressor, and not the worth of the enslaved person: "Why on earth are we so anxious to have them flogged immediately, to have their legs broken on the spot? We do not abandon our rights by postponing the exercise of them."[107] In fact, Seneca's conceptualization of the enslaved character is one of a precarious cradle of "greed" and "hate."

> Slaves require a clothing and food allowance; you have to look after the appetites of all those greedy creatures, you have to buy clothes, you have to keep a watch on those hands ever ready to steal things; you have to make use of the services of people who are always breaking down in tears and who hate us. How much happier is a man whose only obligation is to someone whom he can easily deny – himself! But since we don't have that much self-reliance, we should at least reduce our inherited wealth so that we are less exposed to the damage Fortune can inflict on us.[108]

The Stoic philosopher designates as a happier existence not to have to be surrounded by such emotional "creatures." Most importantly, while the representation of the enslaved person as "breaking down in tears" somewhat acknowledges the emotional impact of unfreedom, this "breakdown" is transformed into hate, and these "tears" are fundamentally depicted as an annoyance for the master. Thus, Seneca's statements about the institution of slavery concentrate on the character and the "happiness" of the slaveholder. Overall, Seneca's thought on the master–enslaved relationship underlined that authoritative power and social order would be better sustained when higher beings treated lesser beings with "clemency,"[109] racialist discourse that would be replicated in nineteenth-century White abolitionism.

Attitudes toward physical punishment of the enslaved in the ancient Roman world normalized the excruciating pain of enslaved people. As described by Plutarch, Cato the Elder's norms for slaveholding granted

---

[106] Seneca, "On Anger," in *Greek and Roman Slavery*, edited by Thomas Wiedemann (New York: Routledge, 2003), 169.
[107] Seneca, "On Anger," 173.
[108] Seneca, "The Tranquillity of the Mind," in *Greek and Roman Slavery*, edited by Thomas Wiedemann (New York: Routledge, 2003), 89.
[109] See Keith Bradley, *Slavery and Society at Rome* (New York: Cambridge University Press, 1994), 5.

much value to the whip as an icon of master supremacy, to violence as a tool of domination, and to slaveholding authority over the bodies of enslaved people, such as the regulation of their energy by promoting long sleep and the sexual exploitation of the enslaved,[110] again advocating for the institutional systemization of "passions" and sexual violence for the continuation of slavery. Meanwhile, a fiction by Apuleius pointed to the pervasiveness of brutal physical punishment toward enslaved people in ancient Roman society. "The men there were indescribable – their entire skin was coloured black and blue with the weals left by whippings, and their scarred backs were shaded rather than covered by tunics which were patched and torn."[111] Even Galen commented on the penalization of the enslaved through the lens of medicine, warning that not delegating physical punishment toward enslaved people could be a source of malady for, not the enslaved themselves, but for the masters. "If a man adheres to the practice of never striking any of his slaves with his hand, he will be less likely to succumb later on, even in circumstances most likely to provoke anger."[112] Corporeal violence toward the enslaved was standardized as a necessary measure to keep the emotions of enslaved people on a tight rein, and the discursive source of concern was fixated with the "emotional toll" on the slaveholders who tortured enslaved people.

Plotinus defined "virtue" as one entirely emerging from reason and detached from the passions. "So understood, virtue is a mode of Intellectual-Principle, a mode not involving any of the emotions or passions controlled by its reasonings, since such experiences, amenable to morality and discipline, touch closely – we read – on body."[113] This characterization of virtue leads to a persistent use of the metaphor of "slavery to passions," culminating with a hierarchy of virtue that in turn justifies the unequal division of "wealth and property."

He has learned that life on earth has two distinct forms, the way of the Sage and the way of the mass, the Sage intent upon the sublimest, upon the realm above, while those of the more strictly human type fall, again, under two classes, the one reminiscent of virtue and therefore not without touch with good, the other mere

---

[110] Plutarch, "Cato the Elder," in *Greek and Roman Slavery*, edited by Thomas Wiedemann (New York: Routledge, 2003), 175.
[111] Apuleius, "Metamorphoses," in *Greek and Roman Slavery*, edited by Thomas Wiedemann (New York: Routledge, 2003), 170.
[112] Galen, "The Diseases of the Mind," in *Greek and Roman Slavery*, edited by Thomas Wiedemann (New York: Routledge, 2003), 173.
[113] Plotinus, *The Six Enneads* (Grand Rapids, MI: Christian Classics Ethereal Library, 1975), Sixth Ennead, Eighth Tractate.

populace, serving to provide necessaries to the better sort. But what of murder? What of the feebleness that brings men under slavery to the passions? Is it any wonder that there should be failing and error, not in the highest, the intellectual Principle, but in Souls that are like undeveloped children?[114]

According to Plotinus, the souls of Men who are "enslaved" by passions are like the ones of "undeveloped children," again tying the idea of slavery to infantilization. Moreover, this notion of souls that are lacking in "virtue" and human development is offered as justification of the economic obligation of a social class of producers, the "mere populace." The Greco-Roman world concocted an emotional economy in which the enslaved are never allowed to be children as children or adults as adults. It is an inevitable, degraded, and permanent infancy that set the framework for the modern racialization of childhood and the uninterrupted economic exploitation of the emotional Other.

Diogenes Laërtius delivered the most categorical statement of the Stoic stance on emotional slavery: "for that freedom is a power of independent action, but slavery is a deprivation of the same. That there is besides another slavery, which consists in subjection, and a third which consists in possession and subjection."[115] Stoicism denied the actuality of slavery by continually relativizing its relevance with the prevalence of "slavery to passions," while also defining enslavement as a product of Fortune.[116] The early Christian Church would transform the discourse of "slavery by Fortune" into "slavery by Divine Providence" and would generate much knowledge production about the spiritual "benefits" of the enslaved condition.[117]

SLAVERY TO SIN: EMOTIONAL JUSTIFICATIONS OF SLAVERY IN CHRISTIAN THOUGHT AND THE MEDIEVAL WORLD

The advent of Christian thought[118] not only acknowledged slavery, but also applied tropes of enslavement to contextualize spiritual teachings. Both the Old and the New Testaments depict slavery as a laudable

---

[114] Plotinus, *The Six Enneads*, Second Ennead, Ninth Tractate.
[115] Diogenes Laërtius, *The Lives and Opinions of Eminent Philosophers* (London: George Bell and Sons, 1901), 303.
[116] Hunt, "Slavery in Greek Literary Culture," 45.
[117] Robin Blackburn, *The Making of New World Slavery: From the Baroque to the Modern, 1492–1800* (London: Verso, 1998), 36.
[118] It is important to mention that the advent of Christian thought not only was grounded on Jewish texts but was also influenced by Egyptian, Greco-Roman, and Nubian

condition, celebrating spiritual emancipation in Exodus, commemorating the crucifixion of the enslaved as the death of Christ, and exalting the metaphor of "slavery to the Lord."[119] Psalm 123 equates the adoration of God to the expected docility of an enslaved person.

> To you I lift up my eyes,
> O you who are enthroned in the heavens!
> as the eyes of servants look to the hand of their master,
> as the eyes of a maid to the hand of her mistress,
> so our eyes look to the LORD our God,
> until he has mercy upon us.[120]

The metaphor of "slavery to the Lord" is framed by the narrative of Exodus: after emancipation, God became the exclusive "master of men."[121] Similarly, the Gospel of Matthew likens the preparation of the soul for the "coming of the Son of Man" to the obedience of a submissive enslaved person. The consequences of infringing the duties of a loyal enslaved person are ruthless.

> Who then is the faithful and wise slave, whom his master has put in charge of his household, to give the other slaves their allowance of food at the proper time? Blessed is that slave whom his master will find at work when he arrives. Truly I tell you, he will put that one in charge of all his possessions. But if that wicked slave says to himself, "My master is delayed," and he begins to beat his fellow slaves, and eats and drinks with drunkards, the master of that slave will come on a day when he does not expect him and at an hour he does not know. He will cut him in pieces and put him with the hypocrites, where there will be weeping and gnashing of teeth.[122]

The description of the repercussions of "disobedience" of the enslaved highlights the emotional responses to punishment, but the fault is the enslaved person's alone. This fear-provoking passage aims to clarify the paybacks of being a "faithful and wise slave," mindful and emotionally prepared for the new coming of Christ. While the Gospel of Matthew visualizes the "weeping" of the "wicked slave," the Pauline Epistles, like Psalm 123, openly intertwine the ideal condition of "slavery to Christ" with religious feelings. "For you were called to freedom, brothers and

---

religious traditions. See Michael A. Gomez, *Reversing Sail: A History of the African Diaspora* (New York: Cambridge University Press, 2005), 16.

[119] Ilaria L. E. Ramelli, *Social Justice and the Legitimacy of Slavery: The Role of Philosophical Asceticism from Ancient Judaism to Late Antiquity* (Oxford: Oxford University Press, 2016), 81.

[120] *The New Oxford Annotated Bible* (Oxford: Oxford University Press, 2010), Psalm 123.

[121] Hezser, *Jewish Slavery in Antiquity*, 328.

[122] *The New Oxford Annotated Bible*, Matthew 24:45.

sisters; only do not use your freedom as an opportunity for self-indulgence, but through love become enslaved to one another. For the whole law is summed up in a single commandment, 'You shall love your neighbor as yourself.'"[123] Love is deemed a feeling that binds Christians to their faith and to each other, and slavery is pictured as a desired spiritual practice of religious fraternity. Although the "docile" enslaved person is constructed as an ethical model of faith in God, Christ, and the universality of humanity, the trope of slavery simultaneously illustrates the adverse nature of being "enslaved by sin."[124] "So then, with my mind I am a slave to the law of God, but with my flesh I am a slave to the law of sin."[125] The slavery of the "flesh" to sin and wealth, as expressed in biblical texts, is evidently rooted in the Stoic rhetoric of "slavery to passions," and so a new paradigm prolonged the reach of the dominance of slaveholding economic regimes.

The Epistle to the Ephesians categorically normalizes slavery and dictates a distinct code of conduct for enslaved people and masters, in which the enslaved were advised to both "fearfully" and "enthusiastically" serve their enslavers.

Slaves, obey your earthly masters with fear and trembling, in singleness of heart, as you obey Christ; not only while being watched, and in order to please them, but as slaves of Christ, doing the will of God from the heart. Render service with enthusiasm, as to the Lord and not to men and women, knowing that whatever good we do, we will receive the same again from the Lord, whether we are slaves or free. And, masters, do the same to them. Stop threatening them, for you know that both of you have the same Master in heaven, and with him there is no partiality.[126]

Since God is regarded as the "Master" of all, biblical texts not only relativize slavery, but also commend the obedient service of the enslaved as a paradigm for religious faith and as an advantage in divine judgment and deliverance. Enslaved people must obey their enslavers as they do Christ, "doing the will of God from the heart." The expectations over enslaved feelings are high: they must both "fear" the Master and show "enthusiasm" in their own exploitation. Not only do the scriptures encourage a parallelism between the omnipresence of master authority and the omnipresence of God, but they also summon the historical

---

[123] *The New Oxford Annotated Bible*, Galatians 5:13.
[124] Glancy, "Slavery and the Rise of Christianity," 460.
[125] *The New Oxford Annotated Bible*, Romans 7:24.
[126] *The New Oxford Annotated Bible*, Ephesians 6:5.

discourse of "trembling" enslaved bodies as experiencing a spiritual deliverance enacted by divine will. The symbiotic link between these two principles sets a precedent for the discursive legitimization of the omnipresence of racialized emotional policing in the Atlantic world.

Early Christianity strikingly granted much significance to the emotional religious experiences tied to the subservience to God: love as instructed in the commandments of the New Testament, disinterested anger toward undue actions, ritualization of guilt, and joyous liturgical tribute to Christ.[127] Within the celebration of religious love, love was to be felt in a sublime emotional level and to be perceived both as a grace of God and as a proof of faith.[128] Certainly, this tradition led to the performativity of religious experiences as beyond the emotional ordinary, the interpretation of religious conversion as a "joyous relief," and the understanding of confession (or testimony) as a pleasurable revelation of scriptural insight.[129] Religious experiences were furthermore represented as carrying ecstatic out-of-worldly sensations with sensual undertones.[130]

Gregory of Nyssa brought an early voice of antislavery thought in *Homilies on Ecclesiastes*. His emotional rationale was grounded on the narrative of Genesis.

> God said, let us make man in our own image and likeness. If he is in the likeness of God, and rules the whole earth, and has been granted authority over everything on earth from God, who is his buyer, tell me? Who is his seller? To God alone belongs this power: or rather not even to God himself. For his gracious gifts, it says, are irrevocable. God would not therefore reduce the human race to slavery, since he himself, when we had been enslaved to sin, spontaneously recalled us to freedom. But if God does not enslave what is free, who is he that sets his own power above God's?[131]

The bishop not only justifies his thinking with the biblical description of the divine creation, but also points to the "irrevocability" of God's gifts, since God had liberated humanity from "slavery to sin." Furthermore, Gregory of Nyssa validates the common origin of humanity

---

[127] Hubert Knoblauch & Regine Herbrik, "Emotional Knowledge, Emotional Styles, and Religion," in *Collective Emotions*, edited by Christian von Scheve & Mikko Salmela (Oxford: Oxford University Press, 2014), 361.
[128] Nancy Martin & Joseph Runzo, "Love," in *The Oxford Handbook of Religion and Emotion*, edited by John Corrigan (Oxford: Oxford University Press, 2007), 313–318.
[129] Douglas J. Davies, *Emotion, Identity, and Religion: Hope, Reciprocity, and Otherness* (Oxford: Oxford University Press, 2011), 51, 216, 220.
[130] Angelika Malinar & Helene Basu, "Ectasy," in *The Oxford Handbook of Religion and Emotion*, edited by John Corrigan (Oxford: Oxford University Press, 2007), 246.
[131] Gregory of Nyssa, *Homilies on Ecclesiastes* (Berlin: Walter de Gruyter, 1993), 74.

with the universality of emotions and bodily sensations. "Your origin is from the same ancestors, your life of the same kind, sufferings of soul and body prevail alike over you who own him and over the one who is subject to your ownership – pains and pleasures, merriment and distress, sorrows and delights, rages and terrors, sickness and death."[132] In this instance, emotions are pictured as "sufferings" of the soul, but this passage still amalgamates passions and bodily sensations. Throughout his work, Gregory of Nyssa refers to emotions as a way to cultivate a normative code of religious devotion.

> Thus those whose soul's eyes are blinded by error in this recent age have made vanity their God. To sum up, whatever a person submits his reason to, making it slave and subject, he has in his sickness made that into a god, and he would not be in this state if he had not attached himself to evil by love.[133]

According to *Homilies on Ecclesiastes*, "vanity" is an emotional state that can be described as a sinful "love of oneself." This love can in turn be defined as a disease for its emotional "attachment to evil." Gregory of Nyssa categorizes "vanity" as an emotional sickness that "submits reason" to slavery and deviates from the adoration of the authentic God. The bishop demystifies the "proper" manner to love God in his interpretation of *Song of Songs*: the rhetorical model of Christ as a groom and the soul/Church as a bride symbolizes the necessity of the soul to transform passionate love toward the self (and its bodily urges) to a mindful "passion" of the spirit toward God.[134] *Homilies on Ecclesiastes* also explicitly comments on the desired control of passions by stressing the limits of freedom.

> What the more devout understanding is disposed to think is this: that the good gift of God, that is, freedom of action, became a means to sin through the sinful use mankind made of it. For unfettered free will is good by nature, and nobody would reckon among good things anything which was constrained by the yoke of necessity. But that free impulse of the mind rushing unschooled towards the choice of evil became a source of distress for the soul, as it was dragged down from the sublime and honourable toward the urges of natural passions.[135]

Therefore, Gregory of Nyssa denounces the elimination of "spiritual" freedom by emphasizing the universality of emotions and warning against

---

[132] Gregory of Nyssa, *Homilies on Ecclesiastes*, 75.
[133] Gregory of Nyssa, *Homilies on Ecclesiastes*, 135.
[134] Niklaus Largier, "Medieval Mysticism," in *The Oxford Handbook of Religion and Emotion*, edited by John Corrigan (Oxford: Oxford University Press, 2007), 365.
[135] Gregory of Nyssa, *Homilies on Ecclesiastes*, 50.

"freedom of action" degrading into a "means to sin" and unbridled passions. In sum, although Gregory of Nyssa condemns slavery as an "evil" institution, his rhetoric paradoxically still draws from and normalizes the relativist notion of "slavery to sin." Likewise, during a sermon on the Epistle to the Ephesians, John Chrysostom echoed this antislavery stance grounded on the discourse of "slavery to sin," denoting the institution of slavery as the "fruit of sin" and "result of greed, of degradation, or brutality," while also conceptualizing enslavement as a "post-flood" institution.[136]

Nonetheless, prominent Christian theorists immortalized the Stoic doctrine of "slavery to passions" and extended it to the premise of "slavery to sin" in order to validate the institution of slavery in the pursuit of eternal life and to advocate for legal distinctions between masters and the enslaved, all under the veil of biblical exegesis.[137] Augustine became the normative voice of religious intellectual production about the institution of slavery. *The City of God* notoriously portrayed slavery as a favorable condition, an early worldly punishment for the original sin.[138]

> And obviously it is a happier lot to be a slave to a human being than to a lust; and in fact, the most pitiless domination that devastates the hearts of men, is that exercised by this very lust for domination, to mention no others. However, in that order of peace in which men are subordinate to other men, humility is as salutary for the servants as pride is harmful to the masters. And yet by nature, in the condition in which God created man, no man is the slave either of man or sin. But it remains true that slavery as a punishment is also ordained by that law which enjoins the preservation of the order of nature, and forbids its disturbance.[139]

Augustine depicts slavery as a lesser detriment to happiness in comparison to "slavery to lust for domination." While lust and pride "devastate the hearts of men," the cleansing "humility" intrinsic to the enslaved condition generates an "order of peace." Augustinian thought equates this "order of peace" with the "preservation of the order of nature," justifying the unnatural enslavement of God's creation with the motive of the law that regulates it as a social practice. *The City of God* reinforces the notion of the "order of slavery" with the paradoxical reasoning of the inherent freedom of the enslaved person. "For the evils inflicted on the

---

[136] Chris L. De Wet, *Preaching Bondage: John Chrysostom and the Discourse of Slavery in Early Christianity* (Oakland: University of California Press, 2015), 1.
[137] See Glancy, "Slavery and the Rise of Christianity," 473.
[138] Blackburn, *The Making of New World Slavery*, 36.
[139] Augustine, *The City of God* (London: Penguin, 2003), 493.

righteous by then-wicked masters are not punishments for a crime but tests of virtue. The good man, though a slave, is free; the wicked, though he reigns, is a slave, and not the slave of a single man, but – what is far worse – the slave of as many masters as he has vices."[140] The earthly experience of slavery is conceptualized as a set of "tests of virtue" that have the potentiality of purifying the soul from the original sin. On the contrary, sinful slaveholders could possibly have many passions as their "masters." Augustine contends that passions are of a demonical influence, consolidating the parallelism of "slavery to passions" and "slavery to sin."

> Thus the mind of the demons is in subjection to the passions of desire, of fear, of anger, and the rest. Then is there any part of them free and capable of wisdom, which can make them acceptable to the gods, and of service to man by offering an example of morality? How can there be, if their mind is subdued under the oppressive tyranny of vicious passions, and employs for seduction and deception all the rational power that it has by nature, with all the more eagerness as the lust for doing harm gains increasing mastery?[141]

The Augustinian theory of "oppressive tyranny of vicious passions" would influence the medieval understanding of the demonic and would extensively relativize and legitimize the condition of slavery. The later Franciscan movement commemorated the contemplation of imagery of the crucifixion of the enslaved as the iconography of the sacrifice of Christ, as the emotional incarnation of spiritual suffering.[142] In *The Governance of God*, Salvian, almost contemporaneously to Augustine, rendered enslaved people as fearful of "bad earthly masters," in comparison to the wealthy who did not dread the divine master and were therefore more likely to satisfy their carnal desires in excessive and "uncontrolled" ways.

> So why are you rich men finding fault with your slaves? You're behaving exactly as they are, since they may well be running away from a bad master, but you from a good one. And then you accuse your slaves of uncontrolled gluttony. This sin is rarely true of a slave, because they lack the means to satisfy it – but it is frequent with you, since you have the means.[143]

---

[140] Augustine, *The City of God*, ccxii.   [141] Augustine, *The City of God*, cdlxv.
[142] Largier, "Medieval Mysticism," 374.
[143] Salvian, "The Governance of God," in *Greek and Roman Slavery*, edited by Thomas Wiedemann (New York: Routledge, 2003), 59.

The Emotional Foundations of Racialized Slavery

While the sacred texts of the three dominant monotheistic religions do not explicitly allude to racialized categories as markers of difference,[144] these religious canons did trivialize slavery and propelled ideas rooted in exclusionary politics. The Islamic Sharia Law would standardize the enslavement of Dar al-Kufr, or "pagans," by Dar al-Islam, the "faithful people of Islam."[145] This code of religious morality led to Africa and Eastern Europe becoming a significant source of enslaved people during the Middle Ages, regardless of their conversion.[146] Not only did the enslaved condition tend to be disaffected by conversion, but the Muslim offspring of enslaved parents would usually still be regarded as unfree,[147] and, just as in ancient Greco-Roman sources, the political unit of the household criminalized those who lived in the sidelines.[148] Eventually, *abd*, the Arabic term for an enslaved person, would be strongly tied to Blackness.[149] Internal African slavery since the ancient world had targeted regional "outsiders,"[150] was premised on the unfreedom of military enemies,[151] and grew during medieval times to being a fundamental component of the economic systems and political alliances of States.[152] Meanwhile, medieval jurists throughout Europe documented ancient Roman law and its figure of *patria potestas* as the foundation of the *ius commune*. Consequently, the *ius commune* contemplated slavery as merely a severer gradation of subjugation in the context of general society in Europe,[153] further solidifying societal apathy toward the condition of slavery during the Middle Ages.[154] Within medieval

---

[144] David Brion Davis, *In the Image of God: Religion, Moral Values, and Our Heritage of Slavery* (New York: Vail-Ballou Press, 2001), 144.

[145] David Robinson, *Muslim Societies in African History* (New York: Cambridge University Press, 2004), 63.

[146] Paul E. Lovejoy, *Transformations in Slavery: A History of Slavery in Africa* (New York: Cambridge University Press, 2000), 16.

[147] Bernard Lewis, *Race and Slavery in the Middle East: A Historical Inquiry* (Oxford: Oxford University Press, 1990), 9.

[148] Ehud R. Toledano, *As if Silent and Absent: Bonds of Enslavement in the Islamic Middle East* (New Haven, CT: Yale University Press, 2007), 24–30.

[149] Davis, *In the Image of God*, 141.

[150] Patrick Manning, *The African Diaspora: A History through Culture* (New York: Columbia University Press, 2009), 52.

[151] Lovejoy, *Transformations in Slavery*, 22.

[152] Sean Stilwell, *Slavery and Slaving in African History* (New York: Cambridge University Press, 2014), 32.

[153] R. H. Helmholz, "The Law of Slavery and the European *Ius Commune*," in *The Legal Understanding of Slavery: From the Historical to the Contemporary*, edited by Jean Allain (Oxford: Oxford University Press, 2012), 21.

[154] Alice Rio, *Slavery after Rome, 500–1100* (Oxford: Oxford University Press, 2017), 216.

slaveholding networks that targeted Africans,[155] there are primary sources that allude to the desirability of West African enslaved women for their "lustrous Black skin."[156] The enslaving "trade" networks throughout the "Old World" would only further propagate with the increasingly globalized and capitalistic demand of tropical goods.[157]

Medieval intellectual production of the Atlantic world continued disseminating discourses of emotional enslavement, while also providing insight into the role of slavery in engendering medieval chains of being. The fourteenth-century Ethiopian Christian epic *Kebra Nagast* channeled religious imagery of slavery in the "Parable of the Two Slaves."

> A certain king had two slaves; one was arrogant and strong, and the other was humble and weak. And the arrogant overcame the humble one and smote him all but killed him, and robbed him, and the king upon his throne saw them. And the king descended and seized the arrogant slave, beat him and crushed him, bound him in fetters and cast him into a place of darkness. Then he raised up his humble and weak slave, embraced him and brushed away the dust from him, washed him and poured oil and wine on his wounds and set him upon his horse and brought him into his city; and he set him upon his throne and seated him on his right hand. The king is in truth Christ, the arrogant servant is Satan, and the humble servant is Adam.[158]

This parable based on Genesis constructs Adam as a "humble and weak slave" of Christ, while Satan represents an antithetical enslaved person due to his "arrogance." Satan's "arrogance" is subjected to the divine punishments of violence, captivity, and exile. Thus, *Kebra Nagast* displays the relativism of slavery, the biblical dichotomy of the faithful-wicked enslaved, and the principle of "slavery to sin." The passage establishes a gradation of states of slavery and depicts the "arrogance" of the enslaved as innately demonic. Following the biblical framework, the transgression of the enslaved person who steps out of the boundaries of enslaved humility is considered a religious abomination, one that strays away from the spiritual love of Christ.

---

[155] Robinson, *Muslim Societies in African History*, 64. During the Middle Ages, economies of enslavement that targeted Africans expanded "Old World" networks of commercial exchange.
[156] Michael Gomez, *African Dominion: A New History of Empire in Early and Medieval West Africa* (Princeton, NJ: Princeton University Press, 2018), 36.
[157] Matthew S. Hopper, *Slaves of One Master: Globalization and Slavery in Arabia in the Age of Empire* (New Haven, CT: Yale University Press, 2015), 15.
[158] Miguel F. Brooks, trans., *A Modern Translation of Kebra Nagast (The Glory of Kings)* (Lawrenceville: Red Sea, 2002), 144.

The Emotional Foundations of Racialized Slavery 33

The *Muqaddimah* by Ibn Khaldun appeared in 1377 as an early manifestation of geographical determinism, the principle that diverse climates produce differentiated populations with a distinct set of behaviors. His definition of Blackness is precisely focused on emotional impulsivity.

> Heat dominates their temperament and formation. Therefore, they have in their spirits an amount of heat corresponding to that in their bodies and that of the zone in which they live. In comparison with the spirits of the inhabitants of the fourth zone, theirs are hotter and, consequently, more expanded. As a result, they are more quickly moved to joy and gladness, and they are merrier. Excitability is the direct consequence.[159]

According to Khaldun, the ardor of Africa's "hot zone" affects Black bodies and "spirits." Heat produces an "excitability" that is prone to "quick" bursts of "joy and gladness." This "excitability" is constructed as the "direct consequence" of an "expanded" spirit. Thus, Khaldun projects emotional impulsivity as emerging from a "spirit" that has been "expanded" by heat, foreshadowing the use of deterministic language of science to impose a racial hierarchy of emotional volatility. A fundamental pillar of geographical determinism would precisely be that heat is presumed to affect both "temperament and formation." Heat may temporarily disturb a newcomer to a hotter climate, but it is intrinsic to the "formation" of those born in hotter climates, dominating their racialized "temperament." The onerous mark of emotional "excitability" would be consequently unavoidable for Black and Brown bodies.

Medieval European literature insistently incorporated references to slavery as tropes of religious conversion and "emotive" national conquests and defeats. In *The Divine Comedy*, Dante Alighieri exclaimed: "Slave Italy! Hostel of grief!," fusing a metaphor of slavery with a figurative proclamation of national suffering.[160] *The Decameron* by Giovanni Boccaccio not only alluded to "slavery to Love" and "slavery to the Lord," but also narrated the tale of a nurse who "wept long and bitterly" on realizing she had become enslaved, until she comprehended that "tears were useless."[161] *The Canterbury Tales* by Geoffrey Chaucer displayed much commentary about the institution of slavery, especially in

---

[159] Ibn Khaldun, *The Muqaddimah: An Introduction to History* (Princeton, NJ: Princeton University Press, 1377), 63.
[160] Dante Alighieri, *The Divine Comedy* (New York: W. W. Norton & Company, 2013), 88.
[161] Giovanni Bocaccio, *Decameron* (Hertfordshire: Wordsworth, 2004), 113.

the final tale of the book, "The Parson's Tale." This text about penitence includes a reference to the biblical narrative of the Curse of Ham. "And furthermore, understand well that conquerors or tyrants often make thralls of those who were born of as royal blood as those who have conquered. This word of thralldom was unknown until Noah said that his grandson Canaan should be servant to his brethren for his sin."[162] Chaucer's dissertation about conquerors and the conquered further evaluates the "order of slavery."

> But certainly, since the time of grace came, God ordained that some folk should be higher in rank and state and some folk in lower, and that each should be served according to his rank and his state. And therefore, in some countries, where they buy slaves, when they have converted them to the faith, they set their slaves free from slavery.[163]

"The Parson's Tale" asserts not only that there is a God-sanctioned "order by rank and state" but that this "order" is also affected by religious conviction. Hence, Chaucer affirms that, while conversion could justify the emancipation of enslaved people, their "sinfulness" or lack of adherence to the faith vindicates their subjugation. Moreover, "The Monk's Tale" inherits the Stoic doctrine of slavery being a product of Fortune.

> Masters, therefrom a moral may you take,
> That in dominion is no certainness;
> For when Fortune will any man forsake,
> She takes his realm and all he may possess,
> And all his friends, too, both the great and less;
> For when a man has friends that Fortune gave,
> Mishap but turns them enemies, as I guess:
> This word is true for king as well as slave.[164]

Chaucer endorses the medieval persistence of the relativism of slavery, intellectualizing the slippery slope from the condition of the master, or "dominion," to the status of the enslaved person as one tied to the role of Fortune in the shift from friend to foe. The Chain of Being is dreadfully variable, or so did the European elite claim. Now, this "variability" still depended on the slaveholding assessment of the religious devotion of the enslaved.

Scholasticism further diffused Aristotelian thought on slavery and augmented the tie of slavery to "femininity" and "sin." *Summa*

---

[162] Geoffrey Chaucer, *The Canterbury Tales* (New York: Dover, 2004), 514.
[163] Chaucer, *The Canterbury Tales*, 514.   [164] Chaucer, *The Canterbury Tales*, 211.

theologica by Thomas Aquinas conceived exorcisms as acts "by which man is wholly freed from the slavery of the devil."[165] The Scholastic writer stated in a letter that Jewish "guilt" had resulted in their "perpetual slavery."[166] Aquinas also validated the rationality behind the heredity of slavery in matrilineal lineage. "Now slavery is a condition of the body, since a slave is to the master a kind of instrument in working; wherefore children follow the mother in freedom and in bondage; whereas in matters pertaining to dignity as proceeding from a thing's form, they follow the father, for instance in honours, franchise, inheritance, and so forth."[167] This influential figure of the medieval clergy constructs slavery as a bodily status and simultaneously ties the corporeal to the figure of the Mother. On the contrary, the concepts of dignity and honor, connected to the soul, are found within the realm of the Father. This reasoning extends the reach of the ancient notion of slavery as a corporeal ailment outside the sphere of "masculine" rationality.

During the Renaissance, there was a free Black African "presence" in Europe, and ideas about "Blackness" were fluctuating.[168] Isabelle D'Este infamously purchased "exotic" enslaved Africans for them to "model" for her financed "works of art," setting a pattern for the intersection of art and racialized exploitation.[169] In *The Oration on the Dignity of Man*, Giovanni Pico della Mirandolla regarded "slavery to appetites and to senses" as obstacles to the pursuit of knowledge and as a sign of inhumanity, fostering the Renaissance's recalling of the ancient discourse of "slavery to passions."

If you see someone who is a slave to his belly, crawling along the ground, it is not a man you see, but a plant; if you see someone who is enslaved by his own senses, blinded by the empty hallucinations brought on by fantasy (as if by Calypso herself) and entranced by their bedeviling spells, it is a brute animal you see, not a man.[170]

---

[165] Thomas Aquinas, *Summa theologica* (New York: Benziger, 1922), 41.
[166] Blackburn, *The Making of New World Slavery*, 45.
[167] Aquinas, *Summa theologica*, 181.
[168] Kate Lowe, "Introduction: The Black African Presence in Renaissance Europe," in *Black Africans in Renaissance Europe*, edited by T. F. Earle & K. J. P. Lowe (New York: Cambridge University Press, 2009), 2–11.
[169] David Bindman & Henry Louis Gates, Jr., *The Image of the Black in Western Art: From the "Age of Discovery" to the Age of Abolition: Artists of the Renaissance and Baroque* (Cambridge, MA: Harvard University Press, 2010), 102.
[170] Giovanni Pico della Mirandolla, *Oration on the Dignity of Man* (New York: Cambridge University Press, 2012), 131.

It has been theorized that Michelangelo's *Nakedness of Noah* exemplifies a historical rupture in the interpretation of the Curse of Ham, with Noah shifting from a "first Christ" to a "second Adam."[171] Indeed, the Age of Exploration led to the opportunistic parallel reading of the Curse of Ham, the Table of Nations, and the dispersion of the Tower of Babel as divine puzzles of racial differentiation.[172]

THE EMOTIONAL RACIALIZATION OF THE GLOBALIZATION OF SLAVERY

In the thirteenth century, King Alfonso X's Siete Partidas responded to the resurgence of ancient Roman law in the Middle Ages and would precisely preserve this canonical influence by eventually infiltrating the colonial legislation on slavery in the Spanish colonies,[173] prescribing an emotional political economy in the Atlantic world. The Siete Partidas consolidated the notion of "slavery to passions" with the principle of "slavery to sin" through its legal conceptualization of "avarice."

> A King Should Not, in His Heart, Covet Excessive Riches: And they said of it, besides, that a man who eagerly desires to collect great treasures, but not for the purpose of doing good with them, although he may have them in possession, is not their master, but their slave; since avarice prevents him from making use of them in a way which would be to his credit. A man of this kind is said to be guilty of avarice, which is regarded by God as a great and mortal sin, and a serious and evil condition in the world.[174]

While the title of the law is limited to the "King," the content of the law conveys the universality of "emotional slavery," as generating "a serious and evil condition in the world." The wording expresses "avarice" as the legal and spiritual transgression that represents both a passion and a sin, in turn making Man (and even a King) enslaved. Furthermore, while this regulation uses discourses of emotion to feature the condition of the King,

---

[171] Benjamin Braude, "Michelangelo and the Curse of Ham: From a Typology of Jew-Hatred to a Genealogy of Racism," in *Signs of Race: Writing Race across the Atlantic World: Medieval to Modern*, edited by Taylor Beidler (New York: Palgrave Macmillan, 2005), 79.

[172] See Stephen R. Haynes, *Noah's Curse: The Biblical Justification of American Slavery* (Oxford: Oxford University Press, 2002), 6.

[173] William D. Phillips, Jr., *Slavery in Medieval and Early Modern Iberia* (Philadelphia: University of Pennsylvania Press, 2014), 21.

[174] Robert I. Burns, ed., *Las Siete Partidas, vol. 1: The Medieval Church: The World of Clerics and Laymen* (Philadelphia: University of Pennsylvania Press, 2001), 281.

another law does the same to encompass the "ideal" behavior of those governed by a monarch.

> How the People Should Fear the King, and What Difference There is Between Fear and Dread: For as wise men once stated, there is no distinction between him who is a prisoner in chains, and in power of his enemies, and him who is the slave of his own will, so that he is obliged something on account of which he will deserve punishment. For, undoubtedly, he who commits an offence subjects himself to the slavery of the penalty which he deserved to undergo on account to it. And with this agrees what the Apostle St. John said, namely, that whoever commits sin is its slave.[175]

Therefore, the Siete Partidas consistently fuses legal transgressions with the condition of being "enslaved by passions and sin," which in turn facilitates an elaborate justification of the power of masters to inflict systematic bodily harm in the enslaved by "their own will." King Alfonso el Sabio's legal framework prohibits a master from filing complaints "against his slave" and orders the slaveholder to instead "exercise his rights over him by punishing him by reproof, or by blows, in such a way as not to kill or cripple him."[176] Along the same lines, if an enslaved person caused "dishonor" on another master, the enslaver of the "dishonorable" enslaved person had to "deliver" them to the "wronged" party, so that the other master could exercise his right to "punish him with blows in such a way as not to kill or maim him."[177] Following the ancient Roman legal framework, the bodily penalization of enslaved people by slaveholders was abstracted as exercising a right and ridding the State of the onus of discipline and punishment of the enslaved population. Still, the State did have the authority and capacity of torturing the enslaved to acquire information against their "masters."[178]

The Siete Partidas also highlights the discourse of the infantilization of the enslaved person, by reiterating the vulnerability of "emotionally immature" enslaved people to being corrupted by the adult rationality of slaveholders. This legal framework forbid children from summoning their parents and, intriguingly, the same law established that emancipated persons could not legally summon "those who enfranchised them," since formerly enslaved people were expected to "always reverence and honor"

---

[175] Burns, ed., *Las Siete Partidas*, vol. 1, 352.
[176] Robert I. Burns, ed., *Las Siete Partidas, vol. 2: Medieval Government: The World of Kings and Warriors* (Philadelphia: University of Pennsylvania Press, 2001), 539.
[177] Robert I. Burns, ed., *Las Siete Partidas, vol. 5: Underworlds: The Dead, the Criminal, and the Marginalized* (Philadelphia: University of Pennsylvania Press, 2001), 1358.
[178] Burns, ed., *Las Siete Partidas*, vol. 5, 1460.

their former enslavers.[179] This law thus regards the act of deliverance as a deed of paternalism and indissoluble familial ties. Furthermore, the Siete Partidas constructs the "corruption of a slave" as a legal transgression: "What Penalty Those Deserve Who Corrupt Slaves, Making the Good Ones Bad, and the Bad Ones Worse: And what we stated in this law and concerning those who corrupt the slaves of others applies also to those who corrupt the sons, daughters, grandsons, granddaughters, or servants of a household."[180] Hence, the Siete Partidas depicts enslaved people as elements of a domestic sphere that could be "corrupted" by another domestic sphere, while also maintaining an enslaved person within an infantile stage of emotional development. To protect the home from "perversion" was to safeguard the economic future of the Master.

The European conquest of the Americas would be precisely endorsed by the interplay of ideas of corruption of emotions and blood. The colonies of the Americas would inherit the reverberations of the Iberian fixation on *"limpieza de sangre,"* a fusion of religious and genealogical intolerance that ostracized *"conversos"* and *"moriscos,"* and this fascination led to the *"averiguación de limpieza,"* an inquest into the "cleanliness" of blood and the verification of a pure bloodline of Christian "ancestry."[181] The conquest of the "New World" was framed by symbolic acts of possession that were in turn centered on the notion of *"res nullius,"* the seizure of land that was considered common property, acts such as ritualistic invasion, cartographic renaming, and Eurocentric territorial disputes.[182] From there, globalized modernity would sophisticate a Eurocentric hierarchy of nations based on opportunistic projections of History, Language, and the development of States, forming a historical geography.[183] Even before the conquest of the Americas, the Catholic Church had legitimized slavery with discourses of the Reconquista, providing the Portuguese state with religious authorization to "trade" in African ports.[184] In 1455, Pope Nicholas V released the papal bull

---

[179] Burns, ed., *Las Siete Partidas*, vol. 2, 606.

[180] Burns, ed., *Las Siete Partidas*, vol. 5, 1392.

[181] Barbara Fuchs, "A Mirror across the Water: Mimetic Racism, Hybridity, and Cultural Survival," in *Signs of Race: Writing Race across the Atlantic World: Medieval to Modern*, edited by Taylor Beidler (New York: Palgrave Macmillan, 2005), 9–10.

[182] J. H. Elliot, *Empires of the Atlantic World: Britain and Spain in America, 1492–1830* (New Haven, CT: Yale University Press, 2016), 30–34.

[183] Ranajit Guha, *History at the Limit of World-History* (New York: Columbia University Press, 2002), 12.

[184] Gwendolyn M. Hall, *Slavery and African Ethnicities in the Americas: Restoring the Links* (Chapel Hill: University of North Carolina Press, 2005), 7.

The Emotional Foundations of Racialized Slavery

Romanus Pontifex, which authorized and justified enslavement as a method of propagation of Christianity.[185] In 1493, the papal bull Inter Caetera by Pope Alexander VI extended its sanction to the Americas, conceiving non-Catholic lands as "barbaric" and declaring the expansion of Catholic faith as the priority of conquering and colonizing missions.[186] Genocide and contagion were "interdependent forces"[187] that engendered a panorama of bloodstained conquest.[188] The European conquest of the Americas was marked by genocidal violence through enslavement, mass killings, and family separations, which in turn led to an exacerbation of the "susceptibility" of indigenous populations to disease.[189]

Bartolomé de las Casas emerged as a figure who spread "passionate" denunciations of maltreatment by Spanish conquistadores and the intrinsic "vulnerability" of the indigenous populations of the Americas, while also preliminarily propelling the idea of Africa being a source of "naturally" (and stronger) enslaved people.[190] In *Brevísima relación de la destrucción de las Indias*, the friar interweaved accounts of mass killings of indigenous people with religious imagery: "Considérese agora, por Dios, ... qué obra ésta y si excede a toda crueldad e injusticia que pueda ser pensada; y si les cuadra bien a los tales cristianos llamarlos diablos, y si sería más encomendar los indios a los diablos del infierno que es encomendarlos a los cristianos de las Indias."[191] The portrayal of Spanish colonizers as "cruel devils" is accentuated by the emotional responses to the genocidal slaughters of indigenous populations.

---

[185] Nicolaus V, "Romanus Pontifex (1455)," in *European Treaties Bearing on the History of the United States and Its Dependencies*, edited by Frances G. Davenport (Washington, DC: Carnegie Institution, 1917), 16.

[186] Alexander VI, "Inter Caetera (1493)," in *European Treaties Bearing on the History of the United States and Its Dependencies*, edited by Frances G. Davenport (Washington, DC: Carnegie Institution, 1917), 73.

[187] David E. Stannard, *American Holocaust: The Conquest of the New World* (Oxford: Oxford University Press, 1992), xii.

[188] See Norman M. Naimark, *Genocide: A World History* (Oxford: Oxford University Press, 2017), 35. The death toll of this genocide is estimated to have reached 70 million out of 80 million indigenous people in the continent.

[189] Ben Kiernan, *Blood and Soil: A World History of Genocide and Extermination from Sparta to Darfur* (New Haven, CT: Yale University Press, 2007), 100.

[190] See David Eltis, *The Rise of African Slavery in the Americas* (New York: Cambridge University Press, 2000), 15.

[191] Bartolomé de las Casas, *Brevísima relación de la destrucción de las Indias* (Barcelona: Linkgua, 2017), 76. Translation to English: "Consider now, for God, ... what wrongdoing, and if it exceeds all cruelty and injustice that can be conceived, and if it fits well to call those Christians devils, and if it would be better to entrust the indigenous people to the devils of Hell than to entrust them to the Christians of the 'Indies.'"

"¡Cuántas lágrimas hizo derramar, cuántos suspiros, cuántos gemidos, cuántas soledades en esta vida y de cuántos damnación eterna en la otra causó, no solo de indios, que fueron infinitos, pero de los infelices cristianos ... en tan grandes insultos, gravísimos pecados y abominaciones tan execrables!"[192] De las Casas conveyed the enslaved indigenous experience in the Americas as one that was encompassed by a distressed display of emotions expressed through "tears," "sighs," and "moans." These expressions were "contagious," since, while indigenous populations were compelled to incessant "tears" in life, the Spanish colonizers would be punished to eternal grief for their "sins" and "abominations."

The Leyes de Burgos of 1512–1513 responded to claims of maltreatment of indigenous populations by authenticating and regulating the transformation of the "amorphous *repartimiento*" into a tributary encomienda system in the Spanish colonies,[193] while also providing insight into the animalization and depersonalization of indigenous populations. This set of laws decreed that indigenous populations had to be "relocated" to the towns settled by their "*encomenderos*," had to receive religious instruction, were "allowed" to attend their "*areytos*," or cultural gatherings, had to be clothed and fed by the colonizers, and were not to be physically abused or called "dogs," among other regulations that bring light to the systematic harm and animalization of indigenous populations.[194] The amendments of 1513 ruled that single indigenous women had to remain under the authority of their parents in order to avoid the rise of "*malas mugeres*," coded language used in gendered discourses of inherent "female" sexual deviance.[195] The Leyes de Burgos were not motivated by the aim to protect the indigenous populations that were being subjected to mass killings, but instead were a legal code that elucidated the configuration (and abuse) of a racialized hypersexual Other.

---

[192] De las Casas, *Brevísima relación de la destrucción de las Indias*, 41. Translation to English: "How many tears were shed, how many sighs, how many moans, how many solitudes in this life, and how many eternal damnations in the other life were caused, not only for the indigenous people, which were infinite, but for the unhappy Christians ... in such great insults, grave sins, and such execrable abominations."

[193] James Lockhart & Stuart B. Schwartz, *Early Latin America: A History of Colonial Spanish America and Brazil* (New York: Cambridge University Press, 1983), 94.

[194] "Leyes de Burgos de 1812," Archivo General de Indias, Patronato, Legajo 174.

[195] "Ordenanzas de 1513," Archivo General de Indias, Patronato, Legajo 174. Translation to English: "bad women."

The model of the sugar plantation based on racialized slavery in the Portuguese colonies in the Atlantic Islands would soon become the paradigm of modern globalized markets in the Atlantic world,[196] and historical and religious ideas about the negative value of the color black were rhetorically utilized to assert the essential "inferiority" of Africans.[197] Monogenism and polygenism surfaced as biblical interpretations of the origins of non-Whiteness. Polygenism argued for a multiplicity of creations; in other words, people of color either were "pre-Adamite" or belonged to a different form, outside the divine creation or outside the human species.[198] Many polygenists held that Blackness must have emerged from human sexual encounters with apes. Meanwhile, monogenism looked in the Book of Genesis for answers[199] to the puzzle of the "degeneration" of the divine (and thus "White") creation into a multiplicity of races: the assassination of Abel by Cain, the Curse of Ham, and the survival and dispersion of "monsters" after the Flood were all named as instances of divine fury that transformed the color of the dermis of those predisposed to slavery. The theory of the "Curse of Cain" constructed Blackness as the instigation of homicidal fraternal violence, while the most influential "Curse of Ham" isolated a biblical mention of a lineage eternally punished to slavery and randomly racialized this ambiguous reference to an evil transgression.[200] The myth of survival after the Flood served as a rationalization of the extermination of "sinful" bodies of color. Regardless of the religious theory, the connection between race and deviance was predestined according to speculative biblical exegesis, and racialized Atlantic slavery was validated by religious interpretations that proclaimed sinfulness as the essence of Blackness, globalizing the emotional discourse of "slavery to sin."

---

[196] Davis, *Inhuman Bondage*, 87.
[197] David M. Goldenberg, *The Curse of Ham: Race and Slavery in Early Judaism, Christianity, and Islam* (Princeton, NJ: Princeton University Press, 2003), 2.
[198] Robert Wald Sussman, *The Myth of Race: The Troubling Persistence of an Unscientific Idea* (Cambridge, MA: Harvard University Press, 2014).
[199] David N. Livingstone, *Adam's Ancestors: Race, Religion & the Politics of Human Origins* (Baltimore, MD: Johns Hopkins University Press, 2008), 14.
[200] The "Curse of Ham" is a historical misnomer as the passage in Genesis places the curse on Ham's son, Canaan, and all of his descendants after Ham saw Noah's "nakedness" while the patriarch was drunk. What was the essence of Ham's transgression in the divine gaze and why the punishment is granted to Canaan and his descendants, and not Ham, are key questions of the theological debate about Genesis. See Goldenberg, *The Curse of Ham*, 141–177.

The Middle Passage was premeditated to be an agonizing experience of terror, overcrowding, dispossession, and disorientation.[201] While the European design of the Atlantic "trade" of enslaved people was distinguished by intended control of the State by taxation, subsidization, and monopoly contracts, the African coordination of the "trade" relied on resistance to the monopoly of one European nation and the constant variation of "prices" and currencies,[202] though much of the Atlantic slaveholding economy was marginal to legal transactions. The image of the "Slave Ship Broadside" has incarnated the abominable forced mobilization of millions of Africans, turning the Atlantic Ocean into a site of memory of genocide, generational trauma, and identity for the African diaspora.[203] This image has also been contemporarily used in public discourse and general education to emotionally depersonalize the enslaved through the fetishization of Black pain. The twentieth-century scholarly debate about the "numbers" of the Middle Passage (and the significance of statistics about enslaved mortality for historiography)[204] would mirror how the captains of slaveholding ships dehumanized the enslaved, depicting enslaved death by "numbers." Captains of enslaving ships wrote in their journals entries of enslaved people "departing this life" from "disease," hiding their negligence and murderous attacks.[205] The representation of enslaved mortality during the Middle Passage in slaveholding primary sources conceived an unfeeling collective unit and itemized their lifeless bodies. This painful generational memory of the detached (and therefore sinister) gaze of the White colonizer as Black people are thrown to the Atlantic Ocean was and is a key driving force of Black revolutionary movements.

Philosophical inquiries of the early modern world evidence an exacerbation of the European preoccupation with the mutability of the

---

[201] Stephanie E. Smallwood, *Saltwater Slavery: A Middle Passage from Africa to American Diaspora* (Cambridge, MA: Harvard University Press, 2007), 35.
[202] Herbert S. Klein, *The Atlantic Slave Trade* (New York: Cambridge University Press, 1999), 103.
[203] "Description of a Slave Ship," Princeton University, Firestone Library, Rare Books and Special Collections, Oversize 2006-001BE.
[204] The key scholarly debate about the "numbers" of the Middle Passage was sparked by the controversial publication of *The Atlantic Slave Trade: A Census* by Philip D. Curtin. The "census" debate in instances emphasized "empirical data," disregarding the history of premeditated erasure, corruption, and trauma, which makes any "number" conservative and non-encompassing. See Philip D. Curtin, *The Atlantic Slave Trade: A Census* (Madison: University of Wisconsin Press, 1969).
[205] Smallwood, *Saltwater Slavery*, 122.

condition of slavery after the encounter with the "New World." Thomas More's *Utopia* cautioned about the perils of a wealth based on gold, stating that it delivered the uncertainty of class mobility and the volatility of the vulnerability to the condition of slavery.

> Which if it should be taken from him by any fortune, or by some subtle wile and cautel of the law (which no less than fortune doth both raise up the low and pluck down the high), and be given to the most vile slave and abject drivel of all his household, then shortly after he shall go into the service of his servant as an augmentation or overplus beside his money.[206]

Meanwhile, *The Prince* by Niccolò Machiavelli represented Italy as historically "enslaved" and assessed the significance of "political slavery."

> And if, as I said, it was necessary in order that the power of Moses should be displayed that the people of Israel should be slaves in Egypt, and to give scope for the greatness and courage of Cyrus that the Persians should be oppressed by the Medes, and to illustrate the pre-eminence of Theseus that the Athenians should be dispersed, so at the present time, in order that the might of an Italian genius might be recognized, it was necessary that Italy should be reduced to her present condition, and that she should be more enslaved than the Hebrews, more oppressed than the Persians, and more scattered than the Athenians; without a head, without order, beaten, despoiled, lacerated, and overrun, and that she should have suffered ruin of every kind.[207]

Machiavelli contends that historical slavery and "degradation" are vital for a calculated "emotive" narrative of political deliverance and the ascent of a powerful ruler. The role of slavery is symbolic, since it boosts the tale of triumph of the sovereign. The intervention of the Prince in History is the establishment of stability and social hierarchy, outlined by the art of war.[208] The philosopher concludes that the ideal ruler comprehends that "his" is not a "profession of goodness."[209] The understanding that "grief" can materialize from the intended good justifies the framing of politics as a perpetual war. It is an eternal figurative battle of perceived emancipation and imposed inequality.

Elizabethan rhetoric merged English patriotism, Protestantism, and appropriation of metaphors of slavery by portraying the Pope as scheming for the English "to be subjects and slaves to aliens and strangers" and Catholic nations as desiring "to overthrow our most

---

[206] Thomas More, *Utopia* (Hertfordshire: Wordsworth, 1997), 84.
[207] Niccolò Machiavelli, *The Prince* (London: Richards, 1903), 103.
[208] Machiavelli, *The Prince*, 57.   [209] Machiavelli, *The Prince*, 60.

happy estate and flourishing commonwealth, and to subject the same to the proud, servile and slavish government of foreigners and strangers."[210] Contemporaneously, William Shakespeare's *Hamlet* used the trope of slavery to express the despair behind the impassioned "tears" of the titular character.

> O, what a rogue and peasant slave am I!
> Is it not monstrous that this player here,
> But in a fiction, in a dream of passion,
> Could force his soul so to his own conceit
> That from her working all his visage wann'd,
> Tears in his eyes, distraction in's aspect,
> A broken voice, and his whole function suiting
> With forms to his conceit? and all for nothing![211]

The metaphor of "slavery to passions" was reinforced later in the play: "Give me that man that is not passion's slave, and I will wear him in my heart's core, ay, in my heart of heart, as I do thee."[212] Similarly, in *El ingenioso hidalgo Don Quixote de la Mancha*, not only did Miguel de Cervantes Saavedra explore the "paradoxical symbiosis" of Quijote and his "servant" Sancho, but tropes of slavery are recalled by "female" characters to articulate the "feminine" experience of love.[213] The Ethiopian hagiography *Gädlä Wälättä Petros* characterized the "just" will of God as knowing the "innermost feelings" of the saint when "supplying" a better "servant."

Do you see the justness of God's understanding? He chased away the young servant girl who had accompanied Walatta Petros into exile but drew close this young servant woman who had been far away, and made her stay with Walatta Petros. He truly is all-powerful. He acts as he pleases and what he decides he carries out. Nobody can argue with him. He removes what is nearby and brings close what is distant. Truly, he scrutinizes the heart and the kidneys.[214]

---

[210] As quoted in Michael Guasco, *Slaves and Englishmen: Human Bondage in the Early Modern Atlantic World* (Philadelphia: University of Pennsylvania Press, 2014), 21.
[211] William Shakespeare, *Hamlet* (London: Heinemann, 1904), 60.
[212] Shakespeare, *Hamlet*, 72.
[213] Miguel de Cervantes Saavedra, *El ingenioso don Quijote de la Mancha, Tomo II* (Barcelona: Gobchs, 1832), 13, 158.
[214] Gälawdewos, *The Life and Struggles of Our Mother Walatta Petros: A Seventeenth-Century African Biography of an Ethiopian Woman*, edited by Michael Kleiner & Wendy Laura Belcher (Princeton, NJ: Princeton University Press, 2015), 113. This translation defines the "heart and the kidneys" as "innermost feelings," following a biblical metaphor in Revelation 2:23.

The Emotional Foundations of Racialized Slavery

The tropes of emotional slavery patently reverberated throughout texts of the early modern Atlantic world. Notably, *Leviathan* by Thomas Hobbes defined the social contract as being bound by laws or "chains": "But as men, for the atteyning of peace, and conservation of themselves thereby, have made an Artificiall Man, which we call a Common-wealth; so also have they made Artificiall Chains, called *Civill Lawes*."[215] And the triumph of the discourse of the irremediable nature of slavery arose from the modern significance of the social contract and the taxonomical codification of laws.

From antiquity to the early modern world, the doctrines of "slavery to passions" and "slavery to sin" served as foundations for the conquest, domination, and enslavement of the "emotionally deviant." The scholarly debate about the racialization of slavery has been primarily focused on why Black Africans became the target of Atlantic slavery and has been mostly concerned with the historical "ruptures," mainly connected to the advent of Eurocentric Christianity, leading to the emergence of a "new" manifestation of bondage, a now racialized slavery.[216] What this debate has not brought to light is that the answer to this inquiry lies in the long-lived institutional conflation of "emotional difference," identifiable "biological difference," and predisposition to slavery. While there has been scholarship on how the modern construction of those who were Black and enslaved inherited the weight of the ancient notion of the "infantilized and animalized"[217] enslaved person, there has been a fundamental gap in the scholarship, a silence on the inexorability between the ancient and medieval emotional justifications of the institution of slavery and the ascent of modern racialist thought. It is not that racialized Atlantic slavery represented a new manifestation of enslavement responding to ideological shifts or simply inheriting the legacies of the slaveholding practices of the ancient and medieval worlds. It is instead that the long-lived emotional

---

[215] Thomas Hobbes, *Leviathan, or The Matter, Forme & Power of a Commonwealth, Ecclesiasticall and Civill* (New York: Cambridge University Press, 1651), 149.

[216] The most cited theory in this debate is the one introduced by David Eltis in *The Rise of African Slavery in the Americas*. According to Eltis, the European dependence on slavery relied on the foreignness of "non-Europeans," when "white slavery" would have been "cheaper" and "developed more quickly" in the Atlantic world, and thus the racialization of slavery was due to the religious unity of European Christians. See Eltis, *The Rise of African Slavery in the Americas*, 17, 70. Meanwhile, the theory of Winthrop Jordan linked the European preoccupation with "heathenism" to the religious connotations of the color black. See Winthrop D. Jordan, *White over Black: American Attitudes toward the Negro* (Chapel Hill: University of North Carolina Press, 2012), 7.

[217] See Davis, *In the Image of God*, 128.

justifications of slavery were the intentional driving force and framework of the early modern racialization of slavery and the symbiotic rise of the social (and scientific) constructs of "race." For the imperial design, Blackness opportunistically embodied the recognizable "biological difference" of the "naturally enslaved" and incarnated the fatal mark of emotional criminality. The escalation of anti-Black slavery ultimately heightened the ancient normativity that stipulated that passions had to be systematized in order to discipline those "enslaved" by emotions.

Through parallelisms that tied the domestic and political spheres, the ancient Greek and Roman worlds conceptualized the enslaved as "surrogate bodies" that could not be injured and constructed the exercise of citizenship as a right tied to the non-foreign emotional aptitude for self-governance and the governmental paternalistic power of domination over the enslaved. These emotional justifications set the framework for both the modern racialization of childhood and the paradoxical emotional infantilization and animalization of those who were Black and enslaved. These rationalizations also shaped the political model of the institutional insistence of emotionally aligning with the master hypothetically "bothered" by the burden (and "emotional toll") of "having to exercise" violence on the enslaved. The Christian teachings about slavery extended the relativism of "slavery to passions" to justify slavery as an institution of spiritual liberation from essentially "sinful" emotions, and the urgency of "deliverance" would soon be appropriated by political defenses of Atlantic conquest, colonization, and enslavement. Christian thought overwhelmingly endorsed the omnipresence of the emotional policing of enslaved humility and religious obedience. The enduring discourses of subservient emotional deficiency relativized slavery to conceal the institutional exclusionary convenience of equating the "emotional difference" and the "biological difference" of those "fit for slavery." The intellectual history of the Eurocentric ancient and medieval worlds advocated for the detection of an emotional Other and for the systematization of passions to regulate the enslaved in order to configure an imperial emotional economy. And the forced globalization of the early modern world made it Law to subdue a racialized emotional Other. In the opportunistic imperial gaze, Black passions became erratic, demonical, and "feminine" in opposition to "masculine" reason, and Blackness in turn became the "biological" proof of absence of emotional self-discipline. Racialized slavery arose to keep Blackness in perpetual subjection to penalizing violence, in everlasting institutional suspicion provoked by its attributed irrational, sinful, and fundamentally emotional nature. Black communities would be increasingly codified as racialized emotional entities that had to be regulated (and perpetually saved, yet never saved) by those "emotionally superior" and thus worthy of the joys of political citizenship and economic inclusion. The imperial economies of the Atlantic world would engender their wealth from racialized emotions that could be injured again and again.

In the eighteenth century, the premise of emotional difference would systematically acquire the deterministic language of science. This turn was also grounded on the shift from the scientific fascination with the "four humors" to the fixation with the "four temperaments." The classical understanding of different bodies being predominantly affected by one of the four humors (yellow bile, blood, black bile, and phlegm) was spread by Galenic thought and, by the seventeenth century, led to the assertion of primacy of one of the four temperaments (choleric, sanguine, melancholic, and phlegmatic) in different peoples of distinct "nature," a "temperament" being assumed to be an emotional "predisposition" due to the "condition of the nervous system."[218] Carl Linnaeus, considered the "father of taxonomy," delineated "variations" of *Homo sapiens* in his influential 1735 *Systema naturae* and strengthened the influence of the notion of the "four temperaments" within the rise of scientific racism.

> *Homo Sapiens.* Diurnal; varying by education and situation.
> *Wild Man.* Four-footed, mute, hairy.
> *American.* Copper-coloured, choleric, erect. Hair black, straight, thick; nostrils wide, face harsh; beard scanty; obstinate, content free. Paints himself with fine red lines. Regulated by customs.
> *European.* Fair, sanguine, brawny. Hair yellow, brown, flowing; eyes blue; gentle, acute. Inventive. Covered with close vestments. Governed by laws.
> *Asiatic.* Sooty, melancholy, rigid. Hair black; eyes dark; severe, haughty, covetous. Covered with loose garments. Governed by opinions.
> *African.* Black, phlegmatic, relaxed. Hair black, frizzled; skin silky; nose flat; lips tumid; crafty, indolent, negligent. Anoints himself with grease. Governed by caprice.[219]

---

[218] Alberti, *Matters of the Heart*, 18, 33.
[219] Carl Linnaeus, *A General System of Nature, through the Three Grand Kingdoms of Animals, Vegetables, and Minerals, Systematically Divided into Their Several Classes, Orders, Genera, Species, and Varieties with Their Habitations, Manners, Economy, Structure, and Peculiarities*, vol. 1 (London: Lackington, Allen, and Co., 1735), 9.

Linnaeus's taxonomy, which would serve as the framework for modern legal codification, utilized the deterministic language of science in order to validate a racialist hierarchy premised on "temperamental" difference. His definitions of his continental categories include racialized generalizations about physical attributes and establish severe lines of emotional distinction. According to Linnaeus, Europeans are "sanguine" and "governed by law," indicating the highest Eurocentric principles of the eighteenth century: legal methodization and "masculine" rationality. In contrast, Asians are "melancholic" and "governed by opinions," and indigenous populations are "choleric" and "regulated by customs." Consequently, Asians are portrayed as "rigid," conceited, and greedy, and the indigenous are depicted as irritable and stubborn. Linnaeus generated a hierarchy of emotional degradation from the "inventiveness" and "gentleness" of Whiteness, and this hierarchy creates a slope of generalizations about dress, from "close vestments" to the nakedness of a "greasy" Black body. Since Africans are conceptualized as "phlegmatic," "indolent," "negligent," and "governed by caprice," Europe is propelled as a site of "gentle" law and "inventiveness" that should govern over lethargic, self-destructive, and emotionally "capricious" African bodies. Linnaeus's taxonomy is the quintessence of the globalization of a scientific (and legalist) hierarchy of racialized feelings, where capricious emotions are ruthlessly punished.

A mother and a daughter. Drums. She is suckling. An eternal glimpse into life with you. Your smell is endless. Your warmth is undying. Because you are not him. You were never his. The corners of her mouths hint at a smile. She was never his.

2

Scientific Racism and Emotional Difference

> Now, to know such things is very useful to anyone as an encouragement to concentrate on regulating his passions. For since, with a little well-directed effort, one can change the movements of the brain in animals devoid of reason, it is clear that this can be done even more successfully in human beings, and that even those who have the weakest souls could acquire a very absolute command of all their passions, if one were to take the trouble to train them and guide them properly.
> —René Descartes, *The Passions of the Soul*

While defining the "body of a living man" as an "automaton,"[1] *The Passions of the Soul*, the last text published by René Descartes in 1649, still explored the dual power of the passions over the body and the soul. Written in the context of the slaveholding regime of the Dutch Golden Age, this text contended that with "little well-directed effort" even the "weakest souls" could regulate their passions after "guidance" and "training."[2] This "little well-directed effort" had to emerge from reason.

Again, our passions cannot be directly aroused or banished by the action of our will; but they can be indirectly, by the representation of things that are habitually associated with the passions we want to have, and that are contrary to those we wish to reject. Thus, to arouse boldness in oneself, and banish terror, it is not enough to will to do so: we must instead set ourselves to consider the reasons, objects, and examples that will persuade us that the danger is not all that great.[3]

---

[1] René Descartes, *The Passions of the Soul* (Oxford: Oxford University Press, 2015), 196.
[2] Descartes, *The Passions of the Soul*, 218. [3] Descartes, *The Passions of the Soul*, 214.

According to Descartes, passions are not directly ruled by an act of "will," but instead self-control arises from rationality, a rationality that operates as "guidance" for the "soul." It is precisely this scientific captivation concerning "guiding the soul" toward reason and away from passions that propelled the "essentialism"[4] of scientific racism from the eighteenth century to the early twentieth century. Rationality was incarnated in those who were White, privileged, and dominant in the climatic context of Atlantic slavery and colonialism. The "weakest souls" simply required "guidance," an emotional "education" that scientific racism would guarantee to be never-ending.

Scientific racism was ultimately premised on the notion that different "races" feel differently. Proponents of scientific racism opportunistically advocated for Atlantic slavery and colonialism with elaborate rationalizations grounded on theories of racialized emotional difference. The current of biological determinism, which affirmed that distinct racialized categories had dissimilar biological compositions, concocted intricate theories of chemical and physiological differentiation in racialized emotional beings. Within this current, craniology organized a chain of being by correlating skulls not only to cognitive capacity, but also to a distinctive set of emotional behaviors, and eugenics disregarded resistance against racial extermination as mere unproductive "sentimentalism." Geographical determinism, or the current that proposes that different climates lead to different "temperaments," contended that hotter climates produce emotional impulsivity, indolence, and sexual deviance. This attribution of emotional instability and corporeal negligence to tropical beings was reinforced by the notion of "tropical fever," or the claim that heat and contagion in the tropics resulted in disease and symbiotic aggressive sexual behaviors. Historical determinism, or the current that proclaims that racialized groups represent an "anthropological present" and offer the opportunity to study the "primitive" origins of "mankind," conceptualized diverse "races" in dissimilar stages of emotional development, or collective progress toward civilized emotions.

All currents of scientific racism, influenced by slaveholding discourses, premeditatedly hesitated in their characterization of the emotions of the racialized Other as either unbridled, resilient, or cautiously simulated. All currents used the deterministic language of science to mask this intended hesitation. All currents infiltrated one another, making scientific racism a

---

[4] Ann Juanita Morning, *The Nature of Race: How Scientists Think and Teach about Human Difference* (Berkeley: University of California Press, 2011), 13.

"purpose," in which scientists, physicians, philosophers, historians, and slaveholders were influenced by (and responded to) one another, profiting from their "purpose." All currents reinforced the same racial hierarchy of "emotional difference" and vindicated the contemporaneous Eurocentric pursuits of regulation of the racialized bodies of the enslaved and the colonized as a progressive triumph in "human feeling." Structured by the imperial gaze, the ascent of scientific racism, and the effect of scientific constructs of "race" in the "order" of inequality, led to the political fulfillment of the inescapability of the surveillance, captivity, and "guidance" of Black emotions.

THE AGE OF WHITE SENTIMENTALITY

Seventeenth-century rationalism relentlessly antagonized emotions in a binary opposition to the fulfillment of truth through reason. Both Descartes and Baruch Spinoza, rationalist thinkers of the Dutch Golden Age, upheld this oppositional symbiosis. Spinoza's definition of emotions in *Ethics* refers to both their influence in the body and the ideas that emerge from them: "By emotion (*affectus*) I understand the modifications of the body by which the power of action in the body is increased or diminished, aided or restrained, and at the same time the ideas of these modifications."[5] The philosopher theorized emotionality with the same principle of "everything in so far as it is itself endeavors to persist in its own being."[6] Not only do emotions strive to persist, but they are also fundamentally grounded on desire: "All emotions have reference to desire, pleasure, or pain, as the definitions which we gave them show. But desire is the nature and essence of everything."[7] Therefore, Spinoza argues that all "modifications of the body" are rooted in desire, but that the ideas or "images" of emotions and "external causes" affect the specificity of the emotion. For example, Spinoza claims that love and hatred are variations of pleasure and pain that are modified "by the idea of an external cause."[8] According to Spinoza, human beings recognize these "images" since childhood.

For we find that children, inasmuch as their bodies are, so to speak, in equilibrium, will laugh and cry merely because they see others laugh or cry; and whatever they see any one do they immediately desire to imitate, and they desire all things for themselves which they see give pleasure to others: clearly because the images of

---

[5] Baruch Spinoza, *Ethics* (London: J. M. Dent & Sons, 1910), 85. [6] Spinoza, *Ethics*, 91.
[7] Spinoza, *Ethics*, 124.   [8] Spinoza, *Ethics*, 95.

things, as we said, are the very modifications of the human body or modes in which the human body is affected by external causes and disposed for doing this or that.[9]

Ethics contends that, since childhood is a state of constant exercise of desire and mimicry, Men should endeavor to regulate their emotions in order to gain sovereignty over themselves and cultivate their rational productivity. Spinoza appropriates the notion of "slavery to passions" and translates it to "servitude to emotions": "Human lack of power in moderating and checking the emotions I call servitude. For a man who is submissive to his emotions is not in power over himself."[10] Hence, the crux of the principle of "servitude to emotions" is that the persistence of emotions is at conflict with the self-preservation of Men. Spinoza states that to live in virtue is to be steered by reason to "preserve one's being."[11] The zenith of reason is "the knowledge of God" and of virtue is "to know God."[12] Men who govern themselves through reason show all virtue.

Nothing, I say, can be desired by men more excellent for their self-preservation than that all with all should so agree that they compose the minds of all into one mind, and the bodies of all into one body, and all endeavor at the same time as much as possible to preserve their being, and all seek at the same time what is useful to them all as a body. From which it follows that men who are governed by reason, that is, men who, under the guidance of reason, seek what is useful to them, desire nothing for themselves which they do not also desire for the rest of mankind, and therefore they are just, faithful, and honourable.[13]

According to Spinoza, "self-preservation" is reached through the "guidance of reason," and thus self-government, by only pursuing collective and "useful" desires, since it is in individual aspirations that Men find their ruin. Spinoza's understanding of government is one in which Men who are not "liable to passions" will "always necessarily agree in nature."[14] Virtuous Men will acknowledge that "desire which arises from pleasure or pain" and is rooted in the body "has no advantage to man as a whole."[15] Spinoza further stresses that "desire which arises from reason can have no excess."[16] The thinker concludes that the "power of the mind of reason" to control emotions is sublime[17] and that a Man who is ruled by reason will enjoy freedom only "in a state where he lives according to common law than in solitude where he is subject to no law."[18] Spinoza's

---

[9] Spinoza, *Ethics*, 107.
[10] Spinoza, *Ethics*, 141.
[11] Spinoza, *Ethics*, 158.
[12] Spinoza, *Ethics*, 159.
[13] Spinoza, *Ethics*, 155.
[14] Spinoza, *Ethics*, 161–163.
[15] Spinoza, *Ethics*, 183.
[16] Spinoza, *Ethics*, 183.
[17] Spinoza, *Ethics*, 199.
[18] Spinoza, *Ethics*, 190.

thought refers to the notion of "servitude to emotions" in order to propose that law is the one that gathers the collective, rational, and nonexcessive desires that stimulate the self-preservation of Men.

The Scientific Revolution not only led to the rise of the methods of modern science, but also constructed emotions as bases of biological degeneration. Influenced by Galen's analysis of feelings and voluntary motion as "effects of the soul,"[19] Andreas Vesalius conceptualized God as "a benevolent founder of cities, who takes thought not merely for the society at present existing but also for a very long time," therefore portraying the longevity of the human body and the natural world as created by divine benevolence.[20] When describing human reproduction, the anatomist affirmed "the Creator of the world added to all these organs of generation a strong desire to copulate and a very individual faculty of pleasure for the purpose of generation, bestowing upon the soul that will be concerned with this pleasure a remarkable and indescribable appetite for experiencing it."[21] While sexual "pleasure" is of divine creation for survival, sexual "appetite" impacts the soul and the body, generating a debilitating urgency. Furthermore, in *The History of Life and Death*, Francis Bacon, a philosopher deemed instrumental in the development of the scientific method, depicted envy as instigating biological degradation: "By envy the worst passion, the spirits, and by them the body are hurt and weakened, being always in action and working, for envy is said to keep no holidays."[22] The Scientific Revolution then further diffused discourses about unbridled emotions being biologically deteriorative.

The philosophy of the Enlightenment and its "nationalistic" doctrines resulted in the acceleration of the rise of "modern racism."[23] In *An Essay Concerning Human Understanding*, philosopher and physician John Locke categorized happiness as the "right" regulation of emotions: "But the forbearance of a too hasty compliance with our desires, the moderation and restraint of our passions, so that our understandings may be free, to examine and reason unbiased give its judgment, being that

---

[19] Galen, *On the Natural Faculties* (Cambridge, MA: Harvard University Press, 1916), 3.
[20] Andreas Vesalius, *De humani corporis fabrica libri septem* (Novato: Norman, 2017), 143.
[21] Vesalius, *De humani corporis fabrica libri septem*, 144.
[22] Francis Bacon, *The History of Life and Death* (London: I. Okes, 1638), 173.
[23] Franklin W. Knight, "Introduction: Race and Identity in the New World," in *Assumed Identities: The Meanings of Race in the Atlantic World*, edited by John D. Garrigus & Christopher Morris (Arlington: University of Texas at Arlington Press, 2010), 8.

whereon a right direction of our conduct to true happiness depends."[24] Moreover, Locke proposed that this "restraint" of passions had to be accomplished even when Man was not monitored by the State: "Nor let any one say, he cannot govern his passions, nor hinder them from breaking out, and carrying him into action; for what he can do before a prince, or a great man, he can do alone, or in the presence of God, if he will."[25] In *A Treatise on Human Nature*, David Hume alleged that the "causes" of passions are the same in animals as in humans, though humans have "superior knowledge and understanding" and thus comprehend "right and property."[26] While all beings that are not "agitated with violent passions" have an urgent "desire of company," human beings display "the most ardent desire of society, and [are] fitted for it by the most advantages."[27] Hume suggests a reversal of the principle of "slavery to passions": "Reason is and ought only to be the slave of the passions, and can never pretend to any other office than to serve and obey them."[28] The thinker bases his argument on his conception of passions as "an original existence" that "contains not any representative quality, which renders it a copy of any other existence or modification."[29] The philosopher declares that it is thus "impossible" for passions to be "contradictory to truth and reason."[30] Yet Hume does judge that these "original existences" can be transformed by society and culture, defaulting into the same narrative of the principle of "slavery to passions": "nothing has a greater effect both to increase and diminish our passions, to convert pleasure into pain, and pain into pleasure, than custom and repetition."[31] Most importantly, Hume explores the role of power as producer of distinct emotions in the enactment of authority versus the experience of slavery. Enslavement is portrayed as an existence of perpetual longing and pain. To be a slaveholder is constructed as having the capacity of "satisfaction" of all desire.

For the same reason, that riches cause pleasure and pride, and poverty excites uneasiness and humility, power must produce the former emotions, and slavery

---

[24] John Locke, *An Essay Concerning Human Understanding* (London: Tegg & Son, 1836), 172.
[25] Locke, *An Essay Concerning Human Understanding*, 172.
[26] David Hume, *A Treatise on Human Nature* (Oxford: Clarendon, 1738), 326.
[27] Hume, *A Treatise on Human Nature*, 363.
[28] Hume, *A Treatise on Human Nature*, 415.
[29] Hume, *A Treatise on Human Nature*, 415.
[30] Hume, *A Treatise on Human Nature*, 415.
[31] Hume, *A Treatise on Human Nature*, 422.

the latter. Power or an authority over others makes us capable of satisfying all our desires; as slavery, by subjecting us to the will of others, exposes us to a thousand wants, and mortifications.[32]

While Ibn Khaldun spread ideas grounded on geographical determinism in the medieval world, Montesquieu preserved these discourses of racialized emotional impulsivity in the foundational thought of the French Enlightenment. *The Spirit of the Laws* by Montesquieu emphasized the role of "human nature" in political theory and again established a dichotomy between "self-preservation" and unregulated passions.

Brutes are deprived of the high advantages which we have; but they have some which we have not. They have not our hopes, but they are without our fears; they are subject like us to death, but without knowing it; even most of them are more attentive than we to self-preservation, and do not make so bad a use of their passions. Man, as a physical being, is like other bodies governed by invariable laws. As an intelligent being, he incessantly transgresses the laws established by God, and changes those of his own instituting. He is left to his private direction, though a limited being, and subject, like all finite intelligences, to ignorance and error: even his imperfect knowledge he loses; as a sensible creature, he is hurried away by a thousand impetuous passions.[33]

The philosopher conceived "brutes" as generally geared toward "self-preservation" and a better "use" of their "passions" (because of the absence of "hopes" and "fears"), while Man is individually prone to legal "transgressions" and "impetuous passions." Due to the "private direction" of individuals, monarchies are irremediably despotic. Montesquieu proclaims that, while the power of despotic monarchies is fueled by passions, such as "fear" and "desire," the supremacy of a republican government is based on collective education. The thinker argues that it is because of this link between despotism and the passions that the road to political "virtue" is one of "self-renunciation, which is ever arduous and painful."[34] Montesquieu contends that the passions that arise in republicanism are not as excessive, since "love of the republic" not only is "conducive to a purity of morals," but also enables Men not to "abandon" themselves to "ordinary passions."[35] Furthermore, the philosopher asserts that despotic states are grounded on the "abuse of servitude," in which a "slave appointed by his master to tyrannize over other wretches of the same condition, uncertain of enjoying tomorrow the

---

[32] Hume, *A Treatise on Human Nature*, 315.
[33] Montesquieu, *The Spirit of the Laws* (London: George Bell & Sons, 1748), 3.
[34] Montesquieu, *The Spirit of Laws*, 36.   [35] Montesquieu, *The Spirit of Laws*, 43.

blessings of today, has no other felicity than that of glutting the pride, the passions, and voluptuousness of the present moment."[36] Despotic monarchies enforce a master–enslaved relationship with the People, which is sustained through imprudent "pride" and an enslaved dependency on the satisfaction of passions. Montesquieu further critiques how "women are subject to very little restraint" in monarchies and represent an "object of luxury" that must remain in a "state of the most rigorous servitude," while republicanism generates a society in which "women are free by the laws and restrained by manners."[37] Republicanism is visualized as a political statement of unfettered rational "masculinity."

The philosopher extends geographical determinism to pronounce that, in warmer climates, there is an inclination toward passionate despotism.

In warm climates, where despotic power generally prevails, the passions disclose themselves earlier, and are sooner extinguished; the understanding is sooner ripened; they are less in danger of squandering their fortunes; there is less facility of distinguishing themselves in the world; less communication between young people, who are confined at home; they marry much earlier, and consequently may be sooner of age than in our European climates.[38]

Montesquieu conflates the agricultural notion of "ripening" in both the exercise of passions and the culmination of childhood. The philosopher contends that peoples from hotter climates are "sooner of age," therefore hypersexualizing racialized childhood. This conflation in turn is used as a claim for differentiated political jurisdictions for populations from warmer climates. "It be true that the temper of the mind and the passions of the heart are extremely different in different climates, the laws ought to be in relation both to the variety of those passions and to the variety of those tempers."[39] The philosopher constructs both the "mind" and the "heart" as susceptible to emotions in warmer climates: these "differences" within these passions disturb the overall character and "hopes" of a population and hence their capacity to be governed by law. Montesquieu's conception of the "South," in opposition to his view of the climate in France, is one predisposed toward immorality, legal transgressions, and emotional excess. "If we draw near the south, we fancy ourselves entirely removed from the verge of morality; here the strongest passions are productive of all manner of crimes, each man endeavouring, let the means be what they will to indulge his inordinate

---

[36] Montesquieu, *The Spirit of Laws*, 107.
[37] Montesquieu, *The Spirit of Laws*, 111.
[38] Montesquieu, *The Spirit of Laws*, 68.
[39] Montesquieu, *The Spirit of Laws*, 238.

desires."[40] Montesquieu's geographical determinism stresses the discourse of the noxious impact of hot climate on human emotions, pointing to a tendency toward "criminal" disorder and consequently legitimizing more forceful political institutions in racialized spaces.

> The heat of the climate may be so excessive as to deprive the body of all vigour and strength. Then the faintness is communicated to the mind; there is no curiosity, no enterprise, no generosity of sentiment; the inclinations are all passive; indolence constitutes the utmost happiness; scarcely any punishment is so severe as mental employment; and slavery is more supportable than the force and vigour of mind necessary for human conduct.[41]

Montesquieu's theory is grounded on a paradox that is central and insistent in modern geographical determinism: the racialized body born in hotter climates produces the "strongest" and most "criminal" passions, yet heat also engenders an extreme "passivity" of the body and the mind, even in the expression of "sentiment." This tension allows for the ambiguity of a racialized body that is "spirited" for some scenarios and not for others, tension that would legitimize the inevitability of the ritualization of Black criminalization and exploitation, buttressed by racialized legal taxonomies. This principle hides its ambiguity by declaring that Blackness mobilizes passions toward fruitless and precarious ambitions or "hopes." The "happiness" of the racialized body lies in its corporeal "indolence," and slavery is deemed more probable than spontaneous Black labor and intellectual production. While Montesquieu affirms that "excess of heat enervates the body, and renders men so slothful and dispirited," which makes slavery seem as "more reconcilable to reason,"[42] the philosopher also states that the end of slavery would lead to the "happiness" of White political societies.

> He sees the happiness of a society, of which he is not so much as a member; he sees the security of others fenced by laws, himself without any protection. He perceives that his master has a soul, capable of enlarging itself: while his own labours under a continual depression. Nothing more assimilates a man to a beast than living among freedmen, himself a slave. Such people as these are natural enemies of society; and their number must be dangerous.[43]

According to Montesquieu, the "collective happiness" that emerges from the conclusion of slavery is due to the elimination of a catalyst: the risk of having "unhappy" enslaved enemies within political societies.

---

[40] Montesquieu, *The Spirit of Laws*, 241.
[41] Montesquieu, *The Spirit of Laws*, 241.
[42] Montesquieu, *The Spirit of Laws*, 258.
[43] Montesquieu, *The Spirit of Laws*, 262.

Thus, the racialized categorization of human groups is advocated as a step in the development of distinctive legal frameworks that protect imperial political jurisdictions from "social evils" and racialized bodies from themselves. Montesquieu's thought immortalized the notion that racialized groups felt differently and hence had to be governed differently, antislavery thought that primarily validated Atlantic imperialism and racially premised exploitation.

Multiple foundational scientific texts of biological determinism used monogenism as an uncomplicated starting point of their rationale for theories of biological (and emotional) degradation. It is indeed in mid-eighteenth century when scientists started to more consistently speak of (and further fabricate) "races of humans."[44] During the second half of the eighteenth century, scientists and physicians developed racialist theories that generated standardized archetypes of racialized and gendered bodies that were assumed to produce distinct "sensibilities" and "feelings."[45] Texts of biological determinism theorized that racialized bodies were biologically and emotionally degenerated and referred to monogenism as a framework to denote emotions as sources of biological degradation from a strictly White divine creation. Comte de Buffon's *Natural History* indeed evidences the influence of monogenism in late eighteenth-century biological determinism, since Buffon mainly proposed that the divine creation was "White" and that the racialized body is a later "degeneration" by "corruptive causes." "White then appears to be the primitive colour of Nature, which climate, food, and manners, alter and even change into yellow, brown, or black; and which, in certain circumstances, re-appears, though by no means equal to its original whiteness, on account of its corruption from the causes here mentioned."[46] The naturalist conceives "climate, food, and manners" as the origins of corporeal "corruption," intersecting biology and morality.

Buffon's racialism also reproduced gendered discourses from humoralism. Humoralism conceived women as biologically colder, as having a corporeal tendency to moisture, and thus as more "hysterical" and prone to "weeping"; within the four humors, women were deemed to be

---

[44] Paul Lawrence Farber, *Mixing Races: From Scientific Racism to Modern Evolutionary Ideas* (Baltimore, MD: Johns Hopkins University Press, 2011), 28.
[45] Frevert, "Defining Emotions," 7.
[46] Comte de Buffon, *Buffon's Natural History Containing a Theory of the Earth, a General History of Man, of the Brute Creation, and of Vegetables, Minerals, etc.*, vol. 4 (London: H. D. Symonds, 1797), 324.

"phlegmatic,"[47] just as Linnaeus classified Africans in 1735. Buffon explored the biological "benefits" of marriage in regulating the passions, since "continence" could "create irritations so violent, that reason and religion will not be sufficient to counteract the impetuosity of the passions which they excite, and thus man may be reduced to a level with the brutes, which, under impression of such sensations, become furious and ungovernable."[48] Having portrayed the sexuality of "brutes" as "furious," the naturalist further demarcated *"furor uterinus"* as a "kind of mania, which disorders their reason and bereaves them of all sense of shame."[49] Buffon's theory of degradation not only constructs sexual "disorder" as inciting uncontrollable and bestial passions that make racialized beings "ungovernable," but also emphasizes the absence of feelings of shame when alluding to "manic female sexuality," away from White rationality. Black women are rendered not only as more "fertile" but also as less inclined to pain during childbirth. "The negro women are very fruitful; in child-birth they experience little difficulty, and require not the smallest assistance; nor of its effects do they feel any consequence beyond the second day. As nurses and mothers they deserve great encomiums, being exceedingly tender of their children."[50] Buffon's representation of Black women underlines "fertility," pain tolerance, and predisposition for maternal care, which could conveniently be extended to the care for others. This discourse not only validated the imperial designation of Black enslaved women as caregivers, but also resulted in the long-lived global history of medical disdain and structural violence against Black communities to this day. His categorical definition of Blackness is undeniably premised on "emotional difference."

He adds, that the understanding of the Negroes is exceedingly contracted; that numbers of them seem to be even entirely stupid, and can never be made to count more than three; that they have no memory, and are as ignorant of what is past, as of what to come; that the most sprightly ridicule the others with a tolerable grace; that they are full of dissimulation, and would sooner perish than divulge a secret; that they are commonly mild, humane, tractable, simple, credulous, and even superstitious; that they possess fidelity and courage, and might with proper discipline make a tolerable figure in the field. If the Negroes are deficient in genius, they are by no means so in their feelings; they are cheerful or melancholy, laborious or inactive, friendly or hostile, according to the manner in which they are treated. If properly fed, and well treated, they are contented, joyous, obliging,

---

[47] Alberti, *Matters of the Heart*, 18, 20. [48] Buffon, *Buffon's Natural History*, vol. 4, 50.
[49] Buffon, *Buffon's Natural History*, vol. 4, 50.
[50] Buffon, *Buffon's Natural History*, vol. 4, 283.

and on their very countenance may we read the satisfaction of their soul. If hardly dealt with their spirits forsake them, they droop with sorrow, and will die of melancholy.[51]

Buffon contends that Black minds have reduced cognitive capacities and utilizes his speculations about arithmetic and time to epitomize their "lack" of intellectual production. The thinker proclaims that Black Africans have a tendency to both "dissimulation" and emotional "excess." Opportunistically, they are "joyous" when they are "properly cared for." This elaborate justification of slavery evidences the paradigm of scientific racism of stressing the categorical affirmation of the "emotional difference" of Blackness, while also vaguely pointing to "dissimulation" as a source of uncertainty and perpetual suspicion. Blackness is depicted as either feeling intensely or putting on a performance of feeling intensely (or too little). At the same time, when Black bodies feel, their feelings are extreme and lack nuance: they are either "cheerful" or "melancholic." Comte de Buffon's theory of degradation mobilizes a chain of being grounded on monogenism, and this hierarchy is ruthless against Black people, who are not allowed to "weep" in childbirth and who would be subjected to institutional distrust if they dared to do so.

Modern capitalistic theory would precisely arise from hierarchical understandings of "emotional difference." *The Theory of Moral Sentiments* by Adam Smith contended that "the rich," in the "gratification of their own vain and insatiable desires," were guided by an "invisible hand" to produce mass employment/productivity "without intending it," in turn contributing to the progress of the "interest of the society" and the "multiplication of the species."[52] This is echoed in *The Wealth of Nations*, where the economist affirms that the "selfish" capitalist is "led by an invisible hand to promote an end which was no part of his intention."[53] Therefore, the notions of the "free market" and the "invisible hand" theory emerge from the conceptualization of the "rich" as being beneficially driven by "vain and insatiable desires." This emotional tendency of the capitalist toward self-interest is construed as advantageous to society as a whole. The modern sentiments of the White elite were ennobled by the economic stagnation of the oppressed.

---

[51] Buffon, *Buffon's Natural History*, vol. 4, 291.
[52] Adam Smith, *The Theory of Moral Sentiments* (London: Millar & Kincaid, 1761), 273–275.
[53] Adam Smith, *An Inquiry into the Nature and Causes of the Wealth of Nations*, vol. 2 (London: W. Strahan & T. Cadell, 1776), 35.

Indeed, the Enlightenment has been deemed the Age of Sentimentality due to its tendency to convey Eurocentric standards of social order and morality through emotional discourse. *Observations on the Feeling of the Beautiful and Sublime* by Immanuel Kant established a racial hierarchy of "feeling" and constructed Blackness as the emotionally "ridiculous" and thus lowest in the hierarchy: "The Negroes of Africa have by nature no feeling that rises above the ridiculous."[54] Kant's philosophy, which was highly influential in scientific racism, also depicts Black spirituality as fetishistic and again as the most "ridiculous" in "human nature."

> The religion of fetishes which is widespread among them is perhaps a sort of idolatry, which sinks so deeply into the ridiculous as ever seems to be possible for human nature. A bird's feather, a cow's horn, a shell, or any other common thing, as soon as it is consecrated with some words, is an object of veneration and of invocation in swearing oaths. The blacks are very vain, but in the Negro's way, and so talkative that they must be driven apart from each other by blows.[55]

This major exponent of the Enlightenment conceives Black spirituality as nonsensical for being a "sort of idolatry" toward "common things" of no value. Furthermore, Kant characterizes Blackness as having a propensity toward "vanity," more specifically, "vanity" manifesting in a lowly "Black way," since "modernity" celebrated White vanity as advantageous. The philosopher also represents Black communities as so excessively "talkative" that violence is the only recourse. White violence against Black pride, that is.

The Age of Sentimentality likewise utilized emotional discourse to rationalize the modern ethics of racialized legal and epistemological taxonomies. With much intentionality in a climatic moment of the history of Atlantic slavery, the framework of the Enlightenment prolonged the influence of taxonomical racialization in its encyclopedic approaches to "emotional difference." For example, the 1798 US edition of the *Encyclopedia Britannica* included the following "unhappy" profile of Blackness: "Vices the most notorious seem to be the portion of this unhappy race: idleness, treachery, revenge, cruelty, impudence, stealing, lying, profanity, debauchery, nastiness, and intemperance."[56] Within this context, the *Discourse on the Origin and Basis of Inequality among Men* by

---

[54] Immanuel Kant, *Observations on the Feeling of the Beautiful and Sublime and Other Writings* (New York: Cambridge University Press, 2011), 4.
[55] Kant, *Observations on the Feeling of the Beautiful and Sublime*, 59.
[56] "1798 U.S. edition of the *Encyclopedia Britannica*," as quoted in Simon Gikandi, *Slavery and the Culture of Taste* (Princeton, NJ: Princeton University Press, 2011), 6.

Jean-Jacques Rousseau formulated a moral parallelism between intellectual pursuit and disease.

> Allowing that nature intended we should always enjoy good health, I dare almost affirm that a state of reflection is a state against nature, and that the man who meditates is a degenerate animal. We need only call to mind the good constitution of savages, of those at least whom we have not destroyed by our strong liquors; we need only reflect, that they are strangers to almost every disease, except those occasioned by wounds and old age, to be in a manner convinced that the history of human diseases might be easily written by pursuing that of civil societies.[57]

While Rousseau does seemingly redirect the narrative of degeneration toward "civil societies," the philosopher perpetuates the discourse of "savages" having a biological composition unaffected by pain, illness, or intellectual curiosity. Moreover, Rousseau proceeds to paint love as a "factitious sentiment, engendered by society, and cried up by the women with great care and address in order to establish their empire," which is also described as based "on certain notions of beauty and merit which a savage is not capable of having."[58] Not only does the thinker conceptualize "civilized love" as degenerative, but Rousseau also points to "women" and their premeditated "empire" as the actual source of corruption and to "savages" as those entirely exempt from feeling love. The philosopher argues that it is "society alone" that has imposed "impetuous ardor" to "love itself as well as to all the other passions," which is rendered as why populations from the Caribbean are "who have as yet deviated least from the state of nature, are to all intents and purposes the most peaceable in their amours, and the least subject to jealousy, though they live in a burning climate which seems always to add considerably to the activity of these passions."[59] Rousseau's text validates ideas of geographical determinism, and still apparently hesitates in the role of heat in the conception of the "savage." This is due to the fact that the "love of self" of the "savage" is represented as muted due to the inclination toward self-preservation. Yet "tropical" emotions are still understood as unrestrained due to the "burning climate" and thus utterly "uncivilized".

The *Discourse of Inequality* goes beyond and affirms that the "savage man" and "civilized man" differ the most in their understanding of "supreme happiness," since, while the "savage man" clings to "repose

---

[57] Jean-Jacques Rousseau, *The Social Contract and the First and Second Discourses* (New Haven, CT: Yale University Press, 2002), 93.
[58] Rousseau, *The Social Contract and the First and Second Discourses*, 109.
[59] Rousseau, *The Social Contract and the First and Second Discourses*, 109.

and liberty," the "civilized man" is constantly laboring, perpetually in motion, and "proud of his slavery[;] he speaks with disdain of those who have not the honor of sharing it."[60] The "civilized man" is who is truly "enslaved": Rousseau appropriates the metaphor of slavery and spreads imagery of a White elite that is too productive and hence too encumbered. In *On the Social Contract*, Rousseau again highlights emotions when proclaiming that "Gods would be necessary to give laws to men, since only a superior intelligence would be necessary who could see all the passions of men without experiencing any of them."[61] Therefore, Rousseau constructs "feminine" sentiment and "masculine" labor as corruptive and "enslaving" forces, but conceptualizes education and reformed politics as a divine deliverance for the "civilized," a deliverance that could not save the "savages" from themselves or from their unnamed slavery.

The Enlightenment also produced a multiplicity of philosophical texts grounded on the debate between monogenism and polygenism. While monogenism inspired Comte de Buffon's theory of degradation, Voltaire would be one of the most notorious polygenists of the French Enlightenment, hypothesizing Blackness as emerging from cross-species sexual encounters. The philosopher avidly mocked the premise of monogenism in his writing. Though monogenism never claimed that Blackness was the "image of God," and, on the contrary, advocated for theories of degeneration from the "sublime beauty" of the "White creation," polygenists, like Voltaire, held on to the "absurdity" of this interpretation of Genesis.

C'est une grande question parmi eux s'ils sont descendus de singes, ou si les singes sont venus d'eux. Nos sages ont dit que l'homme est l'image de Dieu. Voilà une plaisante image de l'Être éternel, qu'un nez noir épaté avec peu ou point d'intelligence! Un temps viendra sans doute où ces animaux sauront bien cultiver la terre, l'embellir par des maisons & par des jardins, & connaître la route de astres.[62]

The Age of Sentimentality certainly manufactured emotionally charged diatribes and scholarly debates in relation to the religious interpretations

---

[60] Rousseau, *The Social Contract and the First and Second Discourses*, 137.
[61] Rousseau, *The Social Contract and the First and Second Discourses*, 180.
[62] Voltaire, *Les lettres d'Amabed* (London, 1769), 53. Translation to English: "It is a great question among them if they descended from the apes or if the apes came from them. Our wise men have said that man is the image of God. Here is a pleasant image of the Eternal Being: a flat black nose with little or no intelligence! A time will undoubtedly come when these animals will know how to cultivate the earth, embellish their houses and their gardens, and become acquainted with the route of the stars."

about the "origins" of racialized groups. Likewise, in *Sketches of the History of Man*, philosopher Lord Kames, another infamous polygenist of the Scottish Enlightenment, disregarded Comte de Buffon's monogenist theories as "mere suppositions": "Doth M. Buffon think it sufficient to say dryly, that such varieties may possibly be the effect of climate, or of other accidental causes?"[63] Exponents of polygenism tended to use defensive language that ridiculed the theory of one divine creation, by emphatically animalizing the Black body and in turn stressing the "disgust" of authors toward the idea of sharing the same "origin" with a "beast-like" Other. This repulsion was represented as a deeply personal emotion and was meant to be prolonged by persuaded readers. Monogenists and polygenists certainly disagreed on the biological ties between Blackness and Whiteness, and polygenists scorned monogenists for including animalized Africans in the advent of human life. Now, it would be a fallacy to regard monogenism as intellectual production that, in juxtaposition to polygenism, was grounded on what linked Whiteness and Blackness. On the contrary, monogenism was captivated with what radically separated Blackness from an originally White "divine image" and usually claimed this massive separation was due to deterioration: Blackness as an unhealthy, tainted, corrupted, emotionally perilous humanity. Whether defined as "bestial" by polygenists or "degraded" by monogenists, Blackness was deemed an enormous step down from humanity and its expressive capacities.

Many examples of emotional differentiation within eighteenth-century historical determinism were delineated by a colonizing gaze, such as in the influential book *History of Jamaica* by Edward Long, a British slaveholder in Jamaica. Long's definition of Blackness not only animalizes Africans, but also relentlessly hypersexualizes and essentializes their bodies as solely made for reproduction. "Secondly, A covering of wool, like a bestial fleece, instead of hair. Thirdly, The roundness of their eyes, the figure of their ears, tumid nostrils, flat noses, invariable thick lips, and general large size of the female nipples, as if adapted by nature to the peculiar conformation of their children's mouths."[64] Long's animalization of Black bodies is reinforced by the historian's emphasis on "smell." "Fifthly, Their bestial or fetid smell, which they all have in a greater or

---

[63] Lord Kames, *Sketches of the History of Man*, vol. 1 (Edinburgh: Creech, 1774), 73.
[64] Edward Long, *The History of Jamaica; or, General Survey of the Ancient and Modern States of That Island: With Reflections on Its Situation, Settlements, Inhabitants, Climate, Products, Commerce, Laws, and Government* (London: Lowndes, 1774), 352.

less degree."[65] His definition of Blackness stresses excess: excess in hair, breasts, lips, fluids, smell. This fixation with "excess" extends to larger characterizations of emotional deviance, immorality, and unproductivity.

> In general, they are void of genius, and seem almost incapable of making any progress in civility or science. They have no plan or system of morality among them. Their barbarity to their children debases their nature even below that of brutes. They have no moral sensations; no taste but for women; gormondizing, and drinking to excess; no wish but to be idle.[66]

Long's portrayal of Black "masculinity" denotes backwardness, depravity, sexual aggressiveness, indolence, and paternal "barbarity." Black "masculinity" is depicted not only as unremitting in carnal desires, including eating and drinking, but also as showing "barbarity" in the conception of childhood. The representation of Black "femininity" again renders the Black body as exempt from the pain of childbirth. "Their women are delivered with little or no labour; they have therefore no more occasion for midwives, than the female oran-outang, or any other wild animal. A woman brings forth her child in a quarter of an hour, goes the same day to the sea, and washes herself."[67] Black motherhood nonchalantly "washes herself" with quotidian ease. The insistence on Black immunity from suffering aims to emotionally depersonalize Blackness and to legitimize the appropriation of Black bodies by White colonizers as sites of imperial morbidity. Still, Long's categorization of Blackness hesitates about the physical "prowess" of Black bodies.

> In short, their corporeal sensations are in general of the grossest frame; their sight is acute, but not correct; they will rarely miss a standing object, but they have no notion of shooting birds on the wing, nor can they project a straight line, nor lay any substance square with another. Their hearing is remarkably quick; their faculties of smell and taste are truly bestial, nor less so their commerce with the other sex; in these acts they are libidinous and shameless as monkies, or baboons.[68]

According to Long's hateful words, Black sexuality has no "shame" and is thus bestial and aberrant. Black bodies are inclined toward physicality, but are not that good at it. They have sensorial advantages, but do not have the cognitive capacity to know what to do with them. They consequently need to be guided in their own physical "prowess,"

---

[65] Long, *The History of Jamaica*, 352.
[66] Long, *The History of Jamaica*, 352.
[67] Long, *The History of Jamaica*, 380.
[68] Long, *The History of Jamaica*, 383.

directed toward mass production. The burden of the White colonizer, He says, is to overcome his "disgust" toward the "gluttonous, malodorous, shameless" Black body in order to deliver imperative emotional guidance.

The long-lived categories of scientific racism are remnants of the racialist assessment of emotional distinction. Johann Blumenbach infamously conceived the term "Caucasian," inspired by the Mount Caucasus, which, according to the scientist, not only "produces the most beautiful race of men," but also is the space "with the greatest probability to place the autochthones of mankind."[69] Blumenbach questions whether human beings and animals express the same emotions, concluding that, while "weeping from sadness is common to animals and man," laughing from joy and its effects in the muscles of the face is unique to human beings.[70] The naturalist abruptly brings up a "peculiar" emotional difference: the "hymen." Blumenbach proposes that the "hymen" has been "granted to woman-kind perhaps much more for moral reasons, than because it has any physical uses."[71] Then, the thinker constructs societal concepts of "genitalia" as indicating the limits of humanity and animalism: "The hymen, the guardian of chastity, is adapted to man who is alone endowed with reason; but the clitoris, the obscene organ of brute pleasure, is given to beasts also."[72] "Feminine" sexual pleasure is deemed animalistic, while the "hymen" is constructed as a locus of "civility," a dichotomy that matches Blumenbach's Blackness/Whiteness binary and therefore subjugates the Black body as excessively "feminine," sexually unbridled, and emotionally inhuman.

Not only would the categories of scientific racism generate theories about race, gender, and sexuality, but these classifications also would structurally racialize childhood precisely during the advent of the Age of Innocence, an age that exempted enslaved children. *Outlines of a Philosophy of the History of Man* by Johann Gottfried Herder affirmed that "maternal love" is the foundation of humanity and proceeded to criticize how "savages" perpetuated the "brutal customs" of lactating children over their shoulders and "ending infancy" too soon. The

---

[69] Johann Friedrich Blumenbach, "De generis humani varietate nativa (1775)," in *The Anthropological Treatises of Johann Friedrich Blumenbach*, edited by Thomas Bendyshe (London: Anthropological Society, 1865), 269.
[70] Blumenbach, "De generis humani varietate nativa," 89.
[71] Blumenbach, "De generis humani varietate nativa," 89.
[72] Blumenbach, "De generis humani varietate nativa," 90.

philosopher held that only a longer childhood could lead to societal development.[73]

Thus to destroy the wilderness of men, and habituate them to domestic intercourse, it was requisite, that the infancy of the species should continue some years: Nature kept them together by tender bands, that they might not separate and forget each other like the brutes, that soon arrive at maturity. The father becomes the instructor of his son, as the mother had been of her infant; and thus a new tie of humanity is formed. Here lies the ground of a necessary *human society*, without which no man could grow up, and the species could not multiply.[74]

Herder's historical determinism claims that first "maternal love" nurtures the humanity of the infant through "tender bands," while the Father introduces his "son" to "civility" and law. It is through this political insertion that Man could be free because He would "become the most savage of all creatures, if he do not quickly perceive the law of God in the works of Nature, and strive as a child to imitate the perfections of his father."[75] The philosopher hesitates: the "civilized" child is brought "quickly" to the "law" of the Father, while the "savage" matures too early and too late. The racialized timeline of infancy is therefore intricate, ambivalent, and exclusive. Herder goes beyond and states that "brutes are born in the great terrestrial family, and the slavish fear of laws and punishments is the most certain characteristic of the brute in man."[76] Therefore, maternal love is tied to human infancy, while the stern direction of the Father is linked to "civilization" and comprehension of the law and religion. Fear toward the primacy of the law produces a "slavish" and animalized soul within this "great terrestrial family." Consequently, slavery and colonialism are contextualized as familial ties, and "savagery" is "feminized." Herder uses this framework to affirm that Blackness had never shown "invention" or an intention to "contribute" to (or occupy) the "West."[77] The thinker proclaims that the "disposition" of Black bodies leaves clues in their "external marks."

According to the rules of physiognomy, thick lips are held to indicate a sensual disposition; as thin lips, displaying a slender rosy line, are deemed symptoms of a chaste and delicate taste; not to mention other circumstances. What wonder then,

---

[73] Johann Gottfried Herder, *Outlines of a Philosophy of the History of Man* (London: Hanfard, 1803), 179.
[74] Herder, *Outlines of a Philosophy of the History of Man*, 179.
[75] Herder, *Outlines of a Philosophy of the History of Man*, 184.
[76] Herder, *Outlines of a Philosophy of the History of Man*, 184.
[77] Herder, *Outlines of a Philosophy of the History of Man*, 259.

that in a nation, for whom the sensual appetite is the height of happiness, external marks of it should happen?[78]

Herder proposes that the behavior and "external marks" of infants presage their "civility" and shame, or lack thereof. "Thick lips" are reckoned as an "external mark" of "sensual appetite" dominating the pursuit of "happiness," while "thin lips" connote "chastity." The racialized body is unalterably hypersexualized, and it is the one to blame for the disruption of infancy, not slaveholding regimes. It is not the Father who allows for "civility": it is the Body itself.

Scientific racism in the United States during the eighteenth century further essentialized the Black body as possessing "external marks" of "uncivilized" emotions. For example, in *An Essay on the Causes of the Variety of Complexion and Figure in the Human Species*, Samuel Stanhope Smith contended that "field slaves" were biologically different from "domestic slaves" due to the fact that the latter were exposed to the "elegance and beauty" of the "civilized" slaveholding family.

> The field slaves are, in consequence, slow in changing the aspect and figure of Africa. The domestic servants have advanced far before them in acquiring the agreeable and regular features, and the expressive countenance of civilized society. – The former are frequently ill-shaped. They preserve, in a great degree, the African lips, and nose, and hair. Their genius is dull, and their countenance sleepy and stupid. –The latter are straight and well-proportioned; their hair extended to three, four, and sometimes six to eight inches; the size and shape of the mouth handsome, their features regular, their capacity good, and their look animated.[79]

Smith argues that the enslaved who were exploited within the domestic sphere gained physical characteristics that were "agreeable" or pleasant for the slaveholding beholder. Even more, "domestic slaves" were closer to embodying the "animation" and the "expressive countenance of civilized society," while "field slaves" were less expressive and "slow" in distancing themselves from an "ugly" Africa. Smith enforces White hegemonic beauty standards of hair length, facial features, and emotional expression to create a racialized ladder of the enslaved. Moreover, the minister also professed that, if indigenous populations had not responded to political and economic competition, they would have remained lethargic. "The character of a savage is indefinitely improvident. Nothing he abhors so much as labor, when he is not under the immediate impulse of

---

[78] Herder, *Outlines of a Philosophy of the History of Man*, 269.
[79] Samuel Stanhope Smith, *An Essay on the Causes of the Variety of Complexion and Figure in the Human Species* (Edinburgh: Elliot, 1788), 91–92.

some imperious appetite, or passion."[80] Thus, Smith asserts that "passion" is the only "impulse" that interrupts the "indefinite improvidence" of indigenous populations. The minister crafts a vision of the United States in which the racialized have "dull" faces and vitalities that do not "express" their unregulated emotions in a "civilized" manner.

In addition to proposing human gradations based on arbitrary facial angles, European craniology held that the racialized were a link to the animal world and hence were more prone to being mesmerized with "chewing," their passions being centered on the mouth as aggressively sexual Others. Anatomist Petrus Camper established a hierarchy of humanity and beauty based on the "facial line."

Voilà donc bien établis les deux extrêmes pour l'obliquité de la Ligne Faciale, c'est à dire, depuis 70 jusqu'à 100 dégrés. Ils constituent tout la gradation depuis la tête du [racial slur] jusqu'à la beauté sublime de l'Antique Gréc. Si vous descendez audessous de 70 dégrés vous avez un Orang Outang, un Singe; si vous descendez plus bas encore vous aurez un Chien, enfin un Oiseau, une Bécasse dont la Ligne Faciale se trouve presque parallèle à la ligne horizontale.[81]

Like other craniologists of his time, Camper intertwines the deterministic language of science with references to "sublime beauty." His hierarchy affirms continuity from Blackness to apes and from apes to "stupid" animals, using language that compels emotional affiliation and admiration toward White "beauty," canons, and political elites.

Medical treatises of the eighteenth century endorsed geographical determinism to frame emotional pathologies and prognoses. Texts of geographical determinism proclaimed that populations from hotter climates were lazier, more violent, more emotionally transient, and more sexually deviant. These texts were influenced by the imperial notion of "tropical fever," which simultaneously referred generally to "tropical diseases," more specifically to contagion of sexually transmitted diseases, and symbolically to "social evils" and sexually aggressive behavior, legitimizing imperial sexual violence as emerging from the victim. While a

---

[80] Smith, *An Essay on the Causes of the Variety of Complexion and Figure*, 15.
[81] Petrus Camper, *Dissertation physique sur les différences réelles que présentent le traits du visage chez les hommes de différents pays et de différents ages; sur le beau qui caractèrise les statues antiques et le pierres gravées* (Utrecht: B. Wild & J. Altheer, 1791), 42. Translation to English: "They are then well established, the two extremes for the obliquity of the facial line, namely, from 70 to 100 degrees. These constitute all the gradation from the head of the black man to the sublime beauty of an Ancient Greek. If one descends from 70 degrees, you have an orangutan, a monkey; if one descends even more, you will have a dog, a bird, whose facial line is almost parallel to a horizontal line."

White colonizer could temporarily catch the "fever," inflict sexual violence on the colonized, and later rid himself of it, the "fever" was innate to the racialized body and stamped a "deviant" soul forever. This fascination with "tropical contagion" led to the publication of many medical treatises that spread theories of geographical determinism. *A Treatise on Tropical Diseases; on Military Operations; and on the Climate of the West Indies* by Benjamin Moseley declared that "females" reach maturity and "decay" earlier in warmer climates, racializing Black childhood and hypersexualizing the Black body.[82] Furthermore, the physician suggests that multiple elements of warm climates influence the "emotional difference" and the "idleness" of Caribbean populations. "Powerful as the dominion of passion and impatience is, indolence must prevail, where perpetual sameness of the seasons blunts the edge of energy, and where climates relaxes the muscular fibers, and debilitates the nerves."[83] Both the tropical heat and the "sameness of the seasons" weaken the nervous system and have repercussions on the productivity and the regulation of passions. Moseley highlights his assertion about the inclination of Blackness toward dissimulation and criminality, reverberating the insistent theory of scientific racism that Black people are either feeling intensely or being dishonest about the intensity of their emotions.

> A negro, – *Parthis mendacior*, – deliberates; and never makes an spontaneous reply. When a question is asked, he generally desires to have it repeated, pretending not to understand it, that he may have time to prepare an answer. A lie once determined on, no pain nor punishment can shake him. Detected in committing a theft, he is not disconcerted; and, when any thing which he has stolen is found on him, he denies all knowledge of the fact.[84]

Moseley's theory of emotional dissimulation echoes Montesquieu's argument about racialized legal jurisdictions. Punishment did not alter the emotional disguise intrinsic to Blackness, and thus the penalization of Black communities had to be forceful and legally aggravated. Geographical determinism fueled the institutional suspicion toward racialized beings who were either emotionally uncontrolled or camouflaged. The same nervous system that is hindered by climate cautiously strategizes its trickery. Slaveholding regimes would read this theory of the

---

[82] Benjamin Moseley, *A Treatise on Tropical Diseases; on Military Operations; and on the Climate of the West Indies* (London: T. Cadell, 1792), 95.
[83] Moseley, *A Treatise on Tropical Diseases*, 103.
[84] Moseley, *A Treatise on Tropical Diseases*, 105.

emotional deception of Blackness as making the enslaved deserving of the continual escalation of genocidal violence.

Some of these medical treatises of the turn of the century not only engendered a chain of emotional being, but also more specifically disseminated an analogous racial gradation of pain tolerance, chemical imbalance, and pathological sexuality. In *An Account of the Regular Gradation in Man and in Different Animals and Vegetables*, physician (and polygenist) Charles White alleged that there are racial distinctions in menstruation. "It is the general opinion of physiologists that females menstruate more in warm climates than in cold; twenty-four ounces being the quantity in the warmest climates, eighteen ounces in Greece, from ten to four in this country, and two ounces in the coldest."[85] Due to gendered religious interpretations, these "racial distinctions" intrinsically construct racialized bodies as "dirtier" and more "sinful." This theory also follows the pattern of scientific racism of claiming that the "excessive" Black body produces an exorbitant amount of fluids and "filthy" emotions. Highlighting his support for polygenism, White also contends that Black people have many similarities with apes, such as their "inclination" to suffer in cold weather,[86] to have less sense of touch than their White counterparts,[87] to walk in a manner that "resembles that of an ape,"[88] and, recalling the theory of many craniologists, to "have stronger powers of mastication than Europeans."[89] White even alludes to societal constructs of "genitalia" to "support" his argument on the closeness of Africans to simians, denoting a bestial sexuality.

> That the penis of an African is larger than that of a European, has, I believe been shown in every anatomical school in London.... I found with some surprise, that, the testes and scrotum are less in the African than in the European. They are still less, proportionally, in the ape. That the penis should be larger, and the testes and scrotum smaller, in the order thus stated is another remarkable instance of gradation.[90]

White's preoccupation with Black sexuality also infiltrates his portrayal of Black childhood. "Negroes are shorter lived than Europeans. All observations confirm the fact, that the children of negroes are more

---

[85] Charles White, *An Account of the Regular Gradation in Man and in Different Animals and Vegetables* (London: Dilly, 1799), 58.
[86] White, *An Account of the Regular Gradation in Man*, 59.
[87] White, *An Account of the Regular Gradation in Man*, 71.
[88] White, *An Account of the Regular Gradation in Man*, 79.
[89] White, *An Account of the Regular Gradation in Man*, 82.
[90] White, *An Account of the Regular Gradation in Man*, 60.

early and forward in walking than those of Europeans; likewise they arrive at maturity sooner. The males are often ripe for marriage at ten, and the females at eight years of age."[91] In the age that paraded White children as the paradigm of innocence, White declared that the end of childhood of Black girls is the age of eight years old, normalizing imperial sexual violence against Black minors. Indeed, the political displays of "feelings" toward the protection of innocence in legal jurisdictions were and are centered on Whiteness.

Eighteenth-century philosophical and scientific intellectual production set a hierarchy of "emotional difference" grounded on the racialization of "self-preservation." Proponents of scientific racism proclaimed that, in the name of the self-preservation of Men, emotions had to be politically regulated in racialized populations and colonial spaces, setting the framework for the ascent of eugenics. Following ancient and medieval precedents, those who governed over themselves had the "nuisance" of ruling over emotional Others, enacting political justice and economic order. The racialization of "self-preservation" allowed for the intensification of the imperial urgency for emotional policing, and scientific racism responded to this urgency by emphasizing racialized "external markers" as the measures of "emotional difference." Both monogenists and polygenists argued for an inhuman Blackness that could not signify the "image of God," essentializing and codifying the "external markers" of Blackness as unwarranted, as a sensorial annoyance for Whiteness. Those "effortlessly identifiable," "biologically different" enslaved people, those to be perpetually suspected, those whose emotions were unbridled were irremediably Black. And a whole political apparatus and economic system were built on this emotional hierarchy shaped by the enormous scope of influence of racialist ideas. The political apparatus of Empires was guided by the principle that legal jurisdictions had to be differentiated (and thus forcefully unjust) in order to adapt to the emotional "composition" of colonized and racialized populations. The capitalistic economic system rationalized the "free" market as emerging from the beneficial "desires" of the White elite. With a long history of imperial intellectual production theorizing desire as hazardous, capitalistic systems made desire inherently productive only when felt by White "financiers," making capitalistic exploitation invincible. Meanwhile, the racialized emotions of hypersexualized enslaved people were to be monitored. Their pain was nonexistent

---

[91] White, *An Account of the Regular Gradation in Man*, 60.

or exaggerated. Their childhood was fleeting and yet never-ending. Eighteenth-century scientific racism encompassed and mobilized key discursive paradoxes that made Black emotional deficiency ambiguously inevitable. Heat impacts the Black body to be emotionally expressive in instances and inexpressive in others. The emotional Other cannot control or understand emotions, and yet can be calculative and meticulously hide or perform their feelings when used for maleficence. This ambiguity sets the stage for racialized policing that suspects a Black self that essentially and predictably cannot feel properly. The intricate mythologies of the "emotional" intersections of race, gender, sexuality, and age would only be exacerbated in the nineteenth and twentieth centuries. More and more, scientific racism devised how to keep the emotionally racialized at the brink of death.

EMOTIONAL DIFFERENTIATION IN RACIALIST THOUGHT OF THE NINETEENTH AND EARLY TWENTIETH CENTURIES

Nineteenth-century scientific racism articulated an even more explicit enthrallment toward "specific" emotions and their expression: love, weeping, fear, anger, and "deviance" would be at the center of the theorization of race. *History of the Female Sex* by Christoph Meiners painted a picture of Black love as an anomaly.

A negro may love his wife with all the affection that it is possible for a negro to possess, but he never permits her to eat with him, because he would imagine himself contaminated, or his dignity lessened by such a condescension; and at this degrading distance, the very negro slaves in the West Indies keep their wives, though it might be presumed that the hardships of their common lot would have tended to unite them in the closest manner.[92]

Imposing binary gendered constructs, Meiners questions the capacity of Black families for love and affection, claiming that, although Black husbands seem to feel "some" love for their wives, a "degrading distance" points to a lesser capability of love in comparison to White Men. The philosopher and historian indicates a "fear" of "contamination" as the origin of this "distance" and critiques the "failure" of the enslaved to breach this remoteness, holding that the African diaspora should be instead "unified" by the experience of slavery. Therefore, not only does

---

[92] Christoph Meiners, *History of the Female Sex: Comprising a View of the Habits, Manners, and Influence of Women, among All Nations, from the Earliest Ages to the Present Time* (London: Colburn, 1808), 53–54.

Meiners's historical determinism craft a racialized hierarchy of love, but his privileged and speculative standpoint also introduces a categorical judgment of the allegedly "unloving" emotional responses of the enslaved to their condition. Meiners further condemns the assumed patriarchal hierarchy within Black communities and the "expectation" of Black women to be "on their knees."

> The poorest and meanest negro, even though he be a slave, is generally waited upon by his wife, as by subordinate being, on her knees. – On their knees the negro women are obliged to present to their husbands tobacco and drink; on their knees they salute them when they return from hunting or any other expedition; lastly, on their knees they drive away the flies from their lords and masters while they sleep.[93]

The insistence of the author on the perpetuity of these practices regardless of class and enslaved status manifestly aims to add to the tone of derision. The essence of this theory is that Black men are absurdly conceited and do not know how to love "their women." Black wives spend a lifetime on the ground, serving undeserving "emotionally inferior men." Not only are Black wives represented as perpetually "on their knees" for their husbands, but the societal gendered expectation of labor is rendered as distinctive from European societies. "From these occupations not even the wives and concubines of kings are in general exempted, but they may be seen laboring in the fields like the rest of their country-women."[94] Meiners speculates and claims that Black "women" were not allowed to be in the same "hut" as their "husbands" if they were menstruating and were "totally excluded from the conjugal embrace" during the time of pregnancy and lactation.[95] For the most part, Meiners portrays gendered relations within Black communities as plagued by the supposed imposition of subservience in Black women. Still, the thinker also vacillates: on one hand, Black women are inappropriately subordinated and "masculinized" with labor, but, on the other hand, "the negroes suffer themselves, exactly like the Americans, to be governed by their wives, and to be maltreated by the daughters of their princes."[96] Thus, according to Meiners, Blackness commits multiple transgressions to "Western masculinity": they do not perform at "elevating their women" (literally from the floor), and they simultaneously allow "non-self-governing" beings to

---

[93] Meiners, *History of the Female Sex*, 53–54.
[94] Meiners, *History of the Female Sex*, 55.
[95] Meiners, *History of the Female Sex*, 53–54.
[96] Meiners, *History of the Female Sex*, 62.

govern over "men." This text encompasses how Whiteness was fixed as the paradigm of familial love. Bourgeois families that truly cultivate the innocence of their children, the economic stability of "their women", and the patriarchal authority of their Men. Racialized families that fail at nurturing meaningful bonds by perpetrating a tyranny of retrograde gendered relations.

The theories of Meiners are in fact grounded on the hypersexualization of all women of color. The *History of the Female Sex*'s depiction of "Orientals" proposes that the "dispositions" and "relations of the sexes" in the "East" engender the "most unlimited authority on the one hand, and the most abject slavery on the other."[97]

The females of the East are in general just what they are considered by their most passionate admirers, children of destitute souls, or creatures with but half a soul, destined for mere animal enjoyment, and the propagation of the species. Incomprehensible as the want of love in the Orientals under these circumstances may appear, the profound contempt which these very people entertain for a sex so essential to their happiness, may nevertheless be very easily accounted for.[98]

Meiners claims that "happiness" in the "East" is driven by sexual pleasure and that "females of the East" are mere objects of desire as "children of destitute souls." The thinker proceeds to declare that it is due to their perennial infantilized state that they are "destined for mere animal enjoyment."

In beings so childish, rude, ignorant, and uncultivated as the females of the East, in whom, no less than in the men, the climate has implanted as insatiable appetite; the propensity to every kind of sensual gratification, and all the passions of little, unpolished, and debased minds, must be infinitely stronger than in the women of our division of the globe: because the innate vices are neither eradicated by the cultivation of the heart and understanding, nor suppressed by useful industry; but on the contrary, are powerfully inflamed and excited by confinement, and the illusions of those very passions.[99]

While "Western women" are refined by their eagerness to support the enterprise of their Men, "uncultivated Eastern women" have instead been unfailingly infantilized because of the climate. Influenced by geographical determinism, Meiners describes "females of the East" as "insatiable." Their pursuit for "sexual gratification" is "stronger" than in White women, and their sexual fantasies are augmented by "confinement."

---

[97] Meiners, *History of the Female Sex*, 100. [98] Meiners, *History of the Female Sex*, 102.
[99] Meiners, *History of the Female Sex*, 102.

Meiners builds an image of not only an infantile complacency with exploitation, but also a symbiotic voracious carnal yearning for subjection to bondage. The rendering of "Orientals" openly rationalizes the pedophilic fulfillment of these "sexual fantasies" of enslavement in all racialized/colonized spaces.

With a high readership among slaveholders, scientific racism lethally branded the lives of the enslaved, and advocates of scientific racism did not just theorize in laboratories and offices. Instead, their experimentation directly distressed the lives of their "objects of study." Georges Cuvier, now lauded as a "founding father of paleontology," infamously dissected the body of "Sara Baartman," who was enslaved, sexually exploited, and paraded as a naked site of observation throughout Europe. In fact, Cuvier conducted a postmortem examination of "Sara Baartman" with the intentionality of scientific racism in 1815, after having previously nonconsensually "evaluated" their enslaved body while still alive.[100] Not only did Cuvier prolong the exploitation of the Black enslaved body with a postmortem narrative, but the naturalist also advanced an elaborate theory about "degradation" grounded on monogenism. Cuvier affirmed that Blackness was "closest to the beast," must have escaped the Flood, and must have been "separated" from Whiteness for much time, theory that assured that "sin" and animalized "deviance" were completely disentangled from Whiteness.

La plus dégradée des races humaines, celle des [racial slur], dont les formes s'approchent le plus de la brute, et dont l'intelligence ne s'est élevée nulle part au point d'arriver à un gouvernement régulier, ni à la moindre apparence de connaissances suives, n'a conservé nulle part d'annales ni de traditions anciennes. Elle ne peut donc nous instruire sur ce que nous cherchons, quoique tous ses caractères nous montrent clairement qu'elle a échappé à la grande catastrophe sur un autre point que les races caucasique et altaïque, dont elle était peut-être séparée depuis long-temps quand cette catastrophe arriva.[101]

---

[100] Sabrina Strings, *Fearing the Black Body: The Racial Origins of Fat Phobia* (New York: New York University Press, 2019), 95.

[101] Georges Cuvier, *Recherches sur les ossemens fossiles, où l'on rétablit les caractères de plusieurs animaux dont les révolutions du globe ont détruit les espèces*, Tome Premier (Paris: D'Ocagne, 1812), 289. Translation to English: "The most degraded of the human races, that of black people, whose form is the closest to the beast and whose intelligence never reached a regular government, nor the minimal appearance of knowledge, nor did it conserve registers or ancient traditions. It cannot then teach us what we are looking for, although all of their characters clearly show us that it escaped the great catastrophe in another location from the Caucasian and the Altaic race, where it was perhaps separated for a long time when this catastrophe arrived."

Like Cuvier, the "legacies" of multiple exponents of scientific racism are far-reaching due to their political and economic influence. Racialist Benjamin Rush, signer of the Declaration of Independence and carceral "reformer" who conceptualized Blackness as a disease, was a member of the Philadelphia Society for Alleviating the Miseries of Public Prisons that "convinced" the Commonwealth of Pennsylvania to approve the construction of the Eastern State Penitentiary in 1822, first prison in the United States to fully impose "solitary confinement."[102] He claimed not only that solitary confinement encouraged "delicacy," "reflection," and "repentance"[103] but also that it was fundamental to the societal invisibility of punishment, avoiding public emotional responses to penalization.[104] It could seem superficially contradictory that a key manufacturer of the modern (and racialized) prison system had an "antislavery" stance. It is actually not a contradiction. Before advocating for the mass application of solitary confinement, the influential "social reformer" had written a statement about slavery in the British colonies in the Caribbean, arguing that Black people were "savages" who lacked the "civilized" emotions tied to "friendship" and "gratitude."

> Friendship and Gratitude are founded upon the Wants and Weaknesses of Man in a State of Society. If any of the Negroes appear to be Strangers to these Virtues, it must be ascribed to their independent Mode of Life, as Savages, which exempts them from most of those Weaknesses, and artificial Wants, which are introduced by civilized Life.[105]

The exemption of Blackness from "artificial Wants" or emotional depth was attributed to their "independent" political order far away from collectively "civilized" societies. Since their "mode of life" was "independent," their state was driven by the absence of virtuous emotions. This

---

[102] Lauren-Brooke Eisen, *Inside Private Prisons: An America Dilemma in the Age of Mass Incarceration* (New York: Columbia University Press, 2018).

[103] "To Thomas Eddy from Benjamin Rush, Philadelphia, October 19, 1803," in *Letters of Benjamin Rush, vol. 2: 1793–1813*, edited by Lyman Henry Butterfield (Princeton, NJ: Princeton University Press, 2019), 875.

[104] Benjamin Rush, "An Enquiry into the Effects of Public Punishments upon Criminals and upon Society," as quoted in *Cruel and Unusual: The Culture of Punishment in America*, edited by Anne-Marie Cusac (New Haven, CT: Yale University Press, 2009), 37.

[105] "A Vindication of the Address, to the Inhabitants of the British Settlements, on the Slavery of the Negroes in America, in Answer to a Pamphlet Entitled, 'Slavery not Forbidden by Scripture; or A Defence of the West-India Planters from the Aspersions Thrown out against Them by the Author of the Address' (1773) by Benjamin Rush, 1746–1813," Princeton University, Firestone Library, Rare Books and Special Collections, Lapidus 4.32.

emotional deficiency was due to lack of emotional "progress." "The Degrees of Natural Affection, Love of Liberty, and Resentment, discovered by the Negroes, are always proportioned to the Progress they had made in political, and domestic Happiness, in their own Country."[106] Rush thus held that "civilized emotions" arise from "progress in political and domestic happiness," one yet unknown by the Black Caribbean, population mostly oblivious to the "love of liberty." Rush further clarifies his stance when condemning despotism, reaffirming the lesser "love of liberty" in Black communities. "Despotic Governments always require severe Laws. It is the same in Domestic Slavery: The natural Love of Liberty which is common to all Men, and the Love of Ease which is peculiar to the Inhabitants of Warm Climates, can only be overcome by severe Laws and Punishments."[107] Rush translates geographical and historical determinism into an "antislavery" plea that targets the "love of ease" afflicting the Black enslaved body. So, it is not contradictory that a key manufacturer of the modern (and racialized) prison system was "antislavery." At the end of the day, Rush was an "antislavery" slaveholder.

In *Medical Inquiries and Observations upon the Diseases of the Mind*, the physician claimed that love "always renders a woman awkward, but it polishes the manners of men."[108] Furthermore, Rush argues that "fear of death" is only remedied by "just opinions of the divine government, and of the relation we sustain to the great Author of our being."[109] The physician recommends constant reading of biblical texts as a way toward "fortifying the mind against this fear." It is through scriptural study and "constant employment" that Men conquer the "fear of death," since "fear, like vice, is the offspring of idleness."[110] Rush then conceives White Christian "masculinity" as a source of "polished" loving and ties groups that he deemed to be inclined to "idleness," or "love of ease," to suffer from an illiterate "fear of death." Even more, Rush contends that the control of anger is fundamental to societal order. According to Rush, anger is "not only contrary to religion and morals, but to liberal manners," and he proclaims: "The term gentleman implies a command of this passion, above all others."[111] According to the carceral

---

[106] "A Vindication of the Address."   [107] "A Vindication of the Address."
[108] Benjamin Rush, *Medical Inquiries and Observations upon the Diseases of the Mind* (Philadelphia: Grigg and Elliot, 1835), 313.
[109] Rush, *Medical Inquiries and Observations upon the Diseases of the Mind*, 324.
[110] Rush, *Medical Inquiries and Observations upon the Diseases of the Mind*, 326.
[111] Rush, *Medical Inquiries and Observations upon the Diseases of the Mind*, 336.

"reformer," White "masculinity" governs its passions and is guided by both religion and liberalism. Rush declares that he once believed there was not a "single remedy," besides religion, that could alleviate the "diseases induced by the baneful passions," but that he had found one in the "frequent convivial society between persons who are hostile to each other," pledging that "it never fails to soften resentments, and sometimes to produce reconciliation and friendship."[112] The physician portrays "civility" within class struggle as an "antidote" to the passions. Rush's theory reinforces the White potential for governability of passions with a dose of piety and capitalism, consistently extracting the racialized and the colonized from this narrative in his intellectual production.

Rush's insight into the origins of unbridled "sexual appetite" in turn brings light to his conceptualization of racialized Otherness. According to the thinker, "diseases in the sexual appetite" are triggered by "excessive eating, more especially of high seasoned animal food,"[113] "intemperance in drinking," and "idleness."[114] The first remedy proposed by Rush is "Matrimony; but where this is not practicable, the society of chaste and modest women."[115] The physician conceives "female" sexuality as the catalyst of sexual deviance and matrimony as an institution to subdue aberration. Moreover, the sexual appetite emerging from eating "seasoned meat" can be naturally eliminated with a diet of unseasoned vegetables.[116] Not only does "temperance in drinking" do the trick, but also "constant employment in bodily labour or exercise" decreases "venereal excitability and promote healthy excitement."[117] That, or a "cold bath."[118] Rush likewise states that "salivation, by diverting morbid excitability from the genitals to the mouth and throat, would probably be useful in this disease."[119] The physician highlights that sexual appetite can be eliminated by "avoiding all dalliance with the female sex"[120] and a "close application of the mind to business, or study of any kind, more especially to the mathematics."[121] "Female" sexuality and the racialized

---

[112] Rush, *Medical Inquiries and Observations upon the Diseases of the Mind*, 340.
[113] Rush, *Medical Inquiries and Observations upon the Diseases of the Mind*, 348.
[114] Rush, *Medical Inquiries and Observations upon the Diseases of the Mind*, 349.
[115] Rush, *Medical Inquiries and Observations upon the Diseases of the Mind*, 349.
[116] Rush, *Medical Inquiries and Observations upon the Diseases of the Mind*, 350.
[117] Rush, *Medical Inquiries and Observations upon the Diseases of the Mind*, 351.
[118] Rush, *Medical Inquiries and Observations upon the Diseases of the Mind*, 351.
[119] Rush, *Medical Inquiries and Observations upon the Diseases of the Mind*, 352.
[120] Rush, *Medical Inquiries and Observations upon the Diseases of the Mind*, 352.
[121] Rush, *Medical Inquiries and Observations upon the Diseases of the Mind*, 353.

"love of ease" are regarded as the instigators of sexual deviance in Rush's writings, and the proponent of scientific racism teaches a fatal lesson of what would happen if labor with capitalistic aims and mathematical structure did not rule the logos of Men, if carcerality did not dominate societal interactions: White "masculine" sexuality would tragically go from healthy to diseased. The lauded "social reformer" emphasized the role of racialized "emotional deficiency" in his gradations of societal "progress" and mental health, while also concretizing a carceral apparatus where "indolent" and essentially "ill" Black prisoners were forced to "contemplate" their emotional crimes in solitude.

Throughout the nineteenth century, scientific racism would precisely construct "appetite" (whether sexual or generally carnal) as the catalyst for emotional abomination and manipulation. Philosopher Arthur Schopenhauer would echo the heteronormative representation of women as deviants in scientific racism, by arguing that "all women" have an innate tendency for "dissimulation": while men pursue "direct domination," women acquire "indirect domination" and use men via "coquetry and mimicry."[122] While "dissimulation" would be simultaneously "feminized" and racialized by scientific racism, the field of craniology would also racialize notions about "excessive eating." "It is obvious that the more the skull is increased in size, the less marked does this inclination appear; and that the larger the cavities for lodging the organs of taste and smell are, the greater, on the other hand, must be the obliquity of the face."[123] Hyppolyte Cloquet alleged a correlation between his formula for the racialized angles of the facial line, lower cognitive capacity, and "prominent" sensory appetites (taste and smell), linking them to a hypersexualized mouth, an animalized nose, and a "gluttonous" state of being.

Historical determinism regarded emotions as indicators of societal, economic, and political development. This framework contended that different racialized groups epitomized distinctive stages of "progress" in human development, rendering racialized groups as perennially paralyzed in time. Historical determinism interrelated the collective "emotional development" of societies and the "emotional development" of an individual from child to adult, positioning Blackness in a never-ending "emotional infancy." Georg Wilhelm Friedrich Hegel's *The Philosophy of History* affirmed that "to *explain* History is to depict the passions of

---

[122] Arthur Schopenhauer, *Essays and Aphorisms* (London: Penguin, 1970).
[123] Hippolyte Cloquet, *A System of Human Anatomy* (Boston: Wells and Lilly, 1830), 105.

mankind."[124] This influential text argues that historical action toward freedom is mobilized by "passions, private aims, and the satisfaction of selfish desires" and that "these natural impulses have a more direct influence over man than the artificial and tedious discipline that tends to order and self-restraint, law and morality."[125] Yet the philosopher warns that Men cannot be "free by nature" and that "savages" cannot pursue freedom from their passions. "Examples of a savage state of life can be pointed out, but they are marked by brutal passions and deeds of violence; while, however rude and simple their conditions, they involve social arrangements which (to use the common phrase) *restrain* freedom."[126] While, in White societies, passions lead to historical movement, the brutality and aggression of the emotions of "savages" restrict their liberty and political development. Hegel's portrayal of the "emotional difference" of Blackness lies in the potential for "destruction."

> Every idea thrown into the mind of the Negro is caught up and realized with the whole energy of his will; but this realization involves a whole sale destruction. These people continue long at rest, but suddenly their passions ferment, and then they are quite beside themselves. The destruction which is the consequence of their excitement, is caused by the fact that it is no positive idea, no thought which produces these commotions; – a physical rather than a spiritual enthusiasm.[127]

The Black body is theorized as an inherently erratic entity due to the "fermentation" of emotions. This "fermentation" is caused by the nonexistence of both rationality and productivity, leading to "destruction" due to the potency of the physical "commotion" produced by "fermented" passions. In other words, the Black body is understood as being in repose only to then explode with devastating feelings. Hegel affirms that this "commotion" is strictly carnal, and not spiritual. The philosopher proceeds to claim that it is because of this defect in "self-control" that Black communities were "capable of no development or culture," even treating English abolitionists as "enemies" and proclaiming that "we may conclude *slavery* to have been the occasion of the increase of human feeling among the Negroes."[128] Hegel states that the condition of being subjected to slavery by Europeans is the first instance of "human feeling" in African populations, their highest emotional feat in their narrative relegated to the margins of History. The philosopher holds that slavery in Africa is "even worse," that the "essential principal of slavery" is that

---

[124] Georg W. F. Hegel, *The Philosophy of History* (New York: Cosimo, 1837), 13.
[125] Hegel, *The Philosophy of History*, 20.   [126] Hegel, *The Philosophy of History*, 40.
[127] Hegel, *The Philosophy of History*, 98.   [128] Hegel, *The Philosophy of History*, 98.

"man has not yet attained a consciousness of his freedom, and consequently sinks down to a mere Thing – an object of no value," and that the "moral sentiments" of Black people are "quite weak, or more strictly speaking, non-existent."[129] Hegel concludes that only the institution of slavery as imposed by Europeans elevates the condition and "human feeling" of Africans, uplifting them to some level of tainted subjectivity.

> But thus existing in a State, slavery is itself a phase of advance from the merely isolated sensual existence – a phase of education - a mode of becoming participant in a higher morality and the culture connected with it. Slavery is in and for itself *injustice*, for the essence of humanity is *Freedom*; but for this man must be matured. The gradual abolition of slavery is therefore wiser and more equitable than its sudden removal.[130]

Hegel conceptualizes racialized Atlantic slavery as a process of education or sophistication of emotions. Black nations have not "matured" on their own due to their own "barbarous" and fluctuating passions. Not only are African populations denoted as geographically and historically segmented from Europe, but this isolation, and its symbiotic "fermentation of emotions," is represented as resulting in an exclusively "sensual existence." A gradual abolition of slavery is prescribed for the diseased Black Body with its festering passions. Still, the time of recovery appears unending, and Hegel infamously silences Africa in the production of History. "What we properly understand by Africa, is the Unhistorical, Undeveloped Spirit, still involved in the conditions of mere nature, and which had to be presented here only as on the threshold of the World's History."[131] Africa's positioning in the "threshold of the World's History" is unaffected and yet "affected" by the master status of Europeans. Hegel's historical determinism places Africans in an anthropological "primitive" present of an "undeveloped" emotional character and hence historical inaction. Their bare existence just requires unhurried emotional education.

Multiple eminent historians of the nineteenth century precisely visualized slavery as an institution that above all controlled the societal negligence of Black emotions. Thomas Carlyle disputed the abolition of slavery in Great Britain and represented the freed "black man of the West Indies" as working only half an hour per day due to his "fortune": "The fortunate black man! Very swiftly does he settle his account with

---

[129] Hegel, *The Philosophy of History*, 96.
[130] Hegel, *The Philosophy of History*, 99.
[131] Hegel, *The Philosophy of History*, 99.

supply and demand; not so swiftly the less fortunate white man of these tropical localities. He, himself, cannot work; and his black neighbor, rich in pumpkin, is in no haste to help him."[132] The historian depicts freed Black communities as both privileged and selfish for they do not help the "poor white man" with a "biological constitution" that "impedes" him to labor in the tropical heat. Carlyle imagines a "regulated" Caribbean with "happy" enslaved people in "adequate numbers": "All "happy" enough; that is to say, all working according to the faculty they have got; making a little more divine this earth which the gods have given them. Is there any other 'happiness' – if it be not that of pigs fattening daily to the slaughter?"[133] Carlyle's choice of words both pleads for the restoration of slavery and hints at the extermination of Blackness, paradigm of his work.

Crania Americana by polygenist Samuel George Morton demonstrated how North American craniology emphasized "emotional difference" in the context of racial tensions in the history of the United States. Morton's definition of the "Caucasian race" places it at the zenith of the cranial hierarchy by diagnosing its skull as one with "well-proportioned features" and "distinguished for the facility with which it attains the highest intellectual endowments."[134] Meanwhile, the skull of the indigenous "American race" is categorized as "small, wide between the parietal protuberances, prominent at the vertex, and flat on the occiput," and, in "their mental character, Americans are averse to cultivation, and slow in acquiring knowledge; restless, revengeful, and fond of war, and wholly destitute of maritime adventure."[135] In contrast, according to Morton, the "Ethiopian race" displays "the head long and narrow, the forehead low, the cheek bones prominent, the jaws projecting, and the chin small" with a cranial line that affects its demeanors: "the negro is joyous, flexible, and indolent; while the many nations which compose this race present a singular diversity of intellectual character, of which the far extreme is the lowest grade of humanity."[136] Morton highlights notions about the "intellectual endowments" of Europeans, refraining from mentioning any passions and therefore implying emotional self-control. Now, indigenous populations are "fond of war" because they are "revengeful,"

---

[132] Thomas Carlyle, *The Selected Works of Thomas Carlyle* (Rome: Bibliotheca Cakravarti, 2014), 471.
[133] Carlyle, *The Selected Works of Thomas Carlyle*, 477.
[134] Samuel George Morton, *Crania Americana* (Philadelphia: Dobson, 1839), 2.
[135] Morton, *Crania Americana*, 3.   [136] Morton, *Crania Americana*, 3.

while Black bodies are in the "lowest" rank of the hierarchy because of their emotional erraticism: they are so "joyous" that they are left without vigor. Morton's hierarchy patently is a White supremacist's emotional geography of the United States, in which craniology rationalizes political commentary about monolithic "emotional behaviors."

Morton also compartmentalizes and emotionally pathologizes further subdivisions of people of color. According to the craniologist, the "true character" of "Turks" is "marked by violence of passion, cruelty and vindictiveness," while he adds that they would "assume an elevated literary rank were it not for the trammels of superstition and fatalism."[137] On the contrary, Mexicans "show" little emotion and "generously" give their gold to colonizers because of their "lack" of understanding of its value, even though it "cost them much labor to obtain."[138] The "vindictive" Iroquois force "their women to work in the field and to carry burthens," pay "little respect to old age," "opt" to suicide without vacillation, and are "untiring in the pursuit of an enemy, and remorseless in the gratification of their revenge."[139] The racialized are depicted as innately cruel and unknowing of capitalistic transactions. Lowest in this emotional hierarchy, Black bodies are essentialized as having a predisposition toward constant "amusement."

The Negroes are proverbially fond of their amusements, in which they engage with great exuberance of spirit; and a day of toil is with them no bar to a night of revelry. Like most other barbarous nations their institutions are not unfrequently characterised by superstition or cruelty. They appear to be fond of warlike enterprises, and are not deficient in personal courage; but, once overcome, they yield to their destiny, and accommodate themselves with amazing facility to every change of circumstance.[140]

Morton hypothesizes the "barbarous" excitability of Blackness toward "superstition," unrestrained festivity, malice, and even "fondness" of war. Their "exuberance of spirit" is due to the fact that their emotions are mobilized only toward emotional impulsivity itself. Blackness is simultaneously fatally marked by its emotional adaptability, an assertion convenient to polygenist proslavery thought. Furthermore, the thinker contends that what Black communities lack in "invention" they surpass in "imitation."

---

[137] Morton, *Crania Americana*, 43.
[138] Morton, *Crania Americana*, 151.
[139] Morton, *Crania Americana*, 191.
[140] Morton, *Crania Americana*, 87.

The Negroes have little invention, but strong powers of imitation, so that they readily acquire the mechanic arts. They have a great talent for music, and all their external senses are remarkably acute. With respect to their intellectual character there is much diversity of opinion; some authors estimate it at a very low scale, whilst others insist that the germ of mind is as susceptible of cultivation in the Negro as in the Caucasian. That there is considerable difference in this respect in the different tribes is pretty generally admitted; but, up to the present time, the advantages of education have been inadequately bestowed on them, and instances of superior mental powers have been of extremely rare occurrence.[141]

According to the craniologist, Black musical talent is owed to sensorial stimulation, negating intellectual production. Morton acknowledges the "potential" of Black populations as a source of "entertainment" for White people, but disavows its value under the premise of imitation. *Crania Americana* thus paints Blackness as a continuous oscillation between emotional excess and mimicry. The framework of imitation is inevitable: Blackness either "fails" or "imitates."

In *The Races of Men: A Fragment*, Robert Knox, the Scottish anatomist notoriously linked to the Burke and Hare murders,[142] declared: "Men are of various Races; call them Species, if you will; call them permanent Varieties; it matters not. The fact, the simple fact, remains just as it was: men are of different races. Now, the object of these lectures is to show that in human history race is everything."[143] Knox later elaborated: "With me, race, or hereditary descent, is everything; it stamps the man."[144] According to Knox, his murderous anatomical studies justified his sociological commentary, claiming that Black history is "simply a blank – St. Domingo forming but an episode": "Can the black races become civilized? I should say not; their future history, then, must resemble the past. The Saxon race will never tolerate them – never

---

[141] Morton, *Crania Americana*, 88.
[142] William Burke and William Hare murdered sixteen people over a twelve-month period in Edinburgh, and Robert Knox later claimed that he "asked no questions" when he purchased cadavers from them; see Lisa Rosner, *The Anatomy Murders: Being the True and Spectacular History of Edinburgh's Notorious Burke and Hare and of the Man of Science Who Abetted Them in the Commission of Their Most Heinous Crimes* (Philadelphia: University of Pennsylvania Press, 2010). The "success" of Knox's lectures, offered three times per day to around 500 students per lecture, was precisely rooted in the access to "fresh anatomical subjects"; see Caroline McCracken-Flesher, *The Doctor Dissected: A Cultural Autopsy of the Burke and Hare Murders* (Oxford: Oxford University Press, 2011).
[143] Robert Knox, *The Races of Men: A Fragment* (Philadelphia: Lea & Blanchard, 1850), 10.
[144] Knox, *The Races of Men*, 13.

amalgamate – never be at peace."[145] Knox pronounces that the "Saxon race" will never live in emotional harmony with Blackness. The White race would not "be at peace," and "future history" had to culminate this war of races and consequently Black stagnation. The Haitian Revolution is mentioned as "but an episode," a footnote among a "blank" history. Scientific racism certainly produced political commentary responding to the revolutions of the enslaved. While the Haitian Revolution is seemingly acknowledged as a victory, this enslaved triumph is recalled to amplify the insult. Hence, the "non-existence" of Black history makes the Haitian Revolution the butt of the joke. Likewise, the anatomist affirms that only the "Western fine arts" can be classified as Art and exalts Whiteness by celebrating the objective of White Art as "to call forth the grand sentiments, feelings, and passions of the soul."[146] *The Races of Men: A Fragment* is a passionate plea for White supremacy and the extermination of Blackness in the pursuit of "concord" and the cultivation of "grand sentiments." Likewise, scholar Ernest Renan would later proclaim that the "Black race" was a "race of workers of the land" and that Europeans were a race of "masters and soldiers," limiting political and military leadership to White sovereignty.[147] To the promoters of scientific racism, race was indeed everything: racism was the key motivation of their research and scholarship.

Nineteenth-century scientific racism surely produced influential advocacy for racial extermination and against "miscegenation" on emotional grounds. *The Moral and Intellectual Diversity of Races* by Arthur de Gobineau fundamentally asserted that racial "mixture" is intrinsically "injurious."[148] Gobineau's proclamation of the "Arian race"[149] as a "master race," which would later infamously influence the leadership of the Nazi Party, is substantiated by argumentation like "the races rise in the scale of beauty" with evidence as solid as the "noble proportions of a Charlemagne, the expressive regularity of features of a Napoleon, or the majestic countenance of a Louis XIV."[150] His position as an aristocrat outside academic production did not impede him from engaging in

---

[145] Knox, *The Races of Men*, 162.   [146] Knox, *The Races of Men*, 278.
[147] Ernest Renan, *La réforme intellectuelle et morale de la France* (Paris: Callman Levy, 1871), 94.
[148] Arthur de Gobineau, *The Moral and Intellectual Diversity of Races, with Particular Reference to Their Respective Influence in the Civil and Political History of Mankind* (Philadelphia: Lippincott, 1853), 241.
[149] Gobineau, *The Moral and Intellectual Diversity of Races*, 457.
[150] Gobineau, *The Moral and Intellectual Diversity of Races*, 379.

biological determinism. His diatribes about the inferiority of "dark races" include theories about Black bodies having a "tendency to fat" and an animalized bone structure. "The dark races are the lowest on the scale. The shape of the pelvis has a character of animalism, which is imprinted on the individuals of the race ere their birth, and seems to portend their destiny."[151] "Miscegenation" would threaten the "Aryan race" because it would introduce agents of animalism and spark the deterioration of Whiteness. Gobineau's depiction of the "dark races" highlights discourses of emotional difference, declaring a fluctuating nature of Black emotions.

> To these traits he joins a childish instability of humor. His feelings are intense, but not enduring. His grief is as transitory as it is poignant, and he rapidly passes from it to extreme gayety. He is seldom vindictive – his anger is violent, but soon appeased. It might almost be said that this variability of sentiments annihilates for him the existence of both virtue and vice. The very ardency to which his sensibilities are aroused, implies a speedy subsidence; the intensity of his desire, and prompt gratification, easily forgotten. He does not cling to life with the tenacity of the whites. But moderately careful of his own, he easily sacrifices that of others, and kills, though not absolutely bloodthirsty, without much provocation or subsequent remorse. Under intense suffering, he exhibits a moral cowardice which readily seeks refuge in death, or in a sort of monstrous impassivity.[152]

Gobineau contends that "dark races" are perpetually infantile due to their forceful "variability of sentiments." The aristocrat's portrayal of "dark races" emphasizes notions of animalism, monstrosity, and "childish" emotional impulsivity. The ever-changing nature of Black emotions is due to the pursuit of "prompt gratification" without rationality: even the act of killing is devoid of reason or provocation. Their inherent desire, aggression, and inclination to slaughter are transient and "forgotten." The "ardency" of Black emotions is such that "intense suffering" leads to "monstrous impassivity." Again, Black communities are presumed to be inhumanly unfeeling toward their own torment. Ultimately, Gobineau claims Blackness does not "cling" to life, swiftly overcomes "grief," does not feel "remorse," and can "cowardly" perpetrate murder (or self-harm) without notice. The Black body is configured as being resilient from grief due to its "biological" expression of emotion: cold-hearted and devoid of nobility. Black religious experiences are not spared, being represented as entirely sexualized. "With regard to his moral capacities, it may be stated that he is susceptible, in an eminent degree, of religious emotions; but

---

[151] Gobineau, *The Moral and Intellectual Diversity of Races*, 443.
[152] Gobineau, *The Moral and Intellectual Diversity of Races*, 445–446.

unless assisted by the light of the Gospel, his religious sentiments are of a decidedly sensual character."[153] While "dark races" are deemed imprudently sensual, the "White man" is admired for his "love of life."

> The white man is also characterized by a single love of life. Perhaps it is because he knows better how to make use of it than other races, that he attaches to it a greater value and spares it more both in himself and in others. In the extreme of his cruelty he is conscious of his excesses; a sentiment which it may well be doubted whether it exists among the blacks. Yet though he loves life better than other races, he has discovered a number of reasons for sacrificing it or laying it down without murmur. His valor, his bravery, are not brute, unthinking passions, not the result of callousness or impassivity: the principal of which is expressed by the word "honor."[154]

The French aristocrat stresses the White utilitarian view of life, consciousness of "excesses," and lack of indulgence in "brute, unthinking passions." Gobineau concocts an intricate racial hierarchy of "love of life," in which Whiteness becomes the paradigm of knowing how to "love life" with true cognizance of its "value" and "use." In fact, this hierarchy places Asians as intermediaries who are distinguished for their "sense of practical usefulness,"[155] while still missing Black "exalted sentiments" and White "inventiveness" and "honor," generating a precedent for the contemporary "model minority" archetype. Gobineau proceeds to further single out honor as a "feeling" derivative of Whiteness.

> But this feeling – we might call it instinctive – is unknown to the yellow, and unknown to the black races: while in the white it quickens every noble sentiment – the sense of justice, liberty, patriotism, love, religion – it has no name in the language, no place in the hearts or other races. This I consider as the principal reason of the superiority of our branch of the human family over all others.[156]

Gobineau's theory of the supremacy of the "Aryan race" is assumed as vindicated by the "instinctive" emotional "superiority" of White "masculinity," which elevates "honor," conquers "impassivity," nurtures the "noble sentiments" of modernity, and better comprehends the "value" of life (and, most importantly, the "value" of the lives of others). The dominant "Aryan race" is the one that can then make decisions about the outcomes of the rest of the "human family." The aristocrat fundamentally contends that "nations degenerate only in consequence and in

---

[153] Gobineau, *The Moral and Intellectual Diversity of Races*, 447.
[154] Gobineau, *The Moral and Intellectual Diversity of Races*, 452.
[155] Gobineau, *The Moral and Intellectual Diversity of Races*, 450.
[156] Gobineau, *The Moral and Intellectual Diversity of Races*, 453.

proportion to their admixture with an inferior race."[157] Gobineau essentially categorizes "miscegenation" as a "death-blow" to the "only natural ties that can bind large masses of men, homogeneity of thoughts and feelings."[158] His "anti-miscegenation" theory stands on the White elitist aspiration for "emotional homogeneity" toward "sentimental" greatness.

Among advocates for racial extermination and against racial "mixing," such as Knox and Gobineau, Charles Darwin is often perceived as a misunderstood antislavery icon. The official narrative about Darwin, supported by scholarship and his representation in mainstream education, proposes that Darwin's intellectual production was "pure, untainted science" with "humanitarian roots,"[159] inspired by abolitionist fervor and absolutely disentangled from the rise of Social Darwinism. In fact, some scholars argue that Darwin's theories about a "common ancestor" were his "contribution" to his family's "commitment" to the abolition of slavery.[160] Now, history has shown that being denominationally antislavery does not preclude from being anti-Black (or even being truly antislavery). Arthur de Gobineau was theoretically "antislavery" and above all fervently racist, thinking the institution of slavery intrinsically encouraged "miscegenation." And Benjamin Rush was also "antislavery," not because he was against Black exploitation, but because he was against the contemporaneous "institution" of slavery instead of other carceral enslaving methods to regulate the "love of ease" of Black communities. And so was Darwin: against the "idea" of slavery and still primarily hateful toward Black emotionality and consequently Black freedom.

While *On the Origin of the Species* signified the self-aware foundation of Social Darwinism, it is the later *The Expression of the Emotions in Man and Animals* that corroborates Darwin's conceptualization of race. Darwin first conceives "weeping" as an infantile "expression": "Weeping seems to be the primary and natural expression, as we see in children, or suffering of any kind, whether bodily pain short of extreme agony, or

---

[157] Gobineau, *The Moral and Intellectual Diversity of Races*, 455.
[158] Gobineau, *The Moral and Intellectual Diversity of Races*, 455.
[159] See Adrian Desmond & James Moore, *Darwin's Sacred Cause: How a Hatred of Slavery Shaped Darwin's Views on Human Evolution* (New York: Houghton Mifflin, 2009), xix.
[160] See James Lander, *Lincoln & Darwin: Shared Visions of Race, Science, and Religion* (Carbondale: Southern Illinois University Press, 2010), 4.

mental distress."[161] Then, the naturalist adds a gendered layer to the understanding of "weeping."

> With adults, especially of the male sex, weeping soon ceases to be caused by, or to express bodily pain. This may be accounted for its being thought weak and unmanly by men, both of civilized and barbarous races, to exhibit bodily pain by any outward sign. With this exception, savages weep copiously from very slight causes.[162]

Darwin constructs "weeping" as a marker of children, women, and all "savages," therefore lifting White "masculinity" as the one that is able to desist from and rid itself of "weeping" as an expression of "bodily pain." Even though "barbarous races" share the "thought" of weeping as "unmanly," only Men from "civilized races" are able to show emotional self-control and be the paradigm of emotional refinement. Furthermore, the naturalist claims that the impetuous "weeping" of "savages" is sparked by "slight causes."

> I saw in Tierra del Fuego a native who had lately lost a brother, and who alternately cried with hysterical violence, and laughed heartily at anything which amused him. With the civilized nations of Europe there is also much difference in the frequency of weeping. Englishmen rarely cry, except under the pressure of the acutest grief; whereas in some parts of the Continent the men shed tears more readily and freely. The insane notoriously give way to all their emotions with little or no restraint.[163]

Darwin's hierarchy places "Englishmen" at the top tier of emotional self-regulation and correlates the emotional predisposition to "weeping" in "savages" and the "insane." When describing the emotional response of a "native" to familial loss, it is represented as oscillating from "hysterical" crying to "hearty laughter." Darwin renders the "uncivilized" not only as perversely laughing during familial grief but also as crying in "violent ways." The parallelism between the "hysterical emotional violence" of "savages" and the "insane" is reinforced throughout the text. "Patients suffering from acute mania likewise have paroxysms of violent crying or blubbering, in the midst of their incoherent ravings."[164] Again, the "insane" are prone to not only "violent" tears, but also "impulsive"

---

[161] Charles Darwin, *The Expression of the Emotions in Man and Animals* (London: John Murray, 1872), 156.
[162] Darwin, *The Expression of the Emotions in Man and Animals*, 154.
[163] Darwin, *The Expression of the Emotions in Man and Animals*, 155.
[164] Darwin, *The Expression of the Emotions in Man and Animals*, 156.

joy and laughter.[165] Following craniological precedents, Darwin's conceptualization of joy animalizes the "savage" condition, tying "savagery" to the carnal and "sensual" pleasures of the mouth: "Savages sometimes express their satisfaction not only by smiling, but by gestures derived from the pleasure of eating."[166] Thus, Darwin generates a slanted pyramid of grief and joy, in which the "insane" and "savages" express their emotions violently. Darwin constructs the emotional Others to an English Man, an English Man who knows how to be "devotional" and had consequently reached a "civilized condition."

> Hence it is not probable that either the uplifting of the eyes or the joining of the open hands, under the influence of devotional feelings, are innate or truly expressive actions; and this could hardly have been expected, for it is very doubtful whether feelings, such as we now rank as devotional, affected the hearts of men, whilst they remained during past ages in an uncivilized condition.[167]

The English Man separated from his "past" has evolved toward a "devotional" sentimentality. Darwin's elevation of White "masculinity" and symbiotic animalization of people of color are premised on his model of natural selection. His analysis of the "reddening of the skin" when in "rage" elucidates how this animalization is achieved through syntagmatic association. "The reddening of the skin has been observed with the copper-coloured Indians of South America, and even, as it is said, on the white cicatrices left by old wounds on negroes. Monkeys also redden from passion."[168] By syntagmatic association, apes and people of color are conceived as leaning toward the passion of "rage," and even the "external markers" of "rage" are connected to the Darwinist theory of natural selection. "The lips are sometimes protruded during rage in a manner, the meaning of which I do not understand, unless it depends on our descent from some ape-like animal."[169] Darwin's speculation is that the "animal-like expression" of fury evidences the "animal descent" and "affinity to anthropomorphous apes"[170] of all humanity, and yet "may be more common with savages than with civilized races."[171] Hence, Darwin theorizes "savages" and their "rage" as in an intermediary state between

---

[165] Darwin, *The Expression of the Emotions in Man and Animals*, 199.
[166] Darwin, *The Expression of the Emotions in Man and Animals*, 213.
[167] Darwin, *The Expression of the Emotions in Man and Animals*, 221.
[168] Darwin, *The Expression of the Emotions in Man and Animals*, 240.
[169] Darwin, *The Expression of the Emotions in Man and Animals*, 243.
[170] Darwin, *The Expression of the Emotions in Man and Animals*, 253.
[171] Darwin, *The Expression of the Emotions in Man and Animals*, 252.

apes and "civilized races," setting an evolutionary hierarchy of feelings and a precedent for the modern penalization of "Black rage" and the rise of the contemporary "angry Black woman" archetype.

Darwinist rhetoric on emotions consistently provides racial commentary through vague references to "savages" and "natives." "In Tierra del Fuego a native touched with his finger some cold preserved meat which I was eating at our bivouac, and plainly showed utter disgust at its softness; whilst I felt utter disgust at my food being touched by a naked savage, though his hands did not appear dirty."[172] The naturalist decides to "support" his argument about the variances in the emotion of repugnance by targeting the "native's" unclothed body as the site of "utter disgust." Since Darwin's methodology is "substantiated" on isolated encounters during his travels, brief anecdotes from his friends, and observation of his infant children in his home, the allusions to the systematic "expression of emotions" of the Other are nonsensical, terrifying, and illustrative of the ascent of Social Darwinism. Darwin develops another convoluted racial hierarchy with his examination of the gesture of "shrugging the shoulders": "Englishmen are much less demonstrative than the men of most other European nations, and they shrug their shoulders far less frequently and energetically than Frenchmen and Italians do."[173] The naturalist proceeds to claim that this expression of emotions is hereditary: "it can be hardly doubted that they have inherited the habit from their French progenitors, although they have only one quarter French blood in their veins, and although their grandfather did not often shrug his shoulders."[174] Darwin therefore deterministically alleges that certain expressions of emotions are biologically inherited by "blood."

In perhaps one of the most disconcerting sections of a very disconcerting book, Darwin argues that the "insane" suffer "erection of the hair" of the head in instances of "horror." "The extraordinary condition of the hair in the insane is due, not only to its erection, but to its dryness and harshness, consequent on the subcutaneous glands failing to act."[175] His rationale proposes that there is a correlation between "recovery" in mental heath and the "softening" of "harsh" hair. "In patients in whom the bristling of the hair is extreme, the disease is generally permanent and mortal; but in others, in whom the bristling is moderate, as soon as they

---

[172] Darwin, *The Expression of the Emotions in Man and Animals*, 257.
[173] Darwin, *The Expression of the Emotions in Man and Animals*, 265.
[174] Darwin, *The Expression of the Emotions in Man and Animals*, 267.
[175] Darwin, *The Expression of the Emotions in Man and Animals*, 297.

recover their health of mind the hair recovers its smoothness."[176] Darwin explicitly connects the "bristling of the hair" not only to the "insane," but also to the "lower members of the Order to which man belongs."

> With respect of the involuntary bristling of the hair, we have good reason to believe that in the case of animals this action, however it may have originated, serves, together with certain voluntary movements, to make them appear terrible to their enemies; and as the same involuntary and voluntary actions are performed by animals nearly related to man, we are led to believe that man has retained through inheritance a relic of them, now become useless. It is certainly a remarkable fact, that the minute unstriped muscles, by which the hairs thinly scattered over man's almost naked body are erected should have been preserved to the present day; and that they should still contract under the same emotions, namely, terror and rage, which cause the hairs to stand on end in the lower members of the Order to which man belongs.[177]

By adding illustrations in his volume that connote the racialization of hair as showing the "useless" animal trait of looking "terrible to their enemies," this chapter represents a climax of Darwin's depiction of race: Blackness embodies the most expressive remnants of the evolution from animals. Darwin's exploration of the emotions of "savages" and "natives" aim to categorize the most "primitive" and "animal-like" emotional expressions in order to validate his theory of natural selection, while simultaneously devising a racialized hierarchy of emotional proximity to the animal world. The naturalist was influenced by monogenist texts of biological determinism that advocated for one human origin, only to speculate about how the emotional inhumanity of Blackness had materialized. Likewise, Darwin's analysis of emotions explicitly places the racialized in an intermediary position between "anthropomorphous apes" and "civilized men," with emotional "remnants" that "evidence" the animal descent of humanity. *The Expression of the Emotions in Man and Animals* therefore provides much insight into the Darwinist chain of being by constructing "Englishmen" as the apex of adult "masculinity" and emotional evolution. Darwin establishes a correlation between the manifestation of emotions in the "insane" and in people of color, interconnecting race, violence, and "madness": their muscular responses to emotions are violent, animalistic, and exemplified by pouted lips and "terrible" hair. Consequently, the public and scholarly perception of Social Darwinism as a deviation from Darwinist thought is not based

---

[176] Darwin, *The Expression of the Emotions in Man and Animals*, 297.
[177] Darwin, *The Expression of the Emotions in Man and Animals*, 309.

on his writing as evidence. His theory of natural selection was always meant to be applied to race because he did it himself.

Not only would Darwin's own thought on natural selection lead to the ascent and transcendence of Social Darwinism, but post-Darwinist scientific racism would reverberate Darwin's rhetoric about emotional expression. Physician Paul Broca, who researched "evolution" contemporaneously to Darwin, advocated for craniology to be considered as a current that "ne fournit pas seulement des caractères de premier ordre pour la distinction et la classification des subdivisions du genre humain; elle fournit encore des données précieuses sur la valeur intellectuelle de ces groups partiels."[178] Broca's craniological analysis would lead him to declare that "la conformation physique du [racial slur] est en quelque sorte intermédiaire entre celle de l'Européen et celle du singe."[179] *L'aryen: son rôle social* by Georges Vacher de Lapouge applied Social Darwinism and Henri de Boullainvilliers's theory of right of conquest as validations for eugenics. Vacher de Lapouge claimed that the institution of slavery was intrinsic to the tie between natural selection and conquest. "La plus belle conquête de l'homme ne fut pas le cheval, mais l'esclave, et une longue sélection parmi les individus contraints au travail de la terre est probablement la cause de la formation de races vraiment agricoles."[180] Moreover, the thinker contended that slavery would naturally reemerge after its legal abolition, were it not for an alternate "simplistic" solution: racial extermination.

Il ne faut pas oublier que l'abolition de l'esclavage a été motivée surtout par des considérations chrétiennes, et qu'en somme cette institution, jugée en dehors de toute conception surnaturelle de l'homme, n'a rien de plus anormal que la domestication du cheval ou du boeuf. Il est donc possible qu'elle reparaisse dans l'avenir, sous une forme quelconque. Cela se produira même probablement d'une manière inévitable si la solution simpliste n'intervient pas: une seule race, supérieure,

---

[178] Paul Broca, *Mémoires d'anthropologie*, vol. 1 (Paris: Reinwald, 1871), 7. Translation to English: "not only offers characters of a first order for the distinction and the classification of the subdivisions of the human race, but still provides precious data about the intellectual value of these partial groups."
[179] Broca, *Mémoires d'anthropologie*, 397. Translation to English: "the physical conformation of the black man is somehow intermediate between that of the European and that of the ape."
[180] Georges Vacher de Lapouge, *L'aryen: Son rôle social* (Paris: Thorin, 1899), 359. Translation to English: "The most beautiful conquest of mankind has not been the horse, but the slave, and one long selection among the individuals forced to work the land is probably the cause of the formation of truly agricultural races."

nivelée par sélection, mais nivelée par suppression de la postérité des individus inférieurs ou médiocres."[181]

Francis Galton, the cousin of Darwin who coined the term "eugenics," propelled a political movement toward measuring Black criminality with statistical and therefore "objective" quantification. Opportunistically escalating from biological determinism after the "abolition" of slavery, eugenics proclaimed that the genetic content of entire populations could be delimited and "bettered" through racial extermination. In *Hereditary Genius: An Inquiry into Its Laws and Consequences*, Galton stated that "the Negro race has occasionally, but very rarely, produced such men as Toussaint l'Ouverture [sic],"[182] portraying the Haitian Revolution as an exception like other advocates of scientific racism and thus twisting the revolution of the enslaved against itself, as a burden to the Black Atlantic that, according to Galton, should be no more. Furthermore, Galton advised that "a man's natural abilities are derived by inheritance" and that "it would be quite practicable to produce a highly-gifted race of men by judicious marriages during several consecutive generations."[183] Not only did the Victorian statistician propose racial cleansing through the regulation of the institution of marriage, augmenting the presence of "natural abilities" in Atlantic societies, but he also categorically defined Blackness as ruled by "impulsive passions, and neither patience, reticence, nor dignity."[184] *Inquiries into Human Faculty and Its Development* more specifically demarcated the "character" of the "ideal criminal" as having "vicious instincts," a dislike for "continuous labour," and an "absence of self-control," which he claimed was "due to ungovernable temper, to passion, or to mere imbecility."[185] This text also affirmed that the

---

[181] Vacher de Lapouge, *L'aryen: Son rôle social*, 487. Translation to English: "We must not forget that the abolition of slavery was mostly motivated by Christian considerations and that, as a whole, this institution, judged outside of any supernatural conception of man, is no more abnormal than the domestication of the horse or the ox. It is therefore possible that it will reappear in the future, in some form. It will probably even inevitably happen if the simplistic solution does not intervene: a single race, superior, evened by selection, but evened by suppression of the posterity of inferior and mediocre individuals."
[182] Francis Galton, *Hereditary Genius: An Inquiry into Its Laws and Consequences* (London: Macmillan, 1869), 338.
[183] Galton, *Hereditary Genius*, 1.
[184] Francis Galton, "Hereditary Talent and Character," *Macmillan's Magazine* 12 (1865): 321.
[185] Francis Galton, *Inquiries into Human Faculty and Its Development* (London: Macmillan, 1883), 61.

incarcerated had an "absence of genuine remorse for their guilt" proven by their "excellent appetites," while also arguing that the imprisoned were distinguished by their "hypocrisy" and "utter untruthfulness."[186] Galton utilized the same discourses of emotional erraticism and carnal deficiencies to circumscribe both Blackness and criminality, and then he used the emphasis on the emotionally "devious" nature of criminality to uplift the modern prison system as a benign punishment.

Galton's advocacy for eugenics tended to ridicule detractors as "sentimentalists." "There exists a sentiment, for the most part quite unreasonable, against the gradual extinction of an inferior race."[187] His texts held that "the process of extinction works silently and slowly"[188] through marriage selection and that "there will be no more unhappiness on the whole"[189] after racial extermination. According to this line of eugenicist thought, the racialized regulation of marriage represents a "slow" racial triumph that would rid future societies of "unhappiness." It is due to how allegedly "slow" this model was that the statistician then crafted "sophisticated" eugenicist methodologies to register and generate knowledge production about "Black criminality" like composite portraiture[190] and fingerprinting.[191] Galton contended that fingerprinting was key to monitoring the colonized and racialized, asserting that "their features are not readily distinguished by Europeans; and in too many cases they are characterised by a strange amount of litigiousness, wiliness, and unveracity."[192] Hence, racialized generation of statistical data was a eugenicist project in itself: only the racialized would be suspected, policed, and measured. The "data" would reveal only the "criminality" of Black communities opportunistically presumed to be "undistinguishable." Galton's criminological "achievements" intentionally institutionalized racialized metrics in order to police and socially incapacitate the corporeal sources of "impulsive passions" through the racialization of forensic science, criminal profiling, and the carceral landscape.

Likewise, Cesare Lombroso, regarded as a "pioneer" of criminology, would further stress the claim for the need of policing to be rooted in

---

[186] Galton, *Inquiries into Human Faculty and Its Development*, 61.
[187] Galton, *Inquiries into Human Faculty and Its Development*, 308.
[188] Galton, *Inquiries into Human Faculty and Its Development*, 308.
[189] Galton, *Inquiries into Human Faculty and Its Development*, 309.
[190] Francis Galton, "Composite Portraits," *Journal of the Anthropological Institute of Great Britain and Ireland* 8 (1878): 132–142.
[191] Francis Galton, *Finger Prints* (Bloomington: Indiana University Press, 1892).
[192] Galton, *Finger Prints*, 149.

racial profiling. *Crime: Its Causes and Remedies* argued for the racialization of childhood and the imposition of geographical determinism in the Law, targeting a hypersexualized racialized minor and normalizing pedophilic imperial sexual violence: "An attempted rape upon a twelve-year-old girl is a different thing in the south, where sexual maturity comes early, from what it is in the north, and the question of the age of consent must be differently decided for different climates."[193] Moreover, the criminologist states that there is "less sexual differentiation" in "savages" and "habitual criminals," while also declaring that criminality is distinguished by "insensitivity to pain, lack of moral sense, revulsion for work, absence of remorse, lack of foresight (although this can at times appear to be courage), vanity, superstitiousness, self-importance, and, finally, an underdeveloped concept of divinity and morality."[194] Ultimately, Lombroso's key theory is that "the most horrendous and inhuman crimes have a biological, atavistic origin in those animalistic instincts that, although smoothed over by education, the family, and fear of punishment, resurface instantly under given circumstances."[195] Lombroso proclaims that a "criminal" could be identified through "biological" characteristics tied to their racialized animalism and hypersexuality. The ungendered "animalistic instincts" of racialized "criminals" were their high pain tolerance, their conceit, and their unremorseful, non-fearful emotional response to punishment. Punishment had to be harsher because of this lack of "fear," this emotional elasticity. Galton and Lombroso set the eugenicist foundations of the field of criminology and its intersection with the modern prison system, foundations that endorsed mass suspicion, registration, and incarceration of the racialized emotional Other, regardless of their age.

Scientific racism of the turn of the century was also preoccupied with the emotional "complications" that arise from colonialism and immigration. In *The Races of Europe*, William Z. Ripley aimed to address the "question of greatest significance for European civilization."

> There is no question of greater significance for European civilization than the one which concerns the possibility of its extension over that major part of the earth which is yet the home of barbarism or savagery. The rapid increase of its populations is more and more forcing this to the forefront as a great economic problem. No longer is it merely a scientific and abstract problem of secondary importance

---

[193] Cesare Lombroso, *Crime: Its Causes and Remedies* (Boston: Little, Brown, 1911), 247.
[194] Cesare Lombroso, *Criminal Man* (Durham, NC: Duke University Press, 2006), 91.
[195] Lombroso, *Criminal Man*, 91.

as contributory to the theories of the unity or plurality of the human race. Even the United States, with its newly imposed colonial policy through the acquisition of the Philippine Islands and Porto Rico, is called upon to deal with the problem.[196]

Ripley breaks down his "urgent" inquiry into multiple questions, such as would a "single generation of European emigrants" be able to "perpetuate their kind in the equatorial regions of the earth," would they be able to "preserve their peculiar European civilization" in colonized territories, or would they "revert to the barbarian stage of modern slavery – of a servile native population, which alone in those climates can work and live?"[197] Not only did the economist echo both historical and geographical determinism by constructing slavery as a developmental "stage" of hotter climates, but Ripley also intertwined biological and geographical determinism, hypothesizing that different racialized "compositions" respond differently to climate. "In any scientific discussion of the effect of climate upon the human body the racial element must always be considered; and correction must be made for ethnic peculiarities before any definite conclusions become possible."[198] Ripley describes the impact of warmer climates on the human body as accelerating corporeal functions.

What is the first effect of a tropical climate upon the body and its functions? The respiration becomes more rapid for a time, although it soon tends toward the normal; the pulse beats more quickly; the appetite is stimulated; and a surexcitation of the kidneys and the sexual organs ensues; the individual as a rule becomes thinner; the liver tends to increase in size, which is perhaps the cause of a certain sallowness of skin; and in females menstruation is often disturbed, the age of puberty being sooner reached.[199]

According to Ripley, bodily organs become overactive due to heat, which affects the development of "female" bodies, "disturbing" their menstruation and "maturation." This is yet another illustration of the hypersexualization of Black children, who become adults too soon in the perverse eye of the colonizer. After having explicitly racialized childhood, the economist expands upon the tropical "surexcitation of the sexual organs."

One of the most subtle physiological effects of a tropical climate is a surexcitation of the sexual organs, which in the presence of a native servile and morally

---

[196] William Z. Ripley, *The Races of Europe* (New York: Appleton, 1899), 560.
[197] Ripley, *The Races of Europe*, 560–561.   [198] Ripley, *The Races of Europe*, 564.
[199] Ripley, *The Races of Europe*, 574–575.

underdeveloped population often leads to excesses even at a tender age. The elimination of this factor becomes especially important in dealing with the crossing of races and the effects of climate upon fecundity. It is invariably true that the mulatto – a social as well as an ethnic hybrid – suffers from a loss of caste which exposes this class to many temptations.[200]

Ripley's conceptualization of "tropical" sexuality is one that is also accelerated, "fertile," and immoral, with racialized children being marked by the "excesses" of sexuality "at a tender age." The economist connects this portrait of racialized sexuality to the innately "servile" nature of the "morally underdeveloped population," justifying enslavement as an economic measure to restrain this uncontrolled sexual deviance. The ominous proposal of "eliminating this factor" of tropical sexuality to confront the "crossing of races" is followed by the notion of racialized hybridity as a "loss of caste" in the context of sexuality and its "temptations." Black sexuality is to blame for the imperial sexual violence of Atlantic slavery. Moreover, Ripley proceeds to pronounce that "ethnic intermarriage or crossing" must be eliminated, since, "as an element in colonization, and a devious means of avoiding the necessity of acclimatization, it arises to complicate the situation."[201] Ripley elaborates on his theorization of "ethnic crossing" as a "complication," arguing that "a cross between races is often apt to be a weakling": "Mulattoes in any climate lack vitality; and, unless a continual supply of White blood is kept up, they tend to degenerate."[202] Thus, *The Races of Europe*'s theory of emotional acceleration as resulting in racial degeneration affects the very fiber of those of "mixed," or as Ripley would declare, "immoral" ancestry.

The popularization of science during the turn of the century resulted in the translation of racialist theories of emotions for a "general" audience. Ernst Haeckel not only made science more "accessible" for popular consumerism, but also he propagated scientific racism in *The Wonders of Life: A Popular Study of Biological Philosophy*. Haeckel's introduces "passions" as the paradigm of the universality of the effect of "temperature" in "chemical processes," further popularizing geographical determinism: "On the whole, the law holds for chemical processes that they are accelerated by high temperatures and retarded by low ones (like the human passions!), the former have a stimulating and the latter a

---

[200] Ripley, *The Races of Europe*, 562.   [201] Ripley, *The Races of Europe*, 569.
[202] Ripley, *The Races of Europe*, 570.

benumbing effect."[203] The scientist also inserts some commentary on the "value of life" of Black South Africans as "like that of the anthropoid apes, or very little higher."[204] Furthermore, Haeckel conceives "savagery" as unbridled sexual impulsivity and objectification of women. "In most savages and barbarians the satisfaction of their powerful sexual impulse is at the same low stage as in the ape and other mammals. The woman is merely an object of lust to the man, or even a slave without rights, bought and exchanged like all other property."[205] Haeckel's popular science insists on the dissimilarity of Blackness on the basis of the "satisfaction of passions."

While eighteenth- and nineteenth-century scientific racism manifested in intricate validations of racialized slavery, "Western" colonialism, and limitations to the citizenship of people of color, the twentieth century showed an enthrallment with genetics and a centrality of eugenics.[206] The first words of *Heredity in Relation to Eugenics* by Charles Davenport are: "Man is an organism – an animal; and the laws of improvement of corn and of race horses hold true for him also. Unless people accept this simple truth and let it influence marriage selection human progress will cease."[207] Davenport, founder of the International Federation of Eugenics Organizations, advises that the agenda of eugenics should be to encourage "superior races" to "fall in love intelligently."

> The general program of the eugenist is clear – it is to improve the race by inducing young people to make a more reasonable selection of marriage mates; to fall in love intelligently. It also includes the control by the state of the propagation of the mentally incompetent. It does not imply destruction of the unfit either before or after birth. It certainly has only disgust for the free love propaganda.[208]

To "fall in love intelligently" is then the fundamental project for the State to uphold "human progress," besides regulating the reproduction of those who are "mentally defective," which would result only in "mentally defective offspring."[209] While many proponents of scientific racism shaped a hierarchy of love, twentieth-century eugenicists add to this

---

[203] Ernst Haeckel, *The Wonders of Life: A Popular Study of Biological Philosophy* (London: Watts, 1904), 301.
[204] Haeckel, *The Wonders of Life*, 393.   [205] Haeckel, *The Wonders of Life*, 402.
[206] Michael Yudell, *Race Unmasked: Biology and Race in the Twentieth Century* (New York: Columbia University Press, 2014), 2.
[207] Charles Benedict Davenport, *Heredity in Relation to Eugenics* (New York: Holt, 1911), 1.
[208] Davenport, *Heredity in Relation to Eugenics*, 4.
[209] Davenport, *Heredity in Relation to Eugenics*, 66.

framework their advocacy for State policies to enforce the supremacist "rationality of love." Moreover, the biologist affirms that "insanity" is mostly due to a "hereditary predisposition"[210] and that the "excessive bodily energy" of "inferior races" is due to "an inhibitor that prevents persons from achieving the best that is in them."[211] Davenport also states that a "bad environment" mainly disturbs "individuals with an hereditary predisposition toward narcotics," contingent on "the nature of the matings that have occurred in the family."[212] According to the eugenicist, neither a favorable environment nor religion can alter the path of "hereditary predisposition." "Religion would be a more effective thing if everybody had a healthy emotional nature: and it can do nothing at all with natures that have not the elements of love, loyalty and devotion."[213] Thus, Davenport hypothesizes that "human progress" through religion can be attained only with "biological" agents of a "healthy emotional nature" that know "how" to love.

Perhaps Davenport's most elaborate theory is one that combines "ancestry," criminality, and infantilization.

Lack of speech, inability to care for the person or to respond in the conventional fashion to the calls of nature, failure to learn the art of dressing and undressing, inability to count, entire lack of ambition beyond getting a meal, abject slothfulness, love of sitting by the hour picking at a piece of cloth – these are unfortunate traits for a twentieth-century citizen but they constitute a first-rate mental equipment for our remote ape-like ancestors, nor do we pity infants, who invariably have them. So likewise with crimes: – the acts of taking and keeping loose articles, or tearing away obstructions to get at something desired, of picking valuables out of holes and pockets, of assaulting a neighbor who has something desirable or who has caused pain or who is in the way, of deserting family and other relatives, or promiscuous sexual relations – these are crimes for a twentieth-century citizen but they are the normal acts of our remote, ape-like ancestors and (excepting the last) they are so common with infants that we laugh when they do such things.[214]

Davenport establishes a link between the perpetual infantile nature of retrograde "citizens" and their "ape-like ancestors," this tie leading to the irremediable delinquency, indolence, and sexual "promiscuousness" of these "citizens." Like many eugenicists, Davenport avoids an explicit mention of Blackness because he does not have to name what is deemed

---

[210] Davenport, *Heredity in Relation to Eugenics*, 80.
[211] Davenport, *Heredity in Relation to Eugenics*, 64.
[212] Davenport, *Heredity in Relation to Eugenics*, 83.
[213] Davenport, *Heredity in Relation to Eugenics*, 255.
[214] Davenport, *Heredity in Relation to Eugenics*, 262.

the social agent of deterioration: his deterministic approach to emotional "ancestry" clearly delineates what it means to "fall in love intelligently." The thinker precisely proceeds to utilize even more deterministic language of biology to validate his assertions.

> In a word the traits of the feeble-minded and the criminalistics are normal traits for infants and for an earlier stage in man's evolution. There is an aphorism that biologists use which is apt here – ontogeny recapitulates phylogeny. This means that the individual (ontos) in its development passes through stages like those the race (phylum) has traversed in its evolution. The infant represents the ape-like stage.[215]

Infancy embodies a stage of both individual and "racial" evolution, one that some are not able to surpass. Hence, Davenport contends that there are parallelisms between racial "ancestry," infancy, cognitive capacity, and criminal tendencies. The eugenicist correlates "racial development," human evolution, and individual development from childhood to adulthood, evidently influenced by the rhetoric of historical determinism about "emotional development." The biologist reinforces his Social Darwinism by further referencing the "ancestral organs" that "superior" beings have "lost" (i.e., "elongated coccyx (tail), an unusually large appendix, a third set of teeth") and focusing on a "heavy coat of hair" as an "ancestral" undesired trait to argue that "these hairy people represent a human strain that has never gained the naked skin of most people, so imbecility and "criminalistic" tendency can be traced back to the darkness of remote generations."[216] This reasoning pleads for White affiliation to eugenics.

> Our present practices are said to be dedicated by emotion untempered by reason; if this is so, then emotion untempered by reason is social suicide. If we are to build up in America a society worthy of the species *man* then we must take such steps as will prevent the increase or even the perpetuation of animalistic strains.[217]

By defining "social suicide" as "emotion untempered by reason," Davenport generates urgency for his eugenicist theory premised on racialized distinctions in "emotional development." Thus, the war of races is mainly one between reason and emotion. Davenport conceives the eugenicist responses to the potential of "social suicide" as primarily framed by the "rational" overthrow of emotions.

---

[215] Davenport, *Heredity in Relation to Eugenics*, 262.
[216] Davenport, *Heredity in Relation to Eugenics*, 263.
[217] Davenport, *Heredity in Relation to Eugenics*, 263.

As I sit here in my study I will that tomorrow I shoot my dog. But when, tomorrow, I approach the dog to carry out my resolution his signs of fondness for me, the *abandon* with which he throws himself in the most helpless position at my feet, make the act impossible for me. I go to a neighbor and say, "My dog is decrepit and enjoys life no longer. I cannot kill him, will you do me the favor of shooting him?" He says, "I will" and does. We both had the will, why the difference in execution? Was he more resolute, more indomitable than I? It does not follow; simply his reaction to the sight of the dog did not overcome his resolution; mine did. There are various ways in which I might bring myself to view him with indifference by associating him with some wrong, or I might picture more vividly my duty so that it would be a stronger motive than my affection or sympathy.[218]

Davenport's frightening metaphor for eugenics aims to help his audience visualize the "model" institutional practice of governing over emotions when ridding society of its "decrepit dogs." This passage mobilizes emotional empathy toward the eugenicist: He is the one who has the burden of having to kill the "dog," He is the one who has to gather the emotional strength. Reason must defeat "affection or sympathy." According to Davenport, "organized society" must comply with its "responsibility" to avert "the mating that brings together the antisocial traits of the criminal" by fostering the "highest development of the good traits and the inhibition of the bad, surrounding the weak protoplasm with the best stimuli and protecting it from harmful stimuli."[219] Defined as "loving intelligently," Davenport asks White supremacist institutions to be "resolute" and finally kill the "dog."

Early twentieth-century historical determinism in the United States was evidently steered by the eugenicist project of emotional governance. Lothrop Stoddard, member of the Ku Klux Klan and the American Eugenics Society, used his historiography to disseminate his White supremacist ideas, for example, his representation of the Haitian Revolution in *The French Revolution in San Domingo*. "One of the most important considerations for the history of the Revolution in San Domingo is the fact that a majority of the negro population was African-born. It is therefore essential to know something of this majority, born, not under the influence of White supremacy, but in African savagery."[220] His historiographical objective was to portray the victory of

---

[218] Davenport, *Heredity in Relation to Eugenics*, 264.
[219] Davenport, *Heredity in Relation to Eugenics*, 266.
[220] Lothrop Stoddard, *The French Revolution in San Domingo* (New York: Houghton Mifflin, 1914), 53.

the enslaved as a defeat, as the beginning of a historical abomination away from the influence of White supremacy. "The white race had perished utterly out of the land, French San Domingo had vanished forever, and the black State of Haiti had begun its troubled history."[221] In *The Rising Tide of Color against White-World Supremacy*, the historian precisely paints a teleological picture of a White supremacist tragedy. This racialist text contended that Black bodies were fit for slavery due to their "intense emotionalism."

> The black man is, indeed, sharply differentiated from the other branches of mankind. His outstanding quality is superabundant animal vitality. In this he easily surpasses all other races. To it he owes his intense emotionalism. To it, again, is due his extreme fecundity, the negro being the quickest of breeders. This abounding vitality shows in many other ways, such as the negro's ability to survive harsh conditions of slavery which other races have soon succumbed.[222]

Stoddard constructs Black people as distinguished from non-enslaved humanity for their "superabundant animal vitality." This animalization not only hypersexualizes Blackness as "extremely fertile," but also refers to "animal vitality" to recall the antebellum era as one that was still accessible. Stoddard frames the "extreme" nature of Black "emotionalism" as a validation of White imperialism.

> Unless, then, every lesson of history is to be disregarded, we must conclude that black Africa is unable to stand alone. The black man's numbers may increase prodigiously and acquire alien veneers, but the black man's nature will not change. Black unrest may grow and cause much trouble. Nevertheless, the white man must stand fast in Africa. No black "renaissance" impends, and Africa if abandoned by the whites, would merely fall beneath the onset of the browns. And that would be a great calamity.[223]

White colonialism in Africa is legitimized with the notion of Black "unrest." According to Stoddard, individual Black "emotionalism" leads to collective Black "unrest," which in turn can create "trouble" for Whiteness. Africa is depicted as retrograde and incapable of a "renaissance." The White supremacist establishes a dichotomy between the alleged African incapacity to "stand alone" and the "Western" duty to "stand fast" in racialized colonies. The true "calamity" would be for

---

[221] Stoddard, *The French Revolution in San Domingo*, 350.
[222] Lothrop Stoddard, *The Rising Tide of Color against White-World Supremacy* (New York: Charles Scribner's Sons, 1920), 90.
[223] Stoddard, *The Rising Tide of Color*, 102.

Africa to fall in Brown hands. Stoddard provides more insight into the potentiality of this "calamity" in the "colored world."

> Thus, the colored world, long restive under white political domination, is being welded by the most fundamental of instincts, the instinct of self-preservation, into a common solidarity of feeling against the dominant white man, and in the fire of a common purpose internecine differences tend, for the time at least, to be burned away. Before the supreme fact of white political world-domination, antipathies within the colored world must inevitably recede into the background.[224]

Stoddard conceptualizes the "colored world" as dangerously uniting in a "common solidarity of feeling against the dominant white man." This "common purpose" is driven by instincts of "self-preservation." It is "fire." The eugenicist framework of this text is manifest when the White supremacist proclaims that this "fire" must "recede into the background," since the main barriers against "White world-domination" could potentially be the "antipathies within the colored world." But they are not. Stoddard argues that the key obstacle in actuality is not found in the "colored world": "In short, the real danger to white control of Africa lies, not in brown attack or black revolt, but in possible white weakness through chronic discord within the white world itself."[225] Therefore, the historian is advocating against "chronic discord" among White nations and instead for the triumphant formation of a united "White world": "White race-consciousness has been of course perturbed by numberless internal frictions, which have at times produced partial inhibitions of unitary feeling."[226] The true overthrow of the "antipathies within the colored world" would emerge from a "White race-consciousness." It would be a "unitary feeling," guided by the emotional principles of eugenics.

Early twentieth-century historical determinism in the United States was also "self-reflective," exploring the role of the Civil War in the intensification of a "White American" identity, identity framed by White supremacist thought against the "sentimentalism" of abolitionism. In *The Passing of the Great Race; or, The Racial Basis of European History*, Madison Grant asserted that slavery as an institution "often arises to compel the servient race to work and to introduce it forcibly to a higher form of civilization," while also declaring that from "a material point of view slaves are often more fortunate than freemen when treated

---

[224] Stoddard, *The Rising Tide of Color*, 9. [225] Stoddard, *The Rising Tide of Color*, 103.
[226] Stoddard, *The Rising Tide of Color*, 198.

with reasonable humanity and when their elemental wants of food, clothing and shelter are supplied."[227] The eugenicist delineates slavery as a forced insertion of Blackness into civilization that is "fortunate" in a "material point of view." Then, Grant proceeds to state that the aftermath of the legal "abolition" of slavery was mismanaged by the "American." "Instead of retaining political control and making citizenship an honorable and valued privilege, he entrusted the government of his country and the maintenance of his ideals to races who have never yet succeeded in governing themselves, much less any one less."[228] Grant traces this "error" to the "sentimentalism of the Civil War."

> Thus the view that the Negro slave was an unfortunate cousin of the white man, deeply tanned by the tropic sun and denied the blessings of Christianity and civilization, played no small part with the sentimentalists of the Civil War period and it has taken us fifty years to learn that speaking English, wearing good clothes and going to school and to church does not transform a Negro into a white man.[229]

Grant's diatribe on the "sentimentalism of the Civil War" affirms that Blackness is not able to escape its misfortune and expresses disdain toward those who deemed Black populations "unfortunate" relatives of White "civilizations." His deprecation extends to the Americas as a whole in order to illustrate the theoretical absurdity of the notion of the United States as a "melting pot": "What the Melting Pot actually does in practice can be seen in Mexico, where the absorption of the blood of the original Spanish conquerors by the Native Indian population has produced the racial mixture which we call Mexican and which is now engaged in demonstrating its incapacity for self-government."[230] Grant underlines the assumed failure of self-governance in racially "mixed" communities and the unavoidability of "miscegenation" regressing "to the more ancient, generalized and lower type": "The cross between a white man and an Indian is an Indian; the cross between a white man and a Negro is a Negro."[231] This rule is also applied to the concept of "Latin America," which Grant alleges is a "misnomer as the great mass of the populations

---

[227] Madison Grant, *The Passing of the Great Race; or, The Racial Basis of European History* (New York: Scribner's, 1922), 8–9.
[228] Grant, *The Passing of the Great Race*, 12.
[229] Grant, *The Passing of the Great Race*, 16.
[230] Grant, *The Passing of the Great Race*, 17.
[231] Grant, *The Passing of the Great Race*, 18.

of South and Central America is not even European and still less 'Latin,' being overwhelmingly of Amerindian blood."[232]

Grant elaborates on his theory of "race determination" being discernible through purportedly precise physical attributes. For example, the thinker conceives "all blue, gray, or green eyes" as limited to the "Nordic" race of Northern Europe, while "dark colored eyes" are deemed signs of backwardness: "Dark colored eyes are all but universal among wild mammals and entirely so among the primates, man's nearest relatives. It may be taken as an absolute certainty that all the original races of man had dark eyes."[233] "Thick, protruding, everted lips" are considered symptoms of "primitivism."[234] These traits, among others, are denoted as external markers of undesirable elements "in the nation," and the eugenicist proposes that "most practical and hopeful method of race improvement" is through the eradication of these elements "by depriving them of the power to contribute to future generations."[235] According to Grant, racial annihilation would in turn exterminate the agents of criminality in society, keeping only intellectuality and vitality.

> In mankind it would not be a matter of great difficulty to secure a general consensus of public opinion as to the least desirable, let us say, ten percent of the community. When this unemployed and unemployable human residuum has been eliminated together with the great mass of crime, poverty, alcoholism and feeblemindedness associated therewith it would be easy to consider the advisability of further restricting the perpetuation of the then remaining least valuable types. By this method mankind might ultimately become sufficiently intelligent to choose deliberately the most vital and intellectual strains to carry on the race.[236]

Biological racism is premised on the modern political incentive to "make live and let die" instead of the exertion to "let live and make die," as the efficiency of the "death of the other, the death of the bad race, of the inferior race (or the degenerate, or the abnormal) is something that will make life in general healthier: healthier and purer."[237] Eugenics, with its principle of the "rational control of reproduction,"[238] vindicated this

---

[232] Grant, *The Passing of the Great Race*, 61.
[233] Grant, *The Passing of the Great Race*, 24.
[234] Grant, *The Passing of the Great Race*, 31.
[235] Grant, *The Passing of the Great Race*, 53.
[236] Grant, *The Passing of the Great Race*, 54.
[237] Michel Foucault, "17 March 1976," in *Society Must Be Defended: Lectures at the Collège de France, 1975–76*, edited by Mauro Bertani & Alessandro Fontana (New York: Picador, 2003), 255. Foucault's application of this theory is Eurocentric.
[238] Dorothy Roberts, *Fatal Invention: How Science, Politics, and Big Business Recreate Race in the Twentieth-Century* (New York: New Press, 2011), 36.

project by propelling a narrative of war between rationality and sensibility. The proponents of scientific racism waged this war with much initiative: establishing eugenics societies, joining "prison reform" committees, lobbying for supremacist policies, holding public conferences and phrenological evaluations, and conducting human experimentation projects, among other atrocities.[239] Samuel George Morton strived for his *Crania Americana* to reach many physicians in the United States.[240] Harvard professor Louis Agassiz wrote four letters to Lincoln's Civil War Commission in 1863, cautioning that political incorporation of Black communities in the United States would lead to "social disorder" due to the "character of the negro race" being "indolent, playful, sensuous, imitative, subservient."[241] These advocates of racialism were resolute in their agenda because they profited from scientific racism in their slaveholding investments, in their professional successes and connections, and in the advancement of their intellectual production. The exponents of scientific racism are still deplorably reckoned as "pioneers" within their fields and certainly dictated the foundations of institutional racism in economic mobility, political agency, and higher education. More recently, in 1994, Richard J. Hernstein and Charles Murray published their infamous *The Bell Curve: Intelligence and Class Structure in American Life*, expressing their disdain toward the "uproar" in response to previous affirmations of the racialization of intelligence.[242] *Guns, Germs, and Steel: The Fates of Human Societies* by Jared Diamond, published in 1997, ascribed to geographical determinism when it claimed that "different, historical trajectories of Africa and Europe" were rooted in the environment or "stem ultimately from differences in real estate."[243] The vast influence and readership of scientific racism then and now has legitimized the exploitation and genocide of the "least valuable types" throughout three centuries, and the "death of the bad race" is something that is still longed for and acted on.

---

[239] See Roberts, *Fatal Invention*.
[240] "Letter Book of Samuel George Morton: Philadelphia, PA, 1832–1837," Princeton University, Firestone Library, Rare Books and Special Collections, C0199 no. 737q; "Receipts for Crania Americana, 1837–1842," Princeton University, Firestone Library, Rare Books and Special Collections, C0199 no. 736q.
[241] As quoted in Roberts, *Fatal Invention*, 33.
[242] Richard J. Hernstein & Charles Murray, *The Bell Curve: Intelligence and Class Structure in American Life* (New York: Simon & Schuster, 2010), 9–11.
[243] Jared Diamond, *Guns, Germs, and Steel: The Fates of Human Societies* (New York: Norton, 1999), 401.

Today, mainstream education still either omits vast elements of the literary production of proponents of scientific racism or recurs to obscene devil's advocacy in classrooms, perpetrating harm on students of color, particularly those who are descendants of the enslaved. Especially in STEM and social sciences, there is a tendency to teach the history of science, medicine, and statistics through presumed "achievement-based" curricula, perpetuating medical racism. Buffon did this. Then, Cuvier did that. Following Cuvier's precedent, Darwin really did it, changing History forever. And let us not forget Galton. Did you know he was Darwin's cousin? This mediocre framing of the history of scientific racism lies. It absolutely lies, and not only because it hides. It lies because it does not specifically bring light to the key "purpose" of this intellectual production. To speak about Buffon's "contributions" to evolutionary biology without addressing the centrality of his key monogenist theory of degradation is to teach through lies. Many times, through devil's advocacy or through treatment of scientific racism as a footnote of the history of science, negligent educators render proponents of scientific racism stuck in a secluded office or lab, disconnected from the world they were profiting from and not really meaning to be racist, minimizing the intentionality and political agency of their "pioneers." Sometimes, educators even affirm that these promoters of scientific racism were a "product of their time" and responded to key "beliefs" of their era, when historians cannot claim to enter the subjectivities of past historical figures, making this a convenient methodological flaw. Creating hierarchies of maleficence among the proponents of scientific racism who were proslavery or "antislavery," monogenists or polygenists, does not improve the methodology. Advocates of scientific racism who were denominationally "antislavery" or endorsed monogenism mainly contended that Blackness represented a perilous emotional deterioration that had to be fiercely regulated, policed, and exploited. All exponents of scientific racism were unified by a "purpose," the purpose of racialized emotional policing. And this purpose of racialized emotional subjugation goes beyond the legal institution of slavery as it manifested in the eighteenth century. Those who were "antislavery" racists still advocated for the exploitation and emotional purging of Blackness. Hence, devil's advocacy aims to veil the profound impact scientific racism contemporarily has over Black life, death, and emotional oppression.

Scientific racism fashioned a supernatural emotional body that cannot "stand alone" but, when speaking of pain, can always take it. Scientific racism systematically upheld that the main justification for racialized slavery was "emotional difference," since this institution allowed for a perpetual education of "human feelings." Powerful thinkers generated elaborate racial hierarchies of love, imitation, dissimulation, and pain tolerance. Emotional difference, they said, manifested in "external markers," such as lips that were too sexual, bodies that were too gluttonous, "genitalia" that were too visceral. Proponents of scientific racism claimed that Blackness was essentially either emotionally erratic, emotionally resilient, or emotionally performative. The Black body is permanently at fault because it can only imitate feelings, simulate feelings, or simply love wrongly. Even the Haitian Revolution was recalled by advocates of scientific racism as an imitative, short-lived display of greatness that resulted in an even "less tolerable" misery. The framing of Black emotions as imitative creates an inescapable structural surveillance, in which Blackness irremediably reaches an inferior simulation of Whiteness or is simply deemed a failure. Whiteness is inherently "non-imitative." Blackness is only entirely Black if it "fails." This discourse allows not only for the negation of Black intellectual production but also for the appropriation of Black intellectual production as a manifestation of White productivity. Therefore, the criminalizing ambivalence on emotional performativity was key to construct a Black emotional antagonist to suspect, police, and injure. When Black emotions were simulated, the Black body could not be harmed, could not suffer, could not feel pain; grief would soon pass, or the injury was strictly White. When Black emotions were earnest, they were precarious, "fermented" for destruction: these violent emotions required institutional punishment to protect Whiteness from explosive emotional perversion. Because Whiteness has the monopoly over knowing how to love life, to rule over Life.

The field of eugenics was conceptualized as a "rationality of love" against the "sentimentalism" of the Black struggle to breathe. The eugenicist project is primarily one of emotional control for both the racialized and the racialist: to regulate the presence of emotions in capitalistic societies through "intelligent love" and to gather the "emotional strength" for racial extermination and thus "emotional homogeneity." Of course, eugenicist criminologists stressed the discourses of the invariable "lack of remorse" and absence of "fear of punishment" in Black communities, since, this way, Black emotions were deemed worthy of permanently escalating penalization. While Black emotions were criminalized as mobilized only toward the "pleasures" of emotional impulsivity, White intellectual production was commemorated as cultivating "grand sentiments," the grand emotional narratives of modernity. This discursive cultivation of White feelings was normalized through the imperial monopoly over "rational" and "civilizing" emotions. Overall, eugenicist thought was unified by the essentialization of Whiteness as reason and Blackness as emotionalism, a climatic extension of long-lived precedents of the intellectual history of racialized slavery. Racial extermination was rationalized as the long-awaited triumph of Reason over Emotion, the demise of Excess, the downfall of "Black unrest." The Black body was essentially emotional and, therefore, excessively criminal. Black expression of emotions was denoted as intrinsic violence and as deserving of the full force of State penalization. Blackness was Emotion itself, Crime itself. Scientific racism hence incentivized an inescapable scrutiny over Black emotions to be punished, to be hurt – an emotional captivity. This emotional captivity was and is accomplished by a sinister imperial gaze that has no sympathetic response to Black pain, since They are either faking pain or complaining too much about it. They are either deceptive about their emotions or authentically oppressed by them. They are loud, They are angry, They are only joyous when Whiteness intrudes. Their moans must be silenced. Their resistance must be contained. Their enslaved bodies can eternally be at the excruciating brink of death because, at the end of the day, They must be enthusiastically obedient to White feelings.

A mother and a daughter. Drums. Suckling. She is hungry. This is not enough. Her body is ravenous. I can sense it. I can take it. Can I take it? Can I rid you of it? Can I cleanse you of your unbridled appetite? I want you to be happy. But this hunger will not let her.

3

Atlantic Slavery and Its Passionate Transgressions

> Flogged my field Negroes for laziness, scolding, quarreling, etc.
> —Diary of Thomas Thistlewood

Etc. The use of "etc." by Thomas Thistlewood, British colonizer in eighteenth-century Jamaica, is part of the agonizing narrative of the institutional emotional detachment of White slaveholders toward the pain and blood emerging from Black enslaved people. The entries about enslaved punishment in Thistlewood's diary[1] tend to follow the same syntagmatic structure: verb denoting the action of the punishment ("flogged"), the subject to be punished ("Field Negroes"), and, last, the "motive" of the punishment ("for laziness, scolding, quarreling, etc."). His notes about reiterated torture of the enslaved, including his more than one thousand entries about the sexual exploitation of enslaved people, aim to collect a segmented logos of his violent enactment of slaveholding dominance. The structure of the diary is terrifying, in part because of the quantity of entries it has. But it provides only entries of punishment, in many instances of collective penalization. Thus, the diary does not count each crack of the whip in the bloodied back of an enslaved person, followed by each tormented moan. It does not capture each tear falling down an enslaved person's cheek while Thistlewood violently penetrates them and later while they clean the disgusting trace of their enslaver's sadism. Only etcetera remains, a code

---

[1] "Diary by Thomas Thistlewood," Yale University, Beinecke Rare Book and Manuscript Library, OSB MSS 176.

word that allows for the normalization of the horrors lived by those in Thistlewood's slaveholding plantation. Because the contingency of etcetera was theorized as originating from the excessive provocation by Black emotions.

The epistemological triumph of the word "etcetera" can be found in the historiographical conceptualization of the "loving relationship" between Thistlewood and the enslaved "Phibbah."[2] Thistlewood freed "Phibbah" in his will when he died, even though he had fathered their child earlier. All of the instances of sexual contact happened while "Phibbah" was in the condition of slavery, within the power dynamic of master and enslaved person, and consequently without the capacity to consent. The exceptionalism of "Phibbah" among the more than one hundred enslaved people who were sexually exploited by Thistlewood seems of historiographical convenience: it follows the tale of a slaveholder "product" of the ideologies of his time and still finding love in one of the enslaved. This historiographical emotional empathy with the White enslaver parallels the "official history" of the "relationship" between Thomas Jefferson and "Sally Hemings," a minor and his late wife's sibling.[3]

In the *Notes of the State of Virginia*, Thomas Jefferson proclaimed the absence of beauty in the Black body that he consistently sexually exploited.

Are not the fine mixtures of red and white, the expressions of every passion by greater or less suffusions of colour in the one, preferable to that eternal monotony, which reigns in the countenances, that immovable veil of black which covers all the emotions of the other race? Add to these, flowing hair, a more elegant symmetry of form, their own judgment in favour of the whites, declared by their preference of them, as uniformly as is the preference of the Oranootan for the black women over those of his own species.[4]

Jefferson not only animalizes Black women by representing them as the "preference" of the "Oranootan," but also tacitly depicts Black men as aspiring to abuse the "ideal" bodies of White women. Furthermore, his biological determinism uses the metaphor of the "immovable veil of Black" to argue that the "emotions" of the "other

---

[2] See Trevor Burnard, *Mastery, Tyranny, & Desire: Thomas Thistlewood and His Slaves in the Anglo Jamaican World* (Chapel Hill: University of North Carolina Press, 2004).
[3] See Lucia C. Stanton, *"Those Who Labor for My Happiness": Slavery at Thomas Jefferson's Monticello* (Charlottesville: University of Virginia Press, 2012).
[4] Thomas Jefferson, *Notes on the State of Virginia* (Boston: H. Sprague, 1802), 191.

race" are "covered" and thus inaccessible. Nonetheless, the paradoxical text goes on to deconstruct the emotions of enslaved people "covered" by Black skin, following the paradigm of scientific racism of visualizing Black emotions as indecipherable and yet comprehensible to scientific observation.

> They are more ardent after their female: but love seems with them to be more an eager desire, than a tender delicate mixture of sentiment and sensation. Their griefs are transient. Those numberless afflictions, which render it doubtful whether heaven has given life to us in mercy or in wrath, are less felt, and sooner forgotten with them. In general, their existence appears to participate more of sensation than reflection. To this must be ascribed their disposition to sleep when abstracted from their diversions, and unemployed in labour. An animal whose body is at rest, and who does not reflect, must be disposed to sleep of course.[5]

Black love is portrayed as grounded on "desire" instead of a "sentiment" that is "delicate," while the overall "existence" of Blackness is geared toward "ardent" passions instead of "reflection." This definition of Black love aims to propel a specific reading of the racial "composition" of the United States, in which political racial integration is an impossibility. The outward self-representation of Thomas Jefferson animalized and simultaneously disenfranchised Black people, while his intimacy was morbidly fixated with his sexual fantasies with a "racially mixed" enslaved minor. Emphatically, "grief" is essentialized as "transient" in those whose emotions were "covered" by Black skin. And that is why the violence of slaveholding regimes was unremitting and always escalating. Because only through continual and ever-increasing violence could punishment be "functional" and Black grief be incessant. The insistence in proclaiming "loving relationships" between masters and the enslaved has not seemed to die down in history. In the Atlantic world, the erasure of sexual slavery has been achieved by the same emotional discourses of scientific racism that hypersexualized, depersonalized, and criminalized Black people to configure an emotional Other.

Since any expression of Black emotions was denoted as deviant and inherently violent, the enslaved Black body was "ideally" expected by Empires of the Atlantic world to diligently serve through emotional self-containment, where the Body kept Emotions captive. The inescapability of racialized emotional policing thus reverberated in the inexorability of

---

[5] Jefferson, *Notes on the State of Virginia*, 192.

perpetual slaveholding violence against the enslaved, as this violence was constructed as "provoked" by the emotional "excesses" of the enslaved Black body. Slaveholding violence permanently escalated because the racialized enslaved body was ambivalently categorized as deceptive, unfeeling, always irremediably failing to "self-contain." Genocidal slaveholding violence had to verify its harm and mobilize against the "transience" of Black grief. Genocidal slaveholding violence was and is always etcetera: immeasurable, insuperable, omnipresent. The long-lived historical systematization of enslaved passions escalated from general notions of enslaved obedience to the systemic racialized perpetration of intrinsically "non-injurious" enslaved injury as the total foundation of the capitalistic racialization of both labor and the institutional acknowledgment of "productivity." While the perpetuation of slavery was systematically validated with the protection of "happiness" in colonial societies of the Atlantic world, the resistance movements of the enslaved were depicted as passionate transgressions that created "discord," discord with profound economic implications for European empires. Atlantic slavery in the eighteenth and nineteenth century consolidated an imperial emotional economy that was premised on scientific hierarchies of racial differentiation in emotional worth, constituting the capitalistic order of White happiness. In the pursuit of economic productivity and international veneration, Empires imposed the distrusting surveillance and regulation of Black bodies through parallel allegorical classifications for racialized categories, emotional distinctions, and political justifications of slaveholding violence. These racialized lines in turn aimed to silence the intellectual production of the enslaved to perpetuity. Black souls were feeling, breathing, pondering, producing, sobbing. And the "order" of inequality did not write that down.

THE IMPERIAL PROJECTION OF THE FEELINGS AND "PROVOCATIONS" OF ATLANTIC SLAVERY

In 1671, Governor Ferão de Sousa Coutinho of Pernambuco in Brazil wrote an urgent letter to the King of Portugal about the establishment of multiple *mocambos* in Palmares, or communities of formerly enslaved people, originally from Angola, who had escaped from their captivity. The governor of Pernambuco characterized the settlements as "bold" and expressed "fear" that the "example" and "permanence of the *mocambos*" could incite other enslaved people to escape from their "suffering" and "grow to such numbers that they move against the inhabitants of this captaincy, who are so few in relation to their slaves."⁶ This letter ends with a plea for "God" to "succor" Palmares from this "disturbance."⁷ Just as Palmares was constructed as a "disturbance" in colonial Brazil, institutional punishment and legal taxonomies regulating slaveholding economies were manufactured to "succor" colonies from any "discord" affecting their "happiness." Just as the power dynamics in colonial Brazil chiefly revolved around the "fear of Palmares," empires of the Atlantic world aimed to subjugate or eradicate any emotional bodies that "dared being bold," asserting their legally illegitimate right to be free. The revolutions of the enslaved were represented as the ultimate imperial "fear." In actuality, not a "fear" at all, as the Empire never experienced the horrors of enslaving regimes, never at all. Instead, Empires premeditated to project their brutality as "fearful" and Black emotional autonomy as the "terrifying" antagonist to colonial "happiness." The sadistic political discourse of imperial "fear" was continual and perversely punished the Black body – because the enslaved resisted by existing, resisted in life and death.

The calculated political discourse of imperial "fear" toward the revolutions of the enslaved guided the ritualization of slaveholding corporeal punishment in the legal taxonomies of Atlantic slavery. The Code Noir aimed to standardize the institution of slavery in the French Empire in 1685 after more than a century of colonial practice, while doing little to avoid family fragmentation and recurrence of torture.⁸ On the contrary, it established a gradation of State physical penalization for "fugitive" enslaved people based on the amount of pain these punishments produced and culminating in death.

L'esclave fugitif qui aura été en suite pendant un mois à compter du jour que son Maître l'aura dénoncé en Justice, aura les oreilles coupées, & sera marqué d'une fleur de lys sur une épaule: & s'il récidive un autre mois à compter pareillement du jour de la dénonciation, aura le jaret coupé, & sera marqué d'une fleur de lys sur l'autre épaule, & la troisième fois il sera puni de mort.⁹

---

[6] "The War against Palmares: Letter from the Governor of Pernambuco, Ferão de Sousa Coutinho (1 June 1671) on the Increasing Number of Insurgent Slaves Present in Palmares," in *Early Brazil: A Documentary Collection to 1700*, edited by Stuart B. Schwartz (New York: Cambridge University Press, 2010), 264.
[7] "The War against Palmares," 265.
[8] James Pritchard, *In Search of Empire: The French in the Americas, 1670–1730* (New York: Cambridge University Press, 2004), 88.
[9] *Le Code Noir ou Recueil des Réglemens* (Paris: L. F. Prault, 1685), 47. Translation to English: "The slave that is fugitive during a month from that day that his owner denounced him to Justice will have his ears cut, and he will be marked with a fleur-de-lis

The ambiguity of the Code Noir surrounding physical penalization is exemplified by its vague prohibition of torture of the enslaved and the concurrent legal confirmation of the use of the whip by the master: "Pourront pareillement les Maîtres, lorsqu'ils croiront que leurs esclaves l'auront mérité, les faire enchainer & les faire battre de verges ou de cordes, leur défendant de leur donner la torture, ni de leur faire aucune mutilation de membre, à peine de confiscation des esclaves."[10] Since the emergence of African diasporic identities was significantly influenced by the "hybridity" and "adaptability" of the religions of the enslaved,[11] the Code Noir also prioritized the prohibition of the practice of any religion other than the Catholic faith.[12] Legal codes about Atlantic slavery, such as the Code Noir, corroborated the inherence of the State in the body and soul of the enslaved through their taxonomical penalization, which fostered rationalizations that encouraged masters to exercise their sadism in the mutilated bodies of the enslaved. Flogging guided by the prerogative of the enslaver was not deemed torture because the racialized emotional Other was presumed not to feel as much pain or suffering. One blow, two blows, fifty blows. With each blow of the whip, a moan. Each moan and burst of blood verifies the pain, the agony. The emotional detachment and malevolence of the enslaver. But although, in theory, the emotional Other is suspected, is said to be faking it, to be able to withstand it, the whip was still rationalized as the legitimate, institutional, and entirely functional method of punishment of the enslaved. Imperial Law conceptualized the enslaved as a thing for all means, except when addressing punishment. The enslaved became human in the eyes of the Law only to be penalized, to be wounded. So punishment, which made the enslaved a lesser humanity to be demeaned, was thought of as functional on the same Body that could theoretically not be injured by it. The injury was legally appropriated by the master, and slaveholding violence could only escalate to verify Black torment.

---

on one shoulder; and, if he similarly relapses another month from the day of the denunciation, he will have his hamstring cut, and he will be marked with a fleur-de-lis on the other shoulder; and, the third time, he will be punished with death."

[10] *Le Code Noir*, 48. Translation to English: "In the same way, the Masters can, when they believe their slaves deserve it, chain them and whip them with rods or ropes, but it is prohibited to use torture, or to mutilate a member, or they will be punished with the confiscation of slaves."

[11] Albert J. Raboteau, *Slave Religion: The "Invisible Institution" in the Antebellum South* (Oxford: Oxford University Press, 2004), 4.

[12] *Le Code Noir*, 30.

The ambivalence of the Law toward the feeling humanity of the enslaved precisely came under scrutiny during the Somerset case in 1772. The decision of Chief Justice William Murray, Earl of Mansfield, emphasized that the institution of slavery could emerge only from positive law in the British Empire. "The state of slavery is of such a nature, that it is incapable of being introduced on any reasons, moral or political; but only by positive law, which preserves its force long after the reasons, occasion and time itself from whence it was created, is erased from memory."[13] The central claim to decide the case was that the institution of slavery was above all "odious." "It is so odious that nothing can be suffered to support it but positive law. Whatever inconveniences, therefore, may follow from a decision, I cannot say this case is allowed or approved by the law of England; and therefore the black man must be discharged."[14] While this case did not serve as a precedent for the abolition of slavery, it elucidated the legal incongruities surrounding the enslaved condition. The institution was declared as "odious" by Law, but that did not mean that the legal taxonomies of slavery rooted in violence had to be dissolved. Slaveholding regimes simply had to utilize the historical discourses that fueled the racialization of slavery and the exacerbation of scientific racism for the formation of a collective racialized emotional deficiency that is hopeless (and "unhappy") unless it is regulated by an "odious" institution, an institution turned benevolent by its motivation of emotional tutelage.

A taxonomical understanding of master–enslaved relations is likewise manifest in eighteenth-century casta paintings in Spanish colonies, iconography that comprised a racialized hierarchy of familial love. Casta paintings displayed vignettes of a father, a mother, and a child. What separates these vignettes is that they were intended to represent different racial "unions" and the heredity of racialized "traits" in the child. A casta painting aimed to be a taxonomical overview of the racial "composition" of a colonial society. The vignettes tended to have captions that name racialized classifications and to move from Whiteness to Blackness. In this shift from Whiteness toward Blackness, there is an overt racialization of childhood. Darker-skinned children are shown working, wearing less clothing, and being less physically acknowledged by their parents. While

---

[13] "The Case of James Sommersett, a Negro, on a Habeas Corpus, King's Bench: 12 George III, A.D. 1771–72," in *A Complete Collection of State Trials, vol. 20: 1771–1777*, edited by Thomas Bayly Howell (London: T. C. Hansard, 1814).

[14] "The Case of James Sommersett."

casta paintings do not truly encompass racial categories in the Spanish Empire, they do convey much about the institutional discursive racialization of familial love and the innocence of childhood.

Throughout the eighteenth century, multiple sources display a "concern" about the "misery" of the enslaved in the Hispanic Caribbean. A proposed "slave code" for the island of Hispaniola by the Spanish King in 1784 aimed for a "happy dawn" after the "lamentable decadence" caused by the "shameful idleness, independence and pride" of formerly enslaved people who had escaped from their captivity,[15] depicting them as being delinquent, disorderly, and dishonorable in the autonomous expression of their feelings. A year later, a speech by Don Josef Antonio de Unizar of the Supremo Consejo de Indias and the Audiencia de Santo Domingo described the enslaved population of Hispaniola as "miserable" and, even more, rendered the history of slavery as a dispersion of "misery." "Apenas se sacudió el yugo de la esclavitud en Europa mirándose como el lado más infeliz y desdichado, se trasladó esta miseria a las porciones de África en unos pueblos que se contemplaban muy remotos de tal desgracia."[16] The speech further holds that, due to this "misery," slavery should be "modified," without affecting "the State, the agriculture, or their Masters" in order to "compel" the emotions of the "miserable" before the "enemies" of slavery attempt to mobilize the feelings of those under the "yoke of slavery." The Spanish bureaucrat proposes a slight modification of the enslaved condition in response to the emotional "unrest" in the colony of Santo Domingo. This alteration would endeavor to mobilize the emotions of the enslaved in the name of the preservation of the institution of slavery (without distressing the "State" or "Masters," of course). The speech offers an emotional portrait of the enslaved people of Santo Domingo: "Esta gente vil, naturalmente inclinada al Ocio, sin vergüenza, ni conocimiento del honor, los mas de ellos ignorantes de la religión y otros neófitos mal instruidos habiéndose acostumbrado al robo, al asesinato cometiendo las mayores

---

[15] "Proposed Spanish Slave Code in the Americas, 1784–1789," in *Women and Slavery in America: A Documentary History*, edited by Catherine M. Lewis & J. Richard Lewis (Fayetteville: University of Arkansas Press, 2011).

[16] "Discurso sobre Modificación y Límites de la Esclavitud formado por Don Josef Antonio de Unizar del Supremo Consejo de Indias y actual Regente de Audiencia de Santo Domingo, 25/06/1795," Archivo General de Indias, ES.41091.AGI/21.1.15/ESTADO, 13, N.17. Translation to English: "As soon as the yoke of slavery rattled across Europe, becoming the most unhappy and unfortunate region, this misery moved to portions of Africa in some populations that were remote from such misfortune."

crueldades, cortando las cabezas de sus señores de las personas mas visibles, y respetables."[17] The colonial tensions surrounding the condition of slavery are portrayed as simultaneously arising from the revolutions of the enslaved and the Black body, more specifically, its assumed lack of "shame" and inclination to cruelty, indolence, and murder. The Black body is represented as in an everlasting state of "misery," not because of the wretchedness of slavery, but mainly because of its own emotional "underdevelopment" and religious "ignorance." The dispersion of "misery" was then understood not as an unwarranted injury, but instead as a political consciousness of the emotional supremacy of racialized enslavement.

During the eighteenth and early nineteenth century in the Atlantic world, missionary discourse would precisely intersect scientific racism and emotive notions of salvation and religious devotion. "Missionary encounters" in the British colonies would spread ideas of the historical juncture about the "creation of race."[18] Many White missionaries would impose morning prayers that constructed "Black indolence" as punishable by God and commanded the enslaved to have a "joyful" day of exploitation, such as: "Awake, my Soul, and with the sun, Thy daily stage of duty run, Shake off dull sloth, and joyful rise, To pay thy morning sacrifice. Thy precious time mispent, redeem; Each present day thy last esteem: Improve thy talent with due care, For the Great Day thyself prepare."[19] In contrast, formerly enslaved Reverend Ajayi Crowther from present-day Nigeria crafted a parallelism between emancipation and conversion: "the Liberated Africans at present, who seem to be awakened from their foolishness and superstition to serve God, greatly show that they are becoming another people."[20] Formerly enslaved African American preacher John Jea underlined in his sermons the universality of biblical scriptures by declaring that slaveholders utilize torture as a way

---

[17] "Discurso sobre Modificación y Límites de la Esclavitud." Translation to English: "This despicable people, inclined to idleness, without shame, nor understanding of honor, the majority of them ignorant to religion and others poorly taught neophytes, accustomed to theft, to murder, committing the worst cruelties, cutting the heads of their masters, of the most visible and respectable people."

[18] Travis Glasson, *Mastering Christianity: Missionary Anglicanism and Slavery in the Atlantic World* (Oxford: Oxford University Press, 2012), 3.

[19] "Form of Prayer Recommended by the Bishop to Be Used Every Morning on a Plantation," Church Missionary Society Archive, University of Birmingham, Original papers, Miscellaneous Papers (1827–1827, 1843), CW 011.

[20] "Original Papers, Missionaries, Rev. Samuel Adjai Crowther (1828, 1837–1844)," Church Missionary Society Archive, University of Birmingham, CA 10 79/1-32.

to "appease their wrath" and then falsely justify this violence and cruelty with selective biblical references.

> After our master had been treating us in this cruel manner, we were obliged to thank him for the punishment he had been inflicting on us, quoting that Scripture which saith, "Bless the rod, and him that hath appointed it." But, though he was a professor of religion, he forgot *that* passage which saith "God is love, and whoso dwelleth in love dwelleth in God, and God in him."[21]

The scholarly conversation about nineteenth-century Atlantic slavery has explored how its legal frameworks responded to the "problem" of the resistance of the enslaved[22] and how, even in freedom suits, the enslaved had to affirm the "idea of just subjection in slave law" in order to legally plea for "emancipation based on wrongful enslavement."[23] Furthermore, the scholarship has examined how plantation capitalism depended on "productivity analysis akin to scientific management."[24] Not only did the incorporation of new technologies in plantation capitalism during the nineteenth century respond to the resistance of the enslaved, but these new technologies were also "shaped by notions of racially endowed aptitude for different kinds of work."[25] Scholars have argued that the development of slaveholding economies during the nineteenth century contradicts "interpretations of slavery in the Americas" that categorize the institution of slavery as "incompatible with a modern industrialist capitalist economy."[26] Still, it has not been analyzed how the intellectual history of slavery evidences that the racialization of labor, central to the capitalistic project, was driven by scientific ideas of emotional difference, and vice versa. This exchange of ideas propelled the forceful regulation of Black emotions through the racialization of productivity, "vice," and "love."

---

[21] "The Life, History & Unparalleled Sufferings of John Jea, African Preacher, c. 1810 (1773–1810)," Merseyside Maritime Museum, Dx/1646.
[22] Edward B. Rugemer, *Slave Law and the Politics of Resistance in the Early Atlantic World* (Cambridge, MA: Harvard University Press, 2018), 2.
[23] Edlie L. Wong, *Neither Fugitive nor Free: Atlantic Slavery, Freedom Suits, and the Legal Culture of Travel* (New York: New York University Press, 2009), 5.
[24] Caitlin Rosenthal, *Accounting for Slavery: Masters and Management* (Cambridge, MA: Harvard University Press, 2018).
[25] Daniel B. Rood, *The Reinvention of Atlantic Slavery: Technology, Labor, Race, and Capitalism in the Greater Caribbean* (Oxford: Oxford University Press, 2017), 2.
[26] Dale W. Tomich, "Preface," in *Atlantic Transformations: Empire, Politics, and Slavery during the Nineteenth Century*, edited by Dale W. Tomich (Albany: State University of New York Press, 2020), xi.

In fact, "auctions" of the enslaved in nineteenth-century United States conceived an enslaved person with an "excellent character" as one who had been "severely warranted against all vices and maladies" by the "seller."

8. Fanny or Frances ..., aged 22 years, is a first rate washer and ironer, good cook and house servant, and has an excellent character. 9. Emma, an orphan, aged 10 or 11 years, speaks French and English, has been in the country 7 years, has been accustomed to waiting on table, sewing, etc.; is intelligent and active. 10. Frank ..., aged about 32 years speaks French and English, is a first rate hostler and coachman, understands perfectly well the management of horses, and is, in every respect, a first rate character, with the exception that he will occasionally drink, though not an habitual drunkard. All the above named Slaves are acclimated and excellent subjects; they were purchased by their present vendor many years ago, and will, therefore, be severally warranted against all vices and maladies prescribed by law, saved and except Frank, who is fully guaranteed in every other respect but the one above mentioned.[27]

The descriptions of the enslaved intertwine their "character" with notions of productivity, skill, and self-discipline, emphasizing how their "character" and labor are molded by abstinence from "vice." Meanwhile, "Frank" is described as a possible liability because of "occasional drinking" and thus a probable disappointment to the expectation of emotional self-containment. While the discourse of "slavery to passions" was historically utilized to relativize slaveholding practices, the "excellent" enslaved person was one who was purged from pleasures and "depravity." Throughout the primary sources of Atlantic slaveholding, the "ideal" enslaved person was expected to show an absolute lack of emotional volatility, while still being categorized as irremediably emotionally deficient regardless of conduct, since this "deficiency" was key to the affirmation of the urgency for an emotional education of Blackness. The emotions of the enslaved were subjected to systematic imperial surveillance and were commanded to be kept inside a fatally marked Black body. The failure to do so resulted in penalization, and the failure to do so was Black.

Throughout the Atlantic world, many imperial policies were fixated with the regulation of enslaved "love" and the marriages of the enslaved. The "lesser" marriages of the enslaved fell under the legal domain of the master and sustained the slaveholder's control and commodification of

---

[27] "Notice of Slave Auction, New Orleans, 1835," Schomburg Center for Research in Black Culture, Manuscripts, Archives and Rare Books Division, Broadsides Collection.

the reproductive potential of Black wombs.[28] In 1810, the Spanish crown released a *"real cédula"* for their colonies in the Caribbean and the Philippines. This regulation imposed the surveillance by masters of the Sunday "diversions" of enslaved people in order to ensure the "separation of the sexes" and, in the case of any marriages of the enslaved across plantations, stipulated that the enslavers of enslaved "husbands" also had to "purchase" their "wives."[29] This White heteronormative practice was evidently meant as a deterrent of marriages of the enslaved (and revolutionary movements) in the first place. A plantation manual of the United States circa 1840 allowed for marriages of the enslaved within plantations with the rationale of "adding" to the "comfort, happiness & health of those who enter upon it, besides insuring a greater increase."[30] The subterfuge of the "happiness" of the enslaved was used to systemize the institution of marriage for enslaved reproduction. As a matter of fact, this plantation manual prescribed "100 lashes" as punishment if the enslaved requested an annulment of marriage and determined that, after an annulment, the enslaved could not "marry again for 3 years."[31] The slaveholding dominance over enslaved "love" and "happiness" had excruciating repercussions for the enslaved communities of the Atlantic world, tied to displacement, torture, and sexual violence.

Legal decisions about slavery in the Atlantic world legitimized (and systematized) slaveholding violence through the discourse of the inherent emotional aberration of the enslaved. The 1829 decision in the case *The State v. John Mann* in the United States determined that enslaver Elizabeth Jones did not have the right to sue John Mann for assaulting the enslaved "Lydia," who had been "hired out" to Mann. This decision of the Supreme Court of North Carolina was rationalized with the "nature" of the enslaved person as being "doomed" in their "own person."

---

[28] See Tera W. Hunter, *Bound in Wedlock: Slave and Free Black Marriage in the Nineteenth Century* (Cambridge, MA: Harvard University Press, 2017).
[29] "Real Cédula de su Magestad sobre la Educación, Trato y Ocupaciones de los Esclavos, en todos sus Dominios de Indias, e Islas Filipinas, baxo las reglas que se expresan, 1810," Schomburg Center for Research in Black Culture, Manuscripts, Archives and Rare Books Division, Miscellaneous Afro-Latin America Collection, Sc MG 418, Box 1, Folder 4.
[30] "Plantation Manual, 1857–1858," in *Women and Slavery in America: A Documentary History*, edited by Catherine M. Lewis & J. Richard Lewis (Fayetteville: University of Arkansas Press, 2011).
[31] "Plantation Manual, 1857–1858."

The end profit of the master, his security and the public safety; the subject, one doomed in his own person, and his posterity, to live without knowledge, and without the capacity to make any thing on his own, and to toil that another may reap the fruits. What moral considerations shall be addressed to such a being, to convince what, it is impossible but that the most stupid must feel and know can never be true – that he is thus to labour upon a principle of natural duty, or for the sake of his own personal happiness, such services can only be expected from one who has no will of his own; who surrenders his will in implicit obedience to that of another. Such obedience is the consequence only of uncontrolled authority over the body. There is nothing which can operate to produce the effect. The power of the master must be absolute, to render the submission of the slave perfect.[32]

The verdict claimed that the enslaved were internally "doomed" by an absence of will. Enslavement is codified as a voluntary "surrender of will" due to the enslaved person's "uncontrolled authority over the body." The "emotional excess" of the enslaved is regarded as inciting the "absolute power" of the master toward the "perfect submission" of the enslaved. The legal decision abstained from ruling against physical punishment of the enslaved because no one "can anticipate the many and aggravated provocations of the master, which the slave would be constantly stimulated by his own passions" or "the consequent wrath of the master, prompting him to bloody vengeance, upon the turbulent traitor – a vengeance generally practiced with impunity, by reason of its privacy."[33] The enslaved are projected as incessantly "provoking" the master due to their "constant stimulation" by their "passions." Black passions are deemed as culpable of causing the valid "wrath" of the master. Hence, violence against those who were Black and enslaved was assumed to be legitimate, private, protected at all costs with impunity, and, consequently, legally invincible. The aggression of the master was systematically communicated as triggered by the transgressions of the emotional "violence" of the enslaved. The Black body was connoted as the cage of unruly emotions, and intrinsically criminal emotional expression would result in lawful torture. The Black body had to pay for its own "infuriating" passions and had to be hurt repeatedly, time after time, in order to drive Black emotions back to their captivity, captivity held by "doomed" Black skin.

---

[32] "The State v. John Mann, 1829," in *Cases Argued and Determined in the Supreme Court of North Caroline from December Term, 1828, to December Term, 1830*, edited by Thomas Devereaux (Raleigh: J. Gales and Sims, 1831).
[33] "The State v. John Mann, 1829."

As part of a global imperial history in which the enslaved/colonized consistently attempted to appeal to courts to become "legal actors,"[34] the legal complaints by enslaved people in nineteenth-century Cuba indeed aimed to go against the emotional differentiation of the enslaved by emphasizing the suffering caused by the emotional whims of enslavers. Dominga Gangá was consistently sexually exploited by her enslaver, Don Juan Antonio Alemán, which resulted in the birth of four children; when Gangá demanded the emancipation of her children, Alemán prohibited her from seeing her children even though the new slaveholder who exploited her "allowed" her to do so, and she then reached out to the colonial authorities in 1853 to denunciate her anguish and the enslaved status of her children.[35] Also in 1853, María Belén Medina filed a complaint because she begged her enslaver, Don Agustín Medina, to free her son Simón, and he then requested 400 pesos; after paying this sum, he stated that it would be 100 more and that, every day, it would be 100 more.[36] A year later, Juana Valenzuela announced to the authorities that she had been enslaved by (and told she was married to) her enslaver since she was fourteen years old; after sexual abuse led to the birth of a son, he married another woman and advised Juana to "sell herself" for a high price.[37] The vast volume of legal complaints about master brutality highlights imagery of infected wounds, sexual torture since childhood, and psychological violence inflicted through the slaveholding endangerment of enslaved children.[38] These wounds embody the intellectual challenge against the political notion of the emotional elasticity of the enslaved and against the slaveholding discourse that wrongly framed the validity of imperial genocidal violence as protecting the "happiness" of colonies.

Just as the Law responded with disdain to the legal grievances of the enslaved, former "masters" would disregard written complaints of the formerly enslaved, asserting the primacy of their own emotions. In the United States, formerly enslaved "Eliza" requested the emancipation of

---

[34] Frederick Cooper, *Colonialism in Question: Theory, Knowledge, History* (Berkeley: University of California Press, 2005), 173.
[35] Archivo Nacional de Cuba, Gobierno Superior Civil, 948/33490.
[36] Archivo Nacional de Cuba, Gobierno Superior Civil, 948/33487.
[37] Archivo Nacional de Cuba, Gobierno Superior Civil, 1056/37631.
[38] See Archivo Nacional de Cuba, Misceláneos de Expedientes, 1197/T, 224/G, 1391/A; Archivo Nacional de Cuba, Gobierno Superior Civil, 936/33047, 954/33754-A, 954/33752.

an offspring, "Jennie," by former enslaver T. D. Jones in 1860, and Jones responded by explaining why he had not "come to a decision."

> As to letting Jennie go to live with you I can hardly make up my mind what to say. I would be reluctant to part with her. She is petted as you used to be. She is a watchful little spy as you used to be. She has a good disposition, is neither cross, obstinate nor mischievous. She is very useful for her services in the house, for going on errands, and for nursing: & I should miss her very much. Nevertheless I know how to estimate the claims of a Mother and to appreciate the affection of a Mother for her child. A request had been made of me thro' Mr. Henry Morris to let Jennie go with you, but I have not yet come to a decision.[39]

Jones amplifies and centers his emotions when addressing this urgent request. He would miss "Jennie" in a way that rivaled the "affection of a Mother for her child." His "feelings" are linked to how "petted" the enslaved child is, how "Jennie" represents an extension of the enslaved person who "abandoned" him. The enslaved child's "disposition" as a "watchful little spy" is something that Jones longs for, makes "use" of. The paternalistic and patronizing reply by Jones denotes the way that slaveholders strategically spotlighted their own emotions in their responses to complaints of the enslaved and in their projection of the enslaved condition.

Paternalistic masters of the antebellum South certainly contended that all their slaveholding actions were expressions of "love toward their slaves" and that "their slaves loved them back": "My husband's influence over the slaves is very great, while they never question his authority, and are ever ready to obey him implicitly, they love him!"[40] Even more, enslavers attributed the condition of slavery to themselves, imagining White slaveholders as "unhappy slaves": "I am the slave for my negroes – while they are happy and content I am unhappy and the loser by them."[41] White slaveholders fabricated a "happy" existence, where compassionate and encumbered masters provided the enslaved with the privileges of emotional education and of protection from their own aberrant Black passions. Though White enslavers of the Atlantic world claimed that they

---

[39] "Letter, T. D. Jones to Eliza, September 7, 1860," in *Women and Slavery in America: A Documentary History*, edited by Catherine M. Lewis & J. Richard Lewis (Fayetteville: University of Arkansas Press, 2011).

[40] Francis Fearn of Louisiana, as quoted in Eugene D. Genovese & Elizabeth Fox-Genovese, *Fatal Self-Deception: Slaveholding Paternalism in the Old South* (New York: Cambridge University Press, 2011), 60.

[41] Colonel James Morgan of Texas, as quoted in Genovese & Genovese, *Fatal Self-Deception*, 69.

held reciprocal "loving relationships" with the enslaved, they in actuality enacted their bloody dominance over Black enslaved people through torture, mutilation, sexual violence, and death. Hortense Spillers theorized this "human and social irreparability as high crimes against the flesh."[42] Throughout the Americas, masters premeditatedly confronted the resistance of the enslaved by "separating and fractionalizing the various African ethnicities."[43] Even though paternalistic slaveholders asserted that the enslaved were "part of the family," they intentionally fragmented enslaved families. They got to decide who was "welcomed" as part of the "family," part of the economic configuration of the slaveholding "home" they administered and profited from. Functionally premeditated family separations perpetrated by slaveholders sparked stories of passionate pursuits of recently emancipated people to reunite families.[44]

Following geographical determinism, slaveholding regimes simultaneously hypersexualized and asexualized those who were Black and enslaved, as a way to normalize imperial sexual violence, while also proclaiming the slaveholding disgust toward the exploited Black body. While masters fostered the discourse of the eagerness of Black men to rape White women as a way to solidify the criminalization of Blackness, they concurrently instituted a sexual economy to systematically perpetrate their "feverish" sexual fantasies and to regulate the reproductive capacity of the enslaved. In *Women, Race, & Class*, Angela Davis describes how the White "institutionalization of rape" in antebellum slavery and the "myth of the Black male rapist" aided not only the criminalization and mass captivity of Black men but also the systematic sexual exploitation of Black women with impunity.[45] Researchers have studied primary sources of the Portuguese Inquisition in Brazil that report recurrent "same-sex" sexual exploitation of enslaved people by "male" and "female" slaveholders rooted in the White "male" heteronormative access of masterhood to the enslaved, access that extended to White wives.[46] The

---

[42] Hortense Spillers, "Mama's Baby, Papa's Maybe: An American Grammar Book," in *Feminisms Redux: An Anthology of Literary Theory and Criticism*, edited by Robyn Warhol-Down & Diane Price Herndl (New Brunswick, NJ: Rutgers University Press, 2009), 446.
[43] Hall, *Slavery and African Ethnicities in the Americas*, 55.
[44] Heather A. Williams, *Help Me to Find My People: The African American Search for Family Lost in Slavery* (Chapel Hill: University of North Carolina Press, 2012), 13.
[45] Angela Y. Davis, *Women, Race, & Class* (New York: Vintage, 1983), 172.
[46] Lawrence Aidoo, *Slavery Unseen: Sex, Power, and Violence in Brazilian History* (Durham, NC: Duke University Press, 2018).

scholarship has furthermore explored how Black enslaved women were represented by colonizer discourse as "monstrous," "unwomanly," and excessively "fertile," as a way to silence the actual desirability and systemic economic and sexual exploitation of enslaved people.[47] The scholarly conversation has likewise analyzed how the eighteenth-century construction of children as the "embodiment" of "innocence" was fundamentally racialized, and its long-term impact was thus reserved to Whiteness.[48] Scholars have also examined how pregnancy and childbirth of the enslaved functioned as "zones of conflict," in which slaveholders, physicians, and enslaved people battled for sovereignty over the reproductive systems of the enslaved.[49] In fact, Black people were abstracted as "medical superbodies" that compelled the medical gaze for their "fecundity" and "hypersexuality," being in turn expected to perform enslaved labor irrespective of pregnancy or illness.[50]

James Marion Sims advanced a "pioneering" legacy in gynecological research by inflicting unbearable pain on trembling Black enslaved people. In *The Story of My Life*, Sims narrated his recollection of his malevolent experiments to treat vesicovaginal fistula on "Anarcha," "Betsey," and "Lucy," among multiple other enslaved people.

> That was before the days of anesthetics, and the poor girl, on her knees, bore the operation with great heroism and bravery. I had about a dozen doctors there to witness the series of experiments that I expected to perform. All the doctors had seen my notes often and examined them, and agreed that I was on the eve of a great discovery, and every one of them was interested in seeing me operate. The operations were tedious and difficult. The instruments were on the right principle, though they were not as perfect as they were subsequently, and improvements had to be made slowly. I succeeded in closing the fistula in about an hour's time, which was considered to be very good work.[51]

Black enslaved bodies were put on display "on their knees" for the "methodical" eyes of White physicians. Sims lies, claiming these operations took place "before the days of anesthetics" instead of

---

[47] Jennifer L. Morgan, *Laboring Women: Reproduction and Gender in New World Slavery* (Philadelphia: University of Pennsylvania Press, 2004).
[48] Robin Bernstein, *Racial Innocence: Performing American Childhood from Slavery to Civil Rights* (New York: New York University Press, 2011), 4.
[49] Sasha Turner, *Contested Bodies: Pregnancy, Childrearing, and Slavery in Jamaica* (Philadelphia: University of Pennsylvania Press, 2017), 10.
[50] Deidre Cooper Owens, *Medical Bondage: Race, Gender, and the Origins of American Gynecology* (Athens: University of Georgia Press, 2017), 109.
[51] James Marion Sims, *The Story of My Life* (New York: Appleton, 1888), 237.

contemporaneous to that time. The "great heroism and bravery" of those who were forcibly operated on without anesthesia are projected in the autobiography as part of a "triumphant" narrative of the "eve of a great discovery." The role of the agonizing pain of the enslaved in the experiments is soon forgotten, as Sims shifts the focus to how "tedious and difficult" the operations were for him. The excruciating pain of a nonconsensual "object of study" is recounted as a tale of "very good work." The autobiography's chronicle of his medical experiments on the enslaved is focused on his "sacrificial" efforts. "This went on, not for one year, but for two and three, and even four years. I kept all these negroes at my own expense all the time."[52] Sims consistently refers to his "expense" in exploiting enslaved people, veiling the persistent medical sexual oppression of the enslaved. Not only did Sims perform at least thirty nonconsensual operations on "Anarcha," but also his prose framed by biological determinism also degraded the Black body into a site of "loathing" and "disgust." "Anarcha had added to the fistula an opening which extended into the rectum, by which gas – intestinal gas – escaped involuntarily, and was passing off continually, so that her person was not only loathsome and disgusting to herself, but to every one who came near her."[53] While the four years of painful experimentation and medical sexual exploitation were portrayed as a repugnant annoyance for the White physician, the end result was depicted as a "success": the fulfillment of immediate "relief" for the enslaved and a long-term cure for a "suffering humanity."

> In the course of two weeks more, Lucy and Betsey were both cured by the same means, without any sort of disturbance or discomfort. Then I realized the fact that, at last, my efforts had been blessed with success, and that I had made, perhaps, one of the most important discoveries of the age for the relief of suffering humanity.[54]

The medical sexual violence against "Anarcha," "Lucy," "Betsey," and many other enslaved people is rationalized as providing "relief for a suffering humanity" without "any sort of disturbance or discomfort." Sims, just like many other promoters of scientific racism, just like other masters and colonizers of the Atlantic World, contemplated unbearable Black pain and then wrote down its negation. Today, the convenient discourse of "these men were a product of their time" regularly emerges from White privileged mouths. What this principle hides is the

---

[52] Sims, *The Story of My Life*, 241.   [53] Sims, *The Story of My Life*, 240.
[54] Sims, *The Story of My Life*, 246.

emotionally detached and perverse gaze of these "pioneers," who deliberately decided to capitalize from the suffering of the enslaved. The apologetic view of Sims and other perpetrators of human experimentation on the enslaved contends that they "believed" Black people felt less pain. There is no proof that these White privileged leaders in their field "believed" that Black enslaved people were "inferior." In fact, it would be against historiographical methodology to theorize about the intricacies of the subjectivities of historical figures. On the contrary, there is vast evidence that they systematically lied, that they lied to negate and erase the Black pain they witnessed. Their intellectual production and the apologetic public memory about them mobilize sympathy toward the exploiter and silence the Black anguish that guarantees White economic "productivity." This "productivity" is venerated as a remedy for "human" suffering, as the assurance of the happiness of a non-marked humanity, of a humanity that feels correctly.

The imperial retelling of conspiracies of the enslaved during the nineteenth century similarly evoked metaphors of "happiness" to mask the colonizing ferocity against the resistance of the enslaved. For example, the conspiracy of 1821 in Bayamón sparked retaliatory measures from the Spanish State in the colony of Puerto Rico. After learning of the conspiracy, authorities started to infiltrate the bomba dances of the enslaved in order to "observe" the enslaved people's "conduct" and capacity for "diversion."[55] The rationale of this heightened scrutiny was the protection of "peace" and "happiness" in the island, avoiding any "public unrest."[56] Multiple official documents were concerned with any "alteration" of the "tranquility" of their "People" and with any revolutionary tentative by "miserable" enslaved people.[57] Authorities described the conspiracy as a "perverse hope" of the enslaved[58] and later celebrated the fact that it was "happily" discovered.[59] The conception of the enslaved longing for freedom as "perverse hope" corroborates the

---

[55] "Carta de Enrique Balseiro del 1 de octubre de 1825," Archivo General de Puerto Rico, Fondo de Seguridad Pública, 1805–22, Box 370.

[56] "Gobierno Político Superior de la Isla de Puerto Rico, Sección de Gobierno, Negociado Político, Negocio de Seguridad Pública, Carta del 12 de agosto de 1821," Archivo General de Puerto Rico, Fondo de Seguridad Pública, 1805–22, Box 370.

[57] "Carta de Seguridad Pública del 25 de julio 1821," Archivo General de Puerto Rico, Fondo de Seguridad Pública, 1805–22, Box 370.

[58] "Carta de Oteiro del 7 de septiembre de 1821," Archivo General de Puerto Rico, Fondo de Seguridad Pública, 1805–22, Box 370.

[59] "Carta de Seguridad Pública de 1821," Archivo General de Puerto Rico, Fondo de Seguridad Pública, 1805–22, Box 370.

institutional rivalry against the emotions of those who were Black and enslaved. Just like scientific racism essentialized Blackness as emotionality, Empires primarily referred to "emotional crimes," naming "delinquent" emotions as a way to denote Blackness. The yearning for liberty was tied to an emotion ("hope"), and the idea or thought that "modifies" it and makes it "disobedient" was defined as "perverse." According to the imperial gaze, not only did the criminal emotionality of Black resistance spontaneously emerge from the Black body, but the villainous Black Mind under the yoke of the Body turned benevolent emotions into evil.

Likewise in Puerto Rico, the conspiracy of 1822 in Guayama provides insight into the "emotional justifications" of the imperial responses to conspiracies of the enslaved. Two enslaved people were executed for their role in the conspiracy, and this measure was codified as a step toward "escarmentar a los malvados y tranquilizar a los buenos."[60] Official documents categorize these politically assassinated enslaved people: "hombres perdidos e inconsiderados, aventureros sin patria y sin honor han intentando transformar la paz interior en estos pueblos afortunados."[61] In 1848, racial tensions due to the conspiracies of the enslaved, or transgressions of colonial "peace," escalated to the political imposition of the Bando contra la raza africana in Puerto Rico, which determined that, in response to the *"situación aflictiva"* caused by the revolutions of the enslaved in the Atlantic World, any Black person who harmed a White person with a weapon would be killed, regardless of whether they were enslaved or free.[62] The "affliction" instigated by the revolutionary movements of the enslaved was named as the imperial motive for the racialization of the genocidal target of assassinations perpetrated by the State. Enslaved resistance movements were certainly conceptualized as passionate transgressions that triggered the spectacle of imperial genocidal violence as emerging from the Black body, the emotional source of colonial unrest. The revolutions of the enslaved were depicted in contemporary

---

[60] "Capitanía General, Carta del 31 de octubre de 1822," Archivo General de Puerto Rico, Fondo de Seguridad Pública, 1805–22, Box 370. Translation to English: "punish the wicked ones and calm the good ones."

[61] "Seguridad Pública, Carta del 18 de octubre de 1822," Archivo General de Puerto Rico, Fondo de Seguridad Pública, 1805–22, Box 370. Translation to English: "lost and inconsiderate men, adventurers without a motherland and without honor have attempted to transform the inner peace of these fortunate populations."

[62] "Bando contra la raza africana," as quoted in Luis M. Díaz Soler, *Historia de la esclavitud negra en Puerto Rico* (Río Piedras: Editorial de la Universidad de Puerto Rico, 1953), 218. Translation to English: "afflictive situation."

historiography and art as the perpetuation of sheer horror for White women and children,[63] and "maroon landscapes"[64] engendered much White curiosity and displeasure in the Americas. The colonial government of Cuba formally expressed its gratitude to the agency of don Francisco José González in the "almost complete extermination" of *palenques* in the eastern side of the island, thwarting formerly enslaved people from committing their "excesses."[65]

Black enslaved emotionality was indeed projected as incessantly "excessive" by imperial discourse, and institutional violence toward Black enslaved people was conceived as a legitimate reaction to the perilous passions of the enslaved. The inescapability of racialized emotional policing of Atlantic slavery resulted in the political sanctification of the enduring dichotomy between the mind and the body, the Empire and the enslaved. Whiteness was deified as the productivity and rationality of the mind. Any production or historical movement would be due to the White mind imagining it. In contrast, Blackness incarnated the emotional "excesses" of reckless carnal impulses. Black enslaved labor had to be ruled by White emotional supremacy, so that the intellectual production of the enslaved could be appropriated entirely by the dominion of the Master. Through this dichotomy, the White enslaver ennobled his presence, and He would be remembered as prolific and industrious in public memory. Those who were Black and enslaved would be remembered as a faceless collective by power and institutions. Epistemologically, the Master was and is a rational bystander of the emotional deviance of the Enslaved, and any productivity becomes His Own. The emotions to be cultivated, protected, and spotlighted are His Own.

The construction of the Black enslaved person as the "carnal" sanctioned the political legitimization of genocidal violence. Empires proclaimed that it was not that the White slaveholder was sadistic. It was that the unwarranted, violent emotions of the enslaved "provoked" brutal discipline and punishment. Precisely due to the fact that the political conceptualization of the enslaved was, as advocated by the history of scientific racism, of an emotionally defective Other, the imperial construct

---

[63] Davis, *Inhuman Bondage*, 205.
[64] Silviane A. Diouf, *Slavery's Exiles: The Story of the American Maroons* (New York: New York University Press, 2014), 6.
[65] "Certificación para don Francisco José González que gracias a sus conocimientos y eficacia ha conseguido casi el total exterminio de los palenques de negros cimarrones en la parte oriental de esta isla, 1829," Harvard University, Houghton Library, bMS Span 170 (2).

of the "ideal" enslaved person was expected to be deprived of "pleasures," rid of Blackness. Blackness could only "fail." Racialist theories propelled a perpetual institutional disbelief of an either emotionally deceptive or explosive enslaved person, or both. The emotional policing of Atlantic slavery was symbiotically grounded on uninterrupted suspicion of Black pleasure, since pleasure would lead to "fermented" revolutionary emotions rising. The enslaved body was expected to contain the Self, to hold Black emotions captive, to perpetually feel (and yet not exteriorize) grief. The genocide of Atlantic slavery was normalized by the institutional expectation of emotional self-containment by a Black body that Empire claimed could not contain its "dirty" passions, a body where grief was transient and obligatory. Intrinsic racialized nonconformity to this rigid understanding of enslaved discipline was constructed as emotional criminality, which resulted in the omnipresence of genocidal violence in the lived experience of slavery, in the lived spaces of imperial management of racialized populations and their feelings. Enslaving genocide was premeditatedly blamed on the "legitimate" White displeasure toward the transgressive emotional "excesses" of the racialized. And so imperial sexual violence and capitalistic inherence in Black wombs were denoted as emerging from the hypersexual and "heated" Black body. And so the resistance of the enslaved was visualized as going against "happiness," as enslaved people could not understand how "happiness" was achieved. Because enslaved people could not comprehend their own emotions. Or Happiness. The Master did.

The political economy of Atlantic slavery was premised on emotional interventionism, since the institution of slavery represented an emotional education, a never-ending emotional "guidance" toward the deliverance of the Black body from its Blackness. Ferociously upholding the institution of slavery was constructed as guaranteeing "happiness," as bringing "relief" to a "suffering humanity." Blackness was suffering a second-class misery due to its "diseased" and "inhuman" feelings. Whiteness was suffering because of its "duty" not only to globalize a slaveholding "remedy" for "unhappy" Black communities, but also to mass-produce luxury goods and enrich their economies and their private interests. The proclamation of colonial (and thus White) "happiness" was tied to the fulfillment of a racialized capitalistic structure, the systematization of an emotional economy based on the strategic idea of Black excess in order to veil White wastefulness. The strategic myth of "imperial fear" against "menacing" Black passions in order to veil how Empires unremittingly terrorized Black enslaved lives. Imperial Law that supported White inherence in emotional bodies was guided by the principle that violent penalization was necessary and functional in bodies that felt less. In feelings that would remain unscathed, torture had to be ever-present, inevitable, and eternally intensifying. This genocidal violence enriched slaveholding economies that rose as emotionally dominant empires, propagating political agendas for the emotional captivity of Blackness. The intellectual production of the enslaved clamorously condemned the construction of the enslaved as unfeeling and the monopoly of Empires over the definition of "happiness." Their words incarnated the bloody injury that hurt so deeply.

THE EMOTIONAL RESISTANCE OF THE INTELLECTUAL PRODUCTION OF THE ENSLAVED

The intellectual production of the enslaved aimed to convey the perpetual emotional resistance of enslaved communities in the Atlantic World. The antislavery writing of the "Black Atlantic" displays a "radical use of political sentiment."[66] Formerly enslaved abolitionist from present-day Ghana Ottobah Cugoano grounded his antislavery discourse in "religious sentiments" in *Thoughts and Sentiments on the Evil and Wicked Traffic of the Slavery and Commerce of the Human Species: Humbly Submitted to the Inhabitants of Great-Britain*. "What I intend to advance against that evil, criminal and wicked traffic of enslaving men, are only some Thoughts and Sentiments which occur to me, as being obvious from the Scriptures of Divine Truth."[67] While his rhetoric stresses the universality of religion, his writing simultaneously emphasizes the unintelligibility of the lived experience of slavery, experience "conceived" through nothing else but emotional introspection.

All my help was cries and tears, and these could not avail; nor suffered long, till one succeeding woe, and dread, swelled up another. Brought from a state of innocence and freedom, and in a barbarous and cruel manner, conveyed to a state of horror and slavery: This abandoned situation may be easier conceived than described.[68]

[66] Christine Levecq, *Slavery and Sentiment: The Politics of Feeling in Black Atlantic Antislavery Writing, 1770–1850* (Durham: University of New Hampshire Press, 2008).
[67] "Thoughts and Sentiments on the Evil and Wicked Traffic of the Slavery and Commerce of the Human Species: Humbly Submitted to the Inhabitants of Great-Britain (1787) by Cugoano, Ottobah," Princeton University, Firestone Library, Rare Books and Special Collections, Lapidus 4.08.
[68] "Thoughts and Sentiments on the Evil and Wicked Traffic of the Slavery."

Cugoano expresses the recurring nature of the "cries and tears" of the enslaved due to the perpetual "state of horror and slavery." Though it is through "tears" that the enslaved person can "conceive" their lived experience, the emotional intelligibility of the "deep sounding groans of thousands" is reserved to the divine alone.

> The cries of some, and the sight of their misery, may be seen and heard afar; but the deep sounding groans of thousands, and the great sadness of their misery and woe, under the heavy load of oppressions and calamities inflicted upon them, are such as can only be distinctly known to the ears of Jehovah Sabaoth.[69]

Olaudah Equiano's prominent *Interesting Narrative* constructed Atlantic slavery as imperiling "every tender feeling."

> Is it not enough that we are torn from our country and friends to toil for your luxury and lust of gain? Must every tender feeling be likewise sacrificed to your avarice? Are the dearest friends and relations, now rendered more dear by their separation from their kindred, still to be parted from each other, and thus prevented from cheering the gloom of slavery with the small comfort of being together and mingling their sufferings and sorrows? Why are parents to lose their children, brothers their sisters, or husbands their wives? Surely this is a new refinement in cruelty, which, while it has no advantage to atone for it, thus aggravates distress, and adds fresh horrors even to the wretchedness of slavery.[70]

Equiano deprecates the systematic practice of family separations and community fragmentation as intensifying the "gloom" and "wretchedness" of slavery. The thinker denounces the premeditated "loss" of both kinship and solidarity in "sufferings and sorrows." Equiano ultimately condemns Atlantic slavery as a "new refinement in cruelty," mobilizing the politics of "refinement" against those who segregated humanity in a hierarchy of "taste" and "civilized" emotions.

Multiple interviews of enslaved people, held in the twentieth century, convey trauma through emotionally charged tropes, confronting the unfeeling characterization promulgated by scientific racism. Formerly enslaved Charles Crawley described not being able to verbalize the traumatic lived experience of the "auctions" of the enslaved: "I don't like to talk 'bout back dar. It brun' a sad feelin' up me."[71] Likewise, formerly

---

[69] "Thoughts and Sentiments on the Evil and Wicked Traffic of the Slavery."
[70] Olaudah Equiano, "The Interesting Narrative of the Life of Olaudah Equiano, of Gustavus Vassa, the African, Written by Himself," in *Slave Narratives* (New York: Literary Classics, 2000), 79.
[71] "Interview of Mr. Charles Crawley, Ex-Slave, Petersburg, Virginia, February 20, 1937," Library of Congress, Born into Slavery: Slave Narratives from the Federal Writers'

enslaved Minnie Fulkes communicated her difficulty in recounting the punishments her mother was subjected to when protesting sexual exploitation by her enslaver.

> Honey, I don't like to talk 'bout dem times, 'cause my mother did suffer misery. You know dar was an' overseer who use to tie mother up in the barn with a rope aroun' her arms up over her head, while she stood on a block. Soon as dey got her tied, dis block was moved an' her feet dangled, yo' know couldn't toch de flo'. Dis ol man, now, would start beatin' her nekkid 'til the blood run down her back to her heels.... Lord, Lord, I hate white people.[72]

Now, although her interview upholds her "hate" for all "White people," the tone changes when contrasting the treatment toward her mother and the demeanor of her own enslaver: "cause master was good and kind to us."[73] Numerous narratives of formerly enslaved people display shifts in emotional projection when comparing slaveholders they knew or juxtaposing their own experiences with the ones of other enslaved people. For example, the autobiography of Elizabeth Sparks speaks of her former "mistress" in a seemingly apologetic manner: "Bless her. She'us a good woman. Course I mean she'd slap an' beat yer once in a while but she warn't no woman fur fighting fussin' an' beatin' yer all day lak some I know."[74] Still, a paradigm in the narratives of the enslaved is that this iteration of "bless her," in actuality, means "bless me": it is an affirmation and recognition of the daily bodily torture inflicted on other enslaved people who were dear to them. Furthermore, in the case of Sparks, the representation of her "mistress" is also meant to serve as a juxtaposition to and accent on the atrocious punishments perpetrated by her vicious "master": "Beat women! Why sure he beat women. Beat women jes' lak men. Beat women naked an' wash 'em down in brine."[75]

The influential *The History of Mary Prince, a West Indian Slave* was framed as a literary response to the "horrors of slavery" in pursuit of abolitionist compassion. "Oh the horrors of slavery! – How the thought

---

Project, 1936–1938 Collection, File 17. The interviews of the Federal Writer's Project were done and transcribed by White interviewers.

[72] "Interview of Mrs. Minnie Fulkes, Petersburg, Virginia, March 5, 1937," Library of Congress, Born into Slavery: Slave Narratives from the Federal Writers' Project, 1936–1938 Collection, File 17.

[73] "Interview of Mrs. Minnie Fulkes."

[74] "Autobiography of Elizabeth Sparks," Library of Congress, Born into Slavery: Slave Narratives from the Federal Writers' Project, 1936–1938 Collection, File 17.

[75] "Autobiography of Elizabeth Sparks."

of it pains my heart! But the truth ought to be told of it; and what my eyes have seen I think it is my duty to relate; for few people in England know what slavery is."[76] The narrative also shows the paradigm of emotional comparative language and portrays her first "mistress" as a benevolent figure. "Mrs. Williams was a kind-hearted good woman, and she treated all her slaves well. She had only one daughter, Miss Betsey, for whom I was purchased, and who was about my own age. I was made quite a pet of by Miss Betsey, and loved her very much."[77] Prince expresses "love" toward the White child that she was "purchased" for, but she soon intertwines these references to the apparent leniency of her "mistresses" with a contextualization of childhood innocence. "This was the happiest period of my life; for I was too young to understand rightly my condition as a slave, and too thoughtless and full of spirits to look forward to the days of toil and sorrow."[78] The depiction of this episode as the "happiest" in her life not only focuses on "appearances" of her childhood, but also intends to contextualize the hierarchy of sadism in her tales about her former enslavers. The narrative arc of the "benevolence" of slaveholders matches her childhood development and in turn her emotional consciousness of the enslaved condition, affected by "toil and sorrow." The progression in slaveholding brutality corresponds with her own withdrawal from the innocence of childhood and therefore full awareness of her hell. Now, just like many other authors of narratives of the enslaved, Prince ultimately affirms and explicitly stresses that enslaving societies generally engendered White people with "hardened hearts."

No, no! They were not all bad, I dare say, but slavery hardens white people's hearts towards the blacks; and many of them were not slow to make their remarks upon us aloud, without regard to our grief – though their light words fell like cayenne on the fresh wounds of our hearts. Oh those white people have small hearts who can only feel for themselves.[79]

Prince repudiates the slaveholding disdain toward Black "grief" and makes an analogy between psychological abuse and the bodily torture of the enslaved, connoting psychological violence as "cayenne on the fresh wounds of our hearts." The thinker not only emphasizes how White slaveholders disregarded and manipulated enslaved grief, but also

---

[76] "The History of Mary Prince, a West Indian Slave. Related by Herself. To Which Is Added, The Narrative of Asa-Asa, a Captured African (1831)," British Library, 8157.bbb.30.
[77] "The History of Mary Prince."   [78] "The History of Mary Prince."
[79] "The History of Mary Prince."

denotes White people as apathetic because of their emotional individualism, stimulated by the institution of slavery itself. Having clarified that all of her former enslavers carried "hardened hearts," Prince stresses the brutality of her second "mistress."

> The next morning my mistress set about instructing me in my tasks. She taught me to do all sorts of household work; to wash and bake, pick cotton and wool, and wash floors, and cook. And she taught me (how can I ever forget it!) more things than these; she caused me to know the exact difference between the smart of the rope, the cart-whip, and the cow-skin, when applied to my naked body by her own cruel hand. And there was scarcely any punishment more dreadful than the blows I received on my face and head from her hard heavy fist. She was a fearful woman, and a savage mistress to her slaves.[80]

The writer then proceeds to contextualize how the blows from her "fearful and savage mistress," and the act of writing itself, entitled her "naked body" to communicate the painful punishment of her fellow enslaved people.

> He threw her down on the ground, and after beating her severely, he took her up in his arms and flung her among the prickly-pear bushes, which are all covered over with sharp venomous prickles. By this her naked flesh was so grievously wounded, that her body swelled and festered all over, and she died a few days after. In telling my own sorrows, I cannot pass by those of my fellow-slaves – for when I think of my own griefs, I remember theirs.[81]

Therefore, Prince, like many other formerly enslaved people, is compelled to clarify that many of those enslaved were not able to tell their stories because their bodies had to withstand an injury culminating in death. Her words deliberately create space for the corporeal wounds of enslaved souls. Responding to the paternalistic concept of the "happily" enslaved, Prince takes an unequivocal stance: "The man that says slaves be quite happy in slavery that they don't want to be free – that man is either ignorant or a lying person. I never heard a slave say so."[82] *The History of Mary Prince, a West Indian Slave* then precisely incorporates the notion of having "loved" a former enslaver, through the lens of the innocence of an enslaved child, in order to cultivate a forceful stance against that same paternalistic theory of "loving" master–enslaved relationships. Prince condemns the "savagery" and "cruelty" of slaveholding regimes, turning concepts of the emotional criminalization of the enslaved

---

[80] "The History of Mary Prince." [81] "The History of Mary Prince."
[82] "The History of Mary Prince."

against the Empire. This autobiography openly points to the tie between imperial violence and the slaveholding disregard toward Black grief as a mode to normalize White individualism.

Frederick Douglass also utilized emotional rhetoric to translate his autobiographies into abolitionist tools. Among the autobiographies of Frederick Douglass, the 1845 *Narrative of the Life of Frederick Douglass, an American Slave* is the one that mostly explores the conditions of enslaved person and "fugitive."[83] In his *Narrative*, Douglass also highlights how the lived experience of slavery is marked by the emotional disruption of childhood. His narration of his emotional response to his mother's death is evocative of Orlando Patterson's description of "natal alienation."[84] "Never having enjoyed, to any considerable extent, her soothing presence, her tender and watchful care, I received the tidings of my mother's death with much the same emotions I should have probably felt at the death of a stranger."[85] Douglass contextualizes enslaved "natal alienation" as an emotional disturbance in childhood development: this disruption is due not only to his mourning for his emotive bond with his mother, but also to the irreparable emotional unattainability of familial grief in his own terms. When narrating the corporeal punishments that his aunt suffered, Douglass further unveils the role of emotional trauma in his childhood development and adulthood.

> I have often been awakened at the dawn of day by the most heart-rending shrieks of an own aunt of mine, whom he used to tie up to a joist, and whip upon her naked back till she was literally covered with blood. No words, no tears, no prayers, from his gory victim, seemed to move his iron-heart from its bloody purpose. The louder she screamed, the harder he whipped; and where the blood ran fastest, there he whipped longest. He would whip her to make her hush; and not until overcome by fatigue, would he cease to swing the blood-clotted cowskin.[86]

Douglass describes his aunt's enslaver as having an "iron-heart" and in turn extends this heartlessness to the nature of slaveholding in the South as a whole. This passage defines the morbidity of masters as a "bloody purpose." This sinister proclivity to generate pain in a naked Black body is intensified by evidence of suffering. The emotional responses of the

---

[83] Robert S. Levine, *The Lives of Frederick Douglass* (Cambridge, MA: Harvard University Press, 2016), 2.
[84] See Patterson, *Slavery and Social Death*.
[85] Frederick Douglass, *Narrative of the Life of Frederick Douglass: An American Slave, Written by Himself* (Boston: Anti-Slavery Office, 1849), 3.
[86] Douglass, *Narrative of the Life of Frederick Douglass*, 6.

Master are deconstructed as sadistic: there is a morbid sexual desire to hear enslaved moans, to see Black skin be covered by blood. These macabre images are contextualized by Douglass as a premature rite of passage to the adult consciousness of the lived experiences of slavery.

> I remember the first time I ever witnessed this horrible exhibition. I was quite a child, but I well remember it. I never shall forget it whilst I remember anything. It was the first of a long series of such outrages, of which I was doomed to be a witness and a participant. It struck me with awful force. It was the blood-stained gate, the entrance to the hell of slavery, through which I was about to pass. It was a most terrible spectacle. I wish I could commit to paper the feelings with which I beheld it.[87]

This childhood rite of passage is defined as a traumatic and unintelligible "blood-stained gate" to the "hell of slavery." The narratives of the enslaved thus tend to have two storytellers: the "participant" who was emotionally terrorized by the tyranny of the whip, and the "witness" who survived to tell the story, but cannot quite tell it in its entirety. The collective enslaved experience can end only in death.

The *Autobiografía* by Juan Francisco Manzano likewise details the emotional impact of the institution of slavery in the racialized lived experience of childhood. Manzano narrated how he as a child would be locked down in a dark bunker for more than twenty-four hours for "la más leve maldad propia de muchacho."[88] The thinker conveys his desperate hunger, thirst, and dread of darkness when the enslaved child experienced pitiless penalization for his "deviant" emotions. Whenever the tortured child screamed for mercy, the penalty was to be whipped and held captive again.[89] Manzano explains how these aching experiences had an enormous emotional toll by the time he turned thirteen years old.

> Desde la edad de trece a catorce años la alegría y viveza de mi genio, lo parlero de mis labios llamados *pico de oro*; todo se troncó en cierta melancolía, que me hizo con el tiempo característica: la música me embelesaba sin saber por qué; lloraba y gustaba de ese consuelo en hallando ocasión de llorar, que siempre buscaba la soledad para dar rienda suelta a mis pesares; lloraba pero no gemía, ni se me añudaba el corazón sino en cierto estado de abatimiento incurable hasta el día.[90]

---

[87] Douglass, *Narrative of the Life of Frederick Douglass*, 6.

[88] Juan Francisco Manzano, *Autobiografía del esclavo poeta y otros escritos* (Madrid: Iberoamericana, 2007), 87. Translation to English: "the mildest mischief, typical from children."

[89] Manzano, *Autobiografía del esclavo poeta*, 88.

[90] Manzano, *Autobiografía del esclavo poeta*, 88. Translation to English: "From the age of thirteen to fourteen, the joy and liveliness of my temperament, the talkative nature of my

The enslaved child is bound by melancholy, looking for solitude to evade the policing eyes that punished him for his distressed cries. In solitude, he could cry, but not moan. His joyful chatter became a muted weeping that signified his trauma, his consciousness of emotional policing, and his defiant act of identity building. His tears encompassed the constant fears he was exposed to in his life as an enslaved person: "toda ella está regada de lágrimas!... Mi pobre corazón se enfermó a fuerza de sufrir por todo lo que me asustaba."[91] His early exposure to punitive darkness, starvation, bodily torture, and silencing "sickened" his "poor heart." Through his written word, Manzano reclaimed his childhood voice to condemn the racialization of childhood and unleashed his melancholy as an act of emotional resistance to the horrors of Atlantic slavery.

Indeed, many narratives of the enslaved referred to fear and grief as the emotional paradigms of enslaved realities. In her *Narrative*, activist Sojourner Truth conveyed shared enslaved trauma in relation to the ritualization of the "auction." "A slave auction is a terrible affair to its victims, and its incidents and consequences are graven on their hearts as with a pen of burning steel."[92] By emphasizing the perpetual nature of enslaved grief, the speech challenges the racialist notion of the transience of enslaved grief as a justification of genocidal slaveholding violence. Likewise, Solomon Northup deplored the ritualization of "Christmas supper" in the South in order to reaffirm the centrality and permanence of terror and sorrow in enslaved lives. "Such is 'southern life as it is,' three days in the year, as I found it – the other three hundred and sixty-two being days of weariness, and fear, and suffering, and unremitting labor."[93] By attesting to the continuity of fear and grief in enslaved lives, the narratives of the enslaved disrupted the imperial discourses of the

---

lips called 'golden peak'; everything broke down into a certain melancholy, which characterized me with time: music enchanted me without knowing why; I cried and looked for that consolation when finding an opportunity to cry, always looking for solitude to give free rein to my sorrows; I cried but did not moan, nor did my heart get into knots, except in a certain state of incurable melancholy until morning."

[91] Manzano, *Autobiografía del esclavo poeta*, 103. Translation to English: "[my life] all of it watered with tears!... My poor heart fell ill from suffering from everything that frightened me."

[92] Sojourner Truth, "Narrative of Sojourner Truth, a Northern Slave, Emancipated from Bodily Servitude by the State of New York, in 1828," in *Slave Narratives* (New York: Literary Classics, 2000), 585.

[93] Solomon Northup, *Narrative of Solomon Northup: Twelve Years a Slave* (Auburn: Derby and Miller, 1853).

capriciousness of enslaved emotions and the relativism of enslaved suffering, unveiling the imperial conceit driven by the racialized order of White happiness.

The narrative of William Craft and Ellen Craft condemned Southern slavery in the United States as an unfeeling institution, resisting the concept of the unfeeling enslaved. "I know that those who are not familiar with the working of 'the peculiar institution,' can scarcely imagine any one so totally devoid of all natural affection as to sell his own offspring into returnless bondage."[94] Furthermore, the thinkers affirmed that their twenty-three years in slavery had shown them "that the practical working of slavery is worse than the odious laws by which it is governed."[95] William Craft and Ellen Craft repudiated how the institution of slavery was even more hateful than its legal framework, abhorring the pervasiveness of torture against the enslaved.

I have often seen slaves tortured in every conceivable manner. I have seen them hunted down and torn by bloodhounds. I have seen them shamefully beaten, and branded with hot irons. I have seen them hunted, and even burned alive at the stake, frequently for offences that would be applauded if committed by white persons for similar purposes. In short, it is well known in England, if not all over the world, that the Americans, as a people, are notoriously mean and cruel towards all coloured persons, whether they are bond or free.[96]

The racially premised cruelty of the slaveholding South is manifested through its multiplicity of sanctioned acts of physical torture and sexual violence. The text exclaims that, if there is one thought "under the wide canopy of heaven, horrible enough to stir a man's soul, and to make his very blood boil, it is the thought of his dear wife, his unprotected sister, or his young and virtuous daughters, struggling to save themselves from falling a prey to such demons!"[97] The key narrative arc of this autobiography is one of liberation from the "demons" that perpetrate and systemize imperial sexual violence. Ellen Craft's apprehension toward becoming a mother within the enslaved condition and William Craft's longing for marriage are signified as the driving forces of their dangerous escape to freedom.

---

[94] William Craft & Ellen Craft, "Running a Thousand Miles for Freedom; or, The Escape of William and Ellen Craft from Slavery," in *Slave Narratives* (New York: Literary Classics, 2000), 584.
[95] Craft & Craft, "Running a Thousand Miles for Freedom," 589.
[96] Craft & Craft, "Running a Thousand Miles for Freedom," 742.
[97] Craft & Craft, "Running a Thousand Miles for Freedom," 585.

My wife was torn from her mother's embrace in childhood, and taken to a distant part of the country. She had seen so many other children separated from their parents in this cruel manner, that the mere thought of her ever becoming the mother of a child, to linger out a miserable existence under the wretched system of American slavery, appeared to fill her very soul with horror; and as she had taken what I felt to be an important view of her condition, I did not, at first, press the marriage, but agreed to assist her in trying to devise some plan by which we might escape from our very unhappy condition.[98]

The writers tell the story of their deliverance from the "very unhappy condition of slavery" toward the institution of marriage. The memory of the dangerous escape is contextualized with the unbearable impact of enslaved family separations and the dread of "lingering" in "miserable existence under the wretched system" of slavery. This fear is described as "filling the soul with horror" and tying the enslaved mother to her child and her grandchild, binding them all together in horror and undying love.

Incidents in the Life of a Slave Girl by Harriet Ann Jacobs vehemently denounces how young enslaved people "learned" to "tremble" at the Master's presence and how slaveholding sexual violence represents a painful "rite of passage" that racializes childhood.

Soon she will learn to tremble when she hears her master's footfall. She will be compelled to realize that she is no longer a child. If God has bestowed beauty upon her, it will prove her greatest curse. That which commands admiration in the white woman only hastens the degradation of the female slave. I know that some are too much brutalized by slavery to feel the humiliation of their position; but many slaves feel it most acutely, and shrink from the memory of it. I cannot tell how much I suffered in the presence of these wrongs, nor how I am still pained by the retrospect. My master met me at every turn, reminding me that I belonged to him, and swearing by heaven and earth that he would compel me to submit to him. If I went out for a breath of fresh air, after a day of unwearied toil, his footsteps dogged me. If I knelt by my mother's grave, his dark shadow fell on me even there. The light heart which nature had given me became heavy with sad forebodings.[99]

Jacobs condemns the racialization of "beauty," bringing "admiration" for some and "degradation" for others. The autobiography interweaves the depiction of trauma with the narration of the inevitability of sexual violence in a slaveholding regime, which adds to the transcendence of pain and "trembling" in the transition from childhood to adulthood. She did not just tremble: she learned to tremble. The emphasis is placed on the

---

[98] Craft & Craft, "Running a Thousand Miles for Freedom," 696.
[99] Harriet Jacobs, *Incidents in the Life of a Slave Girl* (New York: Open Road, 2016), 28.

systematic lived experience of slaveholding sexual violence as "teaching" the feeling of dread. It is a horror engendered by the sexual criminalization of enslaved childhood. The Master's footsteps monitored her every turn and still do. This policing was centered on the evil paternalistic idea of the sexual belonging of an "emotionally precocious" enslaved child to the Master. The "heaviness" of her heart is fueled by a constant "dark shadow," which follows her to her mother's grave, to the most painful sites of generational trauma. Jacobs then further confronts the pervasiveness of sexual exploitation in enslaved experiences and personifies the racialization of childhood by visualizing two White and Black sisters as children "playing together."

> I once saw two beautiful children playing together. One was a fair white child; the other was her slave, and also her sister. When I saw them embracing each other, and heard their joyous laughter, I turned sadly away from the lovely sight. I foresaw the inevitable blight that would fall on the little slave's heart. I knew how soon her laughter would be changed to sighs. The fair child grew up to be a still fairer woman. From childhood to womanhood her pathway was blooming with flowers, and overarched by a sunny sky. Scarcely one day of her life had been clouded when the sun rose on her happy bridal morning. How had those years dealt with her slave sister, the little playmate of her childhood? She, also, was very beautiful; but the flowers and sunshine of love were not for her. She drank the cup of sin, and shame, and misery, whereof her persecuted race are compelled to drink.[100]

A tragedy looms as these sisters embrace one another. The "joyous laughter" of the enslaved child will be diminished because her path is not full of the "flowers and sunshine of love." Instead, she belongs to the "persecuted race," and her adolescent body will be terrorized by the sadism of her White father. As a survivor of slaveholding sexual violence, her destiny according to the imperial perspective is to carry "sin, and shame, and misery" in her insides. Jacobs connotes the grief effected by the racialization of childhood, beauty, and the generational trauma that harasses an enslaved child's heart and body.

J. W. Loguen, formerly enslaved minister and affiliate of the Underground Railroad, sent a letter expressing his indignation toward his former enslaver Sarah Logue in 1870 after having escaped from his captivity. In this letter, Loguen deplored the fact that Logue "sold" his brother and sister as revenge for his getaway. "You are a woman: but had

---

[100] Jacobs, *Incidents in the Life of a Slave Girl*, 29.

you a woman's heart, you never could have insulted a brother by telling him you sold his only remaining brother and sister, because he put himself beyond your power to convert him into money."[101] The minister conveys his profound abhorrence toward the "heartless" act of this "wretched woman" and simultaneously states that this slaveholding vengeance had not tainted his "value of freedom." "Wretched woman! Be it known to you that I value my freedom, to say nothing of my mother, brothers and sisters, more than your whole body; more, indeed than my own life; more than all the lives of all the slaveholders and tyrants under heaven."[102] Loguen upholds the significance of his liberty and his familial ties over the existence of the tyrants who had decreed a White monopoly over Happiness.

The enslaved fervently resisted the imperial discourse of the inherent "happiness" of Black enslavement. They did so in their narratives, in their recollections, in their furious letters to former enslavers, in their breathing and their death. Their words emotively condemned the omnipresent violence of the "unhappy condition" of slavery. Their writings consistently decried the primacy of emotional policing and differentiation in the racialization of childhood and in the exercise of corporal punishment and sexual violence against the enslaved. Their written works also challenged the slaveholding monopoly over familial emotions and projected fear and grief as uniting the enslaved in a collective sense of community and kinship. The affirmation of enslaved grief as constant and generational opposed the imperial projection of Black grief as ephemeral and in need of forceful penalization. The emotional resistance of the enslaved pervaded their intellectual production within and out of slavery. The music of the enslaved transmitted their longings, their affirmations of their identities, their melodious laments. The intellectual production of the enslaved within capitalistic labor was arrogated by emotionally supremacist slaveholding empires, and their revolutions were constructed by Empires as passionate transgressions that had to be eradicated. For there was no greater displeasure for Whiteness than the emotional "excesses" of the revolutions of the enslaved to be unleashed.

---

[101] "Letter J. W. Loguen to Mrs. Sarah Logue, *The Liberator*, April 27, 1870," in *Women and Slavery in America: A Documentary History*, edited by Catherine M. Lewis & J. Richard Lewis (Fayetteville: University of Arkansas Press, 2011).
[102] "Letter J. W. Loguen to Mrs. Sarah Logue."

THE EMOTIONAL "EXCESSES" OF THE HAITIAN REVOLUTION

Toussaint Louverture's first proclamation decreed "vengeance" in the pursuit of "Liberty and Equality" in the colony of Saint-Domingue.[103] This revolutionary discourse was deemed precarious to the Empires of the Atlantic world, since it represented a framework for emotional reparations for the enslaved. Not only did the enslaved deserve to be free; they also deserved to feel avenged. Nineteenth-century European paintings about the Haitian Revolution accentuated the "Western" discomfort toward the enslaved taking over White spaces. Black semi-naked men with little distinguishing detail violently attack White women and children in extravagant dress. The commotion is not only caused by the fact that the enslaved carry machetes, but also due to their unregulated movement and massive association. The spectator of these chaotic images could almost hear the screams of panicked White women and children and is supposed to empathize with the simulated White "fear" toward Black political agency. Their pale faces are contorted to express their desperation to flee from their worst "nightmare": for the enslaved to feel avenged. The primary sources of the imperial debate surrounding the Haitian Revolution encompass the emotional discourses of the White colonizers of Saint-Domingue before and after the revolution that led to the first Black State in the Americas. These sources evidence that the strategic discourse of White "terror" toward "cannibalistic" Blackness was always ingrained in racial capitalism.

The speeches granted by White colonizers of Saint-Domingue in the late eighteenth century were epic tales of emotional contagion. Monsieur Chacherau, lawyer of the Conseil supérieur de Saint-Domingue, delivered a speech in the western side of the colony that mocked the "generous but blind feeling" he claimed had taken over France.

> Que la France se fasse éclairer *par des gens de bien*, elle sera bientôt convaincue que le Sort de ceux auxquels elle est prête à sacrifier son propre bonheur ... à celui de nos *travailleurs* dans nos villes & dans nos campagnes en France, à celui des Africains mêmes, livrés sous les tyrans d'Afrique ...; elle sera convaincue que ceux qui excitent en el ce sentiment généreux, mais aveugle, ne peuvent recevoir un présent dont ils n'ont jamais connu l'étendue ni les bornes, que pour en abuser, & se replongeroient bientôt eux-mêmes dans l'état dont on veut les tirer, sous lequel

---

[103] "Toussaint Louverture's Proclamation of August 29, 1793," as quoted in C. L. R. James, *The Black Jacobins: Toussaint Louverture and the San Domingo Revolution* (New York: Vintage Books, 1938), 125.

ils sont *nés*, & pour lequel on peut dire qu'ils sont faits, comme tous les peuples de la zone torride.[104]

The sarcastic tone of the speech fuses the notions of "enlightenment" and "goodness" in order to connote abolitionism as a flawed application of French revolutionary thought. According to the speaker, the idea of "sacrificing" French "happiness" was mistaken for a "generous but blind feeling." This abolitionist "feeling" is constructed as misleading, since Africans, they said, could never surpass the "limits" of the "state from which they are born," the mark of geographical determinism that results in Black political tyranny and contagious emotional deception. Even before the major revolution that was to come, antislavery thought was abstracted as epitomizing the "sacrifice" of White "happiness."

Secret correspondence between colonial deputies of Saint-Domingue elucidated their understanding of the Declaration of the Rights of Man and of the Citizen as a source of "terror" for the French colony. "Enfin elle est devenue une espèce de terreur, lorsque nous avons vu la déclaration des droits de l'homme poser, pour la base de la constitution, légalité absolue, l'identité de droits, et la liberté de tous les individus."[105] This "terror" compelled the deputies to "rectify" the discourses about slavery and about the "amis des Noirs" in the colony. "Il falloit cependant rectifier les idées dominantes sur l'importance des colonies, ... sur la nécessité de maintenir l'esclavage et la traite, sur le degré de confiance qu'on pouvoit accorder aux amis des noirs."[106] According to Monsieur de Saint-Chéron, this "rectification" could arise only from the Law.

---

[104] "Vues politiques sur Saint-Domingue, adressées à MM. du Comité de la partie de l'Ouest, par M. Chachereau, avocat au Conseil supérieur de Saint-Domingue (1789)," Bibliothèque nationale de France, département Philosophie, histoire, sciences de l'homme, 8-LK12–999. Translation to English: "May France be enlightened by good people, she will soon be convinced that the Fate of those to whom she is ready to sacrifice her own happiness ... than that of our workers in our cities and our countrysides in France, than that of the Africans themselves, delivered under the tyrants of Africa ...; she will be convinced that those who excite this generous, but blind feeling can only receive a gift of which they have never known the extent nor the limits, only to abuse it, and will soon return themselves to the state from which they are born, and for which one can say that they are made, like all the populations of the torrid zone."

[105] "Correspondance secrète des députés de Saint-Domingue avec les comités de cette île (12 août 1789–9 avril 1790)," Bibliothèque nationale de France, département Philosophie, histoire, sciences de l'homme, 8-LK12–267. Translation to English: "Finally, it became a kind of terror, when we saw the declaration of rights of man pose, as the basis of the constitution, absolute legality, the identity of rights, and the freedom of all individuals."

[106] "Correspondance secrète des députés de Saint-Domingue." Translation to English: "It was, however, necessary to rectify the prevailing ideas about the importance of the

O Loi, image auguste de la Divinité sur la terre, garant sacré du bonheur & de la liberté de l'homme en société, recours assuré du juste & terreur du méchant, c'est toi qui au milieu de inégalités nécessaires de dons de la nature & de la fortune, voyant tous les humains du même œil, établis du moins entr'eux cette précieuse égalité qui seul peut sauver du malheur de haïr & d'être haï; sans toi, sans ton salutaire empire, la terre ne m'offre plus, de touts parts, que le spectacle désolant de la justice & de la soiblesse succombant sous la force ou la ruse, & tous les hommes qui couvrant sa surface, ne sont plus, sans toi, qu'un assemblage vil & malheureux d'oppresseurs & d'opprimés, de maîtres & d'esclaves![107]

This conception of the Law as the "image of God" is interpreted as stimulating "happiness" and "freedom" within "necessary inequalities" and preventing societies from becoming "unhappy masters and slaves." Only the Law could regulate the institution of slavery and bring "happiness" to the colony, since only "unhappiness" would result from unregulated bondage. Only the Law could bring "happiness" through the enforcement of racially premised "necessary inequalities" rooted in "nature" that disobeyed the verbatim language of the Declaration of the Rights of Man and of the Citizen, which never intended to acknowledge the oppression of the enslaved. It was taken for granted that the enslaved would never be Men or Citizens because legal codification was meant to confine the imperial definitions of humanity and citizenship.

The White slaveholders of Saint-Domingue reverberated Montesquieu's geographical determinism when they argued that the "passionate" French colony had to be subjected to a distinct legal framework.

Les Colonies doivent-elles être assimilées aux Provinces Françoises, c'est-à-dire, doivent-elles être soumises aux mêmes Loix? Je ne pense pas qu'on puisse raisonnablement contester la négative, pour peu que l'on fasse attention à la situation géographique & à la différence du climat qui en produit une très-remarquable

---

colonies, ... about the necessity of maintaining slavery and the slave trade, about the degree of confidence which could be granted to the friends of black people."

[107] "Considérations sur les gouvernemens, et principalement sur celui qui convient à la colonie de Saint-Domingue, par M. de Saint-Chéron (1790)," Bibliothèque nationale de France, département Philosophie, histoire, sciences de l'homme, 8-LK12–991. Translation to English: "Oh Law, august image of the Divinity on earth, sacred guarantor of the happiness and freedom of man in society, assured recourse of the righteous and terror of the wicked, it is you who in the midst of necessary inequalities of the gifts of nature and fortune, seeing all human beings in the same eye, established at least among them that precious equality which alone can save from the misfortune of hating and being hated; without you, without your salutary empire, the earth no longer offers me more, on all sides, than the distressing spectacle of justice and solitude succumbing under force or cunning, and all the men who cover its surface are no more, without you, than a vile and unfortunate assemblage of oppressors and oppressed, masters & slaves!"

dans le caractère de ses Habitans; leurs passions, leurs mœurs, leurs usages, ne ressemblent point aux nôtres; leurs besoins différent également. De cette dissemblance dérive incontestablement la nécessité d'un régime approprié à leur nature. Il faut donc reconnoître cette première vérité, que les Loix faites pour la Métropole, ne conviennent point aux Colonies.[108]

The conceptualization of France and the colony of Saint-Domingue as "incompatible" legal jurisdictions was reckoned justifiable due to the differences in climate and therefore in "passions." This emotional differentiation is fixed in "nature" and results in dissimilar "needs." Hence, the "need" for the legal permissibility of slavery is depicted as inherent to the "nature" of an emotionally erratic population, the "need" for the emotional "guidance" of slavery.

Vocal free people of color of the colony of Saint-Domingue, categorized by the Empire as of "racially mixed" ancestry, highlighted familial sentiments in their claim for French citizenship. In 1790, Julien Raimond, one of the leaders of the movement of the free people of color, spoke in front of the National Assembly and denounced the "aristocracy of White people" in Saint-Domingue.

Voilà, Messeigneurs, voilà de quelle manière est respecté le premier des principes que vous avez rappellé pour la conservation des droits de l'Homme & de Citoyen: "Tous les hommes naissent & demeurent libres & égaux en droits." Ces malheureuses victimes de l'aristocratie des Blancs, qui pouvoient user de second principe que vous avez établi (de résister à l'oppression), ne l'ont jamais mis en usage. Cette retenue de leur part ne prouve-t-elle pas leur douceur, leur éloignement à toute espèce de violence envers leurs pères & leurs frères, & plus encore leur attachement inviolable à la Patrie.[109]

---

[108] "Lettre a MM. Les Commissaires, nommés pour faire le Rapport de l'Affaire des Colonies à 7 Mars 1790," Universidad de Puerto Rico, Recinto de Río Piedras, Biblioteca José M. Lázaro, Colección Josefina del Toro Fulladosa, Colección Nemours de Historia Haitiana, Box FR. Translation to English: "Should the colonies be assimilated to the French provinces, in other words, should they be subordinated to the same laws? I do not think this can be answered reasonably but in the negative, despite the little attention that is given to the geographical situation and to the difference in climate that produces a quite notable one in the character of its inhabitants; their passions, their morality, their customs are not like ours; our needs also differ. From this incompatibility, unquestionably emerges the need for an appropriate regime for its nature. This first truth then needs to be recognized: that the laws of the metropole do not suit the colonies."

[109] "Réclamations adressées à l'Assemblée nationale par les personnes de couleur de Saint-Domingue, par Julien Raimond (1790)," Bibliothèque nationale de France, département Philosophie, histoire, sciences de l'homme, 8-LK12-232. Translation to English: "Here, Sirs, this is how the first of the principles you have recalled for the conservation of the rights of the Man and the Citizen is respected: 'All men are born & remain free & equal in law.' These sad victims of the aristocracy of white people, who could use the second

Raimond denotes free people of color in the colony as "sad victims" of the "aristocracy of White people" and affirms that this population had shown their "gentleness" by not exercising violence against their "fathers and brothers" and by keeping their "inviolable attachment" to France. Likewise, in a speech provided one year later to the National Assembly, free people of color of Saint-Domingue conveyed their wishes to "soften" the emotions of their "fathers," the White colonizers, augmenting the reach of their "gentleness." "Puisse cet exposé sincère de nos maux attendrir le cœur de nos pères! Puissons-nous déformais plus heureux, vous devoir notre premier sentiment de bonheur!"[110] Their speech goes beyond and asks for the "compassion" of a "paternal gaze."

> Votre équité, vos sentimens humains en seront touchés, l'humanité criera au fond de vos cœurs bienfaisans, & vous daignerez jeter sur sous un regard de compassion; & vous nous ferez participer, sinon à la régénération entière de la Nation, ... dumoins à ses bienfaits, à sa protection, en nous mettant à l'abri des vexations arbitraires auxquelles on nous assujettit dans les Colonies. Enfin, Messieurs, ne laissez pas plus long-temps dans l'oppression & le désespoir, sous les coups les plus terribles du despotisme, des Français qui méritent vos regards paternels comme tels & comme hommes libres.[111]

The speakers conceive their cause as a shift in the "paternal gaze," a turn that musters political "sentiments" toward the population of the free people of color of Saint-Domingue, ends their "arbitrary vexations," and allows them to participate in the "benefits" of the imperial "regeneration." This "paternal gaze" is novel and revolutionary.

---

    principle, which you have established (to resist oppression), never used it. This restraint on their part, does it not prove their gentleness, their remoteness to every kind of violence toward their fathers and brothers, and still more, their inviolable attachment to their country."

[110] "Adresse à l'Assemblé nationale par les hommes de couleur libres de Saint-Domingue (1791)," Bibliothèque nationale de France, département Philosophie, histoire, sciences de l'homme, 8-LK12–946. Translation to English: "May this sincere exposition of our ills soften the hearts of our fathers! May we become happier, owing you our first feeling of happiness!"

[111] "Adresse à l'Assemblé nationale par les hommes de couleur libres." Translation to English: "Your equity, your human sentiments will be affected, humanity will cry in the depths of your kind hearts, and you will deign to cast a look of compassion; and you will make us participate, if not in the entire regeneration of the Nation, ... at least in its benefits, in its protection, by sheltering us from the arbitrary vexations to which we are subjected in the colonies. Finally, gentlemen, do not allow any longer the oppression and despair, under the most terrible blows of despotism, of Frenchmen who deserve your paternal gaze as such and as free men."

> Nous parlons à nos pères, nous avons le bonheur de leur parler pour la première fois, & c'est dan un siècle éclairé, dans un temps où l'humanité, lasse de croupir sous le joug odieux du despotisme, a fait enfin un effort courageux pour briser les fers honteux dans lesquels elle gémissait & languissait, & elle a recouvré ses droits: nous parlons à des Français, à un peuple sage, qui vient de donner à l'Univers l'exemple mémorable de la plus saine Philosophie.[112]

Hence, the speakers represent the "paternal gaze" as an "enlightened" project: it is a progressive and unparalleled moment in French revolutionary history that culminates the "odious yoke of despotism" and sparks the long-desired fulfillment of "happiness" and familial bond. Still, the achievement of this familial embrace is not a new request, but a long-lived debt. "Les blancs qui donnent à leurs enfans de couleur de quoi subsister, leur sont-ils uns grande grâce? Non: c'est une dette sacrée, c'est celle de la nature."[113] The speakers portray the application of the French Declaration as a paternal "sacred debt" that prejudice had left unpaid and conceptualize racism as a "dishonorable contagion."

> Il faut cependant avouer que ce ne sont pas tous les blancs qui tiennent à ce préjugé ridicule, & que cette contagion déshonorante n'a pas corrompu encore les cœurs vertueux qui habitent les Colonies. Il en est un grande nombre qui plaignent notre sort, & qui ne verraient qu'avec la plus grande satisfaction qu'on y apportât le changement que nous demandons. Nous en avons vus même répandre de ces larmes amères d'un douleur bien sentie qu'arrachait la compassion à l'occasion des mauvais traitemens.[114]

Only "bitter tears" could prove the mobilization of the "paternal gaze" toward their "children" of color. By contextualizing alignment with their

---

[112] "Adresse à l'Assemblé nationale par les hommes de couleur libres." Translation to English: "We speak to our fathers, we are happy to speak to them for the first time, and it is in an enlightened century, at a time when humanity, tired of languishing under the odious yoke of despotism, has finally made a brave effort to break the shameful irons in which she groaned and languished, and she recovered her rights: we speak to the French, to a wise people, who have just given to the Universe the memorable example of the healthiest Philosophy."

[113] "Adresse à l'Assemblé nationale par les hommes de couleur libres." Translation to English: "The white men who give their children of color enough to subsist, are they a great grace? No, it is a sacred debt, it is that of nature."

[114] "Adresse à l'Assemblé nationale par les hommes de couleur libres." Translation to English: "It must be admitted, however, that not all white people have this ridiculous prejudice, and that this dishonorable contagion has not yet corrupted the virtuous hearts which inhabit the colonies. There are many who pity our fate, and who would see with the greatest satisfaction that the changes we ask for were made. We have even seen them shed those bitter tears of a well-felt sorrow torn by compassion on the occasion of the ill treatment."

request for French citizenship as proof that the "dishonorable contagion" had not reached the "virtuous hearts" of the White colonizers, and therefore drawing from the notion of "tropical fever" of geographical determinism, the vocal free people of color put the White "virtue" of their "Fathers" into question.

After the start of the Haitian Revolution, the White slaveholders of Saint-Domingue expressed desperate pleas to the King of France. "Nos propriété sont ravagées; une partie de nos frères sont égorgés; les autres sont réduits à défendre leurs jours contre des hommes auxquels la séduction a mis le fer à la main, et que l'ivresse du sang a rendus furieux."[115] Their appeal conflates the loss of property with the death of "brothers." The instigators of these "slaughters" are denoted as "seduction," "intoxication of the blood," and "fury." Yet the speakers argue that this bloodshed is rationalized with "hypocrisy." "Cependant les hommes qui trament ces complots osent encore se couvrir du masque d'un hypocrite humanité; c'est nous qu'ils accusent de barbarie, lorsqu'ils abreuvent de sang notre terre natale!"[116] The representation of Saint-Domingue as being inundated by "intoxicated blood" blames the alleged duplicity, "savagery," and bellicosity of "simulated" abolitionism. The biological determinism of this text links the inherent "aggression" of Black "blood" to the "deception" of antislavery thought. The deviant nature of Black "blood" and emotionality is deemed contagious, seductive, destructive, and leading to the chaos, the misreading of French revolutionary ideals, and the devastation of imperial lands.

The White slaveholders of Saint-Domingue would long for the return of "harmony" and thus the regulation of the corporeal energy of the enslaved. "Car, Messieurs, le sentiment à imprimer à nos esclaves doit être tel qu'il contienne six cent mille noirs dans la dépendance de soixante mille hommes libres."[117] It is through the "sentiment" of "dependence"

---

[115] "Adresse au Roi, et discours à Leurs Majestés et à la famille royale, par les colons français de l'isle de St.-Domingue, réunis à Paris (1791)," Bibliothèque nationale de France, département Philosophie, histoire, sciences de l'homme, 4-LK12–365. Translation to English: "Our properties are ravaged; some of our brothers were slaughtered; others are reduced to defending their days against men whom seduction has put iron in their hands, and whom the intoxication of the blood has made furious."

[116] "Adresse au Roi, et discours à Leurs Majestés." Translation to English: "However, the men who plan these plots still dare to cover themselves with the mask of a hypocritical humanity; it is they who accuse us of barbarism, when they water our native land with blood!"

[117] "Adresses de l'Assemblée provinciale du nord de Saint-Domingue, du 15 juillet 1791, à l'Assemblée nationale, au roi, aux 83 départements et au directoire ... de la Gironde, sur

that the "order" of inequality could sustain the slaveholding productivity of the richest colony of the Caribbean. Yet the French metropole would need to go beyond the "feeling of its power" to regain the colony and the "hearts" of the colonizers: "Il est un autre vérité non moins indestructible; c'est que lorsqu'une métropole ne veut régir ses Colonies que par le seul sentiment de sa puissance, le cœurs des colons s'aliènent bientôt, & la chute de l'empire suit de près."[118] The White colonizers seized the context of the revolution of the enslaved to ominously demand more military support and economic autonomy, warning of the "fall of the Empire" if their political appeals were not met. This imploration was promoted as a response to the emotional context of colonial turmoil.

Le langage ferme & vrai que nous vous tenons ici, est le cri d'un vérité déchirant, sans doute; mais enfin elle est telle. Quand les propriétés d'une section libre de l'empire, qui en fait la splendeur & la force par ses richesses & sa fidélité, son ébranlées jusques dans leurs fondemens, larmes de l'amertume & les sanglots du désespoir doivent nécessairement s'exhaler.[119]

The "tears," "sobs," and "despair" of the slaveholders of Saint-Domingue certainly became emblems of the colonial "dissonances" arising from the revolutionary thought of the enslaved.

Le secours de la Nation, les efforts du Commerce & notre industrie pourront peut-être les réparer; mais qui tarira nos larmes, sur la mort de plus de mille de nos Concitoyens, victimes de cette cruelle révolte? La sensibilité peut-elle être muette, quand on songe que 15,000 [racial slur] seront détruits avant le retour de l'ordre & de la tranquillité, & que s'ils réussissent dans leurs projets, Saint-Domingue deviendra le tombeau de cinquante mille Français![120]

---

    le décret du 15 mai, en faveur des hommes de couleur libres des colonies," Bibliothèque nationale de France, département Philosophie, histoire, sciences de l'homme, 8-LK12–338. Translation to English: "For, gentlemen, the sentiment to be impressed on our slaves must be such that it contains six hundred thousand black people in the dependence of sixty thousand free men."

[118] "Adresses de l'Assemblée provinciale du nord de Saint-Domingue." Translation to English: "There is another truth no less indestructible; it is that, when a metropole wants to govern its colonies only by the feeling of its power, the hearts of the colonists soon become alienated, and the fall of the empire follows closely."

[119] "Adresses de l'Assemblée provinciale du nord de Saint-Domingue." Translation to English: "The firm and true language that we hold here is the cry of a heartbreaking truth, no doubt; but still it is such. When the properties of a free section of the empire, which makes splendor and strength with its riches and its fidelity, are shaking to their foundations, tears of bitterness and the sobs of despair must necessarily be exhaled."

[120] "Recueil des pièces envoyées ou lues jusqu'au 5 décembre 1791, à l'Assemblée Nationale et au Roi, par les Députés de l'Assemblée générale de Saint-Domingue, relativement au

The "tearful" imagery of Saint-Domingue as the potential "tomb" of French slaveholders intends to compel the "sensibility" of the King of France and the National Assembly toward the "return of order and tranquility." Furthermore, the plight of the colonizer is contrasted with the "softened state" of the enslaved under a "paternal government."

> Un gouvernement paternel avoit adouci depuis plusieurs années l'état des [racial slur], & nous osons dire que des millions d'Européens, que tous les besoins assiègent, que toutes les miseres poursuivent, recueillent moins de douceurs, que ceux qu'on vous peignoit qu'on peignoit au monde entier comme chargés de chaînes & expirant dans un long supplice. La situation des noirs en Afrique, sans propriétés, sans existence politique, sans existence civile, incessamment les jouets de la fureur imbécille des tyrans, qui partagent cette vaste & barbare contrée, est changée dans nos colonies en une condition supportable & douce.[121]

The White colonizers of Saint-Domingue juxtapose the "soft condition" under the "paternal" colonial government with the public abolitionist perception of those in bondage as "exhaling in torture." The slaveholders go beyond and compare the state of the enslaved to the one of Europeans with the latter not being as "sweet," relativizing the condition of slavery. Following the rhetoric of historical determinism, the circumstances of the enslaved in the French colony are deemed "softened" when contrasted to their assumed lack of "civil and political existence" under the "imbecile fury" of "African tyrants." Africans are characterized as outside historical movement due to obsolete political systems and absence of property: the nonexistence of Progress is instigated by the "imbecile" rage of African political leadership. The White colonizers fuse their argumentation about the institution of slavery with

---

désastres de cette malheureuse colonie," Bibliothèque nationale de France, département Philosophie, histoire, sciences de l'homme, 4-LK12–1176. Translation to English: "The help of the Nation, the efforts of Commerce, and our industry may be able to repair them; but who will dry our tears for the death of more than a thousand of our fellow citizens, victims of this cruel revolt? Can sensibility be mute when one dreams that 15,000 black people will be destroyed before the return of order and tranquility, and that if they succeed in their projects, Saint-Domingue will become the tomb of fifty thousand Frenchmen!"

[121] "Recueil des pièces envoyées ou lues jusqu'au 5 décembre 1791." Translation to English: "A paternal government had softened the state of black people for several years, and we dare to say that millions of Europeans, whom all needs besiege, whom all the miseries pursue, receive less sweetness than those whom have been painted to the whole world as loaded with chains and expiring in a long torture. The situation of black people in Africa, without property, without political existence, without civil existence, incessantly the toys of the imbecile fury of tyrants, who share this vast and barbarous country, is changed in our colonies into a tolerable and soft condition."

strategic emotional antagonism of the Black leadership of the Haitian Revolution, and revolutionary thought is consequently implied as emotionally absurd.

The White colonizers of Saint-Domingue also insistently spoke of the Société des amis des Noirs as a cradle of discontent, calling them "hypocritical philanthropists" who negligently filled Saint-Domingue with blood and ashes by being manipulated by the "trickery" of Black emotions.

Jouissez, philantropes hypocrites, jouissez de vos succès! ils sont dignes de vous. La partie du nord de Saint-Domingue n'est plus qu'un tas de cendres, teint du sang des blancs et des noirs. Le [racial slur] a été cruel et stupide, comme le tigre des forêts de l'Afrique; il s'est soustrait au pouvoir de ses maîtres, mais c'est pour établir le despotisme le plus absolu, le despotisme des chefs des hordes de la côte de Guinée. Chaque paroisse de la partie du nord a eu son despote, et ce despote, sans raison, sans morale, n'ayant pour guide qu'une volonté brutale et corrompue, s'est livré à tous les excès de la férocité.[122]

Combining theories of geographical and historical determinism, the Black leaders of the revolution of the enslaved are depicted as animalistic "despots" with much cruelty, immorality, irrationality, and "excessive ferocity." Their "fury" is one step behind full-blown "African cannibalism." "Si les [racial slur] avoient réussi dans leur entreprise, si les vœux de leurs amis avoient été exaucés, Saint-Domingue eût bientôt offert le même tableau que l'Afrique; nous aurions vu les repas sanglants des anthropophages, à moins que la traite des noirs n'eût soustrait les malheureuses victimes aux fureurs de leurs semblables."[123] The slaveholders of Saint-Domingue portray the Black revolutionary leaders as bringing the

---

[122] "Adresses des députés de la commune de St. Malo, à l'Assemblée nationale et au Roi, à l'occasion d'une révolte de noirs, à Saint-Domingue, par MM. Fournier de Varenne, Meslé de Grandclos, Harrington, Guillemaut, Tréhouart de Beaulieu, Ethéart, Murat (1791)," Bibliothèque nationale de France, département Philosophie, histoire, sciences de l'homme, 8-LK12–374. Translation to English: "Enjoy, hypocritical philanthropists, enjoy your success! They are worthy of you. The northern part of Saint-Domingue is nothing but a heap of ashes, stained with the blood of white and black people. The black man has been cruel and stupid, like the tiger of the forests of Africa; he has escaped the power of his masters, but it was to establish the most absolute despotism, the despotism of the chiefs of the hordes of the coasts of Guinea. Every parish in the northern part had its despot, and this despot, without reason, without morals, having for his guide only a brutal and corrupt will, has given himself up to all the excesses of ferocity."

[123] "Adresses des députés de la commune de St. Malo." Translation to English: "If black people had succeeded in their enterprise, if the wishes of their friends had been granted, Saint-Domingue would soon have offered the same picture as Africa; we would have seen the bloody meals of the cannibals had the slave trade not subtracted the unfortunate victims from the fury of their fellows."

emotional "damage" that slavery "saved" them from. This involution toward cannibalism and "Black rage" is a step back in the progress of Saint-Domingue "away" from Africa, progress through the emotional "education" of slavery. This grievance is not limited to the colony, but it in turn extends to imperial France. "Le sort de la nation entière, Sire, est lié à celui des Colonies; si elles périssent, si le vœu des amis des noirs est exaucé, si leurs affreux complots s'exécutent, la France est perdue, le meilleur des rois aura la douleur de régner sur le plus malheureux des peuples."[124] The "royal pain" of governing over "unhappy people" legitimizes the claims of the avaricious enslavers. The enslaved are defined as "réellement, et toute leur vie, des enfans adoptifs, dont nous améliorons la condition, dont nous assurons le bien être; et qui deviendroient en général les plus malheureuses de toutes les créatures, s'ils cessoient un instant d'être la propriété des cultivateurs."[125] The "adoption" of the enslaved as "children" represents a stride away from that emotional involution and from the "unhappiness" of "ceasing for an instant" to be "property." The economic exploitation of Blackness has to be uninterrupted, constant in order to guarantee the "happiness" that convalesces the enslaved self away from their "cannibalistic fury." Evoking the racialization of childhood in scientific racism, the emotional infantilization of Blackness propels White paternal inherence on Black bodies, their aberrant emotions, and their labor.

Meanwhile, vocal free people of color described their plight as the suffering of those most "attached to the Motherland": "dans tout l'empire français, nulle classe d'hommes n'est plus fidèlement attachée a la mère-patrie que celle des citoyens de couleur. La moitié de leur origine fait tout leur trésor, toute leur gloire."[126] This speech projects the "White

---

[124] "Adresses des députés de la commune de St. Malo." Translation to English: "The fate of the whole nation, Sire, is connected with that of the colonies; if they perish, the wish of the friends of black people is granted; if their frightful plots are executed, France is lost; the best of the kings will have the pain of reigning over the most unhappy people."

[125] "Assemblée Coloniale de la partie française de Saint-Domingue, aux quatre-vingt-trois Départemens de la France, aux Places de Commerce et aux Manufactures de la Métropole, au Cap, en séance, le 27 février 1792," Universidad de Puerto Rico, Recinto de Río Piedras, Biblioteca José M. Lázaro, Colección Josefina del Toro Fulladosa, Colección Nemours de Historia Haitiana, Box CM. Translation to English: "really, and all their life, adoptive children, whose condition we improve, whose well-being we ensure; and who would generally become the most unhappy of all creatures, if they ceased for a moment to be the property of cultivators."

[126] "Réflexions politique sur les troubles et la situation de la partie française de Saint-Domingue, publiées par les commissaires des citoyens de couleur de Saint-Marc et de plusieurs paroisses de cette colonie auprès de l'Assemblée nationale et du roi, par Viart,

half" of their "ancestry" as their source of "treasured glory." Even more, the speakers later argue that it was their "inviolable attachment" to France that chiefly triggered their alienation and sidelining by the White colonizers.[127] The accent on the "affection" of the vocal free people of color toward the French Empire aims to counteract any insinuation of engagement with the revolution of the enslaved. "Un observateur impartial, témoin des révolutions de Saint-Domingue, prouvera quand il voudra que les hommes de couleur étoient plus doux et plus humains que les blancs de la colonie: on ne peut même leur reprocher un seul attentat qui n'ait été provoqué par une série d'événemens atroces."[128] The free people of color are characterized as "sweeter" and "more humane" than the White colonizers, drawing from emotional concepts to purge any perception of blame or entanglement with Black revolutionary "discord."

Echoing a key emotional discursive paradigm of Atlantic slavery, the White slaveholders of the colony of Saint-Domingue used the notion of enslaved "happiness" to relativize the institution of slavery in the global economy.

les [racial slur] *en général sont-il malheureux?* = non sans doute; car ils ont échangé un esclavage INTOLERABLE, et l'appareil toujours présent des plus affreux supplices, contre une servitude, à peu-près semblable à celle que le besoin impose, dans tous les pays du monde, à tout être qui n'a point de propriétés, et qu'à Saint-Domingue l'intérêt personnel des maîtres, tend sans cess à adoucir.[129]

Dubourg, Chanlate jeune, F. Ouvrière, 1792," Bibliothèque nationale de France, département Philosophie, histoire, sciences de l'homme, 8-LK12-398. Translation to English: "throughout the French Empire, no class of men is more faithfully attached to the mother country than that of citizens of color. Half of their origin made all their treasure, all their glory."

[127] "Réflexions politique sur les troubles."

[128] "Réflexions politique sur les troubles." Translation to English: "An impartial observer, witness of the revolutions of Saint-Domingue, will be proven when he suggests that the men of color were gentler and more humane than the white men of the colony: we cannot even blame them for a single attack which was not provoked by a series of atrocious events."

[129] "Idées sommaires sur la restauration de Saint-Domingue, présentées à la Nation, au Roi et à la Colonie (1792)," Universidad de Puerto Rico, Recinto de Río Piedras, Biblioteca José M. Lázaro, Colección Josefina del Toro Fulladosa, Colección Nemours de Historia Haitiana, Box RF. Translation to English: "are black people in general unhappy? = probably not; for they have exchanged an intolerable slavery, and the ever-present apparatus of the most dreadful punishments, for a servitude, almost like that which needs impose, in all countries of the world, on every being who has no properties, and that, in Saint-Domingue, the personal interest of the masters constantly tends to soften."

The enslavers deny the "unhappiness" of the African diaspora, having been saved from an "intolerable" slavery. This claim, rooted in relativism of the enslaved condition, falsely states that "all countries in the world" enslave those without "property." Therefore, enslavement is rationalized as arising from the racialized themselves, framing their political existence as in the margins of capitalism due to their own inadequacy. Within the global economy, European slavery is portrayed as more "tolerable," as "softer." This historicist argument generates a hierarchical geography of benevolent proprietorship, imperialism, and punitiveness. Moreover, following geographical determinism, this speech normalizes imperial sexual violence as driven by "heated love." "BIENTOT, dans un climat brûlant, où tout porte à l'amour, a résulté de la fréquentation continuelle des Européens avec les Africaines, une race d'individus d'une autre couleur.... Ces fils de femmes esclaves, naissoient tous esclaves, mais bientôt aussi, l'amour paternel les a gratifies de la LIBERTÉ."[130] Tropical heat leads to "love," lawful "love" solely directed from the White "paternal gaze" toward the Black confined body.

When welcoming French civil commissioners in 1792, sent to restore "order," the White colonizers expressed how their arrival to Saint-Domingue represented a "rebirth" of "hope and joy." "Messieurs les Commissaires Nationaux-Civils, Votre arrivée dans cette Isle infortunée fait renaître l'espérance et la joie, et nous fait éprouver des sentimens d'autant plus doux, qu'ils étoient depuis long-temps étrangers pour nos cœurs."[131] Throughout the speech, the rhetoric draws from geographical determinism to declare that the mere arrival of the French commissioners "sweetens" the sentiments of colonizing hearts, hearts hardened by the deviance of "tropical fever." Furthermore, the White slaveholders signify slavery as a "yoke of a paternal domination." "La majeure parti, la presque totalité de nos malheureux [racial slur], long-temps séduits, ne

---

[130] "Idées sommaires sur la restauration de Saint-Domingue." Translation to English: "Soon, in a burning climate, where everything leads to love, resulted from the continual frequentation of the Europeans with African women, a race of individuals of another color.... These sons of female slaves, are all born slaves, but, soon also, paternal love has gratified them with freedom."

[131] "Discours prononcés dans la Séance publique, tous les corps réunis, le 20 Septembre 1792, jour de l'installation de MM. les Commissaires Nationaux-Civils, et de M. le Governeur, Lieutenant général des Isles Françaises de l'Amérique sous le vent," Bibliothèque nationale de France, département Philosophie, histoire, sciences de l'homme, 4-LK12-21. Translation to English: "Gentlemen, National Civil Commissioners, your arrival in this unfortunate island revives hope and joy, and makes us feel sweeter sentiments, since they had long been strangers to our hearts."

soupirent qu'après le moment ou il leur sera permis de se ranger avec sureté sous le joug d'une domination toujours paternelle, toujours bienfaisante."[132] This narrative constructs emancipation from "paternalistic" slavery as a catalyst of sorrow and unrest for Black enslaved people, who soon, they said, long to return to "paternal" control. Only renewed dominance over "unhappy" enslaved people would lead to the culmination of the "spectacle of horror" of the revolution of the enslaved.

Cette Colonie ci-devant la plus florissante de l'Univers, cette riche portion de l'empire Français, ne peut offrir à vos yeux, qu'un spectacle d'horreur, un spectacle attendrissant. Ses plantations précieuses totalement ravagées, dévastées; tous ses édifices renversés ou dévorés par les flammes, son sol teint et fumant encore du sang de ses malheureux habitans, de tout âge, de tout sexe, de tout etat, qui ont péri sous le fer assassin et parricide.[133]

The revolution of the enslaved is conceptualized as a "parricidal" movement that instigated indiscriminate "terror" and death. This is precisely the image that was "painted" of the enslaved leader, a semi-naked Black man viciously attacking White women and children. White blood soiling the ground. Black blood always imperceptible.

In his proclamation of the abolition of slavery in Saint-Domingue in 1793, French civil commissioner Léger-Félicité Sonthonax visualizes this political step as a shift in the construction of colonial "happiness" from royalism to republicanism, silencing this achievement of the revolution of the enslaved.

La République Française veut la liberté et l'égalité entre tous les hommes sans distinction de couleur; les rois ne se plaisent qu'au milieu des esclaves: ce sont eux qui, sur les côtes d'Afrique, vous ont vendus aux blancs: ce sont les tyrans d'Europe qui voudraient perpétuer cet infâme trafic. La République vous adopte au nombre de ses enfans; les rois n'aspirent qu'à vous couvrir de chaînes ou à vous anéantir.[134]

---

[132] "Discours prononcés dans la Séance publique." Translation to English: "The majority, almost all of our unfortunate black people, long seduced, will not sigh until after the moment when they will be allowed to sit safely under the yoke of a domination, always paternal, always beneficial."

[133] "Discours prononcés dans la Séance publique." Translation to English: "This colony formerly the most flourishing of the Universe, this rich portion of the French Empire, can offer to your eyes only a spectacle of horror, a touching spectacle. Its precious plantations totally ravaged, devastated; all its buildings overthrown or devoured by the flames, its soil stained and still smoking with the blood of its unfortunate inhabitants, of all ages, of all sexes, of all states, who perished under the murderous and parricide blade."

[134] "Proclamation, Nous, Léger-Félicité Sonthonax, Commissaire Civil de la République, délégué aux Iles Françaises de l'Amérique sous le vent, pour y rétablir l'ordre et la tranquillité publique, au Cap, le 29 août, l'an deuxième de la République,"

While the "happiness" of monarchial power was fixed on the permanence of slavery, the French Republic now felt "paternal" sentiments for its newly "adopted children." Sonthonax's rhetoric denotes the legal abolition of slavery as a fatherly triumph of republicanism and the "national regeneration" of the French Revolution, and not of the revolutionary movement of the enslaved who won that victory. The emotions that are spotlighted are the "paternal" feelings of French revolutionary thought as the cradle of Black healing, masking the genocidal violence of the military efforts of the French Empire against the Haitian Revolution.

Meanwhile, the White colonizers of Saint-Domingue continued constructing the revolution of the enslaved as the "reign of drinkers of human blood."[135] The conception of Africans as cannibalistic monstrosities drives the economic logos of the White enslavers. "La prospérité du peuple repose sur le commerce; le commerce repose sur les colonies; les afriquains sont les instrumens nécessaires de leur culture, & les afriquains n'ont aucunes des lumières des hommes d'Europe, parcequ'ils n'ont aucuns de leurs besoins."[136] This speech framed by historical determinism establishes Africans as "instruments" of the manufacturing foundation of the colonial economic structure, claiming their "desires" were not guided by the "lights of the men of Europe." In other words, their "wants" were not part of the victorious narrative of the Enlightenment. While Black bodies were fit to be economic "tools," the emotions of those stepping out of this economic configuration were constructed as necrophilic, desiring to eat White flesh and drink White blood. "Enlightened" White men had the "duty" to profit from Black "instruments" in order to prevent the corporeal consumption of Whiteness, the emotional devastation of imperial lands. In contrast, the White slaveholders envisage the "return" of

---

Bibliothèque nationale de France, Lk12-28. Translation to English: "The French Republic wants the freedom and equality of all men regardless of color; the Kings are only happy among slaves: they are the ones who, on the coasts of Africa, sold you to white people: they are the tyrants of Europe who would want to perpetuate this infamous traffic. The Republic adopts you to the number of its children; the Kings only aspire to cover you with chains or annihilate you."

[135] "Essais sur les causes et les effets de la Révolution, par Page (1795)," Bibliothèque nationale de France, département Philosophie, histoire, sciences de l'homme, 8-LB41-4389.

[136] "Essais sur les causes et les effets de la Révolution." Translation to English: "The prosperity of the people rests on commerce; commerce rests on the colonies; Africans are the necessary instruments of their agriculture, and Africans have none of the lights of the men of Europe because they have none of their wants."

French women to the colony as the revival of the "irresistible empire of interest and feeling."

> Les femmes d'Europe, les femmes françaises reprendront, sur les affections des colons, l'ascendant qu'elles auroient toujours dû posséder exclusivement; elles occuperont, auprès d'eux, la place à laquelle les appellent la nature & les bonnes mœurs; & la France elle-même trouvera, dans le nouvel ordre de choses, un ressort puissant, pour retenir à jamais les colonies dans son système. Qu'elle leur envoie des femmes, & toujours elle leur commandera par l'empire irrésistible de l'intérêt & du sentiment.[137]

The romantic "homecoming" of the French colonizers to their White wives, and therefore the reclaiming of the "rightful" monopoly of "ascendancy" of White women, is portrayed as a cleansing force of "nature" and "morality" that in turn represents a restoration of colonizing power. Hence, the systematic sexual violence against enslaved people was twisted as precariously creating strife for White men.

The rhetoric of the White colonizers of Saint-Domingue consistently fabricated a hierarchy of impassioned violence. An apology of the White slaveholders codified the revolution of the enslaved as being compelled by the "violence of the passions" and the colonial tensions between "three kinds of men."

> *Des hommes blancs,* ou *des Européens,* nos compatriotes, nos vrais frères, nos amis, nos parens, nés parmi nous, ayant nos mœurs et nos habitudes ... Ces blancs tant calomniés étoient, sans comparaison, les hommes les plus actifs, et quoiqu'on en ait dit, les plus généreux. *Des hommes noirs* sortant d'Afrique, d'un caractère généralement bon, amis des blancs, mais essentiellement paresseux, faciles à diriger en tout sens, et sur-tout, vers le mal. Des hommes, enfin, sortant de ces deux premières classes, et connus sous le nom d'*hommes de couleur.* Même avant nos troubles, je les regardois comme bien plus disposés aux vices qu'aux vertus, et comme capables seuls, d'empoisonner la population coloniale.[138]

---

[137] "Essais sur les causes et les effets de la Révolution." Translation to English: "The women of Europe, the French women will recover, by the affections of the colonists, the ascendancy which they should have always possessed exclusively; being close to them, they will occupy the place with which they are called by nature and good morals; and France herself will find, in the new order of things, a powerful spirit to retain the colonies forever in her system. May she send them women, and she always will command them by the irresistible empire of interest and feeling."

[138] "Dernier vœu de la justice, de l'humanité et de la saine politique en faveur des colons de Saint-Domingue, et sur la nécessité et les moyens de rendre à cette colonie sa prospérité, par G. Legal, Première partie (1796)," Bibliothèque nationale de France, département Philosophie, histoire, sciences de l'homme, 8-LK12–526. Translation to English: "White men, or Europeans, our compatriots, our true brothers, our friends, our parents, born among us, having our manners and our habits ... These white men, so calumniated,

This defense elevates the "productivity" and "generosity" of White Men, the "true brothers" in "manners" and "habits," and stresses that Whiteness had been wrongly "calumniated" as sparking the misery of the enslaved. In contrast, Black enslaved people had to be steered from their "essential laziness" toward "friendship" with White Men because free people of color could easily mobilize Blackness toward intrinsic "evil." Free people of color are then hypothesized as more prone to Black "vice" than White "virtue," instigating racial "disharmony" and "poisoning" the colonial population of Saint-Domingue with their "mixed" emotional ancestry.

The discourse of the speakers of the French Empire constantly emphasized the emotional infantilization of Blackness.

Les noirs sont encore au berceau de la liberté; ce sont à cet égard de véritables enfans. Ils ignorent l'usage qu'ils doivent faire de leurs forces, ils les emploieront les uns contre les autres. Nés dans les forêts, leurs goûts, leur habitudes conservent encore quelque chose de sauvage: n'ayant aucune idée de la propriété, de l'inviolabilité des personnes, on les verra se disputer les productions d'une terre abandonnée à elle-même; ils se battront pour le moindre fruit; se feront une guerre continuelle et meurtrière, ou termineront par se vendre eux-mêmes.[139]

This historicist notion of the perpetually infant African propels emotional discourses of Black "savagery" and the African continent as in an unending war and without "property": this war is negligent, self-destructive, and in frantic need of White paternalistic intervention, as Blackness does not comprehend how to use its "forces." Biological determinism likewise influences the racialization of age, and the idea of Africa as still in the "cradle of freedom" legitimizes a never-ending enslaving and colonizing project. Citoyen Deaubonneau evoked this perspective and

---

were, without comparison, the most active men and, whatever may have been said, the most generous. Black men coming out of Africa, of a generally good character, friends of white people, but essentially lazy, easy to lead in any direction, and especially, toward evil. Last, men coming from these first two classes and known by the name of men of color. Even before our troubles, I regarded them as much more inclined toward vices than virtues and as capable alone of poisoning the colonial population."

[139] "Lettre de Michel-Pascal Creuzé à Jean Philippe Garan, député du Loiret, sur son Rapport des troubles de Saint-Domingue, distribué au Corps législatif en ventôse an V (1796)," Bibliothèque nationale de France, département Philosophie, histoire, sciences de l'homme, 8-LK12–521. Translation to English: "Black people are still in the cradle of freedom; in this respect, they are real children. They ignore how to use their forces, they will use them against each other. Born in forests, their tastes and habits still retain something savage: having no idea of property, of the inviolability of persons, they will be seen disputing the productions of a land abandoned to itself; they will fight for the least fruit; they will wage a continual and deadly war, or will end up selling themselves."

further portrayed the revolution of the enslaved as the result of the mobilization of "passions," particularly "self-love." "La postérité jugera les hommes qui ont été influens dans l'affaire des Colonies; nos neveux ne croiront jamais qu'il a existé des êtres, qui, en raisonnant sur de si grands intérêts, prenaient leurs passions pour boussole, et l'effet de leur amour-propre pour des vues infaillibles."[140] Moreover, this speech refers to ideas of geographical determinism in order to categorically justify the economic exploitation of African descendants.

> S'il est démontré aujourd'hui que les seuls Africains ou descendans d'Africains, sont seuls susceptibles de travailler la terre dans ces contrées brûlantes, plus de doute qu'il faille les y attacher; ce serait une erreur grave, de croire que des bras Européens peuvent être utilisés à la culture des plantes indigènes, ou naturalisées au sol des Antilles.[141]

The enslaving subjugation of Black bodies is advocated as thwarting the extinction of White supremacy in the globalization of capitalist economies. Black enslavement keeps White power alive and thriving. Geographical determinism then becomes the premise for the ratification of laws to promote the "dependence" of the African "spirit" and in turn vindicate White emotional dominance. "Le but essentiel est donc de connaître parfaitement l'esprit du cultivateur des Antilles, et ensuite faire des lois propres à maintenir sa dépendance."[142] This "dependence of the African spirit" grants access to the economic "efficiency" of racial capitalism.

Napoleon Bonaparte precisely articulated his rationalization of the restoration of slavery in the French Empire by connecting "emotional difference" and colonial economic productivity. His argumentation demonstrates that the First Consul conceptualized the institution of slavery as

---

[140] "Un mot sur les colonies françaises et particulièrement sur Saint-Domingue, par le citoyen Deaubonneau (1799)," Bibliothèque nationale de France, département Philosophie, histoire, sciences de l'homme, 8-LK9–236. Translation to English: "Posterity will judge men who have been influential in colonial affairs; our nephews will never believe that there have existed beings who, reasoning on such great interests, took their passions for a compass, and the effect of their self-love for infallible views."

[141] "Un mot sur les colonies françaises." Translation to English: "If it is demonstrated today that only Africans or descendants of Africans are the ones likely to work the earth in these scorching countries, there is no doubt that they should be attached to them; it would be a grave error to believe that European arms can be used for the cultivation of native plants, or naturalized on the soil of the Antilles."

[142] "Un mot sur les colonies françaises." Translation to English: "The essential goal is then to know perfectly the spirit of the farmer of the Antilles, and then make suitable laws to maintain his dependence."

the economic foundation for the perpetuity of colonialism, since the emperor assumed that it "pacified" the financial discomfort of the White colonizer toward the potentiality of the "vigor" of Blackness to be "transformed" from "obedience" to "mutiny."

Un homme destiné à passer sa vie dans les colonies doit sentir que, si les Noirs ont pu maintenir dans les colonies contre les Anglais, ils tourneraient leur rage contre nous, égorgeraient les Blancs, menaceraient sans cesse d'incendier nos propriétés, et ne présenteraient aucune garantie au commerce, qui n'offrirait plus de capitaux et resterait sans confiance.[143]

The institution of slavery represented a mechanism to "preserve" emotional control over Black populations, to "appease" colonial White residents by publicly "expunging" enslaved "rage," to stimulate an international sense of "confidence" in imperial efficiency, and thus to project the victory of White emotional supremacy, a conquest larger than life itself. Racialized slavery had to be restored in the Atlantic world as a tactic to inspire transnational economic veneration toward the emotional progression of the French Empire. White happiness depended on it, since Black enslavement kept White dominance alive and thriving, eluding the anticapitalistic anthropophagy of "Black rage."

An exploration of the "origins" of "unhappiness" in Saint-Domingue, written shortly after the independence of Haiti in 1804, disavowed the legitimacy of both the French and Haitian Revolutions. "La garantie de la liberté des blancs est dans l'esclavage des noirs."[144] By arguing that racialized slavery "guarantees" White freedom, the text alleges that the "misfortunes" of the White colonizers surfaced from a flawed reading of French revolutionary thought.

Le Colon qui a pénétré la source de ses malheurs, les causes de la dévastation de Saint-Domingue, peut-il jeter les yeux sur la France, sans que son cœur ulcéré ne se

---

[143] "Au Contre-Amiral Decrès, Ministre de la Marine et des Colonies; Paris, 19 thermidor an X (7 août 1802)," in Napoleon Bonaparte, *Correspondance générale III: Pacifications 1800–1802* (Paris: Fayard, 2006), 1059. Translation to English: "A man destined to spend his life in the colonies must feel that, if black people were capable of maintaining the colonies against the Englishman, they would direct their fury against us, they would slaughter the white people, they would forever threaten to burn down our properties, and they would not present any guarantee to commerce, which would no longer offer any capital and remain without confidence."

[144] "Origine des malheurs de Saint-Domingue, développement du système colonial, et moyens de restauration, par Chotard (1804)," Bibliothèque nationale de France, département Philosophie, histoire, sciences de l'homme, 8-LK12–561. Translation to English: "The guarantee of the liberty of white people is the slavery of black people."

partage aussitôt entre la douleur et l'indignation?... Couvert de son sang, entourré des cadavres de ses parens, de ses amis, le Colon songeait à sa patrie, ... et c'est d'elle que lui venaient tous ses malheurs![145]

The "ulcerated heart" of the "displaced" colonizer feels "pain and indignation" toward the White "corpses" that signify the failed enterprise of reconquering the French colony. According to the former planters of Saint-Domingue, the White blood that "covered them" as relocated colonizers was elicited by "negrophilism":

comme affection exclusive, considéré dans ses effets, est donc une monstruosité politique, dont l'Amérique et l'Europe doivent se garantir. D'après la conduite de tous les Français qui, dans la métropole ou dans les colonies ont professé cette doctrine de sang, cette affection est une lâcheté, qui n'a encore été utile qu'aux ennemis de la France.[146]

The former colonizers of Saint-Domingue proclaimed that abolitionist "negrophilism" was a "political monstrosity," a "doctrine of blood" propelled by the emotional weakness of the "enemies" of the French Empire. "Negrophilism" is hence connoted as the crux of Atlantic revolutions. Even more, the slaveholders introduce another pathology. "J'ai dit qu'on oubliait trop souvent les maux qu'a fait la mulâtromanie. Cette affection, accompagnée de résultats politiques, devenait attentatoire au système colonial: cette affection, vraie ou simulée, de la part de ceux qui voulurent la faire passer en loi, donna lieu aux premiers désordres de Saint-Domingue."[147] This exploration of the "origins of unhappiness" assesses the blame of the Haitian Revolution and concludes that the source of "disorder" was "mulattomania" as a revolutionary aftershock

---

[145] "Origine des malheurs de Saint-Domingue." Translation to English: "Can the colonizer who has penetrated the source of his misfortunes, the causes of the devastation of Saint-Domingue, cast his eyes on France, without his ulcerated heart being immediately ripped between pain and indignation? Covered in his blood, surrounded by the corpses of his parents, of his friends, the colonizer dreamed of his homeland, and it was from her that all of his misfortunes came to him!"
[146] "Origine des malheurs de Saint-Domingue." Translation to English: "as an exclusive affection, considered in its effects, is therefore a political monstrosity, from which America and Europe must be guarded. According to the conduct of all the French who, in the metropole or in the colonies, have professed this doctrine of blood, this affection is a cowardice, which has only been useful to the enemies of France."
[147] "Origine des malheurs de Saint-Domingue." Translation to English: "I said that we all too often forget the evils of mulattomania. This affection, accompanied by political results, became detrimental to the colonial system: this affection, true or simulated, on the part of those who wished to make it pass into law, gave rise to the first disorders of Saint-Domingue."

from France, which in turn ignited "negrophilism." The "political results" of this "mania" were triggered by legal modifications in response to "affections" that could be "true or simulated." The retelling of the Haitian Revolution by the enslaving class of Saint-Domingue is mostly concerned with White emotions that are villainized for being swayed by deceptive Black passions, villainized only to further drive the revolutionary victory of the enslaved to the margins of history.

The primary sources of the Haitian Revolution evidence how Atlantic slavery was conceptualized as an emotional economy that ensured the international standing of European empires and the capitalistic exploitation of colonized spaces. The emotional economy of racialized slavery had to remain uninterrupted, since Black enslavement in the Atlantic world guaranteed the preservation of White happiness and capitalistic confidence. For the French Empire, the perpetual emotional policing of Blackness was crucial to the "profitability" of slavery linked to the permanence of coloniality and racialized oppression, "profitability" well beyond the economic "productivity" of the institution of slavery itself. The preservation of White happiness was ferociously advocated through the relativism of slavery. Those without property had to be enslaved: that was the irremediable global order. Now, coincidentally, to be without property was to be irremediably Black, and vice versa. The imperial gaze proclaimed that the condition of slavery arose from the emotionally underdeveloped "spirit" of Blackness. The end of the emotionally superior slavery led by European empires would represent an emotional involution toward Africa, toward "Black rage." "Black rage" was strategically connoted as cannibalistic, as not only potentially killing Whiteness, but also potentially eating it whole. The enslavement of Black communities then kept White power flourishing and blissful. Not only did the economic order of racialized slavery "guarantee" White advantage, but also ending slavery entailed "sacrificing" White happiness, White life as it was conceived: dominant and wasteful. The discourse of "White terror" had nothing to do with fear at all, as only the enslaved experienced Fear in slaveholding regimes. White "terror" was nothing else than the slaveholding objection to having to subject themselves to the "expense" of respecting Black emotionality.

"Love" toward the enslaved had to be unfailingly and invasively regulated within coloniality, since, while slaveholding "love" was deemed legitimate and as nurturing a "sweeter" Black existence, abolitionism and the resistance of the enslaved were regarded as lethal and simulated transgressions of "love." The revolutions of the enslaved were projected as a selfish turn from an infantile, emotionally undeveloped marginality to the wrongful overthrow of a "paternal" and "gentle" regime, a "parricide" perpetrated by African emotional tyranny. Just as exponents of scientific racism constructed Blackness as inherently emotionally misleading, colonizer discourse denoted antislavery thought as a hypocritical and simulated "love of Blackness." This "love" was sparked by infectious deception, the same deception emerging from the nature of Black emotional bodies. The rhetoric of the White slaveholders of Saint-Domingue ultimately made the victory of the Haitian Revolution all about White people: the White people who made the mistake of being misled by Black emotional performativity of a shared humanity, the White agency (and bloodline) that led to the triumph of the Haitian Revolution. "Black rage" was recalled only as marginal, emotionally inhuman, and, following the mythology of "imperial fear," "terrifying." The revolution of the enslaved was thus primarily regarded as a colonial disruption of sensibility. This disruption went against the imperial monopoly over who could "love," who could love others and themselves. After all, the tale of Atlantic slavery was one of "love." Slaveholders who loved the enslaved too much to let them hurt themselves: that was their monopoly. Loving and happy enslaved people who followed their passions too intensely: the whip would remind them there was a price for breathing. Revolutionary discord that was the consequence of loving a deceptive Blackness. Love was embraced as long as it did not challenge the economic order that sanctioned Whiteness to conceive its happiness in correlation with how much it emotionally dehumanized Blackness.

> *A mother and a daughter. Drums. Suckling. She is sold. She is sold. I am sold. He will take you away. He will take me. He will take. His icy eyes. I close my eyes. I am not sold. He is not. I am with you. She is.*

4

The "Abolition" of an Economic Apparatus of Feelings

> Lift six-foot, seven-foot, eight-foot bunch
> Daylight come and me wanna go home.
> —"Day-O (The Banana Boat Song)"

The perhaps most famous scene from the 1988 film *Beetlejuice*[1] shows the "possession" of Catherine O'Hara's character during a dinner with house guests: the White hostess suddenly cannot control her body and dances in an exaggerated manner, while lip synching to the Jamaican folk song known as "Day-O (The Banana Boat Song)," as sung by Jamaican American singer Harry Belafonte. This contagious possession soon spreads to all members of the table, and the "comedic value" of this episode of the film is driven by a White-dominated cast being "haunted" by the "exotic" music and voice of a Black man, resonating the deep-rooted mockery of the religions of the enslaved. The jerky and uncoordinated contortions of the cast could distract from further implications beyond the fetishization and commodification of Blackness. Beyond authentic concerns about cultural appropriation lie the historical origins and lyrics of this Jamaican work song.[2] The lyrics speak of laboring "all night on a drink of rum" while carrying heavy loads of bananas ("lift six-foot, seven-foot, eight-foot bunch"). Daylight comes, and they want to go home. The *Beetlejuice* scene both appropriates and silences the pain

---

[1] Tim Burton (dir.), *Beetlejuice* (film), Geffen Company, 1988.
[2] See *Trinidad Carnival: The Cultural Politics of a Transnational Festival*, edited by Garth L. Green & Philip W. Scher (Bloomington: Indiana University Press, 2007), 186–190.

conveyed by the Black longing to go home, while "performing" the presumed absence of self-control of the Black emotional Other.

The setting of "Day-O (The Banana Boat Song)" is a Jamaica with the historical wound of the recent racialized genocide of the Morant Bay Revolution. In 1865, Black Jamaicans protested extreme poverty, racialized taxation, disenfranchisement in the form of property qualifications for voting, and systemic racialized exploitation long after the legal "abolition" of slavery.[3] Governor Edward John Eyre decreed martial law, which resulted in the murder of around four hundred Black Jamaicans and the flogging of around six hundred.[4] The acquittal of Governor Eyre was facilitated by the apologetic pleas of the White English elite, including prominent figures like Charles Dickens and Thomas Carlyle. The Black longing to go home before sunrise encompassed in "Day-O (The Banana Boat Song)" is therefore fueled by the painful historical legacies of the "post-emancipation" era: the perpetuation of the long days of racialized exploitation and the unforgiving punishment of Black expression of anger, the political antagonism of "Black rage." The ridicule of these legacies by Tim Burton's film is revealing. Jerky, sensual, silly. The possession of the White body by the Black "spirit" is abstracted as humorous, as creating levity. Because soon White emotional self-governance brutally takes over everything.

The White abolitionist movement of the eighteenth and nineteenth centuries was similarly a performative affirmation of White emotional "superiority" and "benevolence" over racialized emotional otherness. While the sentimentalist propaganda of White abolitionism highlighted discourses of enslaved "unhappiness" and "broken" familial structures, its emotional imagery was fixed on imperial agendas about the White family unit and capitalist society. Racialized segregation, human experimentation, colonial oppression, and mass incarceration were normalized by the systematic emotional policing and criminalization of the "formerly" enslaved during and after the "post-emancipation" era. The ascent of the modern carcerality of Black emotions was manufactured by the imperial expectation for the Black body to serve by self-containing emotional criminality and for the Empire, as the Master, to inflict ever-escalating genocidal violence on the emotional Other. Prominent works

---

[3] Edward B. Rugemer, *The Problem of Emancipation: The Caribbean Roots of the American Civil War* (Baton Rouge: Louisiana State University Press, 2008).
[4] Dawn P. Harris, *Punishing the Black Body: Marking Social and Racial Structures in Barbados and Jamaica* (Athens: University of Georgia Press, 2017).

of twentieth-century media capitalized on the intensification of archetypes of emotional criminalization and politics of respectability framed by scientific racism as narrative devices, such as the "angry Black woman," the sympathetic token Black best friend, and the "White savior." Similar to the possession scene from *Beetlejuice*, twentieth-century media both arrogated and marginalized Black voices, consolidating archetypes that profited from the emotional penalization of Blackness.

THE SENTIMENTALITY OF WHITE ABOLITIONISM

Scholarship has argued that British "antislavery sentiment" was present during the "first century of imperial expansion," but was thwarted by the power of colonial enslaving systems, which led to British abolitionists shifting their efforts toward the language of "reform."[5] It has further been theorized that it is the "culture of sympathy" of the eighteenth century that made it "fashionable" to speak of the enslaved as exemplifying "wounded innocence."[6] Eighteenth-century "antislavery" rhetoric justified "reform" with insistent imagery of a "suffering humanity."[7] The academic conversation has explored how White abolitionism sustained "gendered assumptions and exclusions"[8] and how the role of "sentiment" in White antislavery and reformist pleas represented a tactic to promote "empathy for the moral justifications, shelters, and alibis" of their "philanthropic" projects.[9] Now, some scholars have concluded that the "intellectual similarities" between White abolitionism and anti-abolitionism were far more than their differences.[10] In response to "enlightened" concepts about liberty, both White abolitionists and anti-abolitionists dismissed the economic value of slavery, emphasizing "race" as a marker for "incapacity."[11] This also explains why the "transformation" of anti-abolitionist discourse about the enslaved "from a tragic

---

[5] See Christopher Leslie Brown, *Moral Capital: Foundations of British Abolitionism* (Chapel Hill: University of North Carolina Press, 2012), 55.

[6] Brown, *Moral Capital*, 48.

[7] Richard B. Newman, *Abolitionism: A Very Short Introduction* (Oxford: Oxford University Press, 2018), 6.

[8] Pamela Scully & Diana Paton, *Gender and Slave Emancipation in the Atlantic World* (Durham, NC: Duke University Press, 2005), 3.

[9] Gerard Laurence Aching, *Freedom from Liberation: Slavery, Sentiment, and Literature in Cuba* (Bloomington: Indiana University Press, 2015), 12.

[10] Margaret Abruzzo, *Polemical Pain: Slavery, Cruelty, and the Rise of Humanitarianism* (Baltimore, MD: Johns Hopkins University Press, 2011), 8.

[11] David Brion Davis, *The Problem of Slavery in the Age of Emancipation* (New York: Vintage, 2014), 6.

figure to a contented one" simultaneously responded to "shifting conceptions of the moral meaning of pain."[12] In fact, it has been contended that the depiction of Black suffering in eighteenth-century White abolitionism was distinguished by the fetishization of the "spectacle" of corporeal pain, the normalization of the master–enslaved relationship, and the animalization of Blackness.[13] Moreover, it has also been stated that there were "parallels" and "borrowings" between minstrelsy and White abolitionism in the United Kingdom and the United States during the nineteenth century.[14] Now, just as evidenced in the intellectual history of scientific racism, the resemblances between White "antislavery" and proslavery thought go beyond "borrowings," "spectacles" of pain, and the trivialization of masterhood. Ultimately, both White abolitionism and anti-abolitionism were compelled by the political proclamation that White capitalist family formations were emotionally superior and had to remain emotionally dominant, regardless of Black enslavement or "freedom." There was never a collective White project to abolish the emotional economy premised on racialized exploitation.

When Anthony Benezet and William Warburton denounced the "calamitous state of the enslaved Negroes" in the British colonies in 1766, the White abolitionists emphasized selective "insensibility" amid recent revolutionary history: "can it be an inquiry indifferent to any how many of those who distinguish themselves as the Advocates of Liberty, remain insensible and inattentive to the treatment of thousands and tens of thousands."[15] Benezet and Warburton construct "inattentiveness" toward suffering as negligent and in opposition to the struggle for Liberty. Furthermore, their plea utilizes emotional imagery to underline the universality of religion: "the groans, the dying groans, which daily

---

[12] Abruzzo, *Polemical Pain*, 6.
[13] Stephen Ahern, "Introduction: The Bonds of Sentiment," in *Affect and Abolition in the Anglo-Atlantic, 1770–1830*, edited by Stephen Ahern (New York: Routledge, 2016).
[14] Robert Nowatzki, *Representing African Americans in Transatlantic Abolitionism and Blackface Minstrelsy* (Baton Rouge: Louisiana State University Press, 2010), 2.
[15] "Caution and Warning to Great-Britain and Her Colonies, in a Short Representation of the Calamitous State of the Enslaved Negroes in the British Dominions: Collected from Various Authors, and Submitted to the Serious Consideration of All, More Especially of Those in Power (1766) by Benezet, Anthony, 1713–1784 & Warburton, William, 1698–1779," Princeton University, Firestone Library, Rare Books and Special Collections, Lapidus 4.28. Benezet and Warburton's claims were collected from multiple authors.

ascend to God, the common father of mankind, from the broken hearts of those deeply oppressed creatures."[16] The trope of "groans ascending" to the "Father" not only condemns the pain of "broken hearts" of the "deeply oppressed creatures," but also implies that slaveholders will be subjected to divine punishment for tormenting animalized beings. The abolitionists proceed to argue that slaveholders had "contributed to enflame every noxious passion of corrupt nature in the Negroes; they have incited them to make war upon another."[17] Therefore, according to Benezet and Warburton, the "calamitous state" of enslaved people had been effected by slaveholders, by those who had fostered an atmosphere of war and violence that sparked the ruin of innately "corrupt" Black bodies with "noxious passions." Their emotional abolitionist discourse is encompassed by their denunciation of enslaved family separations.

> In this melancholy scene mothers are seen hanging over their daughters, bedewing their naked breasts with tears, and daughters clinging to their parents; not knowing what new stage of distress must follow their separation; or if ever they shall meet again; and here what sympathy, what commiseration are they to expect; why indeed, if they will not separate as readily as their owners think proper, the whipper is called for, and the lash exercised upon their naked bodies, till obliged to part.[18]

The "melancholy" of the family separation is conveyed through "tears" flowing over "naked Black breasts." Since "naked Black breasts" had been historically connoted as "monstrous," this image propels "pity" toward the rupture of a familial bond, though incarnated by a still racialized, inherently degraded, and anomalous enslaved Other. This "pity" is thus more specifically directed at the unexpected outcome of a maternal embrace, the fragmentation of a family unit. Benezet and Warburton craft a trope that portrays slaveholding violence as excessive, aiming to first summon the image of the enslaved aching for "sympathy" and then channel that "sympathy" toward the White abolitionist cause itself, outside the emotionally "corrupt" Black body.

Granville Sharp campaigned for White abolitionism in Great Britain by pointing to how the institution of slavery complicates the conception of British common law as framed by "social love."

---

[16] "Caution and Warning to Great-Britain and Her Colonies."
[17] "Caution and Warning to Great-Britain and Her Colonies."
[18] "Caution and Warning to Great-Britain and Her Colonies."

The "Abolition" of an Economic Apparatus of Feelings 173

All laws ought to be founded upon the principle of *"doing as one would be done by"* and indeed this principle seems to be the very basis of the English constitution; for what precaution could possibly be more effectual for that purpose, than the right which we enjoy for being *judged by our peers*, creditable persons of the vicinage; especially, as we may likewise claim the right of excepting against any particular jury-man, who might be suspected of partiality? This law breathes the pure spirit of liberty, equity, and social love; being calculated to maintain that consideration and mutual regard, which one person ought to have for another, however unequal in rank or station.[19]

By binding the concepts of "liberty, equity, and social love" as the main motives of the Law, Sharp critiques slavery as incompatible with the "English constitution." According to the abolitionist, this legal incompatibility should produce British "horror" toward enslavement in the colonies, regardless of their "considerable distance."

These considerations, I say, must inspire us with indignation and horror even though the evil, at present, is at a considerable distance from us. But if the advocates, for the *unnatural and unlawful claims*, against which I contend, should receive such encouragement as to *confirm their pretentions*; the same must inevitably introduce by degrees a Toleration of the West India Slavery, with all its *direful consequences*, into this Kingdom: which, added to the manifold corruptions and depravities into which this Kingdom has already unhappily fallen, will certainly cause our measure of Iniquity to overflow, and, in all probability, draw down upon us some dreadful and speedy *national* calamity, besides that severe judgment, which is already too apparent amongst us, I mean that deplorable *Hardness of the Heart*, and abandoned *Spirit of Injustice*, which has rendered the publication of this remonstrance necessary.[20]

Sharp theorizes the "toleration" of slavery in the British Caribbean colonies as an "unhappy fall" toward the "national calamity" of "hardness of the heart." Hence, his words aim to encourage national "indignation and horror" from a distance, which is reckoned as the origin of the "spirit of justice" and the triumph of "natural law." Precisely to engender "indignation," Sharp stresses the "horror" of the images of the Middle Passage.

---

[19] "A Representation of the Injustice and Dangerous Tendency of Tolerating Slavery: or of Admitting the Least Claim of Private Property in the Persons of Men, in England (1769) by Sharp, Granville, 1735–1813," Princeton University, Firestone Library, Rare Books and Special Collections, Lapidus 4.11.

[20] "An Appendix to the Representation (Printed in the Year 1769) of the Injustice and Dangerous Tendency of Tolerating Slavery, or, of Admitting the Least Claim of Private Property in the Persons of Men in England by Sharp, Granville, 1735–1813," Princeton University, Firestone Library, Rare Books and Special Collections, Lapidus 4.16.

> What! is it then the voice of humanity that we hear pleading in defence of a practice, the very idea of which must excite, in every breast susceptible of the feelings of humanity, amazement and horror! View yon vessel, with sails expanded, ploughing the deep – Contemplate for a moment the scene which it exhibits – Within that receptacle of human misery, are contained hundreds of beings, possessing passions and feelings congenial to thine own. – Behold them bereft of every enjoyment which can render life a blessing; exposed to every outrage which can render existence a curse.[21]

The abolitionist conceptualizes the Middle Passage as the "human misery" of beings with "congenial feelings," emphasizing the universality of passions. His plea explicitly exposes those "susceptible" to emotional reactions of "humanity" to the imagery of the Middle Passage. Moreover, Sharp rejects proslavery claims about the "happiness" of the enslaved person by addressing the lack of consent.

> But, at all events, if the personal happiness or benefit of the Slave is, indeed, the primary object of the Slave Merchant, certainly those philanthropists who engage in this traffic, from such noble and generous motives, must consider the previous consent of the Slave as absolutely necessary to give validity to the purchase: if, therefore, he quits his native country voluntarily, what occasion for whips, and racks, and chains, to enforce obedience and submission?[22]

With a cynical tone, Sharp opposes slaveholding discourse about enslaved "happiness" and repudiates the "enforcement" of the whip as a fundamental contradiction that intends to mask the absence of legal consent. Furthermore, the abolitionist renders the "tyranny" of slavery as driven by a "callous" heart.

> Haughty and unfeeling tyrant! whose heart has long been callous to all the sensibilities which distinguish and which ennoble humanity; in vain would the miserable beings, subject to thy dominion, complain to thee of the pangs they felt, when, with reverted, eyes, they cast the last long lingering look upon their native shores! Engrossed by one fatal passion, the rage of accumulating wealth, how canst thou sympathize with the emotions excited by the various relations of social and domestic *life*; "by all the charities of father, son, and brother?" – Untaught to weep with those that weep, thy mind possesses no congenial feelings with those whose miseries have, in thy estimation, degraded them almost below the condition of humanity.[23]

---

[21] Granville Sharp, "An Essay on the African Slave Trade (1790)," Gloucestershire Archives, 13/5/11.
[22] Sharp, "An Essay on the African Slave Trade."
[23] Sharp, "An Essay on the African Slave Trade."

Sharp conceives masters as ridding and "unteaching" themselves of the "congenial feelings" of humanity of the "miserable" enslaved. All of the passions of slaveholders are amalgamated into one: the "fatal passion" of the "accumulation" of capital. This economic pursuit derails "unfeeling" slaveholders from "weeping" with those who "weep" due to their enslavement. The "callousness" of the master is such that the "noise of the lash" and the "groans and shrieks of the wretched sufferers" do not disrupt their "repose."[24] Therefore, the abolitionist denounces the selective "unteaching" of slaveholding societies to accelerate their "unfeeling" economic growth, even in detriment to the interpretation of the law. Now, a paradox arises when Sharp contextualizes the imperial discomfort surrounding the "political inconveniences" of the abolition of slavery: "the plantations in the West Indies can be cultivated only by Negroes; the climate is fatal to all but African constitutions; and the labour such as that hardy race of men only can support."[25] At the end of the day, Sharp's answer to the "political inconveniences" of the abolition of slavery does not negate the imperial profit from biological determinism at all, but, on the contrary, it emphasizes the permanence of the racialization of labor: "Numerous and well-authenticated facts incontestably demonstrate that, with mild and indulgent treatment, the present number of Slaves in the West-India Islands might not only be preserved from diminution, but would admit of considerable increase."[26] The abolitionist reaffirms that "universal experience proves the soil of every country to be most advantageously improved and cultivated by the voluntary labours of the native inhabitants."[27] Sharp advocates for "voluntary" racialized labor under a "mild and indulgent treatment," under the premise of the "social love" of Law. In the White abolitionist project, there was no plan to eradicate the "fatal passion" of capitalistic racialized exploitation, to revolutionize the power dynamics of imperial domination, or to truly uphold emotional equality. In fact, the actual plan was to enforce and expand racial capitalism, as the "feelings" of those who were enslaved and Black were not "congenial" enough to have a voice in creating a post-emancipation world.

With Granville Sharp as one of the instigators of the Somerset Case, this canonical jurisprudence also highlights the absence of a definition of

---

[24] Sharp, "An Essay on the African Slave Trade."
[25] Sharp, "An Essay on the African Slave Trade."
[26] Sharp, "An Essay on the African Slave Trade."
[27] Sharp, "An Essay on the African Slave Trade."

slavery in positive law. One of the lawyers of the Somerset case, Francis Hargrave, also utilized emotional imagery to persuade the Earl of Mansfield about the moral and emotional destructiveness of slavery.

> From this view on the condition of slavery, it will be easy to decide its destructive consequences. – It corrupts the morals of the master, by freeing him from those restraints with respect to his slave, so necessary for the control of the human passions, so beneficial in promoting the practice and conforming the habit of virtue. – It is dangerous to the master, because his oppression excites implacable resentment and hatred in the slave, and the extreme misery of his condition continually prompts him to risk the gratification of them, and his situation daily furnishes the opportunity.[28]

Hargrave proposes a symbiotic relationship between the "passions" of the master and the enslaved person, again straying away from the alleged avowal of "congenial feelings" of his movement in his argumentation for the Somerset case. While the master loses the "restraint" of "human passions," the "miserable" enslaved develop an "implacable resentment." Thus, this abolitionist dissertation is preoccupied with the "dignity" of British men, warning about the "corruption" of the master and the rising peril of the "hatred" of the enslaved in British colonies.

Akin to proslavery discourse, multiple White "antislavery" petitions claimed that the abolitionist project would jump-start the emotional "education" of Black communities.

> It has not yet been experienced, how far the common principles of action among freemen may awake the industry, or dilate the mind of a Negro: we have therefore no right, no pretence, to insinuate even a doubt that their natures are inferior to us. The love of independence, of gain, of fame; the gratification of pride, vanity, ambition, avarice, and every human passion, would certainly raise among them a spirit of industry and achievement, which would enable them greatly to surpass the labours to which, at present, the lash alone compels them.[29]

This interpretation of the motive of abolitionism is influenced by historical determinism and hence denies the "emotional development" of Blackness. The prospect of abolition is codified as a potential first encounter with "passions" that would possibly engender a previously

---

[28] "An Argument in the Case of James Sommersett a Negro: Lately Determined by the Court of King's Bench: Wherein It Is Attempted to Demonstrate the Present Unlawfulness of Domestic Slavery in England. To Which Is Prefixed a State of the Case. By Mr. Hargrave, One of the Counsel for the Negro (1772) by Hargrave, Francis, 1741?–1821," Princeton University, Firestone Library, Rare Books and Special Collections, Lapidus.

[29] "A Plan for the abolition of Slavery in the West Indies (1772)," Princeton University, Firestone Library, Rare Books and Special Collections, Lapidus 4.12.

stagnant "spirit of industry and achievement." Not only does the text contend that the whip keeps Black emotions dormant, but it also declares that Africa itself does not produce an atmosphere of feeling, mirroring eventual Hegelian thought.

Thomas Clarkson, founder of the Society for Effecting the Abolition of the Slave Trade in Great Britain, famously won a Cambridge University essay prize with the version in Latin of "An Essay on the Slavery and Commerce of the Human Species, Particularly the African." This essay intends to encompass the transatlantic suffering generated by Atlantic slavery.

> To descant but upon a single instance of the kind must be productive of pain to the ear of sensibility and freedom. Consider the sensations of the unhappy man, who is carried off by a ruffian that has been lurking to intercept him in the night. Separated from every thing which he esteems in life, without the possibility of bidding his friends adieu, behold him overwhelmed in tears – wringing his hands in despair-looking back upon the spot in which all his hopes and wishes lay – while his family at home are waiting for him with anxiety and suspense – are waiting perhaps, for sustenance – are agitated between hope and fear – till length of absence confirm the latter, and they are immediately plunged into inconceivable misery and distress.[30]

Enslaved family separations incite "inconceivable misery and distress" on both sides of the Atlantic. This rhetoric delineates the stages of the emotional involution of Atlantic slavery in order to compel empathy toward the "unhappy man" and dismay toward the "ruffian." The description of the family separation is centered on the dismantlement of the patriarchal and capitalistic arrangement of the family unit. Clarkson crafts an imploration for the "ear of sensibility and freedom" to campaign for the abolition of the "slave trade," fueled by notions of the primacy of White "masculinity." The plea ends up being a lot more about the loss of the figure of the Father than the loss of Liberty and Equality.

The Pennsylvania Society for Promoting the Abolition of Slavery would underline the "universality" of emotions by religious principles: "It having pleased the Creator of the world, to make one flesh, all the children of men – it becomes them to consult and promote each other's happiness, as members of the same family, however diversified they may be, by colour, situation, religion, or different states of society."[31] The act

---

[30] "An Essay on the Slavery and Commerce of the Human Species, Particularly the African: Translated from a Latin Dissertation (1786) by Clarkson, Thomas, 1760–1846," Princeton University, Firestone Library, Rare Books and Special Collections, Lapidus 4.16.1.

[31] "The Constitution of the Pennsylvania Society for Promoting the Abolition of Slavery and the Relief of Free Negroes, Unlawfully Held in Bondage: Begun in the Year 1774 and

of deliverance becomes an affirmation of both the divine creation and the "difference" in societal development of those who are forcibly racialized, colonized, evangelized, benefited with the gift of religious "happiness." Likewise, "Slavery, a Poem" by British writer Hannah More first affirms the universality of emotions to then rely on the emotional othering of Blackness.

> Does then th'immortal principle within
> Change with the casual color of a skin?
> Does matter govern spirit? or is mind
> Degraded by the form to which 'tis join'd?
> No: they have heads to think, and hearts to feel,
> And souls to act, with firm tho' erring zeal?
> For they have keen affections, kind desires,
> Love strong as death, and active patriot fires;
> All the rude energy, the fervid flame,
> Of high soul'd passions and ingenuous shame;
> Strong, but luxuriant virtues boldly shoot
> From wild vigour of a savage root.
> Nor weak their sense of honor's proud control
> For pride is virtue in a Pagan soul.[32]

More represents the racialized "Pagan soul" as feeling intensely. The "high soul'd passions" of Blackness are denoted as "rude" and "fervid." While the writer starts this exploration of feelings by announcing the presence of "keen affections" and "kind desires," she goes deeper into the presumed emotional overindulgences of Blackness, reaching its othered "Pagan soul." More later portrays abolitionism as the endeavor to "respect" the universality of emotions.

> The shrieking babe; the agonizing wife –
> She, wretch forlorn! is dragg'd by hostile hands,
> To distant tyrants sold, in distant lands;
> Transmitted mis'ries, and successive chains,
> The sole had heritage her child obtains;
> Ev'n this last wretched boon their foes deny,
> To weep together, or together die.
> By felon hands, by one relentless stroke,
> See the fond links of feeling Nature broke,

Enlarged on the Twenty-Third of April 1787: To Which Are Added the Acts of the General Assembly of Pennsylvania, for the Gradual Abolition of Slavery," Princeton University, Firestone Library, Rare Books and Special Collections, Lapidus 4.35.

[32] "Slavery, a Poem by Hannah More," Princeton University, Firestone Library, Rare Books and Special Collections, Lapidus 3.32.

> The fibers twisting round a parent's heart,
> Torn from their grasp, and bleeding as they part.
> Hold, murderers, hold! Nor aggravate distress;
> Respect the passions you yourselves possess;
> Ev'n you, or ruffian heart, and ruthless hand,
> Love your own offspring – love your native land.[33]

The author depicts Atlantic slavery as denying the African diaspora from "weeping together" in their unifying suffering and "Nature" as "breaking fond links of feeling." The poet urges slaveholding "ruffian hearts" to "respect" the "passions" that they themselves "possess." Abolitionism is then recapitulated as "respectful" toward passions, not people. Slaveholders are essentially summoned to show "respect" toward White feelings, since the emotional expressiveness of Blackness is concurrently ardently differentiated.

Former captain of enslaving ships and self-proclaimed abolitionist John Newton abstracted abolitionism through the lens of English motherhood. Newton claimed his experiences as an enslaving captain substantiated that the "nature and effects of that unhappy and disgraceful branch of commerce" contradict the "feelings of humanity."[34] Newton proposed British maternal sentiment as the most compelling driving force toward the emancipation of enslaved people.

> I am persuaded, that every tender mother, who feasts her eyes and her mind, when she contemplates the infant in her arms, will commiserate the poor Africans. – But why do I speak of one child, when we have heard and read a melancholy story, too notoriously true to admit of contradiction, of more than a hundred grown slaves, thrown into the sea.[35]

Emancipation was therefore conceptualized as a reflection of Eurocentric sentimentality, of White familial bonds, even by those "abolitionists" who had perpetrated the Trade. Meanwhile, French abolitionism constructed the history of conquest and colonization of the Americas as a European, flawed conflation of wealth and "happiness."

> Aux Sociétés Philantropiques et à toutes les amis sensibles, de toutes nos erreurs, la plus funeste à la félicité humaine, est celle d'avoir toujours considéré de grandes richesses comme la réalité du Bonheur; jadis la soif de l'or, fit massacrer les habitans du Nouveau Monde; aujourd'hui la même cupidité nous entraîne à faire

---

[33] "Slavery, a Poem by Hannah More."
[34] "Thoughts upon the African Slave Trade (1788) by Newton, John, 1725–1807," Princeton University, Firestone Library, Rare Books and Special Collections, Lapidus 4.18.
[35] "Thoughts upon the African Slave Trade."

égorger une partie des peuples de l'Afrique, & à leur enlever des esclaves pour cultiver l'Amérique. En sommes-nous plus heureux?[36]

The illusory "happiness" and insatiable "thirst for gold" of the European colonizer serve as catalysts of global massacres and "hatred" from their offspring, augmenting the "vices and miseries of the human race."

Enfin, après avoir rempli les quatre parties du monde de meurtres & de calamités, nous mourrons egoists, malheureux, détestés de tous ceux qui nous environnent, souvent même de nos propres enfans, sans avoir rien fait pour la postérité, que de multiplier les vices & les misères du genre humain. Tels sont les tristes effets de l'insatiable avarice & de la soif toujours renaissante de l'or.[37]

The "insatiable greed" of Empires propelled a globalized expansion of sadness. French abolitionist thought proclaimed that, while enslaved bodies were forced to feel the "pain" of enslavement, slaveholders were marked by a "heart of stone": "Tandis que les Noirs ne respirent que pour la douleur, & souffrent des premiers besoins de la vie, des colons durs & coleres n'ont plus de pitié pour eux: leurs cœurs sont de pierre, & la mort même de ces infortunés cesse de les affecter."[38] French abolitionists pointed to the "insensibilité meurtrière"[39] of masters as the root of despair in the "West." The weight is placed on the "monstrosity" of slaveholding violence, which remains emotionally detached from spectacles of blood and pain. "Ils contemplent en riant les coups de fouet qui sont quelquefois ruisseler le sang de ces malheureux. Les cris de ces infortunés, losqu'on met du sel & du poivre dans leurs plaies, excitent

---

[36] "Le more-lack; ou, Essai sur les moyens les plus doux & les plus équitables d'abolir la traite & l'esclavage des [racial slur] d'Afrique, en conservant aux colonies tous les avantages d'une population agricole (1789) by Le Cointe-Marsillac," Princeton University, Firestone Library, Rare Books and Special Collections, Lapidus. Translation to English: "To the Philanthropic Societies and to all sensible friends, of all our errors, the most disastrous to human felicity is that of having always considered great riches as the reality of Happiness; once the thirst for gold had the inhabitants of the New World massacred; now the same greed leads us to slaughter some of the peoples of Africa, and to take slaves from them to cultivate America. Are we happier for it?"

[37] "Le more-lack." Translation to English: "Finally, after having filled the four parts of the world with murders and calamities, we die egotistical, unhappy, hated by all who surround us, often even by our own children, without having done anything for posterity than to multiply the vices and the miseries of the human race. Such are the sad effects of the insatiable greed and ever-reviving thirst for gold."

[38] "Le more-lack." Translation to English: "While black people breathe only for pain, and suffer from the first needs of life, hard and angry settlers have no pity for them: their hearts are of stone, and the very death of these unfortunates ceases to affect them."

[39] "Le more-lack." Translation to English: "deadly insensibility."

leurs fouris moqueurs ... Monstres!"⁴⁰ The "monstrous" nature of this emotional detachment toward the torture of the enslaved lies in the capacity of masters to have sanctuary from the suffering of the enslaved in their "sumptuous" residences. The emphasis put on White displays of wealth still insists on sustaining a historicist understanding of emotional progress.

> Tyrans cruels, persécuteurs farouches, vous que la Nature ne fit naître que pour devenir les bourreaux du genre humain, quittez vos tables somptueuses, & visitez les cases de vos [racial slur], où tout annonce la peine & la douloureuse indigence! Voyez-les dans la dureté des travaux, nuds, souffrans, exposés à la rigueur d'un soleil brûlant, dégoûtans de sueurs & quelquefois de sang, mêlé des larmes du désespoir!⁴¹

French abolitionism emphasized the contemporaneous apathy of capitalistic production as a way to advocate for the end of its dependence on legal slavery and to still allow for the economic exploitation of the "underdeveloped" Blackness that historical determinism had formulated. In fact, the White elite membership of the Société des amis des Noirs mostly advocated for the gradual abolition of slavery, while purportedly decrying the torture of enslaved people due to the "thirst for gold" and the associated dissemination of enslaved "fear of pain."

> On ne peut rien dire de raisonnable en faveur d'un commerce où tous les crimes sont des instrumens nécessaires; on ne peut pas mieux justifier cette soif de l'or, qui porte à employer l'effroi des supplices pour excéder de travail des créatures humaines, pour mesurer ce que l'on peut en exiger, non sur leurs forces naturelles, mais sur les efforts que arrache aux malheureux, la crainte de la douleur.⁴²

---

[40] "Le more-lack." Translation to English: "They contemplate, laughing, the lashes that are sometimes streaming the blood of these unfortunates. The cries of these unfortunate people, when salt and pepper are added to their wounds, excite their mockery ... Monsters!"

[41] "Le more-lack." Translation to English: "Cruel tyrants, fierce persecutors, you whom Nature only gave birth for you to become the executioners of the human race, leave your sumptuous tables, and visit the huts of your black people, where everything indicates sorrow and painful indigence! See them in the harshness of work, knotted, suffering, exposed to the rigor of a burning sun, disgusted with sweat and sometimes with blood, mixed with tears of despair!"

[42] "Adresse de la Société des amis des noirs à l'Assemblée nationale, a toutes les villes de commerce, à toutes les manufactures, aux colonies, à toutes les société des amis de la Constitution; adresse dans laquelle on approfondit les relations politiques et commerciales entre la Métropole et les colonies, etc. (1791)," Princeton University, Firestone Library, Rare Books and Special Collections, Lapidus. Translation to English: "We cannot say anything reasonable in favor of a commerce in which all crimes are necessary instruments; this thirst for gold cannot be better justified, which leads to the use of the

The institution of slavery was deemed excessive due to its reliance on violence and torture, as it reflected the character of the "monstrous" slaveholder. Yet there was no argument for the political integration of the enslaved within the speeches of French abolitionism. On the contrary, the Société des amis des Noirs stressed racialist notions about the "natural strengths" of Black bodies and the emotional otherness of Blackness. In the text *On the Cultural Achievements of Negroes*, one of the most influential members of the Société, Henri Grégoire, held on to concepts of emotional erraticism from geographical determinism as his way of counteracting slaveholding racism. The cleric claimed that climate "merely aggravates" certain inclinations and does not exclusively determine the advancement of human groups.

> The accusation of indolence, which is not without some degree of truth, is often exaggerated. It is exaggerated in the mouths of those who are in the habit of employing a bloody whip to conduct slaves to forced labor; it is true in the sense that men cannot have a great inclination to industry when they own nothing, not even their own person, and when the fruits of their sweat feed the luxury or avarice of a merciless master. Nor are men inclined to be industrious in regions favored by nature, where her spontaneous products, or work that requires no great effort, provide abundantly for man's natural needs. But whether they are black or white, all men are hardworking when stimulated by the spirit of property, by utility, or by pleasure.[43]

According to abbot Grégoire's philosophy, sense of property is the incentive of human prosperity, and climate does impact but does not erase the capability to minimally overcome the little "inclination to industry" present in warmer climates. Grégoire proclaims that the racialist discourse of the "indolence" of Black bodies is based on "truth," but an "exaggerated" truth. Nevertheless, the abolitionist was more categorical when he later stated that Blackness has little resistance to pleasure and that this lack of moderation is paralleled by an acute endurance to pain,[44] reverberating devastating theories of biological determinism. French abolitionist thought did not provide an alternative to the regime of the "bloody whip" in the generation of productive Blackness, one that could

---

dread of torture in order to exceed the work of human creatures, to measure what may be required of them, not on their natural strengths, but on the efforts taken from the unfortunate, the fear of pain."
[43] Henri Grégoire, *On the Cultural Achievements of Negroes* (Boston: University of Massachusetts Press, 1808), 40.
[44] Grégoire, *On the Cultural Achievements of Negroes*, 40.

"at last" be spontaneously fueled by the "spirit of property" and not by the unfettered tendency to pleasure and painlessness.

US diplomat William Pinkney condemned the "selfish" and "poisonous" practice of slavery in a speech to the House of Delegates of Maryland in 1789: "Eternal infamy awaits the abandoned miscreants, whose selfish souls could ever prompt them to rob unhappy Africa of her sons, and freight them hither by thousands, to poison the fair Eden of liberty with the rank weed of individual bondage!"[45] Pinkney abstracts "liberty" as a divine paradise that has been intoxicated with the "infamous" human destitution of an "unhappy Africa." Moreover, the diplomat constructs slavery as an inherent violation of the laws and ideologies of the United States, isolating the "love of equality" as the foundational "principle of a democracy." "But is the encouragement of civil slavery, by legislative acts, correspondent with the principle of a democracy? Call that principle what you will, the love of *equality*, as defined by some; of *liberty*, as understood by others; such conduct is manifestly in violation of it."[46] Pinkney conceives abolitionism as central to the diplomatic emotional projection of the United States. The diplomat then advises for the end of slavery as a political act that would reverberate in the gratefulness of "millions" toward the United States. Hence, Pinkney advocates for the abolition of slavery solely for the international standing of the United States, as the abolition of slavery was conceived as a statement about the "abolisher" and not about the Black right to freedom.

> Yours too, will be the gratitude of the millions whom this day's vote may give to breathe the air of freedom; yours the flattering approbation of the friends of mankind; and yours the pleasing consciousness of having, under the influence of every nobler sentiment, unloosed the manacles of many a fellow-creature, and led him by the hand to LIBERTY and SOCIAL HAPPINESS![47]

St. George Tucker, professor of law at the College of William and Mary, introduced a proposal for the gradual abolition of slavery in the state of Virginia in 1796, which highlighted the selective morality of the institution of slavery, "such that partial system of morality which confines rights and injuries, to particular complexions; such the effect of that self-love which justifies, or condemns, not according to principle, but to the

---

[45] "Speech of William Pinkney, Esq., in the House of Delegates of Maryland, at Their Session in November 1789 by Pinkney, William, 1764–1822," Princeton University, Firestone Library, Rare Books and Special Collections, Lapidus 4.37.
[46] "Speech of William Pinkney."   [47] "Speech of William Pinkney."

agent."[48] Tucker attacks "self-love" as instigating the "melancholy" of "perpetual warfare" in the continent of Africa: "it is a melancholy, though well-known fact, that in order to furnish supplies of these unhappy people for the purposes of the slave trade, the Europeans have constantly, by the most insidious (I had almost said infernal) arts, fomented a kind of perpetual warfare among ignorant and miserable people of Africa."[49] The emphasis on both the "unhappiness" and the "ignorance" of the racialized drives Tucker to call for the redirection of the "regard for" enslaved "bodies" toward "saving" enslaved "souls" through baptism: "It would have been happy for this unfortunate race of men if the same tender regard for their bodies, had always manifested itself in our laws, as is shewn for their souls in this act."[50] Therefore, Tucker's gradual abolitionism prioritizes the decrease of "self-love" for the collective imperial project of the forced religious conversion of "ignorant" racialized enslaved people.

Former worker of an enslaving ship and plantation owner Thomas Branagan proclaimed himself as an abolitionist writer and stated that the "Lord" would "avenge" African enslaved people. Like other former masters and captains of enslaving ships that shifted into an "abolitionist" role, he conveniently affirmed that his profit from this bloody Trade provided him with authority and "experience" to speak about it and be heard. In a letter written to Napoleon Bonaparte, Branagan declared that the "deep sighs" of "unhappy" enslaved people reached the "Lord," as "patron" of the "afflicted of mankind." His "shift" from "foe to friend" presumedly exempts him from divine "vengeance."

Did the unjust judge, of whom our Saviour, in one of his parabolical discourses, speaks, *avenge the* injured and unfortunate *victim of her adversaries*; and shall not He, who ever is the patron of the widow, the fatherless, and every other species of the afflicted of mankind, avenge and deliver the unhappy sons and daughters of Africa, who, by their deep sighs and doleful groans, cry day and night onto him? Verily he will speedily avenge them.[51]

---

[48] "A Dissertation on Slavery: With a Proposal for the Gradual Abolition of It, in the State of Virginia (1796) by Tucker, St. George, 1752–1827, College of William and Mary," Princeton University, Firestone Library, Rare Books and Special Collections, Lapidus 4.39.
[49] "A Dissertation on Slavery."   [50] "A Dissertation on Slavery."
[51] "A Preliminary Essay, on the Oppression of the Exiled Sons of Africa: Consisting of Animadversions on the Impolicy and Barbarity of the Deleterious Commerce and Subsequent Slavery of the Human Species; To Which Is Added, a Desultory Letter Written to Napoleon Bonaparte, Anno Domini, 1801 by Branagan, Thomas,

Fitting the paradigm of White "antislavery" thought, while the *American Anti-Slavery Almanac* propelled its abolitionist discourse with an accent on the universality of emotions, its rhetoric simultaneously stressed discourses about the "otherness" of Black emotional bodies. In the entry "Two Little Sisters," the nineteenth-century *Almanac* directly speaks to their "young readers."

A TALK WITH MY YOUNG READERS. Little children, love one another. Despise not one of these little ones. Fleecy locks and black complexion cannot alter nature's claim; skins may differ, but affection dwells in black and white the same. Here is a picture of two little (black/small) sisters. They love each other very much. Slaveholders sometimes tear such little children away from their parents and sell them to cruel men who will never let them see their mothers while they live. When you see your kind mother smile sweetly upon you, as you are engaged in your sports, or when she gives you the parting kiss, as you go to your quiet bed, O think of the hapless slave mother, who is in constant alarm, lest the kidnapper should seize her darling babe. When you kneel down at night, pray for the helpless slave child, and its trembling mother.[52]

The *Almanac* narrates a compelling tale of maternal love as a way to introduce familiar imagery for a young White audience. Though the passage underlines the universality of "affection," it also isolates "fleecy locks and black complexion" as the biological "markers" of a racialized Other. Furthermore, the passage refers to the comforts of White children to generate voyeuristic "pity" toward "two little sisters" that could be separated at any moment and toward the continual horror of their "trembling mother." The lens through which the story of the Black sisters is told is through the emotional performativity of the religious devotion and compassionate benevolence of "White innocence."

In another entry called "A Mother's Anguish," the narrative of enslaved children being sold to another slaveholding plantation is likewise framed with a conversation between a White child and her uncle.

Caroline. What is that woman doing, uncle? *Mr. S.* She has an axe in her hand, with which she is killing those little children. *Car.* What made her hate them so? What had they done to her? *Mr. S.* She didn't hate them, my dear. *Car.* I should think she did. What *did* she kill them for? *Mr. S.* I will tell you. She was a slave. She lived in the state of Missouri, a state seven times as large as Massachusetts,

---

1774–1843," Princeton University, Firestone Library, Rare Books and Special Collections, Lapidus Add-1.
[52] "Two Little Sisters, 1837," Schomburg Center for Research in Black Culture, Manuscripts, Archives and Rare Books Division, the American Anti-Slavery Almanac Collection, Sc Rare 326.59-A.

and a thousand miles from here. Those are her own little children, and she loved them very much. When she came home at night, from her day's hard labor, she always hastened to meet her children. It made her feel happy and forget her wretched lot, when she saw them run smiling to meet her, and hold out their little hand to take hold of hers, as you do when your father comes home.[53]

The Black enslaved mother's act of killing her enslaved children with an ax before they are sold to uncertainty is portrayed as an othered act of "love," instead of "hate." The "mother's anguish" is exacerbated by the prospect of losing her only solace from the sufferings of slavery. Enslaved motherhood is depicted as so powerful as to facilitate the disremembering of the enslaved condition. The storytelling of the White uncle draws a parallel between the hypothetical return of the Black mother to her children after a long day of enslaved exploitation and the comfortable entrance of the White Father to his home. This passage further constructs slavery as a matriarchal labor system and "salaried" capitalism as a patriarchal economic configuration. The crime of slavery is disrupting gendered labor and maternal morality. According to the *Almanac*, the locus of inhumanity of the institution of slavery is the separation of enslaved mothers from their children and thus their gendered expectations and emotional growth, which allows the abolitionist publication to establish ties between enslaved family separations and slaveholding emotional detachment.

When she was seized, she shrieked and cried, and the children cried when they saw their mother torn from them, but the slaveholder did not regard their cries. He chained their mother, and drove her away, where she never saw her children again. Can slaves be happy, when they are all the time exposed to such cruel separations?[54]

Though few, the *Almanac* also has entries about the sale of an enslaved father. In these instances, the loss of the enslaved father is represented as an irremediable affliction. "Consider the desolation which would be brought upon your family, if the head of it should be taken away. The slaves suffer, in such cases, FAR MORE than we, for they have few

---

[53] "A Mother's Anguish, 1837," Schomburg Center for Research in Black Culture, Manuscripts, Archives and Rare Books Division, the American Anti-Slavery Almanac Collection, Sc Rare 326.59-A.
[54] "African American Female Slave Being Separated from Her Children by Slave Dealers, 1838," Schomburg Center for Research in Black Culture, Manuscripts, Archives and Rare Books Division, the American Anti-Slavery Almanac Collection, Sc Rare 326.59-A.

pleasures except those they derive from their companions in woe."[55] The absence of "pleasures" engenders "desolation" for enslaved families, and the appeal for the enslaved family clumsily mimics the discourses of the primacy of the White capitalist nuclear family, in which the privation from the Father and the "pleasures" of capitalistic societies is deemed irreparable. Therefore, the projection of enslaved families is far more concentrated on upholding the capitalistic imposition of White patriarchal power than to ever fully acknowledge the individual humanity and sorrow of enslaved progenitors and their children.

The *Almanac* generates urgency toward its cause by consistently alluding to the passing of time, time that inflicts enslaved "anguish" and slaveholding "guilt." "Readers! Another rolling year has brought us together. It has also brought its 365 days of anguish to the slaves, & its 365 days of guilt and infamy to the nation."[56] Moreover, the *Almanac* constantly fuses its abolitionist rhetoric, premised on Black emotional otherness, with religious sentiment: "Let the anti-slavery motto be, *not* 'I am man, and therefore an abolitionist,' but rather this, 'I love God, and therefore I am an abolitionist.'"[57] Likewise, while Harriet Beecher Stowe's *Uncle Tom's Cabin* urged "northerners" to enact their "Christian morality" toward emancipating enslaved people, it still visualized a "White America" teaching the "backward" enslaved to govern a "foreign nation."[58] The *Almanac* similarly defines the institution of slavery as mainly incompatible with Christian ethics. "CHRISTIANS MUST ABHOR SLAVERY, OR RENOUNCE GOD."[59] According to

---

[55] "Slave Being Separated from His Wife and Children, 1838," Schomburg Center for Research in Black Culture, Manuscripts, Archives and Rare Books Division, the American Anti-Slavery Almanac Collection, Sc Rare 326.59-A.
[56] "Tearing up Free Papers, 1838," Schomburg Center for Research in Black Culture, Manuscripts, Archives and Rare Books Division, the American Anti-Slavery Almanac Collection, Sc Rare 326.59-A.
[57] "Instead of being allowed to comfort and assist one another, the slaves are often compelled to hold one of their number, while another wretched being is forced to ply the lash, 1838," Schomburg Center for Research in Black Culture, Manuscripts, Archives and Rare Books Division, the American Anti-Slavery Almanac Collection, Sc Rare 326.59-A.
[58] Tracy D. Davis & Stefka Mihaylova, *Uncle Tom's Cabins: The Transnational History of America's Most Mutable Book* (Ann Arbor: University of Michigan Press, 2018), 2.
[59] "The slave Paul has suffered so much in slavery, that he chose to encounter the hardships and perils of a runway. He exposed himself, in gloomy forests, to cold and starvation, and finally hung himself, that he might not again fall into the hands of his tormentor, 1838," Schomburg Center for Research in Black Culture, Manuscripts, Archives and Rare Books Division, the American Anti-Slavery Almanac Collection, Sc Rare 326.59-A.

the *Almanac*, the institution of slavery is a cradle of sin, and abolitionism is propelled by "hearts" that are "responsive" to God, a translation of the discourse of "slavery to sin" to White abolitionist thought.

> We should mainly urge this consideration, – *that slavery is a sin against God.* A conviction of this we should strive to produce in every heart. For myself, I can freely say that I have no confidence in any other abolitionism than that which is based upon this principle. I would not have the list of abolitionists swelled by a single name however influential, which did not pledge a heart responsive to this truth.[60]

The *Almanac* entry "Emancipated Slaves Can Take Care of Themselves" aims to deliver "testimonies" on the capacity of formerly enslaved people to "acquire" abilities in business and education. These "testimonies" are granted credibility by the status of the "honorable" White "witnesses." "The emancipated people manifest as much cunning and address in business as any class of persons. – Mr. James Howell." "The capabilities of the Blacks for education are conspicuous; so also as to mental acquirements and trades. – Hon. N. Nugent."[61] In a later entry titled "They Can't Take Care of Themselves," the *Almanac* would further confront the proslavery claim that enslaved people would not "take care of themselves" once free.

> When a good-for-nothing husband runs away and leaves a wife and eight children who "can't take care of themselves," duty is plain; drive them into your yard, put your mark on them, and make them your "property." So with all idiots, the blind, the deaf and dumb, the insane, and all other descriptions of persons who "can't take care of themselves." To send them to asylums and alms-houses is all behind the age; we show you a more excellent way; turn them into property, set them on the auction table, knock them off to the highest bidder, make out a bill of sale for each – and overseers and drivers will see that they are *taken care of*![62]

While the ironic tone of this passage decries the indefensibility of "auctions" and "sales" of the enslaved, it also amalgamates categories outside White "masculinity," as there is an evident symbiotic

---

[60] "Young Horse-Racers Torturing a Free Citizen for Amusement, 1838," Schomburg Center for Research in Black Culture, Manuscripts, Archives and Rare Books Division, the American Anti-Slavery Almanac Collection, Sc Rare 326.59-A.

[61] "Emancipated Slaves Can Take Care of Themselves, The Anti-Slavery Almanac, 1839," Schomburg Center for Research in Black Culture, Manuscripts, Archives and Rare Books Division, Sc Rare 326.59-A.

[62] "They Can't Take Care of Themselves, The Anti-Slavery Almanac, 1840," Schomburg Center for Research in Black Culture, Manuscripts, Archives and Rare Books Division, Sc Rare 326.59-A.

"feminization" and infantilization of the formerly enslaved, in addition to the conflated pathologization of Blackness as "madness." The concept of a "good-for-nothing husband" that "runs away" mirrors the Master who has distanced himself from White "civility." By clarifying that women and children, in addition to "all idiots, the blind, the deaf and dumb, the insane," should be institutionally "cared for," the passage hesitates to articulate the level of White supremacist surveillance that enslaved people should be subjected to once emancipated. And this is the crux of White sentimentalist abolitionism: it argued that Atlantic slavery not only disregarded the universality of the presence of emotions, but also overlooked the racialized differentiation of the quality of feelings. All bodies had emotions and natural "legal freedom," but some bodies had pathologies of emotion that had to be regulated and confined by the State. The preoccupation with expectations of White "male" citizenship and White "female" vulnerability is also present in the entry "How Slavery Improves the Condition of Women."

John Ruffner, a slaveholder, had one slave named Piney, whom he, as well as Mrs. Ruffner would often flog severely. I frequently saw Mrs. Ruffner flog her with the broom, shovel, or anything she could seize in her rage. She would knock her down and then kick and stamp her most mercifully, until she would be apparently so lifeless, that I more than once thought she would never recover.[63]

The title "How Slavery Improves the Condition of Women" is thus meant to serve as an ironic juxtaposition to the slaveholding extreme violence toward enslaved women. By using titles such as "How Slavery Improves the Condition of Women" and "They Can't Take Care of Themselves," the *Almanac* appropriates phrases from the anti-abolitionist movement and offers "evidence," or White vows, to dismantle their reasoning. The *Almanac* also censures the lack of protection of enslaved maternity as an infringement of White "civility."

Those who are with child are driven to their task till within a few days of the time of their delivery; and when the child is a few weeks old, the mother must again go to the field. If it is far from her hut, she must take her babe with her. If the child cries, she cannot go to its relief; the eye of the overseer is upon her: and if, when she goes to nurse it, she stays a little longer than the overseer thinks necessary, he

---

[63] "How Slavery Improves the Condition of Women, The Anti-Slavery Almanac, 1840," Schomburg Center for Research in Black Culture, Manuscripts, Archives and Rare Books Division, Sc Rare 326.59-A.

commands her back to her task. Brother, you cannot begin to know what the poor slave mothers suffer on thousands of plantations at the south.[64]

The abolitionist discourse of the *Almanac* ultimately calls on the universality of familial ties to repudiate the miscarriage of White morality in upholding the model values of a White nuclear family with religious devotion, in turn emotionally depersonalizing the enslaved. This breach of morality lies in Whiteness not acknowledging the second-class emotions of Blackness. Therefore, the *Almanac*, just as other major White abolitionist efforts, did not disavow White "male" supremacy, but instead diffused ideas based on the enforcement of a White patriarchal order, capitalistic understandings of the family unit, rationalizations framed by scientific racism, and, most predominantly, the perpetuity of the emotional surveillance of the racialized Other. The *Almanac* summarized its conceptualization of slavery as an emotion in the premise "Sanctified hate. Legalized hate."[65] The problem was that the White slaveholding heart felt "hate," not that slavery disregarded the equality of humanity or that Blackness should not be policed. The inequality of hearts was never in question.

Both White "antislavery" and proslavery movements had no problem in proclaiming that emotions were universal. Under that surface-level admission lies the explicit differentiation of the quality of Black emotionality as one that still required intervention, surveillance, and economic exploitation. The emotional performativity of White abolitionism was self-aware and enthralled with the globalization of White "innocence." This captivation reveals its own displeasure toward the potential loss of the imperial symbiosis between Whiteness, "masculinity," innocence, and capitalism. Both proslavery and "antislavery" thought were fixated on the projection of White capitalistic empires and their paternalistic "guidance" as emotionally dominant. This White emotional supremacy was unified by the determination to show the Atlantic world that White "masculinity" was innately innocent and benevolent in its regulation of Black emotional "inadequacy," whether manifesting as a slaveholding regime or as a "salaried" capitalistic system. The distinction of White

---

[64] "Women at Work in the Field, The Anti-Slavery Almanac, 1840," Schomburg Center for Research in Black Culture, Manuscripts, Archives and Rare Books Division, Sc Rare 326.59-A.

[65] "Sanctified Hate. Legalized Hate, 1840," Schomburg Center for Research in Black Culture, Manuscripts, Archives and Rare Books Division, the American Anti-Slavery Almanac Collection, Sc Rare 326.59-A.

abolitionism was that it represented the legal "abolition" of slavery as a political statement of White capitalist magnanimity, as a cleansing force that verified the "innocence" of White capitalist and "nationalistic" agendas. There was never a White abolitionist project for Black families to be liberated from their economic subjugation and political surveillance. Even more, eighteenth- and nineteenth-century White abolitionist thought was fueled by the vindication of an economic system that exploited Black emotional bodies, that kept emotional racialization as the foundation of the capitalistic order of White elation. White abolitionists mostly advocated for the claim that racialized emotional surveillance simply did not require the legal institution of slavery as it had been known until then. The same White abolitionist fervor toward the otherness of Black emotionality would perpetuate the state-sanctioned enslavement of Black communities, of those who felt passions not quite White.

Emotional discourses within the intellectual production of the enslaved have been silenced within much of the scholarship about antislavery thought. Some scholars even contend that the origins of organized nongradual abolitionism lie in White men.[66] Meanwhile, other scholars rightfully declare that the "heart of the abolition movement" is the resistance of the enslaved.[67] Indeed, all antislavery victories are indebted to the intellectual production of the enslaved, and the legal abolitions of slavery in the Atlantic world were the triumphs of the revolutions of the enslaved. The Constitution of 1801, signed by Toussaint Louverture in the then colony of Saint-Domingue, is not remembered by mainstream historiography as a pioneering document of constitutional history, when it was the first legal document to both permanently abolish slavery and to innovatively prohibit job discrimination by race.[68] Just as the Haitian Revolution has been kept in the margins of History as a "nonevent,"[69] so have the stories of Cécile Fatiman and Sanité Bélair, among others, been kept at an even more "unthinkable" marginality of this "nonevent" in patriarchal heteronormative historiography. The erasure of the legacies

---

[66] See Stanley Harrold, *American Abolitionism: Its Direct Political Impact from Colonial Times into Reconstruction* (Charlottesville: University of Virginia Press, 2019).
[67] See Manisha Sinha, *The Slave's Cause: A History of Abolition* (New Haven, CT: Yale University Press, 2016), 1.
[68] Louis Joseph Janvier, ed., *Les Constitutions d'Haïti (1801–1885)* (Paris: C. Marpon et E. Flammarion, 1886).
[69] Michel-Rolph Trouillot, *Silencing the Past: Power and the Production of History* (Boston: Beacon Press, 1995), 70.

of the revolutions of the enslaved has paralleled the silencing of the uninterrupted continuation of racialized slavery.

MUTATIONS OF IDEAS OF FEELINGS AND RIGHTS IN THE "POST-EMANCIPATION" ERA

The essence of the "afterlife of slavery"[70] is the White entitlement to Black emotional oppression. The "abolition" of slavery was in actuality a political and economic reformulation of the intersection of freedom, citizenship, and emotional criminalization. The majority of the "emancipated" from slavery in the Atlantic world were immediately subjected to systems of obligatory labor. Tens of thousands of recently emancipated people in the United States fell sick from epidemic diseases in the context of the Civil War and died because of their extreme poverty and disenfranchisement.[71] Not only did "apprenticeships" extend the lived experience of slavery in the Atlantic world, but also colonial governments endeavored to maintain those "emancipated" from entering non-plantation regions, as a way to persist in their inherence in their bodies, their movement, and their labor.[72] The "post-emancipation" era corroborates that it was never a disposition of White abolitionism to eradicate the imperial dependence on Black exploitation. The shift from the "order of inequality" to a "new order" was mostly preoccupied with how to introduce limits to othered freedom that preserved racialized sources of exploitative labor and hence the capitalistic subjugation of Black and Brown people. The "formerly" enslaved were still restricted to systemic agricultural exploitation throughout the Atlantic world, and "former" enslavers proclaimed that the "post-emancipation" era had proven their anti-abolitionist objections: that freed Black people would not know what to do with liberty or comprehend the value of capitalistic labor. Black aspirations for citizenship, nonexploitative labor, and economic mobility in the "post-emancipation" era were assessed by White elites as emotional irrationalities against the "value of work," the work of White choosing,

---

[70] Saidiya Hartman, *Lose Your Mother: A Journey along the Atlantic Slave Route* (New York: Farrar, Straus & Giroux, 2008).

[71] Jim Downs, *Sick from Freedom: African American Illness and Suffering during the Civil War and Reconstruction* (Oxford: Oxford University Press, 2012), 7.

[72] Frederick Cooper, Thomas Holt, & Rebecca Scott, "Introduction," in *Beyond Slavery: Explorations of Race, Labor, and Citizenship in Postemancipation Societies*, edited by Frederick Cooper, Thomas Holt, & Rebecca Scott (Chapel Hill: University of North Carolina Press, 2000), 21.

which proved their predictions about the "failures" of abolition, yet another proof of racialized emotional capriciousness.

The genocidal violence of Atlantic slavery had prescribed the Black body to "self-contain" in order to protect White happiness from unruly emotions, while also presuming Blackness to fail in its emotional self-captivity. Once slavery was "abolished," the modern carcerality of Black emotions was further institutionalized, consecrating the imperial emotional suspicion toward the Black body, the genocidal violence of slavery, the inescapability of racialized emotional policing. The Black body per se was expected to be carceral; its Black skin was supposed to hold Black emotionality captive. Black emotionality per se was to be colonized, monitored, recorded, policed. The institutionalization of the modern carcerality of Black emotions extended the reach of emotional surveillance from private-public masterhood to the industrial manufacture of imperialistic carceral landscapes. The Black body became the Black Body: a collective, monolithic, depersonalized emotionality that had to be perpetually reconquered, recolonized, and recriminalized due to the political definition of Black emotional autonomy as the supreme adversary of the industrial capitalistic order of White imperial happiness.

In the United States, the Thirteenth Amendment premeditatedly created a new political regime of punishment of "criminality," which scientific racism had inexorably tied to Black emotionality. "Neither slavery nor involuntary servitude, except as a punishment for crime whereof the party shall have been duly convicted, shall exist within the United States, or any place subject to their jurisdiction."[73] The "duly convicted" with their intrinsic criminality were regarded as deserving of the punishment of enslavement. While Atlantic slavery was projected as a "loving" institution that protected Blackness from its lowly passions before "abolition," it was (and is) now framed as a large-scale punitive response to the inherent absence of emotional self-governance in Black communities, legitimizing the structural carcerality of Black emotions. Masterhood shifted from a seemingly individual exercise of power to an ambiguous collective entity that "conceals" White privilege, since the modern prison system could not claim to "love" Black people, but instead the carceral State was solely compelled to hurt the corporeal sources of emotional deviance, extending the reach of slaveholding genocidal

---

[73] "Thirteenth Amendment," as quoted in Alexander Tsesis, *The Thirteenth Amendment and American Freedom: A Legal History* (New York: New York University Press, 2004), 163.

violence. The institutional suspicion of Black emotions remained profitable and became even more industrialized, recorded, and systematized by technological machinery. In fact, immediately after the "abolition" of slavery, the format of public "auctions" of enslaved people transitioned to the public "sales" of those who had been "duly convicted."

Public Sale – The undersigned will offer for Sale, at the Court House Door, in the city Annapolis, at eleven O' Clock A.M., on Saturday, 22nd of December, a negro man named John Johnson, aged about Forty years. The said negro was convicted the October Term, 1866, of the Circuit Court for Anne Arundel county, for; Larceny, and sentenced to be sold, in the State, for the term of one year, from the 12th of December, 1866. Also a negro man convicted of aforesaid, named Gassaway Price, aged about Thirty years, to be sold for a term of one year in the State. Also, a negro woman, convicted as aforesaid, named Harriet Purdy, aged about twenty-five years, to be sold for a term of one year in the State. Also a negro woman, convicted as aforesaid, named Dilly Harris, aged about Thirty years, to be sold for a term of two years in the State.[74]

An 1868 poster provides insight into the way the South in the United States referred to its "historical past" shortly after the Civil War, while also encompassing discourses about the marketing of Blackness as entertainment.

Tom! The Blind Negro Boy – of Musical Inspiration! Sightless and Untutored from Birth – his very soul overflowing with Musical Genius. This Youth is a Remarkable Phenomenon in one direction only, and that is his Wonderful Aptness for the Piano Forte! There is no Art about him. God has given him a guide, but it is a silent one, that of Nature herself.[75]

This poster constructs "Tom's" talent as disconnected from "Art." It is instead emerging from "Nature," and this "natural" talent is "guided" by "God" for the enjoyment of White audiences. The negation of "Tom's" musical talent is reminiscent of theories of both biological and historical determinism. Not only is "Tom" depicted as outside the historical realm of Art, but also the acknowledged "musical genius" is merely natural/biological, and its "feeling" is misunderstood by "Tom." The poster additionally delivers further "biological" information in its fine print.

This Wonderful Negro Boy, who is now attracting so much attention throughout the country, was blind from his birth; yet he plays the most difficult Operatic

---

[74] "Public Sale," as quoted in Dennis Childs, *Black Incarceration from the Chain Gang to the Penitentiary* (Minneapolis: University of Minnesota Press, 2015).
[75] "Tom Musical Prodigy, 1868," Schomburg Center for Research in Black Culture, Manuscripts, Archives and Rare Books Division, Broadsides Collection.

Pieces, not only brilliantly and beautifully, but with all the taste, expression and feeling of the most Distinguished Artist. He was born in Georgia, and was caressed and petted, as all negro children are about a Plantation in the South, and more particularly those afflicted with so terrible an infirmity as the loss of sight. But when the veil of darkness was drawn over his eyes, as if to make amends for the infliction upon the poor Negro Boy, a flood of light was poured into his brain, and his mind became an Opera of Beauty, written by the hand of God, in syllables of music for the delight of the world. He is presented to the public as surpassing everything hitherto known to the world as a Musical Phenomenon![76]

Enslaved infancy in the South is remembered as a state distinguished by being "caressed and petted." "Tom's" story is one in which the enslaved child is able to overcome the "inability" to serve the Master. "God" makes "amends for the infliction upon the poor" enslaved child by gifting them the "beauty" and "delight" of entertaining the "taste" of White audiences after the "abolition" of slavery. This "flood of light" is reckoned as exceptional, since one cannot be enslaved and a "musical phenomenon," hold darkness and light at the same time.

Vagrancy laws within "Black Codes" fueled convict leasing in the United States during the last decades of the nineteenth century, and, though "Black Codes" were "modeled directly on slave codes," their punishments more explicitly incentivized the policing of Black communities by White authorities.[77] While convict leasing exemplified the continuation of slavery through the escalation of racialized criminalization, it also represented a rupture in the promotion of the "productivity" of the reproductive systems of Black bodies, shifting to ungendered corporate exploitation in a prison setting.[78] The emerging prison industrial complex, instigated by the influence of proponents of scientific racism and by the intensification of eugenics in response to the "abolition" of slavery, would aim to rid societies of "unwanted" Black emotions and to "solve" the problem of urban "visibility" of exploitative carceral labor, veiling the emotional spectacle of unceasing reenslavement. Khalil Gibran Muhammad argues that White commentators of race relations during the Progressive era in the United States intentionally legitimized the racialist criminal justice system with statistical "data" about "Black

---

[76] "Tom Musical Prodigy, 1868."

[77] William A. Darity, Jr., & A. Kirsten Mullen, *From Here to Equality: Reparations for Black Americans in the Twenty-First Century* (Chapel Hill: University of North Carolina Press, 2020), 186.

[78] Talitha L. LeFlouria, *Chained by Silence: Black Women and Convict Labor in the New South* (Chapel Hill: University of North Carolina Press, 2015), 8.

pathology": "The numbers 'speak for themselves' was one frequent refrain, followed by "I am not a racist.'"[79] While the State conceived governmental responses to White criminality as being attentive to the provision of resources to White communities and families, hyper-policed Blackness was "corroborated" through statistical "data" as being worthy of the full force of carceral punitive measures.[80] While White youth had access to rehabilitative "juvenile court interventions" during the Progressive era, Black youth were exposed to adult prisons, convict leasing, longer confinements, and bodily disciplining.[81] White criminality was codified as a "problem" caused by the State's inadequacy in properly nurturing White "innocence," to be solved through an indeed "loving" investment of funding and resources. In contrast, Blackness was signified as "The Problem," yoked by its own criminal feelings.

The Souls of Black Folk by W. E. B. Du Bois precisely explored the emotional weight of the question, "How does it feel to be a problem?" for Black men in the United States.[82] The scholar-activist introduced the theory of "double consciousness" to reply to this aching question.

After the Egyptian and Indian, the Greek and Roman, the Teuton and Mongolian, the Negro is a sort of seventh son, born with a veil, and gifted with second-sight in this American world, – a world which yields him no true self-consciousness, but only lets him see himself through the revelation of the other world. It is a peculiar sensation, this double-consciousness, this sense of always looking at one's self through the eyes of others, of measuring one's soul by the tape of a world that looks on in amused contempt and pity. One ever feels his two-ness, – an American, a Negro; two souls, two thoughts, two unreconciled strivings; two warring ideals in one dark body, whose dogged strength alone keeps it from being torn asunder.[83]

While White southerners relied on the euphemism of the "peculiar institution" to minimize their economic dependence on slavery, "double consciousness" is defined by Du Bois as a "peculiar sensation" tied to the "gift" of "second-sight." In other words, while the concept of the "peculiar institution" intends to conceal, the "peculiar" feeling of the lived

---

[79] Khalil Gibran Muhammad, *The Condemnation of Blackness: Race, Crime, and the Making of Modern Urban America* (Cambridge, MA: Harvard University Press, 2010), 8.
[80] Muhammad, *The Condemnation of Blackness*, 8.
[81] Carl Suddler, *Presumed Criminal: Black Youth and the Justice System in Postwar New York* (New York: New York University Press, 2019), 7.
[82] W. E. B. Du Bois, *The Souls of Black Folk* (New York: Dover, 2012), 1.
[83] Du Bois, *The Souls of Black Folk*, 2–3.

The "Abolition" of an Economic Apparatus of Feelings

experience of Blackness is one that shows the "revelation of the other world." The "gift" of "second-sight" not only shows the foundations of racialized violence in the "American world," but also burdens the Black consciousness of the Self with its cognizance of the "amused contempt and pity" of the gaze of the "other world." The feeling of "two-ness" is endured only through "dogged strength." Du Bois immediately affirms that the "history of the American Negro is the history of this strife, – this longing to attain self-conscious manhood, to merge his double self into a better and truer self."[84] *The Souls of Black Folk* conveys Black "masculinity" as being in emotional turmoil over the "longing" toward reaching the "self-conscious manhood" that has been denied by the "American world."

The institutional carcerality of Black emotions became the vital motivation and reward of White Empires, now allegedly dependent on "salaried" labor, and colonial landscapes were fundamentally structured by the carceral oppression of Black "passions." The legal "emancipation" of enslaved people in the majority of emerging Latin American nations followed the acquisition of independence, but the systemic exploitation of Afro-Latinx communities would persist through White interventionism, racialist frameworks of identity, segregation, and the racialization of labor, poverty, and crime. Even Latin American "liberators" utilized "language of colonial legacies" to propel a discourse of "pessimistic postcolonial diagnosis."[85] Linguistic "colonial legacies" theorized the "vagina" as a "natural vessel" and the anus as the source of "contra natura" depravity, generating a heteronormative colonizing regime of "sin."[86] In the 1920s, the notion of mestizaje, as outlined in *La raza cósmica* by Mexican philosopher José Vasconcelos Calderón, proclaimed the rise of a dominant "mixed" (and, most importantly, light-skinned) race, fostering the societal alienation and economic subjugation of Afro-Latinx communities.[87] The discourse of mestizaje consolidated the structural repercussions of colonial whitening policies, silencing the

---

[84] Du Bois, *The Souls of Black Folk*, 2–3.
[85] Jeremy Adelman, "Introduction: The Problem of Persistence in Latin American History," in *Colonial Legacies: The Problem of Persistence in Latin American History*, edited by Jeremy Adelman (New York: Routledge, 1999).
[86] Zeb Tortorici, "Introduction: Unnatural Bodies, Desires, and Devotions," in *Sexuality and the Unnatural in Colonial Latin America*, edited by Zeb Tortorici (Oakland: University of California Press, 2016), 6.
[87] Ben Vinson III, *Before Mestizaje: The Frontiers of Race and Caste in Colonial Mexico* (New York: Cambridge University Press, 2018), 31.

experiences of Blackness in Latinx identities and framing rhetoric of national regeneration with an institutional fascination toward a racially ambiguous, White-passing "male" body. The political elevation of antihaitianismo, or anti-Black/anti-Haitian sentiment, by dictator Rafael Trujillo led to the devastating Parsley Massacre in 1938. From 1890 to 1950, Brazil experienced dramatic gentrification caused by mass White immigration in its now most wealthy areas, which correlated with the exacerbation of racial segregation and job and housing discrimination toward Afro-Brazilians.[88] The structural racial segregation of Latin America was concurrent to the racialization of crime and poverty, which resulted in high statistics of economic oppression of Afro-Latinx communities, for example, disproportionate numbers of Afro-Colombians living "below the poverty line."[89] The project of institutional carcerality of Afro-Latinx emotions persevered in the destructive effects of military interventionism in Latin America and the long-lived imposition of blatant colonialism, imperial violence, and criminalization of dissent perpetrated by the United States in Puerto Rico.

The colonizing "feminization" of the "dark continent" led to an analogous reading of the Black "female" body and the African continent as entities of emotional erraticism, high pain tolerance, and racially premised exploitation. While Latin American colonial history was synchronous to the "Western" understanding of European modernity,[90] the conquest and colonization of Africa paralleled the escalation of scientific racism. Africa was theorized as a deviant Black "female" body to conquer, penetrate, and hold captive through emotional carcerality. European inherence and "masterhood" over Africa continued well after the "abolition" of Atlantic slavery with systemic colonial exploitation of the African continent, and African colonial history was deeply affected by bloody military disruption.[91] Not only did African nations lead military oppositional movements against European conquest and colonization,

---

[88] See Edward E. Telles, *Race in Another America: The Significance of Skin Color in Brazil* (Princeton, NJ: Princeton University Press, 2004), 197.

[89] Tanya Katerí Hernández, *Racial Subordination in Latin America: The Role of the State, Customary Law, and the New Civil Rights Response* (New York: Cambridge University Press, 2013), 75.

[90] Mabel Moraña, Enrique D. Dussel, & Carlos A. Jáuregui, *Coloniality at Large: Latin America and the Postcolonial Debate* (Durham, NC: Duke University Press, 2008), 6.

[91] Kenneth Kalu & Toyin Falola, "Introduction: Exploitation, Colonialism, and Postcolonial Misrule in Africa," in *Exploitation and Misrule in Colonial and Postcolonial Africa*, edited by Kenneth Kalu & Toyin Falola (New York: Palgrave Macmillan, 2019), 4.

The "Abolition" of an Economic Apparatus of Feelings 199

but also many African resistance leaders sent letters to the imperial States, generating intellectual production of dissent to Eurocentric colonialism.[92] The "missionary and imperial impulses in Africa" were part of a "grand hegemonic project" with the "same civilizing agenda."[93] Africa faced many "colonial genocides" and analogous "epistemicides" and "linguicides,"[94] as incarnated in the mutilated bodies of the racialized, and those who perished, in the colonial enslaving regime of King Leopold II in the Congo. In turn, Ethiopian history as an independent nation was highly politicized by "Western" structures of power.[95] Foreign interventionism in Africa endured after decolonization through the interference of the United Nations in "African affairs,"[96] and White control of land in Africa persisted in many manifestations, including mining, oil extraction, and corporate "land-grabbing."[97] The discursive oscillation between "mimicry" and "menace"[98] normalized a never-ending colonial project in Africa, an everlasting White intervention in proscribed Black feelings.

Twentieth-century African and pan-Africanist philosophy theorized the history of racialized emotional subjugation effected by imperial violence in the Atlantic world. *Black Skin, White Masks* by Frantz Fanon explored the "inferiority complex" of "all colonized people" who "position themselves in relation to the civilizing language."[99] The philosopher deconstructed the notion of the colonizing yearning for "White love."

> I want to be recognized not as *black*, but as *white*. But – and this is the form of recognition that Hegel never described – who better than the white woman to bring this about? By loving me, she proved to me that I am worthy of a white love. I am loved like a white man. I am a white man. Her love opens the illustrious path that leads to total fulfillment.... I espouse white culture, white beauty, white

---

[92] Boniface Obichere, "African Critics of Victorian Imperialism: An Analysis," in *Conquest and Resistance to Colonialism in Africa*, edited by Gregory Maddox (New York: Routledge, 2018).
[93] Raphael Chijoke Njoku & Chima J. Korieh, "Introduction," in *Missions, States, and European Expansion in Africa*, edited by Chima J. Korieh & Raphael Chijoke Njoku (New York: Routledge, 2007), 3.
[94] Sabelo J. Ndlovu-Gatsheni, *Epistemic Freedom in Africa: Deprovincialization and Decolonization* (New York: Routledge, 2018).
[95] Jan Záhořík, "Ethiopia and the Colonial Discourse," in *Colonialism on the Margins of Africa*, edited by Jan Záhořík & Linda Piknerová (New York: Routledge, 2017).
[96] Elizabeth Schmidt, *Foreign Intervention in Africa: From the Cold War to the War on Terror* (New York: Cambridge University Press, 2013), 3.
[97] Mark Langan, *Neo-Colonialism and the Poverty of "Development" in Africa* (New York: Palgrave Macmillan, 2018), 47.
[98] Homi K. Bhabha, *The Location of Culture* (New York: Routledge, 1994).
[99] Frantz Fanon, *Black Skin, White Masks* (New York: Grove Press, 2008), 3.

whiteness. Between these white breasts that my wandering hands fondle, white civilization and worthiness become mine.[100]

Fanon dissects the discourse of the "love" of the White "woman" as the "illustrious path" for Blackness to reach "white civilization and worthiness." Being "loved like a white man" becomes a gateway to marry "white beauty." The sensual exploration of the White "female" body is geared toward the gaze of White "masculinity." It is His love that results in the imperial "recognition" of Whiteness.

In "On Negrohood: Psychology of the African Negro," Léopold Sédar Senghor subversively reverses the racialist narrative of the emotional deficiency of Blackness by countering the epistemological antagonism of emotions. The politician and theorist first refers to the theories of historical determinism, affirming that it is "often said, and not without reason, that *the Negro is a man of Nature.*"[101] Senghor then contextualizes what it means to exist in a "natural" state.

The African negro is as it were locked up in his black skin. He lives in a primordial night, and does not distinguish himself, to begin with, from the object: from tree or peeble, man or animal, fact of nature or society. He does not keep the object at a distance, does not analyze it. After receiving its impression, he takes the object, all alive, into his hands – like a blind man, anxious not to fix it or to kill it. He turns it over and over in his supple hands, touches it, *feels* it.[102]

This text counters the discourses of African primitivism from historical determinism by constructing Africanness as a state of feeling. While historical determinism conceived Black emotionality as "fermented" and destructive, Senghor responds to this discourse by conceptualizing Blackness as authentically feeling and cultivating Nature. European "objective intelligence" separates itself from Nature in order to rationalize methodologies of colonial exploitation. In contrast, Blackness is "locked up" in "Black skin" and does not distance the Self from Nature. Instead, Black emotions "sym-pathize" with Nature.

Let us stay with the *e-motion* of the African negro and take up the thread of fantasy. Here, then, is the subject who leaves his I to *sym-pathize* with the *Thou*, and to identify himself with it. He dies to himself to be reborn in the Other. He

---

[100] Fanon, *Black Skin, White Masks*, 45.
[101] Léopold Sédar Senghor, "On Negrohood: Psychology of the African Negro," in *Logic and African Philosophy: Seminal Essays on African Systems of Thought*, edited by Jonathan O. Chimakoman (Wilmington, DE: Vernon, 2020), 15.
[102] Senghor, "On Negrohood," 17.

does not assimilate it, but himself. He does not take the Other's life but strengthens his own with its life.[103]

Here, to "sym-pathize" represents a process of symbiosis and identification that results in "strength." Therefore, Senghor concurrently repudiates the imperial notions of Blackness as emotionally undeveloped and of emotions as lowly. "This means that an emotion, under its initial aspect as a fall of consciousness, is on the contrary *the rise of consciousness to a higher state of knowledge.*"[104] "On Negrohood: Psychology of the African Negro" reverses the emotional justifications of Black captivity by constructing Blackness as "locked up" in emotional consciousness, consciousness that is advanced and nonexploitative. Just as Senghor deprecated Eurocentric emotional detachment, Steve Biko, activist against the South African apartheid, denounced how White liberals disinterested themselves from "the oppression of Blacks as a problem" by regarding Black pain as an "eye sore spoiling an otherwise beautiful view."[105]

More recent African philosophical texts have also condemned the historical colonization of African intellectual production by making connections between long-lived imperialist exploitation, emotional differentiation, and epistemological silencing. Kwasi Wiredu has argued for the "conceptual decolonization of African philosophy" by "exploiting as much as is judicious" the "resources" of the African "indigenous conceptual scheme," such as Akan philosophy.[106] Emmanuel Chukwudi Eze has claimed that the "prospect" of a "postracial philosophy" necessitates a "recognition that modern philosophy's pretension to universality and cross-cultural values has often been just that: a pretense."[107] *On the Postcolony* by Achille Mbembe denounced how the "political imagination" of Africa has been connoted as "incomprehensible, pathological, and abnormal," as "powerless, engaged in rampant self-destruction," where any "human action" is deemed "stupid and mad, always proceeding from anything but rational calculation."[108] As African philosophers have denunciated, the pathologization of those subjected to colonial oppression in Africa as "insane," neglectful, unintelligible, and

---

[103] Senghor, "On Negrohood," 19. [104] Senghor, "On Negrohood," 26.
[105] Steve Biko, *I Write What I Like* (Oxford: Heinemann, 1987), 22.
[106] Kwasi Wiredu, *Cultural Universals and Particulars: An African Perspective* (Bloomington: Indiana University Press, 1996), 136.
[107] Emmanuel Chukwudi Eze, *Achieving Our Humanity: The Idea of a Postracial Future* (New York: Routledge, 2001), x.
[108] Achille Mbembe, *On the Postcolony* (Berkeley: University of California Press, 2001), 8.

"irrational" has led not only to the painful narratives of imperial exploitation of the racialized but also to African and pan-Africanist intellectual production being reckoned as too emotive, nonacademic, and therefore deserving of its objectionable marginalization in "canonical" philosophy.

The regimes of the structural carcerality of Black emotions in the Atlantic world are evidenced by the hypersexualization of Blackness and the corresponding rise of racial hierarchies of sex tourism. In addition to being dissected by Georges Cuvier for racialist aims, "Sara Baartman" was sexually exploited and animalized in voyeuristic caricatures that spread through European intellectual production as "proof" of African "monstrosity."[109] The caricatures of "Baartman" were used as an imperial tool for the racialization of fat phobia, which essentialized the Black body as "gluttonous" and unruly.[110] The "scientific" observation of "Baartman" in captivity and the normalization of racialized sexual slavery in the nineteenth century mirror the configuration of sex tourism in the Atlantic world during the twentieth century. Sex tourism aligned with an "economy of desire" based on the racialization of "eroticized capital."[111] The racialized demand for "sexual adventures" reverberated the theories of geographical determinism that codified the "fiery" Black body as emotionally capricious and sexually deviant. White colonizers looked for adolescent bodies of color to rape and mutilate, blaming their own assumed exposition to "tropical fever." These Black bodies "full of heat" were in the margins of History, hungry and persecuted. The narrative of sexual enslavement of Black and Brown people persevered after the "abolition" of slavery through the validation of White colonizing rape under the guise of contagious sexual aggressiveness.

The segregationist politics of the Jim Crow South in the United States were precisely framed by White supremacist discourses of racialized emotional delinquency and bodily restriction, overtly enacting the institutional carcerality of Black emotions. The rationalizations of Jim Crow segregation were centered on the constraints of political rights for Black communities in order to concomitantly inhibit interracial sexual rights.[112]

---

[109] Clifton Crais & Pamela Scully, *Sara Baartman and the Hottentot Venus: A Ghost Story and a Biography* (Princeton, NJ: Princeton University Press, 2009), 3.
[110] Strings, *Fearing the Black Body*, 98.
[111] Amalia L. Cabezas, *Economies of Desire: Sex and Tourism in Cuba and the Dominican Republic* (Philadelphia: Temple University Press, 2009), 12.
[112] W. Fitzhugh Brundage, "Introduction," in *The Folly of Jim Crow: Rethinking the Segregated South*, edited by Stephanie Cole & Natalie J. Ring (Arlington: University of Texas at Arlington Press, 2012), 3.

The extension of chain gangs as a manifestation of convict leasing during the Jim Crow era further exacerbated the racialized differentiation of women in the United States: while White women were exempted from chain gangs, Black women were constructed as intrinsically "queer," sexual, and yet asexual "deviants."[113] The Jim Crow South instituted racialized "politics of respectability," which impacted the emotional racialization of childhood.[114] Ralph Thompson remembered in an interview how Black parents tried to protect their children from the suffering of segregation and racialized violence of Jim Crow: "So they tried to shield us from it by sending us or taking us in a different direction, and whatever was going on, they tried to keep it away from us, so to speak."[115] Ferdie Walker recounted how she was exposed to repeated sexual misconduct from White police officers while waiting in bus stops when she was eleven years old: "They'd drive up under there and then they'd expose themselves while I was standing there, and it just really scared me to death. So I had a morbid fear of policemen all of my life and it has not completely gone away."[116] Walker contextualized her lived experience of Jim Crow as both individually traumatic and as part of a collective trauma for Black girls. "But I will *never forget* it, and it always comes back to me every time I get into a really tight experience. That was really bad and it was bad for *all black girls*, you know."[117]

Hence, racialized segregation perpetrated aggravations of generational trauma and aimed to constitute racialized carceral barriers to access to capital and freedom, forming systems of state-wide "loving" nurture toward Whiteness and penalizing colonization of Blackness. White segregated spaces then and now incentivize and monetize emotional detachment (and satisfaction) toward Black suffering and death. Not only did lynching in the United States perpetrate racialized extrajudicial emotional policing, but also its ritualization acted on White supremacist emotional fulfillment of gazing at Black death. This ritualization of Black murder

---

[113] Sarah Haley, *No Mercy Here: Gender, Punishment, and the Making of Jim Crow Modernity* (Chapel Hill: University of North Carolina Press, 2016), 7.
[114] See Jennifer Ritterhouse, *Growing Up Jim Crow: How Black and White Southern Children Learned Race* (Chapel Hill: University of North Carolina Press, 2006), 56.
[115] "Ralph Thompson," in *Remembering Jim Crow: African Americans Tell about Life in the Segregated South*, edited by William H. Chafe, Raymond Gavins, & Robert Korstad (New York: New Press, 2014).
[116] "Ferdie Walker," in *Remembering Jim Crow: African Americans Tell about Life in the Segregated South*, edited by William H. Chafe, Raymond Gavins, & Robert Korstad (New York: New Press, 2014).
[117] "Ferdie Walker."

was consumed as a "spectacle" of "domination" for a White spectatorship, and the White gaze toward this "spectacle" became in turn the "primary representation" of racialized violence for Black communities.[118] Lynching was above all a "cannibalistic" ritual for a White supremacist spectatorship.[119] The "souvenirs," photographs, and postcards of lynching in the Jim Crow South attest to the White emotional satisfaction of Black murder and morbid contemplation of Black death. White families gathered in masses. White parents and children smiling for the camera. The "cannibalistic" smell of death mobilizing their grin.

The narrative of racialized slavery in the Atlantic world had conceptualized enslaved bodies as expendable sites of human experimentation and scientific observation of emotions, and this inexorable connection endured in sinister ways that paralleled the "spectacle" of lynching. The Tuskegee Syphilis Study, which started in 1932 and spanned four decades, was grounded on the exploitative contemplation of hundreds of Black people deteriorating from untreated syphilis. With the intentionality to autopsy their bodies, these Black victims of human experimentation were falsely told that they would be treated for "bad blood," when they were in actuality given aspirin instead of the recommended penicillin.[120] A 1933 letter between organizers of the study reveals their validation of human experimentation on Black communities and their scheme of having Black intermediaries to build "trust," such as Doctor Eugene H. Dibble, Jr., and Nurse Eunice Rivers.

In order that the observation of this untreated group may be completed, it has been decided to attempt to follow the clinical course in the 600 syphilitic and nonsyphilitic Negroes and in case of death attempt to obtain a necropsy. Arrangements for the necropsy have been made with the Tuskegee Institute but if the attempt is to be most successful it is believed that it will be necessary to hospitalize those cases in the event of a terminal illness. The Tuskegee Institute has agreed to furnish free hospitalization to each one of these patients should he become seriously ill, and your cooperation is sought in reporting the serious illness of any one of those Negroes who may consult you. This can probably be best worked out if you will ask Negroes past the age of 25, in the neighborhood of Realtown on the Macon-Tallapoosa County border who consult you for a serious illness, whether they were examined for bad blood by the "Government doctor"

---

[118] Amy Louise Wood, *Lynching and Spectacle: Witnessing Racial Violence in America, 1890–1940* (Chapel Hill: University of North Carolina Press, 2009), 3.
[119] Orlando Patterson, *Rituals of Blood: The Consequences of Slavery in Two American Centuries* (New York: Basic Books, 1999).
[120] Susan M. Reverby, *Examining Tuskegee: The Infamous Syphilis Study and Its Legacy* (Chapel Hill: University of North Carolina Press, 2009), 3.

at Tuskegee Institute. Your alertness in detecting these cases and immediately notifying Doctor Eugene H. Dibble Jr., Tuskegee Institute, Alabama, will do much to make this study a success.[121]

This letter evidences the intentionality of the "necropsy" and the premeditation behind hospitalization. Black bodies would be exploited and held captive under the veil of the institutional legitimacy of a carceral hospital setting, in addition to the enabling role of "trustworthy" Black intermediaries for colonizing aims. A racially premised experiment with the objective to perform autopsies, to premeditate Black death, all with the subterfuge of White "benevolence" and "success." By telling poor Black patients that they suffered from "bad blood," the coordinators of the study opportunistically drew from ideas of biological determinism that were grounded on notions of "corruption," negated access to medical attention and orientation, and instigated contagion to thousands of people of color in this and the Guatemala branch of this project.

Also in 1932, Cornelius Rhoads, prominent pathologist and oncologist from the United States, wrote a letter to a friend about his medical research in the colony of Puerto Rico, which encompassed his emotional criminalization of Puerto Ricans and his understanding of his "duty" as a colonizing physician.

I can get a damn fine job here and am tempted to take it. It would be ideal except for the Porto Ricans – they are beyond doubt the dirtiest, laziest, most degenerate and thievish race of men ever inhabiting this sphere. It makes you sick to inhabit the same island with them. They are even lower than Italians. What the island needs is not public health work, but a tidal wave or something to totally exterminate the population. It might then be livable. I have done my best to further the process of extermination by killing off 8 and transplanting cancer into several more. The latter has not resulted in any fatalities so far. The matter of consideration for the patients' welfare plays no role here – in fact, all physicians take delight in the abuse and torture of the unfortunate subjects.[122]

Rhoads emphasizes notions of Puerto Rican "laziness" and "criminality" as framed by geographical determinism, discourses that have long oppressed Puerto Ricans as racialized colonial and carceral subjects. The conception of Puerto Ricans as biologically "degenerate" is introduced as justification of a eugenicist project, whether by a "tidal wave" or by

---

[121] "R. A. Vonderlehr to Dr. H. T. Jones, Tallassee, Alabama, November 20, 1933," as quoted in *Tuskegee's Truths: Rethinking the Tuskegee Syphilis Study*, edited by Susan M. Reverby (Chapel Hill: University of North Carolina Press, 2000), 87.

[122] "The Cornelius Rhoads Letter," as quoted in Daniel Immerwahr, *How to Hide an Empire: A History of the Greater United States* (New York: Macmillan, 2019).

"transplanting cancer." Rhoads paints a picture in which doctors "take delight" in maleficence toward "unfortunate subjects" of racialized human experimentation. The history of human experimentation in Puerto Rico includes two major birth control pill trials in the 1950s, with uninformed "participants" of color taking exorbitant hormonal doses,[123] and the systematic sterilization of Puerto Ricans. Racialized nonconsensual sterilization in the United States likewise became generalized in the same historical juncture, and civil rights activist Fannie Lou Hamer, who was a survivor of this systemic institutional violence, referred to racialized forced sterilization as "Mississippi appendectomies," denouncing the pervasive nature of this eugenicist project.[124] The painful narrative of medical maleficence shows up not only in personal letters of medical eugenicists but also in the medical records of state-sanctioned human experimentation and in the countless denunciations of Black activism. Powerful White medical providers "took delight" in perpetrating medical maleficence against Black communities in the name of institutional "success." But medical maleficence was not conceptualized as such, since the rise of medical specialization was grounded on scientific racism and the medical exploitation of Black bodies, all for the fulfillment of a healthier, happier White body.

The historical racialization of poverty and crime in the United States was enforced by discourses of emotional difference in bodies that were deemed "biologically" vicious and lethargic. The scholarship has explored how capitalist "democracies" conceived low-income communities as both "marginal and central to the social order" and how the intentionality of "poverty governance" was to ensure the "cooperation and contributions of weakly integrated populations."[125] Prison systems adhered to a convenient "invisibility" in "modern democracies."[126] The policies of the criminal justice system in the United States, unlike matters of air quality or workplace safety, have not been historically guided by

---

[123] Laura Briggs, *Reproducing Empire: Race, Sex, Science, and U.S. Imperialism in Puerto Rico* (Berkeley: University of California Press, 2002), 124.

[124] Dorothy Roberts, *Killing the Black Body: Race, Reproduction, and the Meaning of Liberty* (New York: Random House, 2016), 90.

[125] Joe Soss, Richard C. Fording, & Sanford F. Schram, *Disciplining the Poor: Neoliberal Paternalism and the Persistent Power of Race* (Chicago: University of Chicago Press, 2011), 2.

[126] Albert W. Dzur, Ian Loader, & Richard Sparks, "Punishment and Democratic Theory: Resources for a Better Penal Politics," in *Democratic Theory and Mass Incarceration*, edited by Albert W. Dzur, Ian Loader, & Richard Sparks (Oxford: Oxford University Press, 2016), 2.

"experts" of societal reintegration, but have instead followed a White "penal populism."[127] Scholars have analyzed how, since the "post-emancipation" era, the US government has steadily used mass incarceration to regulate "poverty, inequality, unemployment, racial conflict, citizenship, sexuality, and gender."[128] Black "urban" spaces have increasingly been "entangled" with spaces of "confinement," building a "carceral landscape."[129] Throughout the second half of the twentieth century, a combination of prejudiced mandatory minimum sentencing and "three strikes" laws resulted in outstanding racialized sentences for petty crime and misdemeanors in the United States,[130] and inmates who received life sentences tended to experience "accelerated aging"[131] in a prison system that is meant to hurt, punish, and take life. More and more, prison labor has backtracked rights attained by union strikes and offered corporations either free or extremely cheap labor to compete in capitalist economies.[132]

The contemporary movement for prison abolitionism has inherited the condemnation of the racialization of emotions in the prison narratives of influential revolutionaries of the Civil Rights movement. The "Letter from Birmingham Jail" by Martin Luther King, Jr., famously denounced the emotional "timetable" of the "White moderate."

I have almost reached the regrettable conclusion that the Negro's great stumbling block in his stride toward freedom is not the White Citizen's Counciler or the Ku Klux Klanner, but the white moderate, who is more devoted to "order" than to justice; who prefers a negative peace which is the absence of tension to a positive peace which is the presence of justice; who constantly says: "I agree with you in the goal you seek, but I cannot agree with your methods of direct action"; who paternalistically believes he can set the timetable for another man's freedom; who lives by a mythical concept of time and who constantly advises the Negro to wait for a "more convenient season."[133]

---

[127] Rachel E. Barkow, *Prisoners of Politics: Breaking the Cycle of Mass Incarceration* (Cambridge, MA: Harvard University Press, 2019), 1–5.
[128] James W. Kilgore, *Understanding Mass Incarceration: A People's Guide to the Key Civil Rights Struggle of Our Time* (New York: New Press, 2015), 1.
[129] Dan Berger, *Captive Nation: Black Prison Organizing in the Civil Rights Era* (Chapel Hill: University of North Carolina Press, 2014), 21.
[130] Peter K. Enns, *Incarceration Nation: How the United States Became the Most Punitive Democracy in the World* (New York: Cambridge University Press, 2016).
[131] Marieke Liem, *After Life Imprisonment: Reentry in the Era of Mass Incarceration* (New York: New York University Press, 2016), 4.
[132] Gordon Lafer, "The Politics of Prison Labor: A Union Perspective," in *Prison Nation: The Warehousing of America's Poor*, edited by Paul Wright & Tara Herivel (New York: Routledge, 2003), 120.
[133] Martin Luther King, Jr., *Why We Can't Wait* (New York: Penguin, 2000), 72–73.

King deplores the paternalism of the "White moderate," condescendingly expecting Black activists to compartmentalize their emotions in the "stride toward freedom" and advising patience in a group that is innately conceptualized as "too impatient." Any progress in restorative justice is detained by the empty promise of a "more convenient season," "more convenient" than the one framed by Black "impatience." Meanwhile, *The Autobiography of Malcolm X* decries the inhumane conditions of prison, deprecating the condition of being "caged."

> Any person who claims to have deep feeling for other human beings should think a long, long time before he votes to have other men kept behind bars – caged. I am not saying there shouldn't be prisons, but there shouldn't be bars. Behind bars, a man never reforms. He will never forget. He never will get completely over the memory of the bars. After he gets out, his mind tries to erase experience, but he can't. I've talked with numerous former convicts. It has been very interesting to me to find that all of our minds had blotted away many details of years in prison. But in every case, he will tell you that he can't forget those bars.[134]

Malcolm X argues that a person with "deep feeling" toward others would not sanction the environment of the prison system in the United States. This "deep feeling" is the core value of his separatist movement. The "bars" of the prison cell create an unavoidable burden, the agonizing image of captivity that encompasses Black generational trauma. The "memory of the bars" is Black captivity itself. George Jackson also expounds the "inevitability of prison," but increases the scope of the experience of being "caged" to much before the "memory of the bars."

> It always starts with Mama, mine loved me. As testimony of her love, and her fear for the fate of the man-child all slave mothers hold, she attempted to press, hide, push, capture me in the womb. The conflicts and contradictions that will follow me to the tomb started right there in the womb. The feeling of being captured ... this slave can never adjust to it, it's a thing that I just don't favor, then, now, never.[135]

George Jackson names an allegorical first encounter with Black captivity: the enslaved womb. Jackson was born enslaved because Black motherhood is born enslaved, binding his mother and her child forever and before. She vehemently "captured" her Black child in her womb to prevent the "fate of the man-child." This fearful "capture" is unique to

---

[134] Malcolm X, *The Autobiography of Malcolm X* (New York: Random House, 1964), 176.

[135] George Jackson, *Soledad Brother: The Prison Letters of George Jackson* (Chicago: Lawrence Hill, 1994), 4.

the Black experience of perennial slavery. The dread toward the incarceration of the "man-child" is equivalent to the matrilineality and irrevocability of slavery itself. Likewise, *Assata: An Autobiography* by Assata Shakur conveys the dehumanizing body politics of carceral oppression.

> I was growing weaker and weaker. My energy seemed to have gone down the drain. All i wanted to do was sleep. I chided myself for trying to escape from reality instead of facing it. I had seen women in jail sleep their whole time away. I was afraid that was happening to me.... I have seen people in prison gain twenty, thirty, forty, fifty pounds eating out of nerves and boredom. It gets to the point when all you have to look to forward to is the meals. And that in itself is pitiful, because anyone who has ever been in prison knows how terrible the food is. Yet i was gulping that stuff down just like it was Mom's home cooking.[136]

Shakur elucidates how the incarcerated strive to retain their corporeal functions and develop a "pitiful" psychological dependence on sleep and food. Anxiety and "boredom" regulate the prisoners' relationship with their own bodies and their own psyches. Hence, prison narratives written by Black political prisoners tend to emphasize the "inevitability of prison" in the structural carcerality of Black emotions, highlighting the inherent emotional tyranny, dehumanization, and oppression of the carceral State, as insistently permeating and distressing Black lives in the United States.

The affirmations of self-love of the Civil Rights movement, the Black Power movement, revolutions for decolonization, and Pan-Africanist thought were regarded as illegitimate "Black rage" by the colonizing institutions of power and were brutally punished. During the 1960s, "Black is beautiful" rose as a slogan of "self-love,"[137] after the history of slavery and colonialism in the Atlantic world had manufactured "Black beauty shame."[138] The State response to the Black Panther Party and to the Attica Prison Revolution paralleled the imperial reactions to the revolutions of the enslaved. Just as the "passionate" revolutions of the enslaved were blamed for the "unhappiness" of colonies, "Black rage" was connoted as the source of the "unrest" within the racialized/colonized, which justified "law and order" policies, police brutality, White flight, statistical policing of Blackness, and colonial barriers to Black citizenship and economic mobility.

---

[136] Assata Shakur, *Assata: An Autobiography* (Chicago: Lawrence Hill, 1987), 121.
[137] Maxine Leeds Craig, *Ain't I a Beauty Queen: Black Women, Beauty, and the Politics of Race* (Oxford: Oxford University Press, 2011), 23.
[138] Shirley Anne Tate, *Black Beauty: Aesthetics, Stylization, Politics* (New York: Routledge, 2009), 79.

Michelle Alexander contends that mass incarceration represents a new "racial caste system," Atlantic slavery and Jim Crow being previous manifestations of such systems that have excluded Black communities from civil and voting rights.[139] Other scholars have pinpointed specific political discourses and governmental administrations that have extended the reach of the carceral State.[140] Contributing to this scholarship, it can be argued that racialized mass incarceration is a direct evolution from the legal "abolition" of slavery that standardized eugenicist state-sanctioned enslavement premised on Black emotional criminalization. It is the perpetuation of slaveholding genocidal violence and racialized emotional policing that constructs Black "emotional violence" as spontaneously "provoking" institutional suspicion and fierce punishment. It is a eugenicist project with the goal of "incapacitating" Black emotionality, concocted by prominent advocates of scientific racism who normalized White profit from the emotional differentiation of Blackness. It is essentially the institutionalization of the prescribed failure of the Black body to attain emotional self-containment as a carceral site: the prison system is then conceived as an apparatus to apprehend and consume the "doomed" emotional carcerality of the Black body. The eugenicist carcerality of Black emotions fundamentally structures the prison industrial complex. The political maleficence toward the emotionally "resilient" Black Body is embedded in the walls and bars of the prison system itself – because Black emotions can take it. The eugenicist design of solitary confinement was aimed toward the self-"contemplation" of Black emotions. Black emotionality could only miscarry this forced contemplation, as structures of power presumed that Black emotions would detonate without notice and would require permanent carceral penalization. While Black lives were expected to "contemplate" and monitor their own emotionality, White emotional supremacy only sadistically gazed at fatally marked, emotionally dehumanized Black "flesh."

Fundamentally, White happiness morbidly and consciously profits from Black pain, avidly enacting the institutional carcerality of Black emotions. Just as Black feelings were dictated to be governed by White rationality, the White penalization of Black Emotions historically rose to

---

[139] Michelle Alexander, *The New Jim Crow: Mass Incarceration in the Age of Colorblindness* (New York: New Press, 2012).

[140] See Elizabeth Hinton, *From the War on Poverty to the War on Crime: The Making of Mass Incarceration in America* (Cambridge, MA: Harvard University Press, 2016); Naomi Murakawa, *The First Civil Right: How Liberals Built Prison America* (Oxford: Oxford University Press, 2014).

sanction every political, economic, and societal enactment of power in the Atlantic world. What needed to be concealed, pushed down, harmed, and yet needed to be there for White emotional privilege to flourish. Black communities were to be kept at the brink of death, assassinated through carceral violence and colonial exploitation, yet they were still needed for the same undesirable labor and role in society as their enslaved ancestors. The role of the emotional villain to elevate the self-indulgence, the wastefulness, the decadence of White joy. The imperial genocidal violence of emotional carcerality is then the essence of the capitalistic racialization of enslaved exploitation and pain. Ultimately, the colonizing order of the structural carcerality of Black emotions is tied to the eugenicist intentionality to exterminate the "annoyance" of "Black rage" in the name of the preservation of White entitled bliss. "Black rage" was the key manifestation of institutional displeasure, and twentieth-century media marketed and profited from this White dissatisfaction toward Black emotional expression.

EMOTIONAL ARCHETYPES IN TWENTIETH-CENTURY HOLLYWOOD MEDIA REPRESENTATIONS OF BLACKNESS

Twentieth-century media inherited the normative epistemological symbiosis of Whiteness, art, and the production of knowledge. The scholarly conversation has elucidated that slavery played an "essential and constitutive role" in the rise of "modernity" and the advent of an "economy of sense and sensibility or taste"[141] and how, within "modernity," "natives" of Africa and the Americas were considered the least "westernizable" and thus the most subordinated by "silencing" in the production of history and knowledge.[142] Scholars have examined how nineteenth-century European art used Blackness as either an "aesthetic tool or novelty" to recall ideas of "conquest" and an intersection of the exotic and erotic,[143] in addition to how there are still two mainstream modes of looking at and packaging the history of art from Africa or the African diaspora in museums of the United States: the "anthropological approach" that preserves Otherness and the "corrective narrative" that alleges to discover

---

[141] Gikandi, *Slavery and the Culture of Taste*, 10.   [142] Trouillot, *Silencing the Past*, 76.
[143] Adrienne L. Childs & Susan H. Libby, "Introduction: Figuring Blackness in Europe," in *Blacks and Blackness in European Art of the Long Nineteenth Century*, edited by Adrienne L. Childs & Susan H. Libby (New York: Ashgate, 2014), 3.

"overlooked" Black art.[144] In sum, the scholarship has analyzed how Blackness embodies a "troubling vision" for the "West."[145] Twentieth-century Hollywood media emotionally depersonalized Blackness and reverberated the emotional policing of a "troubling" Blackness as a monolith and as an expendable source of exploitative labor, hypersexuality, and common entertainment.

The film *The Birth of a Nation*,[146] directed by D. W. Griffith, not only would presage the mainstream media representation of Blackness in the United States but also would mobilize the political agenda that led to the revival of the Ku Klux Klan. The use of blackface in the first feature-length film of all time is strategic and illustrative of the foundational practice of blackface in the birth of film. The transnational rise of blackface minstrelsy was certainly concurrent and "complementary" to the intensification of White abolitionist "fervor."[147] *The Birth of a Nation*, like Madison Grant's *Passing of the Great Race*, is a manifesto against the "sentimentality of the Civil War," a diatribe against Reconstruction, and a defense of White supremacy. The public response to the film led by William Monroe Trotter would compel Griffith's own "emotional" reaction in his subsequent film, titled *Intolerance*. Today, there is still a scholarly debate about how *The Birth of Nation* should be academically assessed. Many scholars have indicated a "duality" in their interpretation of the film, as a film that is both "controversial" and "crucial" to the history of cinema.[148] In other words, mainstream media studies acknowledge the racism in the film only to "clarify" that it should still be understood as a meaningful film for its "form" or aesthetic "value," creating a duality between "narrative" and "style." Other scholars have rightfully criticized how *The Birth of a Nation*'s "melodrama" aimed to "convert the nation to southern sympathy" grounded on "antipathy for the black male sexual threat to white women."[149] The reductionist reading of *The Birth of a Nation* as having a "dual" legacy indeed fails to

---

[144] Bridget R. Cooks, *Exhibiting Blackness: African Americans and the American Art Museum* (Boston: University of Massachusetts Press, 2011), xix.

[145] Nicole R. Fleetwood, *Troubling Vision: Performance, Visuality, and Blackness* (Chicago: University of Chicago Press, 2011), 6.

[146] D. W. Griffith (dir.), *The Birth of a Nation* (film), Epoch Producing Co., 1915.

[147] Nowatzki, *Representing African Americans*, 4.

[148] Melvin Stokes, *D. W. Griffith's The Birth of a Nation: A History of the Most Controversial Motion Picture of All Time* (Oxford: Oxford University Press, 2007).

[149] Linda Williams, *Playing the Race Card: Melodramas of Black and White from Uncle Tom to O. J. Simpson* (Princeton, NJ: Princeton University Press, 2001), 98.

recognize that the film's "form" is central to its White supremacist storytelling.

The gaze of the camera in *The Birth of a Nation* premeditatedly constructs Blackness as innately prone to emotional delinquency and "tastelessness." The notorious "legislature scene" shows actors in blackface eating fried chicken, drinking alcohol, and resting their bare feet over the legislative posts previously occupied by "productive" White politicians. Formerly enslaved people of the South are depicted as "mindlessly" dancing and eating watermelon, not "knowing" what to do with themselves. Following discourses of historical determinism and proslavery thought, their emotional "erraticism" is "heightened" by a lack of consciousness of the "limits of freedom." In the most infamous scene of the film, a "Black man" (again, an actor in blackface) discovers a White teenaged girl in the woods. A close-up of the "Black man" highlights him staring lustfully at her pale, adolescent body. The "Black man" approaches the White teenager and tells her with desire: "You see, I'm a captain now – and I want to marry." In panic, the White girl runs away from the "menacing Black man" and throws herself down a cliff. Later in the movie, the "Black criminal" is apprehended, and he is put on trial by the Ku Klux Klan. Images of the White teenager's funeral invade the linearity of the "trial." Her lifeless body is under a white blanket covered in flowers, and her presence connotes the "innocence" of White childhood, the "honor" of her White family, and the aesthetics of classical art. The "Black man" is found guilty by the Ku Klux Klan, and his cadaver is carelessly thrown onto the porch of the house of a White family with a note showing an image of a skull signed by the "KKK." *The Birth of a Nation*'s essence can be discerned in the camera zooming in to the gaze of the "Black male rapist" and the editorial juxtaposition of the "honorable" cadaver of the White girl and the "disposable" remains of the Black man. The Ku Klux Klan is therefore represented as vigilante justice against the inborn emotional "aggression" of Black "masculinity," the unbridled and hazardous sexual desire of "lawless" Black men toward "pure" White women. The "form" of the film is inexorably connected to (and openly encourages) extreme violence against intrinsically emotionally "deviant" and "expendable" Black people.

Gone with the Wind[150] notoriously replicated the slaveholding celebration of the "happiness" of the antebellum South. The enslaved people

---

[150] Victor Fleming (dir.), *Gone with the Wind* (film), Metro-Goldwyn-Mayer, 1939.

of Tara remain there after the Civil War, and their loyalty toward Scarlett O'Hara is an expression of their "happy" condition. While enslaved men are set to deliver an "Uncle Tom" presence, Prissy, a young enslaved woman, is portrayed as "hysterical" and indolent, screaming herself out of every challenge. Prissy represents a source of annoyance for Scarlett, and audiences are expected to admire Scarlett's patience toward such an emotionally "negligent" enslaved woman/child. In contrast, Mammy is a maternal figure who "adores" (and serves) Scarlett. In one scene of the film, after having helped Scarlett get into a corset and elaborate party dress, Mammy begs Scarlett to eat the meal that she prepared for her. The power dynamics of the scene accentuate Mammy's concern and emotional attachment toward the fulfillment of her "service." Furthermore, Mammy points out that "you can always tell a lady by the way she eats in front of folks like a bird" and not like a "field hand and gobble like a hog," animalizing and "masculinizing" her own enslaved body. In the end, Mammy "wins," and always-supporting actress Hattie McDaniel contemplates the Hollywood megastar Vivien Leigh with a smile as she eats some food prepared by enslaved hands. This scene, in a disconcerting and manipulative manner, characterizes the master–enslaved relationship not only as earnestly "loving" but also as one in which seemingly "domineering" and self-deprecating Black women get what they want.

An analogous figure of *Gone with the Wind*'s Mammy in cinema is *Song of the South*'s Uncle Remus. Although Disney's *Song of the South*[151] was banned from DVD release, its legacies can still be found in the dispersal of imagery of the "happy" enslaved and in the only recently addressed Splash Mountain ride. Not only does *Song of the South* appropriate and dilute the Br'er Rabbit character from enslaved cultural production without any contextualization, but it also crafts one of the most influential images of the "happiness" of the enslaved. Though Disney clumsily tried to excuse itself with the "clarification" that this film aimed to represent the Reconstruction era, an era that terrorized Black communities, the "Uncle Tom–like" emotional dependence of Uncle Remus on the White characters he "serves" is offensive regardless of its time frame. When Uncle Remus starts singing the famous song "Zip-a-Dee-Doo-Dah," flowers whimsically come out of his head, and his surroundings become an idyllic animation world. Uncle Remus expresses hyperbolic joy and delightfully sings: "Mr. Bluebird's on my shoulder / It's the truth, it's

---

[151] Harve Foster & Wilfred Jackson (dirs.), *Song of the South* (film), Walt Disney Productions, 1946.

actual / Everything is satisfactual / Zip-a-dee-doo-dah, zip-a-dee-ay / Wonderful feeling, wonderful day." His imaginary fulfillment of his "wonderful feeling," which only the White children in the film are able to enjoy, keeps him in a perpetual emotionally infantilized state and reverberates the discourses of sublime enslaved happiness and the "satisfaction" of contemplating White agency.

The *Song of the South* was inevitably influenced by the inexorable link between the rise of animation, emotional theories of scientific racism, and, more specifically, the imagery of craniology. With the iconic Mickey Mouse, Hollywood animation arose as a "performative tradition" grounded on "blackface minstrelsy and vaudeville."[152] "Mickey's Mellerdrammer"[153] shows a stage performance of *Uncle Tom's Cabin* led by Mickey and Minnie Mouse. The scene where the characters prepare for their performance demonstrates the racialization of beauty framed by scientific racism. While Minnie Mouse confidently puts white powder on her face and proudly glances at her reflection after putting on a blond wig to play "little Eva," Clarabelle Cow swiftly covers her face with lantern soot to "simulate" a Black enslaved person. Even more repugnant is how Mickey Mouse explodes a firecracker in his mouth in order to apply blackface to represent enslaved girl "Topsy," while also wearing a racialized wig and ragged clothing. The "gender bender" is an anomaly for its time, indicating a blatant attempt at "masculinizing" and ridiculing Black women. The whole animation short film highlights how both "fun" and "funny" it is to emotionally simulate slavery, with much slapstick and chaos along the way. Goofy laughs hysterically at the end of the cartoon when he notices he has blackface too, after being attacked with a chocolate cake by the unimpressed audience craving to be entertained with a "more pleasing" simulation of slavery.

The unavoidable ties among scientific racism, blackface minstrelsy, and early animation are even more apparent in "The Censored Eleven," a set of short animation films from the 1930s and 1940s, mostly from *Merrie Melodies*. These cartoons unfailingly craft Black emotional caricatures that are framed by both blackface and the imagery of craniology. "Sunday Go to Meetin' Time"[154] is a musical cartoon filled with

---

[152] Nicholas Sammond, *Birth of an Industry: Blackface Minstrelsy and the Rise of American Animation* (Durham, NC: Duke University Press, 2015).
[153] Wilfred Jackson (dir.), "Mickey's Mellerdrammer" (cartoon), Walt Disney Productions, 1933.
[154] Friz Freleng (dir.), "Sunday Go to Meetin' Time" (cartoon), Warner Bros. Pictures, 1936.

blackface caricatures and criminalizing typecasts of Blackness: emotionally depersonalized Black children, a "Mammy" character, and preconceived trivializations of Black spirituality. In this cartoon, the "Mammy" serves as a caricature of the "angry Black woman" archetype after finding Nicodemus, the Black protagonist, "playing dice." "Mammy" scolds him while pulling his ear and forcing him to attend church: "You good for nothing! Get yourself to that church! The Devil's gonna get you as sure as you're born!" After escaping church, Nicodemus proceeds to attempt to steal some chickens when he loses consciousness in front of a sign that says "Judge Jailem Court of Justice," which transforms itself into the hellish "Hades Court of Justice." The Devil looks for Nicodemus's "sins" in his book to find his past "crimes": "shooting craps, stealing chickens, missing church, raisin' dickens, stealing watermelons." The Devil exclaims, "That's bad!" and throws him into an inferno full of little devils reminiscent of blackface minstrelsy. The Devil then sings: "You gotta give the Devil his due." Nicodemus regains consciousness and runs to church to purge his "sins." Not only does this cartoon deliberately revert to societal constructs in the United States about the "passionate" behavioral tendencies of Blackness, such as "playing dice," "stealing chickens," and "eating watermelon," but it also conceives these emotional behaviors as inherently both criminal and sinful, echoing religious interpretations of monogenism. The imagery blending the criminal justice system with the "Devil's Court" mocks Black spirituality and makes a political statement about what Black men innately "owe." Therefore, "Sunday Go to Meetin' Time" utilizes discourses of biological and geographical determinism to spread ideas of intrinsic Black criminality, negligence, and absence of emotional self-regulation to give their "due."

Released just two years later, "Jungle Jitters"[155] is a cartoon that also reverberates blackface minstrelsy, but does so in the context of the emotional pathologization of Africa. The cartoon starts with a caricature of "tribal dancing": semi-naked Black men with depersonalized "ape-like" traits and hyperbolic neck rings "hysterically" dance just to waste time. A dog-like, and yet still depicted as White and therefore more human, salesman knocks on the door of the "tribe's" bamboo house, and the African caricatures instantaneously plan to eat him. A "Mammy-like" cook starts to boil the salesman alive, while some cannibalistic Africans angrily await for their meal, and others are in awe of the "modern"

---

[155] Friz Freleng (dir.), "Jungle Jitters" (cartoon), Warner Bros. Pictures, 1938.

possessions that the White dog/salesman has in his suitcase, such as a vacuum cleaner and light bulbs. A sign that reads "The Palace (Temporary): Moving to More Palatial Quarters" connotes the butt of the joke: Africa's "anthropological present." "Jungle Jitters" evokes theories of historical determinism in its representation of a "backward," animalistic, and cannibalistic Africa with an "ethnic" nakedness and ritualistic anger.

"All This and Rabbit Stew"[156] follows the same format of other Bugs Bunny cartoons, but the drawing of his "child-like" archenemy overtly recreates the historical racist illustrations of craniological texts. Following both biological and geographical determinism, the Black "male" character walks in a tediously slow manner, dragging a rifle as a sign of "tropical" indolence and biological negligence. His speech is premeditatedly almost undecipherable, and his reflexes and verbal communication are as unhurried as his walk. In multiple instances, the character transforms into a Black lollipop with the caption "sucker." In the climax of this cartoon, the Black character finally has his prey defenseless when Bugs Bunny distracts him with some dice. The Black archenemy reacts ecstatically to the dice and, behind a bush, gambles his clothing away. Bugs Bunny emerges triumphant with the Black archenemy's clothing, imitating the first scene of the cartoon, walking slowly, dragging his gun, and singing unintelligibly. The Black character reappears naked "from the bush" with an Adamite leaf, exclaiming "Well, call me Adam!," the joke being the "audacity" of the Black man to deem himself the "image of God." As the screen goes to black, Bugs Bunny deliberately takes the leaf with pride, reinforcing the mockery of the Black body and its emotionality. Not only does this cartoon construct an infantilized Black caricature that cannot regulate his emotional impulsivity toward gambling and his own corporeal movement, but it also derives from ideas of monogenism, polygenism, and scientific racism. Twentieth-century media evoked the racialization of childhood, exposing Black children to hateful imagery that they were supposed as spectators to imprint in their own skin. The "family-friendly" market of "fantasy" and "dreams coming true" was never made for them, but at the expense of them.

Twentieth-century media representations also utilized "sympathetic" portrayals of Blackness to mobilize emotions toward "perceptions" of racial progress. "Sympathetic" media representations have been historically manipulated to render the United States as an "enlightened" nation in

---

[156] Tex Avery (dir.), "All This and Rabbit Stew" (cartoon), Warner Bros. Pictures, 1941.

a "postracial era."[157] Films scripted with a "White savior" narrative echoed theories of historical determinism and spotlighted colonizing "love" toward Blackness. Not only did the archetype of the mythical/magical Black supporting character diffuse preconceived notions of "Black paganism" and about the religions of the enslaved, but it also celebrated emotional altruism from Black secondary characters to White protagonists. Multiple films of the twentieth century show a "sympathetic token Black best friend" that is archetypically "louder," "lazier," and more "sexually impulsive" than their White counterparts. On the contrary, Black "sympathetic" leading roles have had to be morally "elevated" in comparison to White protagonists: Sidney Poitier's filmography in the 1960s demonstrates the higher pressures of being emotionally "immaculate" for Black leading actors versus any White characters. "Sympathetic" Black "masculinity" in "mainstream" films tends to be represented through Black characters that are isolated from their Black community and are "doing it for daddy": propelling all of their emotional efforts for the redemption of a White "male" character.[158] Hollywood production companies have historically branded Black films as "unbankable" as a way to retain the exclusion and tokenization of Black thespians and directors in mainstream cinema, upholding the packaging of Blackness in White cinematography.[159] The silencing of Black queer experiences in twentieth-century media is in turn tied to narrative restrictions posed to manifold emotional otherness.

Throughout its history, *National Geographic* spread images of a seminaked "tribal" Africa, appealing to a voyeuristic/apathetic spectatorship of Black poverty and famine. Not only did this magazine particularly depict Africa as an "anthropological present" during the 1970s and 1980s, but it also endorsed disdain toward the fetishized "consumption" of the "nakedness" of Black bodies. "Famine photography" has been used as an "instrument of affective imperatives, the emotive gestures of a mostly American public negotiating the terms of the cadaver of the other."[160] This "affective" imagery framed by historical determinism can

---

[157] Evelyn Alsultany, *Arabs and Muslims in the Media: Race and Representation after 9/11* (New York: New York University Press, 2012), 16.

[158] bell hooks, *Reel to Real: Race, Sex, and Class at the Movies* (New York: Routledge, 1996), 104.

[159] Maryann Erigha, *The Hollywood Jim Crow: The Racial Politics of the Movie Industry* (New York: New York University Press, 2019), 52.

[160] Kimberly Juanita Brown, "Regarding the Pain of the Other: Photography, Famine, and the Transference of Affect," in *Feeling Photography*, edited by Elspeth H. Brown & Thy Phu (Durham, NC: Duke University Press, 2014), 183.

also be found in the twentieth-century cinematographic representation of Africa, such as the film *The Gods Must Be Crazy*.[161] Claiming to be a "comedy" that questions ideas about "civilization," the film epitomizes an instance of cultural exploitation, in this case, of its Black South African actors. It tells the paternalistic story of a "tribe gone wrong" once a form of property (a "Coca-Cola" bottle) is given by the "Gods" (more like thrown from an airplane). The havoc created by the bottle leads to "superstition," mayhem, violence, and the disruption of the "tribal" unit. The message is clear: some human groups are "stuck in time" and too emotionally variable to manage property. The cinematography shows disregard toward naked Black bodies, while it generates an air of ethereal beauty for its blond and always fully clothed White leading actress, with the support of a romantic musical score. This cinematographic mysticism surrounding White women reinforces ideas of protection of White "purity." In contrast, tourism advertisements around the world disseminated discourses of "tropical fever" that hypersexualized Blackness and glorified notions of "paradise," or "emotional detours," guaranteed by the privilege of being served by Black hands. Tropical destinations were (and are) advertised with sweaty and suggestively clothed bodies of color, in correlation with the racialized demand of sex tourism. A disturbing 1978 commercial for Jamaican tourism, titled "Make It Jamaica Again," plagiarizes "Happy Xmas (War Is Over)" by John Lennon and Yoko Ono and changes the lyrics to "Come Back to Jamaica." The commercial spotlights multiple Black Jamaicans who speak to the camera, saying phrases such as, "Come back to hospitality" and "Come back to romance." The theme of "coming back" to "romantic feelings" draws disconcerting connections to Jamaica's colonial past and the history of imperial sexual violence against Black Jamaicans.

The influence of geographical determinism in media is most prominent in the unrelenting hypersexualization of people of color through emotional archetypes. The pervasive archetypes of the "Latin lover," the "fiery Latina," and the "crazy Latina girlfriend" are premised on ideas of aggressive sexual "promiscuity" of racialized populations from hotter climates. Following the discourse of mestizaje, Latin American telenovelas appropriate these same archetypes to uplift light-skinned sex symbols, keeping Black and indigenous faces in the peripheral roles of the asexualized "help." The hypersexualization of Black women in twentieth-

---

[161] Jamie Uys (dir.), *The Gods Must Be Crazy* (film), C.A.T. Films, 1980.

century media emulated the "Jezebel" archetype, "fallen" Black women who "could not be raped" because of their unbridled sexual drive, and the "Sapphire" archetype, sexually "aggressive" and inherently dangerous Black women. Blaxploitation films directed by White men, and thus enacting a "White man's fantasy vision,"[162] perpetuated these discourses of hyperbolically sexually forceful and emotionally criminal Black women within Black spaces of social decay of drug and sex trades, which they had the burden of rescuing as "caregivers," such as the main character of *Foxy Brown*,[163] who was signified as an excessive "whole lotta woman." The beginning of the James Bond film *Live and Let Die*[164] arrogated Blaxploitation imagery in its exposition of New Orleans and "San Monique." A well-attended Black funeral procession in a street of New Orleans plays somber music while a Black woman weeps. After a White bystander is killed, film spectators find out that the coffin and the funeral were always intended for him. The music shifts, and the Black woman joyfully dances in unison with the Black community that serves as a collective antagonist in a film franchise with individual White antagonists. The movie turns to the fictional Caribbean island of San Monique (obviously Haiti), where the Black cast is told to perform a "tribal" dance. Their "frenetic" bodily contortions are portrayed as part of a "ritual" of possession and connoted as a mockery of Haitian vodou. A Black priest uses a snake to kill a White prisoner, which jump-starts the musical opening credits of the film. When Paul McCartney sings the words "live and let die," the head of a naked Black woman transforms into a skull on fire. Not only does the Bond film represent Black communities as cohesively emotionally performative and perilous to White comfort, but the movie is also driven by the eroticization of Black death as tied to spiritual decadence. Likewise, the photographic essay *Jungle Fever*[165] by Jean-Paul Goude, who claimed that he himself suffered from this "ailment," voyeuristically displays digitally altered images of unclothed Black women. Their Black bodies are denoted as "monstrous," hypersexual, and captive (sometimes even in cages), when Goude's photography of White models for Chanel shows their White bodies as whimsical, "innocent," and, of course, fully clothed.

---

[162] Stephane Dunn, *"Baad Bitches" and Sassy Supermamas: Black Power Action Films* (Urbana-Champaign: University of Illinois Press, 2008), 15.
[163] Jack Hill (dir.), *Foxy Brown* (film), American International Pictures, 1974.
[164] Guy Hamilton (dir.), *Live and Let Die* (film), United Artists, 1973.
[165] Jean-Paul Goude, *Jungle Fever* (photographic essay), 1981.

Every single day, US media diffused ideas of the urgent threat of Black emotional criminality, which mimicked "concerns" about "overpopulation" in imperial discourses. Black and Afro-Latinx people were consistently represented in twentieth-century media as "violent, pathological criminals."[166] "Mass media spectacles of race, violence, and crime"[167] both garnered activism for restorative justice and were seized by White political figures as a public demonstration of their efficacy and "sensitivity." The horror "slasher films" of the 1980s aimed to unsettle the comfort of "those who thought white flight away from the urban black and poor and into the welcoming arms of white, middle-class suburban communities would bring them peace."[168] Crime television shows, such as *Cops*, capitalized on a pornographic gaze toward the racialization of poverty, profiling, police brutality, and media representations of addiction. The media unremittingly targeted the emotional tropes of the conniving "welfare queen" and the "failed" single Black mother through coded (yet overt) language, following the paradigm of the Moynihan Report in the rendering of essentialized Black single-parent households as enduring disappointments. Black men were characterized as emotionally "capricious" lawbreakers who could not value the "rightful" gateways to "success," regardless of their socioeconomic status. The emotional criminalization of Black men in media spotlighted the archetypes of the "thug" and the "superpredator": Black "masculinity" was categorized as "monstrous," emotionally treacherous, sexually "aggressive," and aspiring to quick success, not comprehending the "limits of freedom" like the "formerly" enslaved. While White success was celebrated in twentieth-century media, the rich man of color was depicted as chauvinistic, greedy, materialistic, and emotionally dependent on property. White criminality was glamorized, received with awe and curiosity, portrayed as "conflicted," and deconstructed for its "brilliance," with figures such as serial killer Ted Bundy. Black criminality was hyperpoliced, emotionally depersonalized, taken for granted, and presented as essentially "dirty," menacing, and sexually perverse. Even Black victimhood was and is emotionally criminalized. The discourse of "Black-on-Black crime" solidified the power of the "statistical" hyperpolicing of

---

[166] See Christopher P. Campbell, ed., *The Routledge Companion to Media and Race* (New York: Routledge, 2017).
[167] Jonathan Markovitz, *Racial Spectacles: Explorations in Media, Race, and Justice* (New York: Routledge, 2011), 3.
[168] Robin R. Means Coleman, *Horror Noire: Blacks in American Horror Films from the 1890s to Present* (New York: Routledge, 2011), 148.

Blackness and of the notion of Black communities as emotionally self-destructive. White-on-White crime was and is conveniently left unnamed.

Twentieth-century media accumulated capital through the commodification of iconography of racialized emotional differentiation, and Black suffering was fetishized as something to be marketed, packaged, exploited, and consumed as entertainment. The media archetypes of racialized emotions were fueled by White institutional agendas for Black emotional criminalization and exploitation. Following "post-emancipation" intellectual history, these agendas centered White emotionality as righteous benevolence, commemorated the "happiness" of a "past" of slavery, diffused images of a "postracial/post-abolition" world, and normalized imagery of the racialized prison industrial complex as proof of White emotional supremacy. Twentieth-century media, with foundations in blackface minstrelsy and an enthrallment with White "beauty," endorsed the narrative of the "abolition" of racialized slavery and the "law and order" rhetoric that antagonized "Black rage." The pervasive archetypes about Black feelings in twentieth-century media amplified the inescapable emotional surveillance of Black communities as a lucrative product for emotional simulation and mass consumption. The "informational" structures of power profited from the scientific signification of the Black body as emotionally performative, and White joy now ritualistically required leisured amusement based on the emotional dehumanization of Blackness. Hollywood media, enamored with a normative White audience, disseminated tropes of Black emotional "inferiority" in the name of White hilarity. The media archetypes of Black emotional deviance were globalized and influenced by the public relations of political parties, health providers, education systems, and corporations, sanctioning the contemporary emotional economy of racial capitalism in the Atlantic world.

The predominant media archetype of the "angry Black woman" indeed follows the principle of scientific racism that states that Blackness feels violently. Black women are simultaneously "masculinized," ungendered, and hypersexualized, received as both emotionally forceful and indifferent. Their rage is conceptualized as uncontainable and entirely undesirable. The political target is Black "anger" because of its signifying primacy in Black emotional resistance and solidarity; Audre Lorde notably elevated anger as the essence of emotional resistance to racism.[169]

---

[169] Audre Lorde, *Sister Outsider: Essays and Speeches* (New York: Random House, 2007), 124.

The "Abolition" of an Economic Apparatus of Feelings

The emotional archetype of the "angry Black woman" encompasses the consecration of the emotional policing and punishment of Blackness: a Black woman is angry before she speaks, angry before she gestures, punished before she breathes. A priori "Black rage" is codified by carceral landscapes in order to confine the freedom of Black emotionality and to enable the perpetuation of the contemporary emotional economy of racialized enslavement. Black anger was and is radical. It was and is revolution itself. It was and is the substance of the Atlantic.

> *A mother and a daughter. Drums. Suckling. She opens her eyes. He loves children. He is inside. Do not look. Do not look into His Eyes. He loves children. A child with a child.*

5

The Racialization of Emotions in Contemporary Slavery

> It was more than the walls surrounding me, more than the heavy metal door. For weeks, I'd felt trapped by Kut's rules, by the men who claimed ownership over my body, by the feeling there was no way out. Now that feeling wasn't a metaphor. It was my reality. There's something about being trapped that exaggerates the emotions and issues already inside you. The numb, autopilot state I'd been in for weeks melted away. Now I felt everything. Anger when guards shackled my hands and feet like I was some kind of dangerous weapon. Fear of what this murder charge would mean.
> —Cyntoia Brown-Long, *Free Cyntoia: My Search for Redemption in the American Prison System*

Cyntoia Brown-Long's autobiography narrates her emotional journey through the continuities of Black captivity: from child victim of sexual slavery to a prisoner with a murder charge, her victimhood not being acknowledged by the criminal justice system of the United States.[1] Her words about her first weeks in jail facing a murder charge emphasize how the walls that confined her were an extension of how her young Black body had been regulated and harmed by enslavers, with "no way out." Brown-Long describes how, after a couple of weeks in that "numb state" triggered by the continuity of anti-Black exploitation, she then "felt everything": "anger" for her racialized criminalization and "fear" for its painful consequences. Now, according to the contemporary structural carcerality of Black emotions, Black survivors of contemporary slavery

---

[1] Cyntoia Brown-Long, *Free Cyntoia: My Search for Redemption in the American Prison System* (New York: Atria, 2019), 96.

have no right to feel angry or scared. The intersection of contemporary slavery and mass criminalization accuses Black survivors of being the producers of violent anger and the architects of White "fear."

Brown-Long's case did not reach notoriety until Rihanna and Kim Kardashian tweeted about it.[2] When a Black sixteen-year-old girl was indicted with murdering the White man who "purchased" her, the system (the prosecutors and psychiatrists assigned to her case) never addressed her as a survivor of sexual slavery and constantly inquired about her "having sex with men" when she was explicitly affirming that she was being exploited. In fact, they particularly questioned why the Black minor went to the bathroom before killing her perpetrator if she was so "fearful," policing her bodily functions as a natural "marker" of her inherent emotional deviance. Then, she spent fifteen years in the prison system. After celebrities mentioned her case, pictures of a sixteen-year-old Brown-Long with ponytails and a prison uniform circulated online. There was some public outrage in response to a minor killing her abuser in self-defense and then spending half of her lifetime in prison. There was little public discourse about the emotional racialization of childhood, or how racialized survivors of contemporary slavery are emotionally marginalized, criminalized, and overlooked.

Racialized slavery never ended: it lives on to sustain the capitalistic order of White happiness. Then and now, the structural demand for exploitation has been framed by discourses of scientific racism that propel the commodification of Blackness, of those deemed emotionally divergent. The survivors of contemporary slavery in the Atlantic world, with manifestations such as sexual slavery, labor exploitation, mass incarceration, crimmigration, and organ trafficking, tend to be disproportionally part of the racialized who were singled out by Empires as being emotionally excessive and rightfully injured (yet mythically not injured). Following the narrative of "abolition" of racialized enslavement and a legal framework fascinated with "White slavery," the recent intellectual history of international law and media representation about contemporary slavery constructs an "ideal" victim that is young, "female," cisgender, privileged, and very White. Public policy and discourse either mobilize theories about the emotional Other as the threatening perpetrator of contemporary slavery against those who are "pure" (and therefore White) or fuel apathy toward the suffering of those chained by their own

---

[2] See Juno Mac & Molly Smith, *Revolting Prostitutes: The Fight for Sex Workers' Rights* (New York: Verso, 2018), 131.

"primitive cultural norms." The projection of "human trafficking" as a "hidden" and White issue not only allows for claims of "postracial" harmony as emerging from "sacrificial" White emotionality itself, but also facilitates the uninterrupted spotlighting of White emotions, even in conversations about restorative justice. This spotlighting of White emotionality is achieved through White appropriation and commodification of Black emotions. The sustained institutional denial of the visibility of the contemporary emotional economy of racialized slavery in the Atlantic world is driven by the structural emotional alienation of Black trauma, the carceral penalization of racialized emotional "rebellion," and the institutional unwillingness to "sacrifice" White happiness. The emotional policing of Blackness feeds the contemporary emotional economy of racial capitalism and reinforces the racialized hierarchy of those worthy of "rescue," resources, and, overall, wealth, designating racialized bodies in pain as deserving of sadistically being observed as such. To this day, proximity to Blackness still entails being closer and closer to enslavement by emotional inequality. To this day, White happiness is premised on genocidal anti-Blackness. The only thing that has changed is that the White monopoly of emotions now selectively likes to be Black.

EMOTIONAL IMPLORATIONS OF INTERNATIONAL LAW AND MEDIA REPRESENTATIONS ABOUT CONTEMPORARY "WHITE SLAVERY"

The contemporary public discussion about "human trafficking" in richer economies is constrained by a dichotomy between imagining contemporary slavery as an ahistorical, racially foreign issue or as an urgent domestic threat to "White innocence" in a "post-abolition West." Indeed, early anti–"White slavery" campaigns in the United States, championed by moral reformers of the Progressive era, were driven by ideas of the urgency of the "protection" of White "female chastity" and White "childhood innocence," which led to the development of the Mann Act, also known as the White-Slave Traffic Act of 1910.[3] Instead of addressing the "concern" about the alleged rise of "White slavery," the Mann Act was predominantly used to police sexuality, including consensual interracial relationships that crossed state lines.[4] The concept of "White slavery" as

[3] Carrie N. Baker, *Fighting the U.S. Youth Sex Trade: Gender, Race, and Politics* (New York: Cambridge University Press, 2018), 15.
[4] Jessica R. Piley, *Policing Sexuality* (Cambridge, MA: Harvard University Press, 2014), 131.

the undesired aftermath of the legal "abolition" of racialized slavery, "endangering" White women and children, still histrionically guides the recent intellectual history of media representation and international law about contemporary enslavement. Even the most influential Spanish dictionary, the *Diccionario de la Real Academia Española*, currently includes the widely used term *"trata de blancas,"* which translates literally to "trafficking of White women," as the term for "sex trafficking." This racialized, gendered, and heteronormative scope of survivor representation rallies emotional campaigns heightened by ideas of "purity" in White "femininity," establishes a hierarchy of those deserving of empathy, and frighteningly replicates the discourses about "White slavery" of the beginning of the twentieth century, which aimed to regulate the bodies of White women and to normalize the systemic sexual violence against racialized people. Evoking eugenicist thought, the public discussion about "White slavery" mobilizes emotional urgency toward the "jeopardy" of Whiteness due to "unfettered" Black passions.

It was in 1926 that the first international legal definition of slavery materialized, precisely ruled by the allure of "White slavery." The still valid 1926 Slavery Convention defines slavery as the "status of a person over whom any or all of the powers attaching to the right of ownership are exercised."[5] The ambiguity of the convention is intentional. The 1926 Slavery Convention was actually confabulated by Empires as a political tool that was meant to constitute a colonial "Other" and justify White interventionism in Africa.[6] The later 1956 Slavery Convention by the United Nations amended the 1926 convention in order to incorporate the ambiguous category of "practices similar to slavery," which includes sections on debt bondage, serfdom, forced marriage, and child exploitation. The definitions of forced marriage and child exploitation demonstrate the political motive of spreading ideas about an othered "Third World."

(c) Any institution or practice whereby:
  (i) A woman, without the right to refuse, is promised or given in marriage on payment of a consideration in money or in kind to her parents, guardian, family or any other person or group; or

---

[5] United Nations, "Slavery Convention," United Nations, Office of the High Commissioner, 1926.
[6] Jean Allain, "The Legal Definition of Slavery into the Twenty-First Century," in *The Legal Understanding of Slavery: From the Historical to the Contemporary*, edited by Jean Allain (Oxford: Oxford University Press, 2012), 199.

      (ii) The husband of a woman, his family, or his clan, has the right to transfer her to another person for value received or otherwise; or

      (iii) A woman on the death of her husband is liable to be inherited by another person;

  (d) Any institution or practice whereby a child or young person under the age of 18 years, is delivered by either or both of his natural parents or by his guardian to another person, whether for reward or not, with a view to the exploitation of the child or young person or of his labour.[7]

The 1956 Slavery Convention evidently responds to political agendas concerning "tyrannical states" outside the "First World." The reference to "clan" in the definition of forced marriage connotes how this convention conceives this "practice similar to slavery" to be solely perpetrated by the colonized and racialized "outside" the historicist realm of political "modernity." In other words, the convention uses coded language that is driven by the notion of scientific racism that the racialized do not know how to "love properly" and have emotionally turbulent familial structures. In contrast, child exploitation could not be committed by parents or legal guardians, evidencing the convenient lack of inherence of the State in the control of the bodily autonomy of children effected by White guardians, key lobbyists against legal reform in this matter. The concepts of both "marriage" and "childhood" had been historically racialized to signify the hegemony of White familial bonds, and so the convention draws from these principles to distance Whiteness from the contemporary infliction of slavery. Even the notion of "practices similar to slavery" endorses racialized knowledge production about slavery with dissimilar projections of emotional urgency. What is named "slavery" correlates with the "Western" idea of a troubled past that has been overcome. Only "White slavery" is denoted as carrying the suffering of slavery. The nonpressing "practices similar to slavery" can be "found" in the racialized periphery, which "fails" at creating stable societal and political systems. These crimes are reckoned atrocious, while also regarded as intrinsic to the familial bonds, interpersonal relationships, and "cultural norms" of people of color, as such forming part of an insuperable "primitive"

---

[7] United Nations, "Supplementary Convention on the Abolition of Slavery, the Slave Trade, and Institutions and Practices Similar to Slavery," United Nations, Office of the High Commissioner, 1956.

present of distinct emotional economies. Therefore, the 1926 and the 1956 Slavery Conventions were much more interested in concocting a racialized geography of exploitation, progress, and emotional governability to legitimize White industrialist imperialism. After the end of the Cold War, the "politicization" of "human trafficking" transformed this scrutiny of the "structural violence" of the colonized into a media interest in the "individual victim."[8] This shift has emphasized the emotional vulnerability of an affluent and "virginal" White girl.

The 2000 Palermo Protocol by the United Nations substantiates how international law visualizes "human trafficking" as a gendered transgression, an "epidemic" of "White slavery" that threatens "fragile" White women and children. The non-binding Palermo Protocol conceptualizes "human trafficking" under the umbrella of "organized crime."[9] This restrictive perspective hypothesizes a struggle between good and evil: benevolent White nations uniting against enormous (and "inevitably" racially foreign) subterranean economies. The connections between structural inequality, imperial history, and White perpetration are erased. Furthermore, there was much debate in the United Nations about whether the Palermo Protocol should protect all persons or only safeguard women and children.[10] This gendered and heteronormative discussion led to its title: "Protocol to Prevent, Suppress and Punish Trafficking in Persons, Especially Women and Children." The protocol inherits the emotional power of the historicist discourse of the legal duty of States to protect women and children vulnerable to "White slavery."

"Trafficking in persons" shall mean the recruitment, transportation, transfer, harbouring or receipt of persons, by means of the threat or use of force or other forms of coercion, of abduction, of fraud, of deception, of the abuse of power or of a position of vulnerability or of the giving or receiving of payments or benefits to achieve the consent of a person having control over another person, for the purpose of exploitation. Exploitation shall include, at a minimum, the exploitation of the prostitution of others or other forms of sexual exploitation, forced labour or services, slavery or practices similar to slavery, servitude or the removal of organs.[11]

---

[8] Jennifer Suchland, *Economies of Violence: Transnational Feminism, Postsocialism, and the Politics of Sex Trafficking* (Durham, NC: Duke University Press, 2015).

[9] See Marie Segrave, Sanja Milivojevic, & Sharon Pickering, *Sex Trafficking and Modern Slavery: The Absence of Evidence* (New York: Routledge, 2017).

[10] Anne T. Gallagher, *The International Law of Human Trafficking* (New York: Cambridge University Press, 2010), 26.

[11] United Nations, "Protocol to Prevent, Suppress and Punish Trafficking in Persons, Especially Women and Children, Supplementing the United Nations Convention against

The Palermo Protocol has predictably caused much confusion in popular opinion, circumscribing a limited scope of emotional panics. Its structure is divided into "act," "means," and "purpose." The "act" section stresses movement, when "movement" is not an essential legal criterion of "trafficking." The "means" category includes the phrase "achieve the consent of a person having control over another person" and affirms in a later section that "consent" is "irrelevant." Last, the reference to "slavery and practices similar to slavery" in the "purpose" section means that the document adheres to and prolongs the reach of the colonizing definitions of the 1926 and the 1956 Slavery Conventions. The absurd engagement of the Palermo Protocol with the notion of consent is detrimental to public discussion about contractual and sexual consent. Researchers have examined how "misconceptions" within law enforcement about the role of consent profoundly affect the identification of victims of exploitation.[12] Legally, a person cannot consent to being exploited or to being the victim of a crime, and the clumsy contextualization of "consent" in the Palermo Protocol fuels racialized victim shaming. The influence of geographical determinism in the emotional depersonalization and hypersexualization of Blackness drives the public discourse that claims that there are racialized Others who are always self-destructive, emotionally resilient, and deviantly willing to hurt their bodies, their future, and White communities. Moreover, due to the alleged political weight of the word "slavery" in an institutionally named "post-racial world," there has been a shift from speaking of "slavery" to "human trafficking." Even more, efforts to speak about "contemporary slavery" of racialized groups are usually received as "sentimentalist" or emotionally exploitative. This rhetoric affects the possibility of the 1926 Slavery Convention being utilized through the application of the 2000 Palermo Protocol. In actuality, recent jurisprudence in international courts after the Palermo Protocol evidence the failure of States to structurally protect their citizens against racialized enslavement and the institutional hesitation to take categorical stances about the topic of contemporary slavery,[13] fostering an uphill legal battle for Black survivors. The 2000 Palermo Protocol, and its connection to the 1926 and 1956 Slavery Conventions, inevitably passes the burden of proof to

---

Transnational Organized Crime," United Nations, Office of the High Commissioner, 2000.

[12] Jessica Elliot, *The Role of Consent in Human Trafficking* (New York: Routledge, 2015).

[13] Allain, "The Legal Definition of Slavery into the Twenty-First Century," 214.

emotionally criminalized survivors with its limited scope, gendered concepts, colonial legacies, and racialized tropes about consent.

In addition to the Palermo Protocol, the Trafficking in Persons Report, prepared annually by the US Department of State, significantly frames public discourse about "human trafficking" as an issue that is utterly foreign, to be found outside the "Western" narrative of emotional progress. The 2019 report starts with a letter by Secretary of State Michael Pompeo, which sets the emotional tone for the whole document: "Right now traffickers are robbing a staggering 24.9 million people of their freedom and basic human dignity – roughly three times the population of New York City. We must band together and build momentum to defeat human trafficking. We must hold the perpetrators of this heinous crime accountable."[14] The letter contextualizes "human trafficking" as a fight between good and evil in which the United States leads the "good fight" and is the frame of reference. This rhetoric mimics the historical military propaganda of the United States, which underestimates structural violence as a mere enemy that can be defeated, trivializing the conflict as a geopolitical one. The language also evokes the "tough-on-crime" approaches of the racialized criminal justice system and legal framework about immigration of the United States. The provided statistic is entirely too conservative, since fragmented numbers of the United Nations for this immeasurable human rights crisis show that there are currently more than a hundred million people under the yoke of exploitation. The report obscenely includes a quote by White supremacist Donald Trump: "This is an urgent humanitarian issue. My Administration is committed to leveraging every resource we have to confront this threat, to support victims and survivors, and to hold traffickers accountable for their heinous crimes. – President Donald J. Trump."[15] The quote reverberates the rhetoric of a "national security" and "criminal justice" issue because he did not have more to say: his White supremacist administration was indeed "committed to leveraging every resource" they had to "confront" and injure the lives of the racialized in the United States.

The tier ranking in the Trafficking in Persons Report can be read as geopolitical propaganda of the United States for the emotional defeat of an undesirable racialized enemy. The Tier 1 is restricted to "countries whose governments fully meet the TVPA's minimum standards for the

---

[14] US Department of State, *Trafficking in Persons Report* (2019).
[15] US Department of State, *Trafficking in Persons Report* (2019).

elimination of trafficking,"[16] the TVPA, or Trafficking Victims Protection Act, being the flawed anti-trafficking legislation of the United States. Following the legacy of the Mann Act, the implementation of the TVPA in the United States is mostly concerned with "sex trafficking" and shaped by paternalistic discourses of gender and sexuality.[17] The tier ranking ends up being a frightening hierarchy of political systems driven by historical determinism, which facilitates the legitimization of the abstinence of provision of humanitarian support by the United States. Tier 1 nations are disproportionately regarded as White, while criminalized Tier 2 and 3 countries tend to have a history of subjugation to White imperialism. Not surprisingly, the United States unfailingly gives itself a final grade of A+, maintaining a Tier 1 status since the inception of the Trafficking in Persons Report in 2001. The self-assessment is self-evident in its sidelining of racialized suffering.

The government continued to demonstrate serious and sustained efforts during the reporting period; therefore the United States remained on Tier 1. These efforts included increasing the number of convictions; increasing the amount of funding for victim services and number of victims served; continuing to seek and incorporate survivor input on human trafficking programs and policies; and launching new public outreach measures to more sectors. Although the government meets the minimum standards, it opened, charged, and prosecuted fewer cases, issued fewer victims trafficking-specific immigration options, and granted fewer foreign national victims of trafficking eligibility to access benefits and services.[18]

The self-assessment underlines vague "achievements" and then proceeds to disclose "setbacks" that are more specific and concerning. The 2019 Trafficking in Persons Report was prepared during the Trump administration, so, while the United States maintains a Tier 1 status, the report accepts the negligence of the US government toward "foreign national victims of trafficking" in relation to access to survivor support and provision of T visas, visas designed for (and rarely granted to) "trafficking" survivors. In fact, the preamble of the report attributes the pervasiveness of "human trafficking" to "cultural norms and practices."[19] Therefore, the Trafficking in Persons Report hides more than it shows: it is another emotional media spectacle in which the United States, one of the top destination countries for "trafficking," triumphs in its

---

[16] US Department of State, *Trafficking in Persons Report* (2019).
[17] Alicia W. Peters, *Responding to Human Trafficking: Sex, Gender, and Culture in the Law* (Philadelphia: University of Pennsylvania Press, 2015), 3.
[18] US Department of State, *Trafficking in Persons Report* (2019).
[19] US Department of State, *Trafficking in Persons Report* (2019).

capitalistic and imperialistic dominance in a globalized world, victory over racialized nations with retrograde "cultural norms" that merit emotional policing. The intentionality of this media spectacle is most evident in the imagery used by the militaristic report: images of malnourished and agonized Black and Brown people, mostly children, laboring under the sun. One of the first images of the report is a photograph of a Black African child watching over cattle. The caption of the photograph states that "in some areas of Africa, traffickers force children to work in agricultural sectors," and, over the image, there is another quote by Pompeo: "We take these stories to heart. We use them as fuel to motivate us to end human trafficking once and for all."[20] Early on, the report represents a monolithic Africa as neglecting to protect childhood innocence, while the White performativity of the emotional empathy of the "heart" as "fuel" parallels the historical White abolitionist spotlighting of White emotionality to commemorate colonizing benevolence. The Trafficking in Persons Report voyeuristically presents image after image of famished Black children in pain, fetishizing an emotionally detached engagement with the topic of contemporary racialized child exploitation, which reaffirms White comfort and triumph over noxious emotions.

The media coverage about contemporary slavery in the twenty-first century emulates the emotional rhetoric of international law, disseminating ideas about "human trafficking" as a transnational "evil" to be "defeated" through prosecution. Mainstream media coverage in Canada, the United Kingdom, and the United States has blamed "organized crime" as the "primary cause" of "human trafficking" and has taken for granted that "more law enforcement" would be the best response to this international issue.[21] The media coverage in newspapers tends to portray the matter either as a foreign and "barbaric" propensity or, even more predominantly, as a hidden domestic (yet still racially "foreign") network that could injure the "girl next door." This imagery is in turn abused by *Lifetime* films and crime drama television series, such as the *Law and Order* and *CSI* franchises. These texts refer to "human trafficking" as the basis of a story line for entertainment, to add a "shock factor," or to authenticate their products as "thrillers," following the precedent of the

---

[20] US Department of State, *Trafficking in Persons Report* (2019).
[21] Girish J. Gulati, "Representing Trafficking: Media in the United States, Great Britain, and Canada," in *From Human Trafficking to Human Rights: Reframing Contemporary Slavery*, edited by Alison Brisk & Austin Choi-Fitzpatrick (Philadelphia: University of Pennsylvania Press, 2012), 54.

2008 blockbuster film *Taken*.[22] The film *Taken*, starring Liam Neeson, tells the story of former CIA agent Bryan Mills, who "bravely" confronts a "White slavery" trade. During the first part of the film, Bryan is trying to reconcile with his seventeen-year-old daughter, Kim, and buys her a small karaoke machine. His effort is overshadowed by Kim's affluent stepfather, who gifts her a pony. The beginning of the film stresses how Bryan feels "emasculated" and not relevant in the life of his daughter, who speaks to him only to get permission to travel from the United States to France. Kim's "White innocence," wealth, and "virginity" are strategically disclosed during the preamble to her abduction in Paris. *Taken* introduces now familiar clichés in films and television episodes about "sex trafficking": the parent who risks it all to save their daughter, the "foreignness" of the location of the abduction (or the destination), the oppositional binary with the United States as a safe sanctuary, the post-9/11 xenophobic depiction of immigrant "traffickers" following the model of James Bond adversaries, and the blockbuster action that eclipses survivor experiences. The other White women subjected to sexual slavery are in fact rarely shown in this film: this is the story of Bryan, who saves his daughter, her "virginity," and his "masculinity" by the end of the film. The happy ending is achieved when Bryan and Kim finally arrive at a US airport, with Kim "unaffected" by the abduction, while Bryan has a cast on his arm, confirmation of the fact that the emotional arc of the film is captivated with the "White male savior." While the film mobilizes emotional empathy toward the vindication of White patriarchy, the death of Kim's best friend Amanda is briefly shown and met with apathy. Her character is rendered as culpable of her own abduction because she unknowingly and "impulsively" introduced Kim and herself to the enslavers and, most importantly, she is not a "virgin." Her Whiteness is disturbed by her "heated" sexuality contrary to Kim's "virginity," hypersexualization structurally attributed to Blackness in the history of film.

It is evident that Hollywood representations of contemporary slavery are fueled by discourses of sexual morality that mold "pure," "model," and very White victims as the ones who are worthy of emotional responses and funding for "rescue." The construction of the "ideal victim" in media and both governmental and nongovernmental campaigns is framed by theories of scientific racism about the intersections of race, gender, sexuality, and age that summon emotional empathy

---

[22] Pierre Morel (dir.), *Taken* (film), 20th Century Fox, 2008.

toward "White innocence." In a surface-level assessment, the "ideal victim" is a young White heterosexual cisgender woman, who must not be "sexually promiscuous." A deeper look at patterns in the media representations of contemporary slavery shows that the "ideal victim" is codified as the antithesis of hypersexual queer Blackness, the antithesis of the never "ideal" Black enslaved person destined to emotionally "fail" and be injured. In contrast, Whiteness is assumed to spark emotional reactions toward anti-trafficking campaigns, highlighting that "it could happen to anybody's child." In this context, "anybody" equals a privileged White person. This imagery is categorized as interesting, upsetting, and profitable because she is White. She not only must be eternally rescued from "menacing" Black men, but, above all, she must be treasured. Further, she must be loved. This imagery inherently promotes victim shaming toward intrinsically hypersexualized Blackness and queerness, perpetuating racialist theories of sexual deviance and therefore taking the sexual consent of Black and Brown bodies for granted: the queer racialized body is to blame for its own systematic exploitation.

Like *Taken*, the campaign "Real Men Don't Buy Girls" by the Demi and Ashton Foundation encompasses the tendency of "anti-trafficking" nongovernmental campaigns to rally emotional empathy toward White "masculinity" within savior tropes. In one of the commercials from this campaign, Justin Timberlake attempts to shave his face with a chain saw, which sparks the voiceover, "Real men prefer a close shave, real men don't buy girls."[23] A close-up of the face of Justin Timberlake mutates into a photograph in a gold frame with a caption that reads "Real Man." The commercial cuts to other gold frames with the same caption, holding photographs of Tom Selleck, Bruce Willis, Harrison Ford, and Piers Morgan. Eva Longoria seductively says, "Piers Morgan is a real man, are you?" Not only does the word choice of "buying girls" objectify survivors and rid them of agency, but it also perpetuates the gendered, heteronormative, and racialized scope of international law, reinforced by the White imagery of the commercial. This campaign evidently connotes "masculinity" as being exclusively White and rewards White "masculinity" for doing the bare minimum, the reward being indulging in the "exotic" affection of a light-skinned Latina. White "masculinity" is constructed as enacting a "White savior" role by simply existing, by continuing to exercise a "toxic masculinity" worthy of a blockbuster, by

---

[23] "Real Men Prefer a Close Shave," Demi and Ashton Foundation, 2012.

detaching itself from the demand of contemporary "White slavery," and by instead fetishizing the hypersexualized desirability of women of color that fuels their racialized enslavement in the first place. The "comedic" (though not funny at all) tone of the campaign presents White perpetration of contemporary slavery as a light, non-threatening issue, garnering endearing emotions toward the White Man for monopolizing "masculinity." The "Black enslaver" is certainly not painted in that light.

The emotional antagonism of Blackness in media about "human trafficking" precisely shapes the format of mainstream news reports and documentaries. The brief documentary "Human Trafficking: Lives Bought & Sold"[24] by BBC News examines contemporary slavery in the United States, United Kingdom, and Nigeria. The survivors of color interviewed in the United States and the United Kingdom are voyeuristically requested to recreate their trauma, being asked triggering and invasive questions by White reporters, such as how many surgeries they had to undergo after "rescue" and whether they would be able to have children. One of the White reporters even affirms that their exploitation will "haunt" survivors forever. The characterization of survivors of color can be summarized as emotionally "damaged" beings with no identity and no "innocence," this "trauma porn" being another manifestation of morbid entertainment and emotional detachment from the personhood of racialized survivors of sexual slavery. While the representation of "trafficking" in the United States and the United Kingdom is of a "hidden" epidemic of exploitation perpetrated by individuals, the depiction of Nigeria is of a "trafficking hub," where systemic exploitation is the Black essence of its emotionally "criminal" population. In fact, the section about Nigeria includes the only interview of an exploiter in the whole documentary, an interview of a Black Nigerian. It had all been leading to this: the documentary ends with the unveiling of the villain, the threat to the "free world," encompassed in the emotional Black Other. This portrayal of Nigeria as a breeding ground of exploitation is present in another news report by BBC News, titled "Trafficked into Prostitution with Black Magic,"[25] which covers the mass exploitation of Nigerians in Italy. The captions of the news report emphasize the role of "juju oaths" performed in Nigeria by Nigerians in its explanation of why those enslaved "would" not "escape" after having been "purchased" in Italy,

---

[24] "Human Trafficking: Lives Bought & Sold," BBC News, 2015.
[25] "Trafficked into Prostitution with Black Magic," BBC News, 2019.

"convinced" that they were "spiritually bound" to their enslavers. A White Italian psychiatrist is interviewed as the "rational" voice that states that, while a "juju oath" might just seem like "superstition" to "us," it is the "reality" of "Nigerians." The White psychiatrist bestows upon himself the role of the "translator" of an essentialized Nigerian emotionality, marked by "Black magic." Depictions of White survivors in media humanize their trauma. In the case of victim-blamed Black survivors, their trauma is either capitalized on or voided as mere "superstitious" emotions. Evoking theories of scientific racism, the emotional antagonists of the struggle against contemporary slavery have been personified by the press and news media as the figures of the "primitive" enslaver and the emotionally "oblivious" enslaved.

Hence, mainstream media in the Atlantic world premeditatedly neglect to promote emotional empathy toward survivors of contemporary slavery, who are disproportionately people of color and thus do not fit the prescriptive role of the "ideal victim," and instead criminalize their emotions. In fact, the few survivor narratives that are highlighted in memoirs and films regularly reproduce the "gendered and racialized narrative of white men rescuing white girls from men of color."[26] When organ trafficking is discussed in news reports, the issue is represented as driven by its "conflicted feelings": the plight of a White elite having to make a "painful" decision that separates life and death and the "fact" that impoverished racialized groups "feel" that selling their organ is their only option, a feeling consequently connoted as proof of their gullibility and recklessness.[27] Furthermore, public debate about "sex trafficking" tends to propagate the myth that victims must be under "physical restraint."[28] A Black sex worker cannot be sexually exploited. Black migrants consent to be exploited, just like they consent to crime. Forced marriage is traditional in some developing countries. They live in those worlds. They eagerly took a wrong path. They belong to a culture with primeval norms. The perception is that racialized survivors of contemporary slavery who were smuggled or participated in sex work before must have "consented to some part" of the exploitation, segregating them from the legal principle of consent having to be informed. Their struggle then is

---

[26] Baker, *Fighting the U.S. Youth Sex Trade*, 167.
[27] See "Tales from the Organ Trade," *CNN*, 2014.
[28] Andrea J. Nichols, *Sex Trafficking in the United States: Theory, Research, Policy, and Practice* (New York: Columbia University Press, 2016), 9.

"beyond the law" because their experiences are "cultural" (a code word for "racial"), erasing the universality of racialized exploitation across the globe. The policing scrutiny over the past emotional "transgressions" of survivors of color results in many being used by media for their "horror stories" as a form of entertainment. The focus is not on what they have to say but on a detailed re-creation of their horror and the connection of their horror to their racialized "backstory" – horrors they have to embody in every speaking engagement, every interview, for consumption. The emotional detachment of a tactless media industry, and its avid audience, pervades the emotional antagonism of the racialized survivors of contemporary slavery because their painful lived experiences verify White comfort.

Essentially, international law and mainstream media propel emotional urgency toward an "imperiled" Whiteness and antagonize an "uncontrolled," "post-abolition" Blackness. The triumph of the narrative of "White slavery" fuels the contemporary consecration of the fight between good and evil, Whiteness and Blackness, Reason and Emotion. Even more, it allows for the emotional appropriation of enslaved pain and victimhood. The enslaved are now White, and their distress corroborates the tragedy of the "abolition" of racialized slavery and the certainty of a "postracial" meritocracy, which in turn sparks discontentment toward the Black survivor who is to blame, who failed at being free "post-abolition." The intention is to seize Black grief, to take over everything, even the narrative of victimhood in racially premised slavery. This "postracial" hyperfixation with White joy as in "peril" aims to hide the continued emotional oppression of Blackness and the victorious indomitability of White emotional privilege. The narrative of "White slavery" verifies the lengths to which structures of power will circumvent the capitalistic "sacrifice" of White bliss.

THE CONTEMPORARY EMOTIONAL ECONOMY OF RACIALIZED SLAVERY IN THE ATLANTIC WORLD

As fostered by the recent intellectual history of international law and media representation, the disregard of the political and economic spheres regarding their perpetration of racialized exploitation is encompassed by public discourse about the visibility of contemporary racialized slavery. "Human trafficking" is a "hidden epidemic" that is "shocking." Meanwhile, during the first decade of the twenty-first century, there were multiple reports of public "auctions" of the enslaved in airports of the

United Kingdom.[29] When footage of an "auction" perpetrated against Black Nigerians in Libya was released by news media, it did not become a major news story.[30] In all privileged regions of the Atlantic world, Black people are structurally in low-paying or unpaid labor, while White people dominate major corporations. Black people are serving, and White people are being served. Not in a fancy restaurant, though: they employ only White people. And this enslaving emotional economy is visible. It is common knowledge that the majority of goods are made through racialized exploitation, but schools and textbooks still teach that slavery is part of an abominable past that has been overcome. The structures of power project contemporary anti-Black exploitation as an issue that pales in comparison to the latest celebrity gossip or major sporting event. They certainly do not want to talk about the fact that racialized slavery never ended. Due to the intellectual history of racialized slavery in the Atlantic world, contemporary racialized enslavement is rooted in emotional anti-Blackness, and the contemporary emotional economy of racial capitalism is propelled by the structural carcerality of Black emotions, carcerality that is unwilling to publicly face the intellectual history of sadistic White delight. And institutional malevolence is visible too.

The key scholarly debate about contemporary slavery is preoccupied with the scope of its definition and how much "emotional weight" it has. *Disposable People: New Slavery in the Global Economy* by Kevin Bales argues that, while the "old slavery" was distinguished by the high prices of the enslaved, lower generation of capital for slaveholders, shortage of the enslaved, and the racialized and long-term nature of slavery, the "new slavery" evidences the low cost of the enslaved, high generation of slave-holding capital, high number of people who are "disposable" and vulnerable to slavery, and the non-racialized and short-term nature of slavery.[31] Orlando Patterson responded to Kevin Bales, claiming that his demarcation of the "old slavery" and "new slavery" is ahistorical and that his statements about the non-racialized nature of the "new slavery" are too categorical, while also affirming that his definition of slavery is too expansive, that theorizing that "all forms of forced labour today amount to slavery" would mean that "the entire history of the world" would be

---

[29] See Louise Shelley, *Human Trafficking: A Global Perspective* (New York: Cambridge University Press, 2010), 1.
[30] See "Migrants Being Sold as Slaves in Libya," *CNN*, 2017.
[31] Kevin Bales, *Disposable People: New Slavery in the Global Economy* (Berkeley: University of California Press, 2012), 15.

conceptualized as "the history of slavery."[32] The main dispute then becomes, What is the "problem" of conceptualizing the history of the world as the history of slavery? The scholarly debate about contemporary slavery shows that antislavery thought is still received as "sentimentalist" and that the institutional narrative of "abolition" of racialized slavery is still prospering through the upholding of a rupture between an "old" and "new" slavery. Contemporary slavery was and is racialized and driven by notions of emotional differentiation. Contemporary slavery was and is motivated by the long-lived institutional disdain toward the pain and emotionality of the racialized and colonized, disdain that has ruled the history of the Atlantic world. What has changed is that the nomenclature of "racialized slavery" became "sentimentalist," its visibility unspoken by capitalist structures of power.

Throughout the Atlantic world, enslaving institutions tend to exploit those who have been historically most marginalized by the structural inequality of feelings due to their racialized emotional disgrace and their state of being as the most expendable to and criminalized by States. They are aware of how White power opportunistically constructs the racialized as more sexually impulsive and subordinate, how the racialized body is the site of fetishized fantasies of imperial sexual violence. They are aware of the institutional indifference toward the continued economic exploitation of the racialized in the name of White indulgence. They are aware of the enlargement of an organ market that mutilates racialized bodies in the name of White elitist survival. They are aware that housing and economic segregation facilitates the veiling of the sadistic emotional detachment of those who benefit from the capitalist order of the contemporary emotional economy of racialized slavery. They profit from the economic and political disenfranchisement of those ostracized for their "emotional difference" due to their interconnected racialized criminalization, sexual orientation, gender identity, immigration status, membership in a religious minority, and exposure to war and conflict. In fact, multiple scholars of contemporary slavery studies argue that debt bondage is the most widespread type of exploitation and is a gateway to other manifestations of slavery.[33] There is a strong connection between debt bondage,

---

[32] Orlando Patterson, "Trafficking, Gender, and Slavery: Past and Present," in *The Legal Understanding of Slavery: From the Historical to the Contemporary*, edited by Jean Allain (Oxford: Oxford University Press, 2012), 334.

[33] Siddharth Kara, *Modern Slavery: A Global Perspective* (New York: Columbia University Press, 2017).

disenfranchisement, and the experiences of homeless queer youth of color, those in the lower ranks of caste systems, those criminalized by school-to-prison pipelines, and those persecuted by the repercussions of White interventionism, medical racism, climate colonialism, and carceral systems. According to the 2015 *U.S. Transgender Survey*, 42 percent of Black trans respondents "experienced homelessness at some point in their lives," and 53 percent of Black trans respondents had been "sexually assaulted at some point in their lifetimes."[34] Black trans survivors are systemically targeted by hate crimes, subjected to sexual slavery, criminalized, and incarcerated in units that do not correspond to their gender identity.[35] The structures of power, grounded on White emotional supremacy, know this. These structures of power devised the structural carcerality of Black emotions. The contemporary emotional economy of racialized slavery in the Atlantic world is ultimately guided by the conscious White profit from the inescapability of anti-Black emotional policing that eugenically punishes "excess." And, every day, it is visible.

Imperial sexual violence has been historically legitimized by discourses of geographical determinism that conceive people of color as sexually "promiscuous," emotionally "aggressive," and hence always criminally consenting. Today, that remains unchanged in the enduring structural carcerality of Black emotions. There is therefore a pervasive stimulus of ideas from scientific racism in the demand of contemporary sexual slavery: intersections of race, gender, and sexuality frame not only who are most vulnerable to the racialized demand of sexual slavery, but also who are most at risk due to their emotional expendability, their hypersexualized desirability, and their subjection to the excruciating oppression of structural emotional inequality. Tourism advertisements are complicit with sex tourism industries and networks of sexual slavery, since these advertisements create a hierarchy of national identities premised on historical determinism. While destinations in Europe, Canada, and the United States are advertised as full of historical and cultural attractions and monuments, regions of Africa, Asia, the Caribbean, and Latin America are still pitched as deserted spaces with sandy beaches, fetishized immersion experiences, and/or "safari" adventures. Instead of concentrating on Eurocentric pedagogical experiences, tourism advertisements

---

[34] *2015 U.S. Transgender Survey: Report on the Experiences of Black Respondents* (Washington, DC: National Center for Transgender Equality, Black Trans Advocacy, & National Black Justice Coalition, 2017).
[35] See "Transgender Life in Jail and on the Street: 'That's my sister,'" *The Guardian*, 2016.

about tropical regions emphasize "rest" and "adventure." According to this imagery, rest is assured by the Black "submissive" hands that deliver that piña colada or that serve as a point of entry to the untouched "animal world." The sense of adventure is situated in the sweaty, semi-naked body of a person of color dancing to "ethnic" music. The tropics are codified as spaces of temporary sexual deviance for White consumers who get a thrilling access to the emotional "imprudence" of Blackness. Corporations and governmental agendas then economically benefit from the outstanding pressures on oppressed communities of color to provide these criminalized "services." In fact, these institutions turn a blind eye to the systematic sexual exploitation and symbiotic criminalization of those who are most marginalized by the enslaving emotional economy, an economy that feeds institutional power.

While public discourse about contemporary slavery emphasizes the notion of racialized "subterranean networks of organized crime" to breed emotive patriotism, the international courts, governments, and mainstream media of the Atlantic world do not strategically elucidate that this enslaving emotional economy that normalizes racialized exploitation and genocidal policing is in fact state-sanctioned. State-sanctioned enslavement is structurally state-perpetrated through the population control of the institutional carcerality of Black emotions. The agricultural system of the United States operationally depends on the enslavement of criminalized migrants from Africa and Latin America,[36] perpetuating ideas of biological determinism for agricultural exploitation. It is common knowledge that major corporations rely on racialized "sweatshop" work, and consumer and political apathy pervades conversations on the subject of the intersection of "sweatshop" work, racialized child exploitation, and carceral landscapes. The structural carcerality of Black emotions prevails because it upholds White happiness and delays its "sacrifice" until further notice. The continual economic exploitation of the racialized, of those categorized as emotionally delinquent and unworthy of economic mobility, is taken for granted, and controversies about the intentional dependence of multinational corporations on racialized labor exploitation and the devaluation of Black labor have not affected their economic monopolies and state sanctions. Furthermore, due to the unrelenting governmental failures in racialized health crises, States also avoid the inclusion of the intersection of human medical experimentation and medical racism in the

---

[36] See Kara, *Modern Slavery*, 28.

transnational conversation about contemporary exploitation. Not only have physicians and medical institutions been complicit in racialized human experimentation and organ trafficking, but there is also little public outrage about how transplant tourism and the organ trade disproportionately affect criminalized people of color. This is of no surprise, since ethical questions about the organ trade and medical experimentation – in other words, questions about the commodification of the human body[37] – are subsumed into larger questions about the genocidal commodification of health. Health systems privilege the White elite through better health care and higher investment in a more than functional body, while fostering Black mortality and eugenicist institutional disregard of Black pain and socioeconomic alienation. The "monumental history of American medical racism" has normalized the racialization of diagnosis and healing.[38] The prevalence of complications in childbirth in Black communities has been pathologized by medical institutions as caused by substance abuse, eating habits, low income, or unmarried status, constructing Black pregnant people as "embodying risk" and as "targets of intervention."[39] To this day, medical systems in the United States and the United Kingdom, to name a few, terrorize the quality of life of Black emotional Others, who are oppressed and criminalized as sites of scientific experimentation and who do not receive proper diagnosis or expedite medical assistance due to the theories of scientific racism that conveniently claim their "supernatural" pain tolerance, their inherent blame in their biological "degeneration," and their deceptive emotional performativity.

Not only does the pervasiveness of state-sanctioned racialized enslavement and genocide dodge public debate, being portrayed as a manifestation of the past, but there is also outstanding resistance from governments in confronting the propensity of racialized domestic slavery and child slavery in the Atlantic world, preserving the domestic sphere as a protected emotional economy. Domestic slavery is a taboo topic due to the normalization of forced marriage, the institutional negligence toward heteronormative gendered violence, and the tendency of powerful White families in the Atlantic world to employ people of color as their "loving

---

[37] See Oliver Decker, *Commodified Bodies: Organ Transplantation and the Organ Trade* (New York: Routledge, 2014).
[38] John Hoberman, *Black and Blue: The Origins and Consequences of Medical Racism* (Berkeley: University of California Press, 2012), 2.
[39] Dána-Ain Davis, *Reproductive Justice: Racism, Pregnancy, and Premature Birth* (New York: New York University Press, 2019), 8.

nannies" and "highly valued help," enacting "antebellum" fantasies. Moreover, ambiguous discourses about "childhood dependence" and "adult power,"[40] allow for the continuance of racialized child exploitation. According to UNICEF, around 168 million children aged five to seventeen were subjected to child labor in 2014, "accounting for almost 11 percent of all children."[41] The restavek system in Haiti is usually named as an appalling anomaly of the Atlantic world, but there is little conversation about how White nations profit from the exploitation of racialized/criminalized children, exploitation that has been normalized because of the emotional racialization of childhood. For example, US foster care agencies accumulate revenue by hiring "private companies to help obtain disability and survivor benefits from abused and neglected children,"[42] and, due to the lobbying of White conservative religious groups, legal frameworks grant much power to legal guardians of minors in relation to their "education" and "upbringing," refusing to clarify the distinction between a "chore" and exploitative labor. Strategically, child labor exploitation is typically not included in statistics of "human trafficking," minimizing the urgency of this human rights violation. If these statistics were included, the current number of enslaved people would be much higher than the couple of tens of millions of people who tend to be named by influential statistics. Now, the reason why they are not included in the conversation is not only because of the fact that the more authentic statistics of contemporary racialized slavery would be deemed too unrealistic or "sentimentalist," but also due to the foundational conceptualization of the domestic sphere as a parallel, "civilizing" emotional economy that comprises racialized exploitative work and that is safeguarded from intervention by Law. The centrality of White familial bonds (and White luxury) still dictates legal frameworks and public discourse about domestic and child slavery in the Atlantic world.

The current public discussion about child soldiers erases their existence in the history of the "West," transforming this conflict into an exclusively

---

[40] Anna Mae Duane, "Introduction: When Is a Child a Slave?," in *Child Slavery before and after Emancipation: An Argument for Child-Centered Slavery Studies*, edited by Anna Mae Duane (New York: Cambridge University Press, 2017), 4.

[41] "Child Labour and UNICEF in Action: Children at the Centre," United Nations Children's Fund, 2014. Official statistics about contemporary exploitation tend to be conservative.

[42] Daniel L. Hatcher, *The Poverty Industry: The Exploitation of America's Most Vulnerable Citizens* (New York: New York University Press, 2019), 4.

"Global South" issue.[43] Now, researchers elucidate that the scope of the experiences of child soldiering goes beyond the context of military conflicts,[44] so the condition of "child soldier" can also be attributed to the many children exploited in drug trafficking throughout the Atlantic world, drug trafficking that in turn feeds the institutional emotional economy. Child soldiers are systemically ostracized by societies through structural racism, genocidal rape, and the criminalization engendered by war conflict and "tough-on-crime" policies. Humanitarian rescue of child soldiers is not common,[45] and Black girl soldiers within "warscapes" tend to be represented in media as gendered and peripheral "camp followers," silencing their lived experiences.[46] Hence, the media tend to marginalize the experiences of Black child soldiers and, even more, the oppression of Black girl and nonbinary soldiers, in military exploitation and drug trafficking due to the political disdain propelled by the racialization of childhood and historicist anti-Blackness. Her image does not fit the emotional slogans of the mainstream "anti-trafficking movement," unless it is to feed White comfort through her emotional otherness. Because she never connotes innocence. She is intrinsically menacing, even without a weapon.

There is recent public uproar in relation to climate change, but international agencies are openly critiquing in vague ways only the connections between climate change and migration, and not enslavement. Climate change has been trivialized in governmental reports as inciting migration due to natural disasters, instead of a more nuanced approach that looks at the multiple lived experiences of survivors of natural catastrophes.[47] The link between climate change and migration is more complex: contemporary slavery is tied to "environmental destruction" due to

---

[43] David M. Rosen, *Child Soldiers in the Western Imagination: From Patriots to Victims* (New Brunswick, NJ: Rutgers University Press, 2015).
[44] Scott Gates & Simon Reich, "Introduction," in *Child Soldiers in the Age of Fractured States*, edited by Scott Gates & Simon Reich (Pittsburgh, PA: University of Pittsburgh Press, 2009), 3.
[45] Mark A. Drumbi, *Reimagining Child Soldiers in International Law and Policy* (Oxford: Oxford University Press, 2012), 2.
[46] Alpaslan Özerdem & Suyanka Podder, "The Long Road Home: Conceptual Debates on Recruitment Experiences and Reintegration Outcomes," in *Child Soldiers: From Recruitment to Reintegration*, edited by Alpaslan Özerdem & Suyanka Podder (New York: Palgrave Macmillan, 2011), 11.
[47] Robert McLerman & François Gemenne, "Environmental Migration Research: Evolution and Current State of the Science," in *Routledge Handbook of Environmental Displacement and Migration*, edited by Robert McLerman & François Gemenne (New York: Routledge, 2018), 11.

the demands of "cheap" labor of wasteful consumer societies,[48] colonial legacies, carceral systems, and the environmental negligence of corporations. Nonetheless, States of the Atlantic world do not defy their corporate gaze, their entrenchment in the contemporary emotional economy of racialized slavery. Scholars foresee that hundreds of millions of people will soon become at-risk "environmental migrants" due to the disruptions generated by climate change.[49] Not only do enslavers consciously target racialized populations affected by natural disasters, but also governmental emergency relief responses are clearly racialized, as evidenced by the catastrophic outcome of Hurricane Maria in Puerto Rico, where more than 4,000 Puerto Ricans died in a racialized genocide perpetrated by the inaction and negligence of the US government toward its colony with a high Afro-Puerto Rican presence. In the racialized aftermath of Hurricane Katrina, George W. Bush actually suspended wage restrictions for two months, and the Department of Homeland Security lifted the regulation that requires employers to "confirm employee eligibility and identity"; these measures, represented by the government as accelerating the rebuilding of New Orleans, instigated the racialized labor exploitation of thousands.[50] While people of color around the world have "contributed the least to climate change," they are the most affected by it.[51] In contrast, mainstream media have spotlighted White emotionality in relation to climate change activism, in figures like Greta Thunberg, erasing long-lived Black and indigenous activism. Climate change is depicted as the fight for the future, and images of a drowning Manhattan aim to elicit urgent feelings of apocalyptic dread. For the racialized/criminalized, climate colonialism has already happened, but their deaths are deemed not more worthy of a tear than inundated real estate and a threatened emotional economy.

Not only does the public debate about climate change and migration hide its ties to contemporary slavery, but also the unconcerned silencing

---

[48] Kevin Bales, *Blood and Earth: Modern Slavery, Ecocide, and the Secret to Saving the World* (New York: Random House, 2016), 8–9.

[49] See Ato Quayson & Antonela Arhin, eds., *Labor Migration, Human Trafficking and Multinational Corporations: The Commodification of Illicit Flows* (New York: Routledge, 2012).

[50] Stephanie Hepburn & Rita J. Simon, *Human Trafficking around the World: Hidden in Plain Sight* (New York: Columbia University Press, 2013), 19.

[51] Lisa Reyes Mason & Jonathan Rigg, "Climate Change, Social Justice: Making the Case for Community Inclusion," in *People and Climate Change: Vulnerability, Adaptation, and Social Justice*, edited by Lisa Reyes Mason & Jonathan Rigg (Oxford: Oxford University Press, 2019).

of racialized exploitation of migrants is corroborated by political discourse about crimmigration. The conceptualization of immigration control in the Atlantic world has become more and more punitive toward the racialized emotional Other in the form of mass deportation or incarceration in capitalistic detention centers.[52] The "crimmigration crisis" in the United States extended mass incarceration to "immigration enforcement and border policing."[53] "Crimmigration" refers not only to the application of criminal law to immigration enforcement but also to the criminalization, stigmatization, and disenfranchisement of migrants and refugees.[54] Not surprisingly, the model of crimmigration is the one that guides survivor rescue, reintegration, and health care, since the agencies that have arrest quotas for "immigration control," such as Immigration and Customs Enforcement in the United States, are the ones that have direct contact with migrant survivors of contemporary racialized slavery. Even when survivors reach out for help, racialized ideas about "victimhood" and "innocence" influence whether victims are designated as such or criminalized by the same system that should be helping them.[55] Governmental resources publicized as rescuing and safeguarding survivors of "human trafficking" in the United States "universally translate to punitive results," prolonging "carceral control" of those most at risk.[56] Even though the United States already had the "largest immigration detention system" with deplorable statistics of captivity of Black and Brown migrants, the Trump administration still augmented the funding for penal detentions and federal prosecutors tasked with charging criminal convictions to migrants and asylum-seekers.[57] In the persistent industrial carcerality of Black emotions that fuels the emotional economy of racial capitalism, many Black migrant survivors of contemporary slavery

---

[52] Mary Bosworth, Alpa Parmar, & Yolanda Vázquez, *Race, Criminal Justice, and Migration Control: Enforcing the Boundaries of Belonging* (Oxford: Oxford University Press, 2017).
[53] Patrisia Macías-Rojas, *From Deportation to Prison: The Politics of Immigration Enforcement in Post–Civil Rights America* (New York: New York University Press, 2016), 9.
[54] Idil Atak & James C. Simeon, *The Criminalization of Migration: Context and Consequences* (Québec: McGill-Queen's University Press, 2018).
[55] Margaret Malloch & Paul Rigby, *Human Trafficking: The Complexities of Exploitation* (Edinburgh: Edinburgh University Press, 2016), 5.
[56] Jennifer Musto, *Control and Protect: Collaboration, Carceral Protection, and Domestic Sex Trafficking in the United States* (Berkeley: University of California Press, 2016), 30.
[57] César Cuauhtémoc García Hernández, *Migrating to Prison: Obsession with Locking Up Immigrants* (New York: New Press, 2019), 11.

are in jails, detention centers, or subjected to re-victimization and enslavement – because their emotions are strategically distrusted by White emotional entitlement.

The current state of the mass incarceration crisis in the United States evidences the aggravation of the emotional policing inherent to racialized slavery, achieving a eugenicist project by centering all the force of State penalization on an emotional Black body and soul. The contemporary carceral politics of "surveillance of Blackness" certainly mimics the vigilance of slavery.[58] Multiple studies about law enforcement in the United States have concluded that current official protocols of police departments are still explicitly grounded on violating the rights of Black communities.[59] The capitalistic criminalization of poverty in the United States leads to the compilation of more debt through high fines, prison charges for basic needs, and loss of job prospects, among other complications due to a criminal record.[60] The carceral landscape rooted in racial capitalism increasingly enables the institutional generation of capital at the expense of Black agony. The United States as a prison nation has heightened the vulnerability of women of color from ostracized communities who are survivors of violence.[61] The high statistics of racialized sexual violence by the police in the United States spark questions about state-sanctioned sexual exploitation, due to the systemic lack of institutional accountability of police officers and the legal legitimacy of strip searches and cavity searches.[62] White public discourse takes for granted that physical punishment and sexual violence are entrenched in the racialized, gendered, and heteronormative prison industrial complex. If not, there would not be "drop the soap" jokes. Thus, racialized torture and sexual abuse are emotionally relativized as part of the prison sentence, and unconcerned White emotional privilege presumes that Black emotional "capriciousness" did something to deserve it. The notion that structural violence needs to escalate for Black emotionality to reach Grief thrives in the

---

[58] Simone Browne, *Dark Matters: On the Surveillance of Blackness* (Durham, NC: Duke University Press, 2015).
[59] Paul Butler, *Chokehold: Policing Black Men* (New York: New Press, 2017).
[60] Peter Edelman, *Not a Crime to Be Poor: The Criminalization of Poverty in America* (New York: New Press, 2017).
[61] Beth E. Ritchie, *Arrested Justice: Black Women, Violence, and America's Prison Nation* (New York: New York University Press, 2012), 17.
[62] Andrea J. Ritchie, *Invisible No More: Police Violence against Black Women and Women of Color* (Boston: Beacon Press, 2017), 104.

hypercarcerality of Black emotions and the ubiquity of anti-Black police brutality.

In *Are Prisons Obsolete?*, prison abolitionist Angela Davis condemns the structural silencing of Black women's experiences in prison, contextualizes that "prison practices are gendered," and contends that taking for granted that "men's institutions constitute the norm and women's institutions are marginal" is to immortalize the "very normalization of prisons that an abolitionist approach seeks to contest."[63] Anticarceral feminism has historically opposed "violent policing and state repression"[64] based on hegemonic ideas of gender and sexuality. Among multiple demands, activists of anticarceral feminism argue that the intersection of Blackness and queerness is subjugated by "amplified" notions of "deviant hypersexuality," exemplified in the "framing of black women as sexual predators of white women in prison" and the "pervasive profiling" of Black trans women as "sex workers."[65] The assumed "un-femininity" of Black cisgender and transgender women by law enforcement and media leads to the silencing of their "death and brutalization" by police violence.[66] In response, the emergence of the Black Lives Matter movement propelled a "Black feminist intersectional praxis,"[67] and the 2015 song "Alright" by Kendrick Lamar was adopted as a chant against police brutality and carceral oppression,[68] with Black activists vocalizing in unison "it's gonna be alright" as an act of emotional restorative defiance. The Black Lives Matter movement and Black anticarceral feminism work toward emotional justice every day, and the affirmation that Black lives do matter explicitly condemns the historical sadism of White emotional supremacy against Black communities. And White happiness perseveres in its victimhood by disallowing Black emotional reparations.

The carceral emotional policing of Blackness extends to the racialization of childhood innocence, with Black children being at high risk for the industrial school-to-prison pipeline and contemporary racialized slavery.

---

[63] Angela Y. Davis, *Are Prisons Obsolete?* (New York: Seven Stories, 2011).
[64] Emily L. Thuma, *All Our Trials: Prison, Policing and the Feminist Fight to End Violence* (Urbana-Champaign: University of Illinois Press, 2019).
[65] Joey L. Mogul, Andrea J. Ritchie, & Kay Whitlock, *Queer (In)Justice: The Criminalization of LGBT People in the United States* (Boston: Beacon Press, 2011).
[66] Keeanga-Yamahtta Taylor, *From #BlackLivesMatter to Black Liberation* (Chicago: Haymarket, 2016), 164.
[67] Barbara Ransby, *Making All Black Lives Matter: Reimagining Freedom in the Twenty-First Century* (Berkeley: University of California Press, 2018).
[68] Fernando Orejuela & Stephanie Shonekan, *Black Lives Matter and Music: Protest, Intervention, Reflection* (Bloomington: Indiana University Press, 2018), 1.

Educational systems both legitimize and standardize racial profiling and carceral methods of disciplining and punishing.[69] Multiple studies corroborate that Black students in the United States are disproportionately disciplined, suspended, and expelled due to "zero tolerance" policies.[70] Black girls are regularly subjected to school arrests and referrals to law enforcement, and notorious cases of Black six-year-olds being arrested for "throwing tantrums"[71] corroborate the omnipotent nature of racialized emotional policing. The contemporary racialization of childhood is further evidenced by the lack of media attention, resources, and "AMBER alerts" in relation to the disappearance of thousands of Black children in the United States every year, Black children who are vulnerable to contemporary racialized slavery. Black teenage victims of police brutality and White emotional supremacy, such as Trayvon Martin and Nia Wilson, have been criminalized by media and legal proceedings, which have scrutinized their entirely legal social media conduct, such as raising the middle finger or holding a cell phone case that looks like a gun, and then denoted this behavior as vicious and downright emotionally illicit. Black children cannot be innocent, cannot be victims, cannot be children. It is still not permissible for the Black child to weep or laugh.

The discourse of the lack of visibility of contemporary racialized slavery normalizes the notion of a "postracial/color-blind" world, in which "racial harmony" is perceptible and emerges from the efforts of "White savior sensibility" with the "sacrificial" ramification of "White emotional injury." It is commonplace to hear White institutions state that racism today is "subtle," attempting to conceal the unbearable oppression of racial capitalism and structural emotional inequality, which is all too familiar to Black communities. This discursive framework facilitates the perpetuation of an enslaving emotional economy in the Atlantic world that structures the sustained capitalistic exploitation, punishment, and regulation of those "emotionally lesser" in the name of White joy. The diverse manifestations of contemporary racialized slavery intersect in the dependence of the enslaving emotional economy on the carceral policing and punishment of Black emotionality. This dependence is framed by the long-lived historical legacies of anti-Black hierarchization, appraisal, and

---

[69] Erica R. Meiners, *Right to Be Hostile: Schools, Prisons, and the Making of Public Enemies* (New York: Routledge, 2007).
[70] Anita Wadhwa, *Restorative Justice in Urban Schools: Disrupting the School-to-Prison Pipeline* (New York: Routledge, 2015).
[71] Monique Morris, *Pushout: The Criminalization of Black Girls in Schools* (New York: New Press, 2016).

judgment of feelings, the eugenicist project to name and ferociously act on emotional "excess." The enduring capitalistic order of White happiness, sustained by the dehumanizing institutional carcerality of Black emotions, not only remains, but thrives. The "postracial" narrative of a bettered Atlantic world aims to veil that the ultimate displeasure of White power would be to forgo the economic and emotional dependence on sadistic Black emotional criminalization. The contemporary emotional economy of racialized slavery in the Atlantic world is prolonged through the carceral industries that hyperpolice Black emotions and terrorize Black lives. The basis of emotional racism has always been "self-preservation," the preservation of decadent White delight. And so Blackness remains at the brink of death, just where White emotional entitlement wants it to be. The contemporary brutality of racialized exploitation and genocidal violence is premeditated, since it allows for the institutionally unchecked continuity of White emotional advantage. White privileged consumers get to purchase the newest devices and fashionable clothing made by enslaved people. They get to enjoy luxurious spaces that are economically prohibitive for Black people and still claim not to be aware of their privilege. Do they ever wonder where are those who are Black? They do not. Because they know exactly where they are.

EMOTIONAL JUSTICE NOW

The inescapable emotional policing of Blackness in the Atlantic world aims for the prescribed futility of the fulfillment of the Black body as a site of emotional containment, where it is intended by White emotional supremacy for shame to infiltrate every intimate relationship of the Black self with their own feelings, where genocidal violence dictates every institutional interaction with the Black Body, always escalating "in response" to the emotional "excesses" of Blackness. And this is the essence of Black captivity in the Atlantic world, then and now. Then, enslavement was defined as the triumph of Reason over Emotion and was scientifically extended to make that victory solely White. Then, White emotional supremacy was codified as that to be institutionally loved, admired, cherished, sanctified, while the intellectual history of the emotional policing of racialized slavery became the criminalizing basis of racial capitalism itself. Then, the carceral emotional economy persecuted "unwarranted" Black emotions that were infinitely suspect of infringing on the gratifications of those who were White, endearing, allowed to be emotionally free and even unhinged. Then, now, then, coexisting, transecting, "sick and tired of being sick and tired,"[72] the enslaved then and now, writing words, writing music, holding hands, moving souls. The institutional "postracial" narrative of the "abolition" of racialized slavery will strategically avoid at all costs the political acknowledgment that slavery is still very much a racialized emotional economy in the twenty-first century, that the racialized and interconnected nature of contemporary slavery and mass incarceration is still very much premised on the ambivalent discourses of emotional difference of scientific racism. The Black body is projected as having both a high pain tolerance and a propensity to complain about pain, which fuels the political emotional depersonalization of Black suffering. The Black body is codified as both emotionally erratic and emotionally resilient, this fluctuation being disguised by inevitable scripts of racialized deception. The result is not only the premeditated inexorable policing of Black emotions perpetrated by racialist structures of power, but also the institutional endorsement of the very visible structural hate against Blackness in the Atlantic world – because the capitalistic order of sadistic White happiness rules over economic mobility and the institutional carcerality of Black emotions. Because the Black emotional antagonist is needed for the White emotional protagonist to be idolized. Because White emotional "productivity" sadistically corresponds with Black emotional devaluation. The Atlantic emotional economic order never stopped relying on the criminalization, exploitation, and emotional expendability of racialized groups for mass production, and the emotional policing of Black lives raises its stakes every single day. Not only has the wealth gap between White and Black families in the United States multiplied by four in the last generations, but also school segregation and Black infant mortality have systematically either risen annually or not decreased at all.[73] Artificial intelligence brings new challenges to intersectional activism against racial oppression, leading to "the New Jim Code": "the employment of new technologies that reflect and reproduce existing inequities but that are promoted and perceived as more objective or progressive than the discriminatory systems of a previous era."[74] "Algorithmic oppression" is grounded on

---

[72] These are influential, compelling words by Fannie Lou Hamer.
[73] Daria Roithmayr, *Reproducing Racism: How Everyday Choices Lock in White Advantage* (New York: New York University Press, 2014), 2–4.
[74] Ruha Benjamin, *Race after Technology: Abolitionist Tools for the New Jim Code* (Cambridge: Polity, 2019), 5–6.

"racism, sexism, and false notions of meritocracy."[75] Inheriting the eugenicist foundations of "data," artificial intelligence engenders a veil of objectivity for racialized criminalization, surveillance, and provision of resources, still enacting and intensifying racial discrimination.

Through social media, White celebrities perform cultural appropriation and Blackfishing, changing their appearance with the pretense to colonize Blackness to reach, in their case, a lessened hypersexualization with the capacity to selectively step out and remain unharmed by the consequences of imperial sexual violence. Blackfishing pays: Ariana Grande, Kim Kardashian, and Kylie Jenner are some of the most followed celebrities on Instagram, accumulating capital from their mocking appropriation of Blackness. Recurring to plastic surgery and tanning, Blackfishing bodies set new "postracial yet very racial" standards of beauty framed by the racialization of what is deemed "beautiful" and what is deemed "imitative." "Thick noses" are degraded as "animalistic," while butt implants and lip fillers in a White body have become the new hegemonic standards of beauty. Contouring, a normalized method of makeup, verifies the desirability of a "thin nose," "bronzer," and over-lined lips, eroticizing the White body with a sprinkle of Black hypersexualization. When Ariana Grande, who has altered her skin tone and her appearance, did her exploitative "7 rings" music video, she did not hypersexualize herself: she indulged in the hypersexualization of the Black body, appropriated a disingenuous brand of Blackness with the veil of White productivity, generated an obscene amount of capital through Blackfishing, and then stepped out, with no repercussions for her or White privileged people like her. Furthermore, Black bodies (and vernaculars) have been monetized as "proxies" for the expression of emotions in social media memes and gifs, intensifying the conception of Black emotions as sources of voyeuristic entertainment and simulated performativity. Hence, Blackness has essentially become disembodied in the White Mind: ideas about Black emotions have been deliberately colonized as instruments of eugenicist renewal of Whiteness, only when felt by an emotionally "innocent," inherently "non-imitative" White body. Blackness has been commodified as a capitalistic conduit to convey White emotional "complexity." Blackness "infuses" the White body with emotional "spontaneity" and even more societal endearment. It is not only still innocent, but also wealthy, productive, invincible. In the gaze of

---

[75] Safiya U. Noble, *Algorithms of Oppression: How Search Engines Reinforce Racism* (New York: New York University Press, 2018), 2.

White emotional supremacy, Black emotions are now cultural capital that is "in fashion" as a way to elude the emotional "rigidity" of Whiteness diffused by scientific racism and consolidating White productivity in every domain, even the one primarily antagonized. When Kylie Jenner dyes her hair, it is major news that feeds her Blackfishing brand. When Megan Thee Stallion is shot, there is media silencing, since, when felt by a Black body, Black emotions are "criminal" and not "worthy" of a tear. Black emotions have become a conduit for the regeneration of an imperial monopoly over the standards of emotional "superiority." White joy, always defined as "non-imitative," endeavors to take over everything, even the delight of Black pride.

While White feelings are celebrated in their newfound Blackness, the emotional policing of the racialized and colonized is silenced in public discourse and academia, since knowledge production consistently and unscrupulously skips Blackness. In universities in the United States, departments tend to have many scholars that specialize in (White) "American" or "European" Studies and only one in African Studies, while many scholars in African nations face "teaching overcrowded classes in dilapidated infrastructures with outdated technologies" due to the "neocolonial exploitation of African states."[76] The incorporation of "voluntourism" in education has become another manifestation of colonizing negligence and of maintaining privilege in White hands – White hands that provide a transactional "service" to Black children to add a line to their résumé. Furthermore, high school textbooks today still include essentialist representations of race.[77] The emotional depersonalization of the enslaved marginalizes the intellectual production about enslaved resistance then and now. Just as the Haitian Revolution was not written then, Haitian subjectivities are not being written now. Just as gender theory silenced women of color then, White feminism hushes Black trans activists today. There is no Advanced Placement exam about African history in the education system of the United States because emotional empathy toward Blackness is "troublesome." What is being silenced and marginalized are Black minds and souls that feel and speak about feeling, outrage toward Black pain. Which is why Atlantic slavery is not remembered as what it was and is: a genocide. Institutions instead set a relaxed gradual "timeline" and deem "emotional" those who cannot

---

[76] Nicholas M. Creary, "Introduction," in *African Intellectuals and Decolonization*, edited by Nicholas M. Creary (Athens: Ohio University Press, 2012), 6.
[77] Morning, *The Nature of Race*, 66.

wait. To protest against the monuments of White supremacists and enslavers is portrayed as "erasing history" instead of affirming a true history of racialized suffering. Black student activists are criminalized, while White supremacists and proponents of contemporary scientific racism are paid honoraria to speak at prestigious universities in the name of the selective institutional reading of the right to free speech, where racial slurs and hateful statements are opportunistically read as "speech" and not as actions of "harassment" or "discrimination." Black students are prescribed to embody trauma narratives, but anti-Blackness is not institutionally regarded as traumatic, since actual Black emotions are irrelevant and yet everything to the system. Black students are expected to withstand devil's advocacy of enslavers and promoters of scientific racism in the classroom. Black students are expected to withstand watching Black voices being kept in a scholarly marginality in the name of a more "emotive," more "beautiful," Whiter history of the world.

Black resistance is in turn regarded as emotionally "excessive," as entirely too "sensitive." The political criticism of "woke/cancel culture" is that it is too emotional, too angry, belittling Black community organizing and activist struggles through social media hashtags. The mainstream media narrative of the summer of 2020 was that the nine minutes and twenty-nine seconds of the assassination of George Floyd by police led to an "uproar" of "violence" and "chaos" in the United States. The emotional criminalization of "Black rage" is blatant when protesting and "looting" are denoted as more violent than structural anti-Blackness. Genocidal violence against Blackness is still legitimate, while attacks against White property are very violent and very, very Black; Kyle Rittenhouse is an innocent child, while Tamir Rice is not. "Black rage" in response to those excruciating nine minutes and twenty-nine seconds, reminiscent of the trauma of the murder of Eric Garner and so many other anti-Black assassinations perpetrated by White police, was patronizingly communicated by mainstream media and White politicians as "understandable" and yet uncalled for. Black Grief is still signified as transient. The part that was "understandable" still spotlighted "cathartic" White emotions that appropriated Black grief, as institutional conversations about social justice always end up being primarily about White people. White performative activism by celebrities, politicians, and corporations inundated social media. White people said they finally "found out" that "silence is not an option." White people, who have monopolized the elitist discourse about who can be "qualified" as "educated," said they finally "found out" that they needed to "educate" themselves about their blatantly obvious privilege and about blatantly visible systemic conflicts. White people said they finally had "uncomfortable" family conversations about racism. This White "reckoning," this White "uncomfortable epiphany" about racism existing, compelled tender emotions toward the "compassionate White ally" for a couple of weeks. And still, even within this context of White "allyship," Black emotions about restorative justice were policed through empty White affirmations of "I hear you" that anticipated applause for the act of "hearing" without having to listen and change, without having to "sacrificially" respect Black emotionality. Even within this context of White "allyship," White people gaslighted Black people on the importance of Black Lives Matter protests not being excessive, not being too much, not being too emotional. Even within this context of White "allyship," the COVID-19 pandemic was being communicated as a universal conflict, primarily spotlighting, yet again, White emotional victimhood. We are all in this together. When Black essential workers were dying in a medically racist landscape, the Black body was to blame for causing its own mortality, its "diabetes," its "hypertension," its incapacity to overcome its own deterministic "gluttony" and emotional "capriciousness." White institutions and public figures are willing to accept that they were silent in their "inadvertent" privilege and to post a black square in social media accounts they monetize, but violently react to actual revelations of their anti-Blackness. Normative White "allyship" disqualifies structural anti-Blackness and capitalizes from the emotional performativity of momentary "White guilt," which soon dissolves into "allyship fatigue." Dismantling the inescapability of anti-Black emotional policing would be a point of no return for White emotional privilege, and Whiteness is not willing to risk it.

The emotional policing and penalization of Black communities is relativized and silenced today through the conceptualization of anti-Blackness as premised on benevolent emotional states of being, such as fear, ignorance, obliviousness, or even an internal struggle of guilt. There is no such thing as collective White guilt, this being another offensive colonization of the language of trauma. If there were, the Atlantic world would be completely different. On the contrary, in the discursive scripts of a "postracial" Atlantic world, emotions are solely mobilized toward the image of an "accidental" racist who is unaware of their own privilege and their own anti-Blackness. Apologetic notions, such as "implicit bias" or "microaggressions," construct the emotional violence of anti-Blackness as minimal or unintentional, while Black emotions are a priori proscribed as explosive, as forever "macro." A physician who provides pain relief to

White pregnant people and does not do so with Black pregnant people does not notice they are doing so, as it is simply an unconscious, unintentional slip. No, it is most certainly not a slip. It is impossible for someone not to notice that they are methodically doing so. It is a choice, a deadly, repeated, beyond noticeable choice. The concept of "unconscious bias" allows for the excusal of those institutionally elevated as the "most educated" as simultaneously the "most oblivious" of that which is very visible and right in front of them: the racialized who serve them and are harmed by them. Racism is not the "fear" toward all that is "different" or "fear" of losing societal standing, but instead anti-Blackness emotes loathing (a completely different emotion) that propels the uninterrupted fulfillment of White emotional entitlement and comfort. It is not fear at all: it is institutionally embedded Hate. It is this visible Hate that explains why, when White supremacists storm a carceral State's Capitol, when White shooters perpetrate a mass killing, the Police do not murder. The normative White emotional supremacy does not injure itself, as the intellectual history of racialized slavery proclaimed that Black feelings are the ones that exist only to be viciously wounded, to embody scorned scars. The institutional emotional identification and societal preoccupation with a nonexistent fearful, ignorant, perhaps remorseful, and always deserving-of-a-second-chance racist conceals structural Hate and the real Fear at hand: the unbearable Fear in Black communities of being killed because "they can take it." Of being killed because their families are regarded as "failures" at loving others and loving themselves. Of being killed because the State does not allow for Black Grief if their children are injured. Of being killed because White institutional power grins while gazing at their death. Of being killed because they do not have enough time for their tears to fall on the ground. Of being killed because emotions are "abominable" when felt by Black hearts. Emotions ferment. Emotions explode. Emotions kill. Revolution is the fight for the right to breathe and feel synchronously.

And emotional justice will be possible only when anti-Blackness is no longer minimized as a microaggression, Black Rage and Joy frame emotional reparations, and Black emotionality is actually spotlighted and listened to when expressed by the Black Body. Emotional justice will be possible only if Black people are allowed to be unapologetically Black (and angry) without being enslaved for their emotions, if Black pain no longer inescapably summons malicious White happiness. Emotional justice will be reached only when Black tears matter. The tears of a mother and a daughter. Going down Black cheeks. As they are crossing the tomb of the Atlantic. Alone and together. As they are raped, mutilated, tortured, killed, hushed, parodied. As they loudly cry for their right to breathe and feel at the same time. As they look at each other and weep when they hear their precious song in their own terms. As they look and defiantly love themselves.

> *A mother and a daughter. Drums. Suckling. Drums. Revolution. She can hear the drums. They beat as one. Dance in sync. I can hear her song. It lifts the dust from the ground. Hope her song can be hers. Cannot hear it herself. She is angry. I am Angry. She is Loved.*

Bibliography

PRIMARY SOURCES

Archives and Libraries

Archivo General de Indias
Archivo General de Puerto Rico
Archivo Nacional de Cuba
Bibliothèque nationale de France
British Library
Gloucestershire Archives
Harvard University, Houghton Library
Library of Congress
Merseyside Maritime Museum
Princeton University, Firestone Library, Rare Books and Special Collections
Schomburg Center for Research in Black Culture, Manuscripts, Archives and Rare Books Division
Universidad de Puerto Rico, Biblioteca Lázaro, Colección Nemours
University of Birmingham, Church Missionary Society Archive
University of Miami, Jamaica Manuscripts Collection
Yale University, Beinecke Rare Book and Manuscript Library

Printed Works

Aesop. *Aesop's Fables*, edited by W. T. Stead. London: Review of Reviews Office, 1896.
Alighieri, Dante. *The Divine Comedy*. New York: W. W. Norton & Company, 2013.
Aquinas, Thomas. *Summa theologica*. New York: Benziger, 1922.
Aristotle. *Rhetoric*. London: T. Cadell, 1823.
— *Nicomachean Ethics*. London: Longmans, Green, and Co., 1869.

Augustine. *The City of God.* London: Penguin, 2003.
Bacon, Francis. *The History of Life and Death.* London: I. Okes, 1638.
Biko, Steve. *I Write What I Like.* Oxford: Heinemann, 1987.
Blumenbach, Johann Friedrich. "De Generis Humani Varietate Nativa (1775)." In *The Anthropological Treatises of Johann Friedrich Blumenbach,* edited by Thomas Bendyshe. London: Anthropological Society, 1865.
Bocaccio, Giovanni. *Decameron.* Hertfordshire: Wordsworth, 2004.
Bonaparte, Napoleon. *Correspondance générale III: Pacifications 1800–1802.* Paris: Fayard, 2006.
Brettler, Marc Z., Michael D. Coogan, Carol A. Newsom, & Pheme Perkins, eds. *The New Oxford Annotated Bible.* Oxford: Oxford University Press, 2010.
Broca, Paul. *Mémoires d'anthropologie,* vol. 1. Paris: Reinwald, 1871.
Brooks, Miguel F., trans. *A Modern Translation of Kebra Nagast (The Glory of Kings).* Lawrenceville: Red Sea, 2002.
Brown-Long, Cyntoia. *Free Cyntoia: My Search for Redemption in the American Prison System.* New York: Atria, 2019.
Buffon, Comte de. *Buffon's Natural History Containing a Theory of the Earth, a General History of Man, of the Brute Creation, and of Vegetables, Minerals, etc.,* vol. 4. London: H. D. Symonds, 1797.
Burns, Robert I., ed. *Las Siete Partidas, vol. 1: The Medieval Church: The World of Clerics and Laymen.* Philadelphia: University of Pennsylvania Press, 2001.
  ed. *Las Siete Partidas, vol. 2: Medieval Government: The World of Kings and Warriors.* Philadelphia: University of Pennsylvania Press, 2001.
  ed. *Las Siete Partidas, vol. 5: Underworlds: The Dead, the Criminal, and the Marginalized.* Philadelphia: University of Pennsylvania Press, 2001.
Butterfield, Lyman Henry, ed. *Letters of Benjamin Rush, vol. II: 1793–1813.* Princeton, NJ: Princeton University Press, 2019.
Camper, Petrus. *Dissertation physique sur les différences réelles que présentent le traits du visage chez les hommes de différents pays et de différents ages; sur le beau qui caractèrise les statues antiques et le pierres gravées.* Utrecht: B. Wild & J. Altheer, 1791.
Carlyle, Thomas. *The Selected Works of Thomas Carlyle.* Rome: Bibliotheca Cakravarti, 2014.
Cervantes Saavedra, Miguel de. *El ingenioso don Quijote de la Mancha, Tomo II.* Barcelona: Gobchs, 1832.
Chafe, William H., Raymond Gavins, & Robert Korstad, eds. *Remembering Jim Crow: African Americans Tell about Life in the Segregated South.* New York: New Press, 2014.
Chaucer, Geoffrey. *The Canterbury Tales.* New York: Dover, 2004.
"Child Labour and UNICEF in Action: Children at the Centre." New York: United Nations Children's Fund, 2014.
Cicero. *Republic.* New York: G. & C. Carvill, 1829.
Cloquet, Hippolyte. *A System of Human Anatomy.* Boston: Wells and Lilly, 1830.
Le Code Noir ou Recueil des Réglemens. Paris: L. F. Prault, 1685.
Craft, William, & Ellen Craft. "Running a Thousand Miles for Freedom; or, The Escape of William and Ellen Craft from Slavery." In *Slave Narratives.* New York: Literary Classics, 2000.

Cuvier, Georges. *Recherches sur les ossemens fossiles, où l'on rétablit les caractères de plusieurs animaux dont les révolutions du globe ont détruit les espèces, Tome Premier.* Paris: D'Ocagne, 1812.
Darwin, Charles. *The Expression of the Emotions in Man and Animals.* London: John Murray, 1872.
Davenport, Charles Benedict. *Heredity in Relation to Eugenics.* New York: Holt, 1911.
De las Casas, Bartolomé. *Brevísima relación de la destrucción de las Indias.* Barcelona: Linkgua, 2017.
Descartes, René. *The Passions of the Soul.* Oxford: Oxford University Press, 2015.
Devereaux, Thomas, ed. *Cases Argued and Determined in the Supreme Court of North Caroline from December Term, 1828, to December Term, 1830.* Raleigh, NC: J. Gales and Sims, 1831.
Diamond, Jared. *Guns, Germs, and Steel: The Fates of Human Societies.* New York: Norton, 1999.
Douglass, Frederick. *Narrative of the Life of Frederick Douglass: An American Slave, Written by Himself.* Boston: Anti-Slavery Office, 1849.
Du Bois, W. E. B. *The Souls of Black Folk.* New York: Dover, 2012.
Equiano, Olaudah. *The Interesting Narrative of the Life of Olaudah Equiano.* Dublin: W. Sleater, 1791.
Fanon, Frantz. *The Wretched of the Earth.* New York: Grove, 2004.
  Black Skin, White Masks. New York: Grove, 2008.
Gälawdewos. *The Life and Struggles of Our Mother Walatta Petros: A Seventeenth-Century African Biography of an Ethiopian Woman,* edited by Michael Kleiner & Wendy Laura Belcher. Princeton, NJ: Princeton University Press, 2015.
Galen. *On the Natural Faculties.* Cambridge, MA: Harvard University Press, 1916.
Galton, Francis. "Hereditary Talent and Character." *Macmillan's Magazine* 12 (1865): 321.
  Hereditary Genius: An Inquiry into Its Laws and Consequences. London: Macmillan, 1869.
  "Composite Portraits." *Journal of the Anthropological Institute of Great Britain and Ireland* 8 (1878): 132–142.
  Inquiries into Human Faculty and Its Development. London: Macmillan, 1883.
  Finger Prints. Bloomington: Indiana University Press, 1892.
Gobineau, Arthur de. *The Moral and Intellectual Diversity of Races, with Particular Reference to Their Respective Influence in the Civil and Political History of Mankind.* Philadelphia: Lippincott, 1853.
Grant, Madison. *The Passing of the Great Race; or, The Racial Basis of European History.* New York: Scribner's, 1922.
Gregory of Nyssa. *Homilies on Ecclesiastes.* Berlin: Walter de Gruyter, 1993.
Haeckel, Ernst. *The Wonders of Life: A Popular Study of Biological Philosophy.* London: Watts, 1904.
Hegel, Georg W. F. *The Philosophy of History.* New York: Cosimo, 1837.
Herder, Johann Gottfried. *Outlines of a Philosophy of the History of Man.* London: Hanfard, 1803.

Hernstein, Richard J., & Charles Murray. *The Bell Curve: Intelligence and Class Structure in American Life*. New York: Simon & Schuster, 2010.

Hobbes, Thomas. *Leviathan, or The Matter, Forme & Power of a Commonwealth, Ecclesiasticall and Civill*. New York: Cambridge University Press, 1651.

Homer. *Odyssey*, vol. 4. London: Nicol and Murray, 1834.

Horace. *Satires and Epistles*. Oxford: Oxford University Press, 2011.

Howell, Thomas Bayly, ed. *A Complete Collection of State Trials*, vol. 20: *1771–1777*. London: T. C. Hansard, 1814.

Hume, David. *A Treatise on Human Nature*. Oxford: Clarendon, 1738.

Hunter, John. *Essays and Observations on Natural History, Anatomy, Physiology, Psychology, and Geology*. London: John van Voorst, 1861.

Jackson, George. *Soledad Brother: The Prison Letters of George Jackson*. Chicago: Lawrence Hill, 1994.

Jacobs, Harriet. *Incidents in the Life of a Slave Girl*. New York: Open Road, 2016.

Janvier, Louis Joseph, ed. *Les Constitutions d'Haïti (1801–1885)*. Paris: C. Marpon et E. Flammarion, 1886.

Jefferson, Thomas. *Notes on the State of Virginia*. Boston: H. Sprague, 1802.

Kames, Lord. *Sketches of the History of Man*, vol. 1. Edinburgh: Creech, 1774.

Kant, Immanuel. *Observations on the Feeling of the Beautiful and Sublime and Other Writings*. New York: Cambridge University Press, 2011.

Khaldun, Ibn. *The Muqaddimah: An Introduction to History*. Princeton, NJ: Princeton University Press, 1377.

King, Martin Luther, Jr. *Why We Can't Wait*. New York: Penguin, 2000.

Knox, Robert. *The Races of Men: A Fragment*. Philadelphia: Lea & Blanchard, 1850.

Laërtius, Diogenes. *The Lives and Opinions of Eminent Philosophers*. London: George Bell and Sons, 1901.

Lewis, Catherine M., & J. Richard Lewis, eds. *Women and Slavery in America: A Documentary History*. Fayetteville: University of Arkansas Press, 2011.

Linnaeus, Carl. *A General System of Nature, through the Three Grand Kingdoms of Animals, Vegetables, and Minerals, Systematically Divided into Their Several Classes, Orders, Genera, Species, and Varieties with Their Habitations, Manners, Economy, Structure, and Peculiarities*, vol. 1. London: Lackington, Allen, and Co., 1735.

Locke, John. *Two Treatises of Government*. London: Whitmore & Fenn, 1690.

An Essay Concerning Human Understanding. London: Tegg & Son, 1836.

Lombroso, Cesare. *Crime: Its Causes and Remedies*. Boston: Little, Brown, & Co., 1911.

Criminal Man. Durham, NC: Duke University Press, 2006.

Long, Edward. *The History of Jamaica; or, General Survey of the Ancient and Modern States of That Island: With Reflections on Its Situation, Settlements, Inhabitants, Climate, Products, Commerce, Laws, and Government*. London: Lowndes, 1774.

Lorde, Audre. *Sister Outsider: Essays and Speeches*. New York: Random House, 2007.

Bibliography

Machiavelli, Niccolò. *The Prince.* London: Richards, 1903.
Manzano, Juan Francisco. *Autobiografía del esclavo poeta y otros escritos.* Madrid: Iberoamericana, 2007.
Meiners, Christoph. *History of the Female Sex: Comprising a View of the Habits, Manners, and Influence of Women, among All Nations, from the Earliest Ages to the Present Time.* London: Colburn, 1808.
Montesquieu. *The Spirit of the Laws.* London: George Bell & Sons, 1748.
More, Thomas. *Utopia.* Hertfordshire: Wordsworth, 1997.
Morton, Samuel George. *Crania Americana.* Philadelphia: Dobson, 1839.
Philo of Alexandria. *The Contemplative Life, The Giants, and Selections.* Mahwah, NJ: Paulist Press, 1981.
Pico della Mirandolla, Giovanni. *Oration on the Dignity of Man.* New York: Cambridge University Press, 2012.
Plato. *Phaedo.* London: Routledge, 1955.
  Phaedrus and Letters VII and VIII. London: Penguin Books, 1973.
  Republic. Cambridge, MA: Harvard University Press, 2014.
Plotinus. *The Six Enneads.* Grand Rapids, MI: Christian Classics Ethereal Library, 1975.
Renan, Ernest. *La réforme intellectuelle et morale de la France.* Paris: Callman Levy, 1871.
Ripley, William Z. *The Races of Europe.* New York: Appleton, 1899.
Rousseau, Jean-Jacques. *The Social Contract and The First and Second Discourses.* New Haven, CT: Yale University Press, 2002.
Rush, Benjamin. *Medical Inquiries and Observations upon the Diseases of the Mind.* Philadelphia: Grigg and Elliot, 1835.
Schopenhauer, Arthur. *Essays and Aphorisms.* London: Penguin, 1970.
Schwartz, Stuart B., ed. *Early Brazil: A Documentary Collection to 1700.* New York: Cambridge University Press, 2010.
Scott, S. P., ed. *The Civil Law, Including the Twelve Tables: The Institutes of Gaius, the Rules of Ulpian, the Opinions of Paulus, the Enactments of Justinian, and the Constitutions of Leo.* Cincinnati, OH: Central Trust Co., 1932.
Senghor, Léopold Sédar. "On Negrohood: Psychology of the African Negro." In *Logic and African Philosophy: Seminal Essays on African Systems of Thought*, edited by Jonathan O. Chimakoman. Wilmington: Vernon, 2020.
Shakespeare, William. *Hamlet.* London: Heinemann, 1904.
Shakur, Assata. *Assata: An Autobiography.* Chicago: Lawrence Hill, 1987.
Sims, James Marion. *The Story of My Life.* New York: Appleton, 1888.
Smith, Adam. *The Theory of Moral Sentiments.* London: A. Millar, A. Kincaid, & J. Bell, 1759.
  An Inquiry into the Nature and Causes of the Wealth of Nations, vol. 2. London: W. Strahan & T. Cadell, 1776.
Smith, Samuel Stanhope. *An Essay on the Causes of the Variety of Complexion and Figure in the Human Species.* Edinburgh: Elliot, 1788.
Spinoza, Baruch. *Ethics.* London: J. M. Dent & Sons, 1910.
Stoddard, Lothrop. *The French Revolution in San Domingo.* New York: Houghton Mifflin, 1914.

The Rising Tide of Color against White-World Supremacy. New York: Charles Scribner's Sons, 1920.

Truth, Sojourner. "Narrative of Sojourner Truth, a Northern Slave, Emancipated from Bodily Servitude by the State of New York, in 1828." In *Slave Narratives.* New York: Literary Classics, 2000.

United Nations. "Slavery Convention." United Nations, Office of the High Commissioner, 1926.

"Supplementary Convention on the Abolition of Slavery, the Slave Trade, and Institutions and Practices Similar to Slavery." United Nations, Office of the High Commissioner, 1956.

"Protocol to Prevent, Suppress and Punish Trafficking in Persons, Especially Women and Children, Supplementing the United Nations Convention against Transnational Organized Crime." United Nations, Office of the High Commissioner, 2000.

"U.S. Transgender Survey: Report on the Experiences of Black Respondents (2015)." Washington and Dallas: National Center for Transgender Equality, Black Trans Advocacy, & National Black Justice Coalition, 2017.

Vacher de Lapouge, Georges. *L'aryen: Son rôle social.* Paris: Thorin, 1899.

Vesalius, Andreas. *De humani corporis fabrica libri septem.* Novato: Norman, 2017.

Voltaire. *Les lettres d'Amabed.* London, 1769.

White, Charles. *An Account of the Regular Gradation in Man and in Different Animals and Vegetables.* London: Dilly, 1799.

Wiedemann, Thomas, ed. *Greek and Roman Slavery.* New York: Routledge, 2003.

X, Malcolm. *The Autobiography of Malcolm X.* New York: Random House, 1964.

Xenophon. *Oeconomicus, or Treatise on Household Management.* Cambridge: J. Hall & Son, 1885.

Secondary Sources

Abruzzo, Margaret. *Polemical Pain: Slavery, Cruelty, and the Rise of Humanitarianism.* Baltimore, MD: Johns Hopkins University Press, 2011.

Aching, Gerard Laurence. *Freedom from Liberation: Slavery, Sentiment, and Literature in Cuba.* Bloomington: Indiana University Press, 2015.

Adelman, Jeremy, ed. *Colonial Legacies: The Problem of Persistence in Latin American History.* New York: Routledge, 1999.

Agamben, Giorgio. *Homo Sacer: Sovereign Power and Bare Life.* Palo Alto, CA: Stanford University Press, 1998.

Ahern, Stephen, ed. *Affect and Abolition in the Anglo-Atlantic, 1770–1830.* New York: Routledge, 2016.

Ahmed, Sara. *The Cultural Politics of Emotion.* New York: Routledge, 2004.

Aidoo, Lawrence. *Slavery Unseen: Sex, Power, and Violence in Brazilian History.* Durham, NC: Duke University Press, 2018.

Alberti, Fay Bound. *Medicine, Emotion and Disease, 1700–1950.* New York: Palgrave Macmillan, 2006.

Matters of the Heart: History, Medicine, and Emotion. Oxford: Oxford University Press, 2010.

Alexander, Michelle. *The New Jim Crow: Mass Incarceration in the Age of Colorblindness*. New York: New Press, 2012.
Allain, Jean, ed. *The Legal Understanding of Slavery: From the Historical to the Contemporary*. Oxford: Oxford University Press, 2012.
Alsultany, Evelyn. *Arabs and Muslims in the Media: Race and Representation after 9/11*. New York: New York University Press, 2012.
Atak, Idil, & James C. Simeon. *The Criminalization of Migration: Context and Consequences*. Quebec: McGill-Queen's University Press, 2018.
Baker, Carrie N. *Fighting the U.S. Youth Sex Trade: Gender, Race, and Politics*. New York: Cambridge University Press, 2018.
Bales, Kevin. *Understanding Global Slavery: A Reader*. Berkeley: University of California Press, 2005.
  Disposable People: New Slavery in the Global Economy. Berkeley: University of California Press, 2012.
  Blood and Earth: Modern Slavery, Ecocide, and the Secret to Saving the World. New York: Random House, 2016.
Barkow, Rachel E. *Prisoners of Politics: Breaking the Cycle of Mass Incarceration*. Cambridge, MA: Harvard University Press, 2019.
Beidler, Taylor, G., ed. *Signs of Race: Writing Race across the Atlantic World: Medieval to Modern*. New York: Palgrave Macmillan, 2005.
Benjamin, Ruha. *Race after Technology: Abolitionist Tools for the New Jim Code*. Cambridge: Polity, 2019.
Berger, Dan. *Captive Nation: Black Prison Organizing in the Civil Rights Era*. Chapel Hill: University of North Carolina Press, 2014.
Bernstein, Robin. *Racial Innocence: Performing American Childhood from Slavery to Civil Rights*. New York: New York University Press, 2011.
Bhabha, Homi K. *The Location of Culture*. New York: Routledge, 1994.
Bindman, David, & Henry Louis Gates, Jr. *The Image of the Black in Western Art: From the "Age of Discovery" to the Age of Abolition: Artists of the Renaissance and Baroque*. Cambridge, MA: Harvard University Press, 2010.
Blackburn, Robin. *The Making of New World Slavery: From the Baroque to the Modern, 1492–1800*. London: Verso, 1998.
Boddice, Rob, ed. *Pain and Emotion in Modern History*. New York: Palgrave Macmillan, 2014.
Bosworth, Mary, Alpa Parmar, & Yolanda Vázquez. *Race, Criminal Justice, and Migration Control: Enforcing the Boundaries of Belonging*. Oxford: Oxford University Press, 2017.
Bradley, Keith. *Slavery and Society at Rome*. New York: Cambridge University Press, 1994.
Bradley, Keith, & Paul Cartledge, eds. *The Cambridge World History of Slavery*, vol. 1. New York: Cambridge University Press, 2011.
Briggs, Laura. *Reproducing Empire: Race, Sex, Science, and U.S. Imperialism in Puerto Rico*. Berkeley: University of California Press, 2002.
Brisk, Alison, & Austin Choi-Fitzpatrick, eds. *From Human Trafficking to Human Rights: Reframing Contemporary Slavery*. Philadelphia: University of Pennsylvania Press, 2012.

Brown, Christopher Leslie. *Moral Capital: Foundations of British Abolitionism.* Chapel Hill: University of North Carolina Press, 2012.
Brown, Elspeth H., & Thy Phu, eds. *Feeling Photography.* Durham, NC: Duke University Press, 2014.
Brown, Vincent. *The Reaper's Garden: Death and Power in the World of Atlantic Slavery.* Cambridge, MA: Harvard University Press, 2008.
Browne, Simone. *Dark Matters: On the Surveillance of Blackness.* Durham, NC: Duke University Press, 2015.
Burnard, Trevor. *Mastery, Tyranny, & Desire: Thomas Thistlewood and His Slaves in the Anglo Jamaican World.* Chapel Hill: University of North Carolina Press, 2004.
Butler, Paul. *Chokehold: Policing Black Men.* New York: New Press, 2017.
Cabezas, Amalia L. *Economies of Desire: Sex and Tourism in Cuba and the Dominican Republic.* Philadelphia: Temple University Press, 2009.
Campbell, Christopher P., ed. *The Routledge Companion to Media and Race.* New York: Routledge, 2017.
Campbell, Gwyn, & Elizabeth Elbourne, eds. *Sex, Power, and Slavery.* Athens: Ohio University Press, 2014.
Childs, Adrienne L., & Susan H. Libby, eds. *Blacks and Blackness in European Art of the Long Nineteenth Century.* New York: Ashgate, 2014.
Childs, Dennis. *Black Incarceration from the Chain Gang to the Penitentiary.* Minneapolis: University of Minnesota Press, 2015.
Cole, Stephanie, & Natalie J. Ring, eds. *The Folly of Jim Crow: Rethinking the Segregated South.* Arlington: University of Texas at Arlington Press, 2012.
Cooks, Bridget R. *Exhibiting Blackness: African Americans and the American Art Museum.* Boston: University of Massachusetts Press, 2011.
Cooper, Frederick. *Colonialism in Question: Theory, Knowledge, History.* Berkeley: University of California Press, 2005.
Cooper, Frederick, Thomas Holt, & Rebecca Scott, eds. *Beyond Slavery: Explorations of Race, Labor, and Citizenship in Postemancipation Societies.* Chapel Hill: University of North Carolina Press, 2000.
Cooper Owens, Deidre. *Medical Bondage: Race, Gender, and the Origins of American Gynecology.* Athens: University of Georgia Press, 2017.
Corrigan, John, ed. *The Oxford Handbook of Religion and Emotion.* Oxford: Oxford University Press, 2007.
Crais, Clifton, & Pamela Scully. *Sara Baartman and the Hottentot Venus: A Ghost Story and a Biography.* Princeton, NJ: Princeton University Press, 2009.
Creary, Nicholas M., ed. *African Intellectuals and Decolonization.* Athens: Ohio University Press, 2012.
Cryle, Peter, & Elizabeth Stephens. *Normality: A Critical Genealogy.* Chicago: University of Chicago Press, 2017.
Curtin, Philip D. *The Atlantic Slave Trade: A Census.* Madison: University of Wisconsin Press, 1969.
Cusac, Anne-Marie. *Cruel and Unusual: The Culture of Punishment in America.* New Haven, CT: Yale University Press, 2009.

Darity, William A., Jr., & A. Kirsten Mullen. *From Here to Equality: Reparations for Black Americans in the Twenty-First Century.* Chapel Hill: University of North Carolina Press, 2020.
Davies, Douglas J. *Emotion, Identity, and Religion: Hope, Reciprocity, and Otherness.* Oxford: Oxford University Press, 2011.
Davis, Angela Y. *Women, Race, & Class.* New York: Vintage, 1983.
  Are Prisons Obsolete? New York: Seven Stories, 2011.
Davis, Dána-Ain. *Reproductive Justice: Racism, Pregnancy, and Premature Birth.* New York: New York University Press, 2019.
Davis, David Brion. *In the Image of God: Religion, Moral Values, and Our Heritage of Slavery.* New York: Vail-Ballou Press, 2001.
  Inhuman Bondage: The Rise and Fall of Slavery in the New World. Oxford: Oxford University Press, 2006.
  The Problem of Slavery in the Age of Emancipation. New York: Vintage, 2014.
Davis, Tracy D., & Stefka Mihaylova. *Uncle Tom's Cabins: The Transnational History of America's Most Mutable Book.* Ann Arbor: University of Michigan Press, 2018.
Decker, Oliver. *Commodified Bodies: Organ Transplantation and the Organ Trade.* New York: Routledge, 2014.
Desmond, Adrian, & James Moore. *Darwin's Sacred Cause: How a Hatred of Slavery Shaped Darwin's Views on Human Evolution.* New York: Houghton Mifflin, 2009.
De Wet, Chris L. *Preaching Bondage: John Chrysostom and the Discourse of Slavery in Early Christianity.* Oakland: University of California Press, 2015.
Díaz Soler, Luis M. *Historia de la esclavitud negra en Puerto Rico.* Río Piedras: Editorial de la Universidad de Puerto Rico, 1953.
Diouf, Silviane A. *Slavery's Exiles: The Story of the American Maroons.* New York: New York University Press, 2014.
Dixon, Thomas. *From Passions to Emotions: The Creation of a Secular Psychological Category.* New York: Cambridge University Press, 2003.
Downs, Jim. *Sick from Freedom: African American Illness and Suffering during the Civil War and Reconstruction.* Oxford: Oxford University Press, 2012.
Drumbi, Mark A. *Reimagining Child Soldiers in International Law and Policy.* Oxford: Oxford University Press, 2012.
Duane, Anna Mae. *Child Slavery before and after Emancipation: An Argument for Child Centered Slavery Studies.* New York: Cambridge University Press, 2017.
Dunn, Stephane. *"Baad Bitches" and Sassy Supermamas: Black Power Action Films.* Urbana-Champaign: University of Illinois Press, 2008.
Dzur, Albert W., Ian Loader, & Richard Sparks, eds. *Democratic Theory and Mass Incarceration.* Oxford: Oxford University Press, 2016.
Earle, T. F., & K. J. P. Lowe, eds. *Black Africans in Renaissance Europe.* New York: Cambridge University Press, 2009.
Edelman, Peter. *Not a Crime to Be Poor: The Criminalization of Poverty in America.* New York: New Press, 2017.
Eisen, Lauren-Brooke. *Inside Private Prisons: An America Dilemma in the Age of Mass Incarceration.* New York: Columbia University Press, 2018.

Elliot, J. H. *Empires of the Atlantic World: Britain and Spain in America, 1492–1830.* New Haven, CT: Yale University Press, 2016.

Elliot, Jessica. *The Role of Consent in Human Trafficking.* New York: Routledge, 2015.

Eltis, David. *The Rise of African Slavery in the Americas.* New York: Cambridge University Press, 2000.

Enns, Peter K. *Incarceration Nation: How the United States Became the Most Punitive Democracy in the World.* New York: Cambridge University Press, 2016.

Erigha, Maryann. *The Hollywood Jim Crow: The Racial Politics of the Movie Industry.* New York: New York University Press, 2019.

Eustace, Nicole. *Passion Is the Gale: Emotion, Power, and the Coming of the American Revolution.* Chapel Hill: University of North Carolina Press, 2008.

Eze, Emmanuel Chukwudi. *Achieving our Humanity: The Idea of a Postracial Future.* New York: Routledge, 2001.

Farber, Paul Lawrence. *Mixing Races: From Scientific Racism to Modern Evolutionary Ideas.* Baltimore, MD: Johns Hopkins University Press, 2011.

Festa, Lynn. *Sentimental Figures of Empire in Eighteenth-Century Britain and France.* Baltimore, MD: Johns Hopkins University Press, 2006.

Fischer, Sibylle. *Modernity Disavowed: Haiti and the Cultures of Slavery in the Age of Revolution.* Durham, NC: Duke University Press, 2004.

Fitzgerald, William. *Roman Literature and Its Contexts: Slavery and the Roman Literary Imagination.* New York: Cambridge University Press, 2000.

Fleetwood, Nicole R. *Troubling Vision: Performance, Visuality, and Blackness.* Chicago: University of Chicago Press, 2011.

Foucault, Michel. *The History of Sexuality, vol. 2: The Use of Pleasure.* New York: Pantheon Books, 1985.

"17 March 1976." In *Society Must Be Defended: Lectures at the Collège de France, 1975–76,* edited by Mauro Bertani & Alessandro Fontana. New York: Picador, 2003.

Fraser, Michael L. *The Enlightenment of Sympathy: Justice and the Moral Sentiments in the Eighteenth Century and Today.* Oxford: Oxford University Press, 2010.

Frevert, Ute. *Emotions in History: Lost and Found.* Budapest: Central European University Press, 2010.

ed. *Emotional Lexicons: Continuity and Change in the Vocabulary of Feeling, 1700–2000.* Oxford: Oxford University Press, 2014.

Frevert, Ute, & Thomas Dixon, eds. *Civilizing Emotions: Concepts in Nineteenth Century Asia and Europe.* Oxford: Oxford University Press, 2015.

Gallagher, Anne T. *The International Law of Human Trafficking.* New York: Cambridge University Press, 2010.

García Hernández, César Cuauhtémoc. *Migrating to Prison: Obsession with Locking Up Immigrants.* New York: New Press, 2019.

Garrigus, John D., & Christopher Morris, eds. *Assumed Identities: The Meanings of Race in the Atlantic World.* Arlington: University of Texas at Arlington Press, 2010.

Gates, Scott, & Simon Reich, eds. *Child Soldiers in the Age of Fractured States.* Pittsburgh: University of Pittsburgh Press, 2009.
Genovese, Eugene D., & Elizabeth Fox-Genovese. *Fatal Self-Deception: Slaveholding Paternalism in the Old South.* New York: Cambridge University Press, 2011.
Gikandi, Simon. *Slavery and the Culture of Taste.* Princeton, NJ: Princeton University Press, 2011.
Glancy, Jennifer A. *Slavery in Early Christianity.* Oxford: Oxford University Press, 2002.
Glasson, Travis. *Mastering Christianity: Missionary Anglicanism and Slavery in the Atlantic World.* Oxford: Oxford University Press, 2012.
Goldenberg, David M. *The Curse of Ham: Race and Slavery in Early Judaism, Christianity, and Islam.* Princeton, NJ: Princeton University Press, 2003.
Gomez, Michael. *Reversing Sail: A History of the African Diaspora.* New York: Cambridge University Press, 2005.
  African Dominion: A New History of Empire in Early and Medieval West Africa. Princeton, NJ: Princeton University Press, 2018.
Goring, Paul. *The Rhetoric of Sensibility in Eighteenth-Century Culture.* New York: Cambridge University Press, 2005.
Green, Garth L., & Philip W. Scher, eds. *Trinidad Carnival: The Cultural Politics of a Transnational Festival.* Bloomington: Indiana University Press, 2007.
Gross, Daniel M. *The Secret History of Emotion: From Aristotle's Rhetoric to Modern Brain Science.* Chicago: University of Chicago Press, 2006.
Grubs, Judith Evans, Tim Parkin, & Roslynne Bell, eds. *The Oxford Handbook of Childhood and Education in the Classical World.* Oxford: Oxford University Press, 2013.
Guasco, Michael. *Slaves and Englishmen: Human Bondage in the Early Modern Atlantic World.* Philadelphia: University of Pennsylvania Press, 2014.
Guha, Ranajit. *History at the Limit of World-History.* New York: Columbia University Press, 2002.
Haley, Sarah. *No Mercy Here: Gender, Punishment, and the Making of Jim Crow Modernity.* Chapel Hill: University of North Carolina Press, 2016.
Hall, Gwendolyn M. *Slavery and African Ethnicities in the Americas: Restoring the Links.* Chapel Hill: University of North Carolina Press, 2005.
Hannaford, Ivan. *Race: The History of an Idea in the West.* Baltimore, MD: Johns Hopkins University Press, 1996.
Harper, Kyle. *Slavery in the Late Roman World AD 275–425.* New York: Cambridge University Press, 2011.
Harris, Dawn P. *Punishing the Black Body: Marking Social and Racial Structures in Barbados and Jamaica.* Athens: University of Georgia Press, 2017.
Harrold, Stanley. *American Abolitionism: Its Direct Political Impact from Colonial Times into Reconstruction.* Charlottesville: University of Virginia Press, 2019.
Hartman, Saidiya. *Lose Your Mother: A Journey along the Atlantic Slave Route.* New York: Farrar, Straus, & Giroux, 2008.
Hatcher, Daniel L. *The Poverty Industry: The Exploitation of America's Most Vulnerable Citizens.* New York: New York University Press, 2019.

Haynes, Stephen R. *Noah's Curse: The Biblical Justification of American Slavery*. Oxford: Oxford University Press, 2002.
Hepburn, Stephanie, & Rita J. Simon. *Human Trafficking around the World: Hidden in Plain Sight*. New York: Columbia University Press, 2013.
Hernández, Tanya Katerí. *Racial Subordination in Latin America: The Role of the State, Customary Law, and the New Civil Rights Response*. New York: Cambridge University Press, 2013.
Hezser, Catherine. *Jewish Slavery in Antiquity*. Oxford: Oxford University Press, 2005.
Hinton, Elizabeth. *From the War on Poverty to the War on Crime: The Making of Mass Incarceration in America*. Cambridge, MA: Harvard University Press, 2016.
Hoberman, John. *Black and Blue: The Origins and Consequences of Medical Racism*. Berkeley: University of California Press, 2012.
hooks, bell. *Reel to Real: Race, Sex, and Class at the Movies*. New York: Routledge, 1996.
Hopper, Matthew S. *Slaves of One Master: Globalization and Slavery in Arabia in the Age of Empire*. New Haven, CT: Yale University Press, 2015.
Hunter, Tera W. *Bound in Wedlock: Slave and Free Black Marriage in the Nineteenth Century*. Cambridge, MA: Harvard University Press, 2017.
Immerwahr, Daniel. *How to Hide an Empire: A History of the Greater United States*. New York: Palgrave Macmillan, 2019.
Ioanade, Paula. *The Emotional Politics of Racism: How Feelings Trump Facts in an Era of Colorblindness*. Stanford, CA: Stanford University Press, 2015.
James, C. L. R. *The Black Jacobins: Toussaint Louverture and the San Domingo Revolution*. New York: Vintage Books, 1938.
Jordan, Winthrop D. *White over Black: American Attitudes toward the Negro*. Chapel Hill: University of North Carolina Press, 2012.
Joshel, Sandra R. *Slavery in the Roman World*. New York: Cambridge University Press, 2010.
Joshel, Sandra R., & Sheila Murnaghan. *Women and Slaves in Greco-Roman Societies*. New York: Routledge, 1998.
Kagan, Jerome. *What Is Emotion? History, Measures, and Meanings*. New Haven, CT: Yale University Press, 2007.
Kalu, Kenneth, & Toyin Falola, eds. *Exploitation and Misrule in Colonial and Postcolonial Africa*. New York: Palgrave Macmillan, 2019.
Kamen, Deborah. *Status in Classical Athens*. Princeton, NJ: Princeton University Press, 2013.
Kara, Siddharth. *Modern Slavery: A Global Perspective*. New York: Columbia University Press, 2017.
Kaster, Robert A. *Emotion, Restraint, and Community in Ancient Rome*. Oxford: Oxford University Press, 2005.
Kiernan, Ben. *Blood and Soil: A World History of Genocide and Extermination from Sparta to Darfur*. New Haven, CT: Yale University Press, 2007.
Kilgore, James W. *Understanding Mass Incarceration: A People's Guide to the Key Civil Rights Struggle of Our Time*. New York: New Press, 2015.
Klein, Herbert S. *The Atlantic Slave Trade*. New York: Cambridge University Press, 1999.

Lander, James. *Lincoln & Darwin: Shared Visions of Race, Science, and Religion.* Carbondale: Southern Illinois University Press, 2010.

Langan, Mark. *Neo-Colonialism and the Poverty of "Development" in Africa.* New York: Palgrave Macmillan, 2018.

Leeds Craig, Maxine. *Ain't I a Beauty Queen: Black Women, Beauty, and the Politics of Race.* Oxford: Oxford University Press, 2011.

LeFlouria, Talitha L. *Chained by Silence: Black Women and Convict Labor in the New South.* Chapel Hill: University of North Carolina Press, 2015.

Lemmings, David, & Ann Brooks, eds. *Emotions and Social Change: Historical and Sociological Perspectives.* New York: Routledge, 2014.

Leonard, A. B. & David Pretel, eds. *The Caribbean and the Atlantic World Economy: Circuits of Trade, Money and Knowledge, 1650–1914.* New York: Palgrave Macmillan, 2016.

Levecq, Christine. *Slavery and Sentiment: The Politics of Feeling in Black Atlantic Antislavery Writing, 1770–1850.* Durham: University of New Hampshire Press, 2008.

Levine, Robert S. *The Lives of Frederick Douglass.* Cambridge, MA: Harvard University Press, 2016.

Lewis, Bernard. *Race and Slavery in the Middle East: A Historical Inquiry.* Oxford: Oxford University Press, 1990.

Liem, Marieke. *After Life Imprisonment: Reentry in the Era of Mass Incarceration.* New York: New York University Press, 2016.

Livingstone, David N. *Adam's Ancestors: Race, Religion & the Politics of Human Origins.* Baltimore, MD: Johns Hopkins University Press, 2008.

Lockhart, James, & Stuart B. Schwartz. *Early Latin America: A History of Colonial Spanish America and Brazil.* New York: Cambridge University Press, 1983.

Lovejoy, Paul E. *Transformations in Slavery: A History of Slavery in Africa.* New York: Cambridge University Press, 2000.

Lydon, Jane. *Imperial Emotions: The Politics of Empathy across the British Empire.* New York: Cambridge University Press, 2020.

Mac, Juno, & Molly Smith. *Revolting Prostitutes: The Fight for Sex Workers' Rights.* New York: Verso, 2018.

Macías-Rojas, Patrisia. *From Deportation to Prison: The Politics of Immigration Enforcement in Post–Civil Rights America.* New York: New York University Press, 2016.

Maddox, Gregory, ed. *Conquest and Resistance to Colonialism in Africa.* New York: Routledge, 2018.

Malloch, Margaret, & Paul Rigby. *Human Trafficking: The Complexities of Exploitation.* Edinburgh: Edinburgh University Press, 2016.

Manning, Patrick. *The African Diaspora: A History through Culture.* New York: Columbia University Press, 2009.

Marchant, Alicia, ed. *Historicising Heritage and Emotions: The Affective Histories of Blood, Stone and Land.* New York: Routledge, 2019.

Markovitz, Jonathan. *Racial Spectacles: Explorations in Media, Race, and Justice.* New York: Routledge, 2011.

Matt, Susan J., & Peter N. Stearns, eds. *Doing Emotions History*. Urbana-Champaign: University of Illinois Press, 2014.
Mbembe, Achille. *On the Postcolony*. Berkeley: University of California Press, 2001.
McCracken-Flesher, Caroline. *The Doctor Dissected: A Cultural Autopsy of the Burke and Hare Murders*. Oxford: Oxford University Press, 2011.
McLerman, Robert, & François Gemenne, eds. *Routledge Handbook of Environmental Displacement and Migration*. New York: Routledge, 2018.
Means Coleman, Robin R. *Horror Noire: Blacks in American Horror Films from the 1890s to Present*. New York: Routledge, 2011.
Meiners, Erica R. *Right to Be Hostile: Schools, Prisons, and the Making of Public Enemies*. New York: Routledge, 2007.
Mogul, Joey L., Andrea J. Ritchie, & Kay Whitlock. *Queer (In)Justice: The Criminalization of LGBT People in the United States*. Boston: Beacon Press, 2011.
Moraña, Mabel, Enrique D. Dussel, & Carlos A. Jáuregui. *Coloniality at Large: Latin America and the Postcolonial Debate*. Durham, NC: Duke University Press, 2008.
Morgan, Jennifer L. *Laboring Women: Reproduction and Gender in New World Slavery*. Philadelphia: University of Pennsylvania Press, 2004.
Morning, Ann Juanita. *The Nature of Race: How Scientists Think and Teach about Human Difference*. Berkeley: University of California Press, 2011.
Morris, Monique. *Pushout: The Criminalization of Black Girls in Schools*. New York: New Press, 2016.
Muhammad, Khalil Gibran. *The Condemnation of Blackness: Race, Crime, and the Making of Modern Urban America*. Cambridge, MA: Harvard University Press, 2010.
Murakawa, Naomi. *The First Civil Right: How Liberals Built Prison America*. Oxford: Oxford University Press, 2014.
Musto, Jennifer. *Control and Protect: Collaboration, Carceral Protection, and Domestic Sex Trafficking in the United States*. Berkeley: University of California Press, 2016.
Naimark, Norman M. *Genocide: A World History*. Oxford: Oxford University Press, 2017.
Ndlovu-Gatsheni, Sabelo J. *Epistemic Freedom in Africa: Deprovincialization and Decolonization*. New York: Routledge, 2018.
Newman, Richard B. *Abolitionism: A Very Short Introduction*. Oxford: Oxford University Press, 2018.
Nichols, Andrea J. *Sex Trafficking in the United States: Theory, Research, Policy, and Practice*. New York: Columbia University Press, 2016.
Njoku, Raphael Chijoke, & Chima J. Korieh, eds. *Missions, States, and European Expansion in Africa*. New York: Routledge, 2007.
Noble, Safiya U. *Algorithms of Oppression: How Search Engines Reinforce Racism*. New York: New York University Press, 2018.
Nowatzki, Robert. *Representing African Americans in Transatlantic Abolitionism and Blackface Minstrelsy*. Baton Rouge: Louisiana State University Press, 2010.

Orejuela, Fernando, & Stephanie Shonekan. *Black Lives Matter and Music: Protest, Intervention, Reflection*. Bloomington: Indiana University Press, 2018.

Özerdem, Alpaslan, & Suyanka Podder, eds. *Child Soldiers: From Recruitment to Reintegration*. New York: Palgrave Macmillan, 2011.

Patterson, Orlando. *Slavery and Social Death: A Comparative Study*. Cambridge, MA: Harvard University Press, 1982.

Rituals of Blood: The Consequences of Slavery in Two American Centuries. New York: Basic Books, 1999.

Perry, Matthew J. *Gender, Manumission, and the Roman Freedwoman*. New York: Cambridge University Press, 2014.

Peters, Alicia W. *Responding to Human Trafficking: Sex, Gender, and Culture in the Law*. Philadelphia: University of Pennsylvania Press, 2015.

Phillips, William D., Jr. *Slavery in Medieval and Early Modern Iberia*. Philadelphia: University of Pennsylvania Press, 2014.

Piley, Jessica R. *Policing Sexuality*. Cambridge, MA: Harvard University Press, 2014.

Plamper, Jan. *The History of Emotions: An Introduction*. Oxford: Oxford University Press, 2012.

Plessis, Paul J. du, Clifford Ando, & Kauis Tuori, eds. *The Oxford Handbook of Roman Law and Society*. Oxford: Oxford University Press, 2016.

Pritchard, James. *In Search of Empire: The French in the Americas, 1670–1730*. New York: Cambridge University Press, 2004.

Quayson, Ato, & Antonela Arhin, eds. *Labor Migration, Human Trafficking and Multinational Corporations: The Commodification of Illicit Flows*. New York: Routledge, 2012.

Raboteau, Albert J. *Slave Religion: The "Invisible Institution" in the Antebellum South*. Oxford: Oxford University Press, 2004.

Ramelli, Ilaria L. E. *Social Justice and the Legitimacy of Slavery: The Role of Philosophical Asceticism from Ancient Judaism to Late Antiquity*. Oxford: Oxford University Press, 2016.

Ransby, Barbara. *Making All Black Lives Matter: Reimagining Freedom in the Twenty-First Century*. Berkeley: University of California Press, 2018.

Reverby, Susan M., ed. *Tuskegee's Truths: Rethinking the Tuskegee Syphilis Study*. Chapel Hill: University of North Carolina Press, 2000.

Examining Tuskegee: The Infamous Syphilis Study and Its Legacy. Chapel Hill: University of North Carolina Press, 2009.

Reyes Mason, Lisa, & Jonathan Rigg, eds. *People and Climate Change: Vulnerability, Adaptation, and Social Justice*. Oxford: Oxford University Press, 2019.

Rio, Alice. *Slavery after Rome, 500–1100*. Oxford: Oxford University Press, 2017.

Ritchie, Andrea J. *Invisible No More: Police Violence against Black Women and Women of Color*. Boston: Beacon Press, 2017.

Ritchie, Beth E. *Arrested Justice: Black Women, Violence, and America's Prison Nation*. New York: New York University Press, 2012.

Ritterhouse, Jennifer. *Growing Up Jim Crow: How Black and White Southern Children Learned Race*. Chapel Hill: University of North Carolina Press, 2006.

Roberts, Dorothy. *Fatal Invention: How Science, Politics, and Big Business Recreate Race in the Twenty-First Century*. New York: New Press, 2011.

Killing the Black Body: Race, Reproduction, and the Meaning of Liberty. New York: Random House, 2016.

Robinson, David. *Muslim Societies in African History*. New York: Cambridge University Press, 2004.

Roithmayr, Daria. *Reproducing Racism: How Everyday Choices Lock in White Advantage*. New York: New York University Press, 2014.

Rood, Daniel B. *The Reinvention of Atlantic Slavery: Technology, Labor, Race, and Capitalism in the Greater Caribbean*. Oxford: Oxford University Press, 2017.

Rosen, David M. *Child Soldiers in the Western Imagination: From Patriots to Victims*. New Brunswick, NJ: Rutgers University Press, 2015.

Rosenthal, Caitlin. *Accounting for Slavery: Masters and Management*. Cambridge, MA: Harvard University Press, 2018.

Rosenwein, Barbara H. *Generations of Feeling: A History of Emotions, 600–1700*. New York: Cambridge University Press, 2016.

Rosner, Lisa. *The Anatomy Murders: Being the True and Spectacular History of Edinburgh's Notorious Burke and Hare and of the Man of Science Who Abetted Them in the Commission of Their Most Heinous Crimes*. Philadelphia: University of Pennsylvania Press, 2010.

Rotman, Youval. *Byzantine Slavery and the Mediterranean World*. Cambridge, MA: Harvard University Press, 2009.

Rugemer, Edward B. *The Problem of Emancipation: The Caribbean Roots of the American Civil War*. Baton Rouge: Louisiana State University Press, 2008.

Slave Law and the Politics of Resistance in the Early Atlantic World. Cambridge, MA: Harvard University Press, 2018.

Sammond, Nicholas. *Birth of an Industry: Blackface Minstrelsy and the Rise of American Animation*. Durham, NC: Duke University Press, 2015.

Scheve, Christian von, & Mikko Salmela, eds. *Collective Emotions*. Oxford: Oxford University Press, 2014.

Schmidt, Elizabeth. *Foreign Intervention in Africa: From the Cold War to the War on Terror*. New York: Cambridge University Press, 2013.

Scully, Pamela, & Diana Paton. *Gender and Slave Emancipation in the Atlantic World*. Durham, NC: Duke University Press, 2005.

Segrave, Marie, Sanja Milivojevic, & Sharon Pickering. *Sex Trafficking and Modern Slavery: The Absence of Evidence*. New York: Routledge, 2017.

Shelley, Louise. *Human Trafficking: A Global Perspective*. New York: Cambridge University Press, 2010.

Sinha, Manisha. *The Slave's Cause: A History of Abolition*. New Haven, CT: Yale University Press, 2016.

Smallwood, Stephanie E. *Saltwater Slavery: A Middle Passage from Africa to American Diaspora*. Cambridge, MA: Harvard University Press, 2007.

Soss, Joe, Richard C. Fording, & Sanford F. Schram. *Disciplining the Poor: Neoliberal Paternalism and the Persistent Power of Race*. Chicago: University of Chicago Press, 2011.
Spillers, Hortense. "Mama's Baby, Papa's Maybe: An American Grammar Book." In *Feminisms Redux: An Anthology of Literary Theory and Criticism*, edited by Robyn Warhol-Down & Diane Price Herndl. New Brunswick, NJ: Rutgers University Press, 2009.
Stannard, David E. *American Holocaust: The Conquest of the New World*. Oxford: Oxford University Press, 1992.
Stanton, Lucia C. *"Those Who Labor for My Happiness": Slavery at Thomas Jefferson's Monticello*. Charlottesville: University of Virginia Press, 2012.
Stilwell, Sean. *Slavery and Slaving in African History*. New York: Cambridge University Press, 2014.
Stokes, Melvin. *D. W. Griffith's The Birth of a Nation: A History of the Most Controversial Motion Picture of All Time*. Oxford: Oxford University Press, 2007.
Strings, Sabrina. *Fearing the Black Body: The Racial Origins of Fat Phobia*. New York: New York University Press, 2019.
Suchland, Jennifer. *Economies of Violence: Transnational Feminism, Postsocialism, and the Politics of Sex Trafficking*. Durham, NC: Duke University Press, 2015.
Suddler, Carl. *Presumed Criminal: Black Youth and the Justice System in Postwar New York*. New York: New York University Press, 2019.
Sussman, Robert Wald. *The Myth of Race: The Troubling Persistence of an Unscientific Idea*. Cambridge, MA: Harvard University Press, 2014.
Tate, Shirley Anne. *Black Beauty: Aesthetics, Stylization, Politics*. New York: Routledge, 2009.
Taylor, Keeanga-Yamahtta. *From #BlackLivesMatter to Black Liberation*. Chicago: Haymarket, 2016.
Telles, Edward E. *Race in Another America: The Significance of Skin Color in Brazil*. Princeton, NJ: Princeton University Press, 2004.
Thuma, Emily L. *All Our Trials: Prison, Policing and the Feminist Fight to End Violence*. Urbana-Champaign: University of Illinois Press, 2019.
Toledano, Ehud R., ed. *As if Silent and Absent: Bonds of Enslavement in the Islamic Middle East*. New Haven, CT: Yale University Press, 2007.
Tomich, Dale W., ed. *Atlantic Transformations: Empire, Politics, and Slavery during the Nineteenth Century*. Albany: State University of New York Press, 2020.
Tordoff, Rob, & Ben Akrigg, eds. *Slaves and Slavery in Ancient Greek Comic Drama*. New York: Cambridge University Press, 2013.
Tortorici, Zeb, ed. *Sexuality and the Unnatural in Colonial Latin America*. Oakland: University of California Press, 2016.
Trouillot, Michel-Rolph. *Silencing the Past: Power and the Production of History*. Boston: Beacon Press, 1995.
Tsesis, Alexander. *The Thirteenth Amendment and American Freedom: A Legal History*. New York: New York University Press, 2004.
Turner, Sasha. *Contested Bodies: Pregnancy, Childrearing, and Slavery in Jamaica*. Philadelphia: University of Pennsylvania Press, 2017.

Vinson, Ben III. *Before Mestizaje: The Frontiers of Race and Caste in Colonial Mexico*. New York: Cambridge University Press, 2018.

Wadhwa, Anita. *Restorative Justice in Urban Schools: Disrupting the School-to-Prison Pipeline*. New York: Routledge, 2015.

Williams, Heather A. *Help Me to Find My People: The African American Search for Family Lost in Slavery*. Chapel Hill: University of North Carolina Press, 2012.

Williams, Linda. *Playing the Race Card: Melodramas of Black and White from Uncle Tom to O. J. Simpson*. Princeton, NJ: Princeton University Press, 2001.

Wiredu, Kwasi. *Cultural Universals and Particulars: An African Perspective*. Bloomington: Indiana University Press, 1996.

Wong, Edlie L. *Neither Fugitive nor Free: Atlantic Slavery, Freedom Suits, and the Legal Culture of Travel*. New York: New York University Press, 2009.

Wood, Amy Louise. *Lynching and Spectacle: Witnessing Racial Violence in America, 1890–1940*. Chapel Hill: University of North Carolina Press, 2009.

Woods, Michael E. *Emotional and Sectional Conflict in the Antebellum United States*. New York: Cambridge University Press, 2014.

Wright, Paul, & Tara Herivel, eds. *Prison Nation: The Warehousing of America's Poor*. New York: Routledge, 2003.

Yudell, Michael. *Race Unmasked: Biology and Race in the Twentieth Century*. New York: Columbia University Press, 2014.

Záhořík, Jan, & Linda Piknerová, eds. *Colonialism on the Margins of Africa*. New York: Routledge, 2017.

Index

1926 Slavery Convention, 227, 230
1956 Slavery Convention, 227–230
2015 U.S. Transgender Survey, 241

Act of 1910, (Mann Act), 226
advertisements, tourism, 219
Aesop, 9
Agassiz, Louis, 108
Alemán, Juan Antonio, 125
Alexander, Michelle, 210
Alexander VI, 39
Alfonso X, 36–37
Alighieri, Dante, 33
"All This and Rabbit Stew" (cartoon), 217
Allegory of the Cave, 14
American Anti-Slavery Almanac, The, 185–190
American Eugenics Society, 103
ancient terms for enslaved people, 8
antihaitianismo, 198
anti-trafficking campaigns, 235–236
apprenticeships, 192
Apuleius, 23
Aquinas, Thomas, 34–35
archetypes in media, emotional, 217–223
Aristotle, 4, 6–8, 14–17, 19
artificial intelligence, 252–253
Atheneaus, 9
atimia, 10
Attica Prison Revolution, 209
auctions, of the enslaved, 122, 135, 141, 194, 239
Augustine, 29–30

Baartman, Sara, 76, 202
Bacon, Francis, 53
Bales, Kevin, 239
Bando contra la raza africana, 131
Beetlejuice, 168–169
Bélair, Sanité, 191
Benezet, Anthony, 171–172
Biko, Steve, 201
birth control pill trials and sterilization (Puerto Rico), 206
Birth of a Nation, The, 212–213
Black Lives Matter movement, 249, 255–256
Black Panther Party, 209
Black Power movement, 209
blackface minstrelsy, 212, 215–216
Blackfishing, 253–254
Blackness, representation in mainstream media and art, 211–212
Blumenbach, Johann, 66
Boccaccio, Giovanni, 33
bomba dances, 130
Bonaparte, Napoleon, 163–164
Boullainvilliers, Henri de, 94
Branagan, Thomas, 184
Brazil, gentrification in, 198
Broca, Paul, 94
Brown-Long, Cyntoia, 224–225
Buffon, Comte de, 58–60, 64
Bundy, Ted, 221
Burgos, Leyes de, 40
Bush, George W., 246

277

Camper, Petrus, 69
Caribbean slave codes, 116–117, 119
Carlyle, Thomas, 82–83, 169
casta paintings, 118–119
Cato the Elder, 22
"Censored Eleven, The"
    "All This and Rabbit Stew," 217
    "Jungle Jitters," 216–217
    "Sunday Go to Meetin' Time," 215–216
Cervantes Saavedra, Miguel de, 44
Chacherau, Monsieur, 146
chain gangs, 203
Chaucer, Geoffrey, 33–34
child soldiers, 244–245
Christian thought, 24–30
Chrysostom, John, 29
Cicero, 17–18
Civil Rights movement, 209
Clarkson, Thomas, 177
climate change, 245–246
Cloquet, Hyppolyte, 80
Code Noir, 116–117
colonial deputies of Saint-Domingue, 147
colonialism in Africa, 198–199
Columella, 20
composite portraiture, 96
COVID-19 pandemic, 256
Civil War Commission, 108
conquest of the Americas, European, 38–39
Consejo de Indias, Supremo, 119
conspiracies, of the enslaved in Puerto Rico, 130–131
Constantine, 18
Constitution of Saint-Domingue of 1801, 191
convict leasing, 195–196, 203
Cops, 221
Craft, Ellen, 142–143
Craft, William, 142–143
Crawley, Charles, 135
criminology, 95–97
crimmigration, 246–248
Crowther, Ajayi, 120
Cuba, nineteenth-century legal complaints of the enslaved, 125
Cugoano, Ottobah, 134–135
cultural appropriation, 14
Cuvier, Georges, 76

Darwin, Charles, 89–94
Davenport, Charles, 100–103

Davis, Angela, 127, 249
Davis, David Brion, 8
"Day-O (The Banana Boat Song)," 168–169
de las Casas, Bartolomé, 39–40
de Sousa Coutinho, Ferão, 115–116
de Unizar, Josef Antonio, 119–120
Deaubonneau, Citoyen, 162
Declaration of the Rights of Man and of the Citizen, 147–148
decolonization, 197, 209
degradation, theory of, 58–60
Descartes, René, 49–51
D'Este, Isabelle, 35
Diamond, Jared, 108
Dibble, Eugene H., Jr., 205
Dickens, Charles, 169
Douglass, Frederick, 139–140
Du Bois, William Edward Burghardt, 196–197
Dutch Golden Age, 130

Earl of Mansfield, 118, 176
Eastern State Penitentiary, 77
Elizabeth I, 43–44
emotions, contemporary scholarship about, 2–4
encomienda system, 40
Encyclopedia Britannica, 61
Enlightenment, 53–58, 60–64
enslavement, contemporary domestic, 243
Epistle to the Ephesians, 26–27, 29
Equiano, Olaudah, 135
Exodus, 25
experimentation, human, 128–130, 204–206
exploitation, contemporary child, 244
Eyre, Edward John, 169
Eze, Emmanuel Chukwudi, 201

family separations, 127
Fanon, Frantz, 199–200
Fatiman, Cécile, 191
feminism, anticarceral, 249
fever, tropical, 50, 69–70
films, Blaxploitation, 220
fingerprinting, 96
Floyd, George, 255
Foucault, Michel, 11
four humors, 47, 58
four temperaments, 47
Foxy Brown, 220

Index

Franciscan movement, 30
Fulkes, Minnie, 135–136

Gädlä Wälättä Petros, 44
Galen, 2, 23, 47, 53
Galton, Francis, 95–96
Gangá, Dominga, 125
Garner, Eric, 255
Genesis, 27, 32, 41, 63
gentrification, in Brazil, 198
Gobineau, Arthur de, 86–89
Gods Must Be Crazy, The, 218–219
Gone with the Wind, 213–214
González, Francisco José, 132
Gospel of Matthew, 25
Goude, Jean Paul, 220
Grant, Madison, 105–107
Grégoire, Henri, 182–183
Gregory of Nyssa, 27–29
Griffith, David Wark, 212
gynecological research, 128–130

Haeckel, Ernst, 99–100
Haitian Revolution, 146, 166–167
    correspondence of colonial deputies of Saint-Domingue, 147
    correspondence of the French Empire, 163–164
    mentions in texts of scientific racism, 85–86, 95, 103–104
    proclamations by French civil commissioners, 159–160
    speeches by free men of color of Saint-Domingue, 149–152, 156–157
    speeches by White colonizers of Saint-Domingue, 146–149, 152–166
Hamer, Fannie Lou, 206
Hargrave, Francis, 175–176
Hegel, Georg Wilhelm Friedrich, 80–82
Herder, Johann Gottfried, 66–68
Hernstein, Richard J., 108
historiography, racialist, 64–66, 73–76, 82–83, 103–107
Hobbes, Thomas, 45
Homer, 8–9
Horace, 20
Hume, David, 54–55
Hurricane Katrina (New Orleans), 246
Hurricane Maria (Puerto Rico), 246

Inquisition, Portuguese, 127
Inter Caetera, 39
International Federation of Eugenics Organizations, 100
ius commune, 31
ius gentium, 18
ius naturale, 18

Jackson, George, 208–209
Jacobs, Harriet Ann, 143–144
Jea, John, 120–121
Jefferson, Thomas, 113–114
Jim Crow era, 202–204
Jones, T.D., 125–126
"Jungle Jitters" (cartoon), 125–126

Kames, Lord, 64
Kant, Immanuel, 61
Kebra Nagast, 32
Khaldun, Ibn, 33
King, Martin Luther, Jr., 207–208
Knox, Robert, 85–86
Ku Klux Klan, 103, 212–213

labor, contemporary forced, 242
Laërtius, Diogenes, 24
Lamar, Kendrick, 249
law
    ancient Roman, 18–20, 36
    early modern, 40, 116–117
    eighteenth-century, 118, 175–176
    medieval, 31–32, 36–38
    nineteenth-century, 123–124, 131, 193
    Sharia, 31
laws, vagrancy, 195
legal complaints, of the enslaved in nineteenth-century Cuba, 125
legislation and jurisprudence about contemporary slavery, current, 230–231
    1926 Slavery Convention, 227, 229
    1956 Slavery Convention, 227–229
    Palermo Protocol, 229–230
    Trafficking Victims Protection Act, 232
Leopold II, 199
Lex Aelia Sentia, 18
limpieza de sangre, 38
Linnaeus, Carl, 47–48, 59
literature
    ancient Greek, 8–10
    ancient Roman, 21, 23

literature (cont.)
    early modern, 39–40, 44–45
    eighteenth-century, 134–135
    medieval, 32–34
    nineteenth-century, 136–144
    twentieth-century, 207–209
Live and Let Die, 220
Locke, John, 53–54
Loguen, J.W., 144–145
Lombroso, Cesare, 96–97
Long, Edward, 64–66
Lorde, Audre, 222
Louverture, Toussaint, 146, 191
lynching, in the United States, 203–204

Machiavelli, Niccolò, 43
Mann Act, 232
Manzano, Juan Francisco, 140–141
marriages, of the enslaved, 122–123
Martin, Trayvon, 250
mass incarceration, 206–207, 210
Mbembe, Achille, 201
media representation, of survivors of contemporary slavery, 233–238
medieval networks, of African enslavement, 31
Medina, Agustín, 125
Medina, María Belén, 125
Meiners, Christoph, 73–76
mestizaje, 197–198
Michelangelo, 36
"Mickey's Mellerdrammer", (cartoon), 215
Middle Passage, 42
military interventionism, 198
missionaries, White, 120
mocambos, 115–116
monogenism, 41, 58–60, 63–64, 76
    Curse of Cain, 41
    Curse of Ham, 34, 36, 41
Montesquieu, 55–58
Morant Bay Revolution, 169
More, Hannah, 178–179
More, Thomas, 43
Morton, Samuel George, 83–85, 108
Moseley, Benjamin, 70
Moynihan Report, 221
Muhammad, Khalil Gibran, 195–196
Murray, Charles, 108

narratives, of the enslaved, 134, 145
    Elizabeth Sparks, 136
    Ellen Craft, 142–143
    Frederick Douglass, 139–140
    Harriet Ann Jacobs, 143–144
    Juan Francisco Manzano, 140–141
    Mary Prince, 136–139
    Olaudah Equiano, 135
    Ottobah Cugoano, 134–135
    Sojourner Truth, 141
    Solomon Northup, 141–142
    William Craft, 142–143
National Assembly, 149–150, 154
National Geographic, 218
natural selection, 89–94
Nazi Party, 86
Newton, John, 179
Nicholas V, 38
Northup, Solomon, 141–142

oikos, 11
organ trafficking, 243

palenques, 132
Palermo Protocol, 229–230
Palmares, 115–116
Pan-Africanism, 209
Parsley Massacre, 198
paterfamilias, 19
paternalism, slaveholding, 126–127
Patterson, Orlando, 10, 139, 239–240
Pauline Epistles, 25–26
Philo of Alexandria, 21
philosophy
    ancient Greek, 6–8, 11–17
    ancient Roman, 17–18, 21–24
    early modern, 35, 42–43, 45, 49–54
    eighteenth-century, 54–58, 60–64, 66–69
    medieval, 32–35
    nineteenth-century, 80–82, 86–89, 94–95, 97–99
    twentieth-century, 199–201
    twenty-first-century, 201
Pico della Mirandolla, Giovanni, 35
Pinkney, William, 183
plantation, model of the sugar, 41
plantation manual, 123
Plato, 7–8, 13–14
Plotinus, 23–24
Plutarch, 22
Poitier, Sidney, 218
political prisoners, 207–209
polygenism, 41, 61–64
Pompeo, Michael, 231, 233

post-emancipation era, 192–195
Prince, Mary, 136–139
prison industrial complex, rise of the, 195–196
Progressive era, 195, 226
Psalm 123, 25
Pseudo-Phocyclides, 9
public discourse, about White slavery, 226–227
Puerto Rico
  conspiracies of the enslaved in, 130–131
  Hurricane Maria, 246

racial profiling, 96–97
racism, contemporary medical, 243
racism, in higher education, 254–255
racism, scientific, 50–51, 72–73, 107–111
  biological determinism, 47–48, 50, 58–60, 66, 68–69, 71–72, 76–80, 83–94, 96–100
  craniology, 50, 69, 80, 83–85, 94
  eugenics, 50, 95–96, 100–105, 107
  geographical determinism, 32–33, 50, 55–58, 69–71
  historical determinism, 50, 64–68, 73–76, 80–83, 103–107
  phrenology, 108
  Social Darwinism, 93–95
Raimond, Julien, 149–150
rationalism, 49–53
Reconquista, 38
Reconstruction, 212
Renaissance, 35–36
Renan, Ernest, 86
republicanism, 55–56, 159–160
revolutions, of the enslaved, 131–132, 191–192
Rhoads, Cornelius, 205–206
Rice, Tamir, 255
Ripley, William Z., 97–99
Rittenhouse, Kyle, 255
Rivers, Eunice, 204
Romanus Pontifex, 39
Rousseau, Jean-Jacques, 61–63
Rush, Benjamin, 77–80, 89

Saint-Chéron, Monsieur de, 147
Saint-Domingue, colonial deputies of, 119
Salvian, 30–31
Santo Domingo, Audiencia de, 119
Scholasticism, 34–35

school-to-prison pipeline, 249–250
Schopenhauer, Arthur, 80
science
  ancient, 2, 23, 47
  early modern, 53
  eighteenth-century, 47–48, 58–60, 66, 69–72
  nineteenth-century, 76–80, 83–86, 89–96, 99–103
Scientific Revolution, 53
segregation, racial, 198, 202–204
Seneca, 21–22
Senghor, Léopold Sédar, 200–201
Shakespeare, William, 44
Shakur, Assata, 209
Sharia law, 31
Sharp, Granville, 172–175
Siete Partidas, Las, 36–38
Sims, James Marion, 128–130
slave codes, in the Caribbean, 116–117, 119
"Slave Ship Broadside," 42
slavery, racialization of, 45–46, 118
  contemporary, 239–240
  early modern, 45–47
Smith, Adam, 60
Smith, Samuel Stanhope, 68–69
Social Darwinism, 93–95
Société des amis des Noirs, 155, 179–183
societies, White abolitionist, 190–191. *See also* names of specific societies
Society for Alleviating the Miseries of Public Prisons, Philadelphia, 77
Society for Effecting the Abolition of the Slave Trade, 177
Society for Promoting the Abolition of Slavery, Pennsylvania, 177–178
Somerset case, 118, 175–176
Song of the South, 214–215
Sonthonax, Léger-Félicité, 159–160
Sparks, Elizabeth, 136
Spillers, Hortense, 127
Spinoza, Baruch, 51–53
State v. John Mann, The, 123–124
Stoddard, Lothrop, 103–105
Stoicism, 24, 26, 29, 34
Stowe, Harriet Beecher, 187
"Sunday Go to Meetin' Time" (cartoon), 215–216
sweatshops, 242
Syrus, Publilius, 17

Taken, 234
taxonomy, 47–48
terror servilis, 18
Thirteenth Amendment, 193
Thistlewood, Thomas, 112–113
Thompson, Ralph, 203
tourism
  sex, 202
  transplant, 243
Trafficking in Persons Report, 231–233
Trafficking Victims Protection Act, 232
Trotter, William Monroe, 212
Trujillo, Rafael, 198
Trump, Donald, 231–232, 247
Truth, Sojourner, 141
Tucker, St. George, 183–184
Tuskegee Syphilis Study, 204–205
Twelve Tables, 20

Underground Railroad, 144
United Nations, 199, 227, 229, 231
US Civil War, 105, 192, 214
US Declaration of Independence, 77
US Department of Homeland Security, 246
US Department of State, 231
US Immigration and Customs Enforcement, 247

Vacher de Lapouge, Georges, 94–95
Valenzuela, Juana, 125
Varro, 17
Vasconcelos Calderón, José, 197
Vesalius, Andreas, 53
violence, imperial sexual, 127–128
Voltaire, 63

Walker, Ferdie, 203
Warburton, William, 171–172
White, Charles, 71–72
White abolitionism, contemporary scholarship about, 170–171, 191
White slavery, public discourse about, 226–227
whitening policies, 197
Wilson, Nia, 250
Wiredu, Kwasi, 201

X, Malcolm, 208
Xenophon, 11–13